Italian Women Writers
from the
Renaissance to the Present

# Italian Women Writers
## from the
# Renaissance to the Present

## Revising the Canon

Edited with an Introduction
by
Maria Ornella Marotti

The Pennsylvania State University Press
University Park, Pennsylvania

Library of Congress Cataloging-in-Publication Data

Italian women writers from the Renaissance to the present : revising the canon / edited
with an introduction by Maria Ornella Marotti.
    p.        cm.
   Includes bibliographical references and index.
   ISBN 0-271-01505-5 (cloth)
   ISBN 0-271-01506-3 (paper)
   1. Italian literature—Women authors—History and criticism. 2. Canon
(Literature)   I. Marotti, Maria Ornella.
PQ4063.I885   1996
850.9'9287—dc20                         95-14888
                                                    CIP

*To my mother, Ester Marotti,*
*and to the loving memory of my aunt, Letizia Taddeo.*

# Contents

## PART III. AT THE TURN OF THE CENTURY: WOMEN WRITERS AT THE MARGINS OF THE CANON

## PART IV. CONTEMPORARY WOMEN WRITERS: TOWARD A NEW CANON

## PART V. WOMEN AS FILMMAKERS: IMAGES OF WOMEN/IMAGES BY WOMEN/IMAGES FOR WOMEN

# Acknowledgments

I wish to thank the Interdisciplinary Humanities Center at the University of California, Santa Barbara, and the Italian Cultural Institute in Los Angeles for awarding me grants for a conference on Italian women writers that gave me the impetus for this volume. I would like also to thank Indiana University Press for permission to reprint Marguerite Waller's article, "Signifying the Holocaust: Liliana Cavani's *Portiere di notte*"; Minnesota University Press for permission to reprint Graziella Parati's article, "From Genealogy to Gynealogy and Beyond: Fausta Cialente's *Le Quattro Ragazze Wieselberger*"; *Quaderni d'Italianistica* for permission to reprint Lucia Re's article, "Mythic Revisionism: Women Poets and Philosophers in Italy Today"; and the University of Nebraska Press for permission to reprint parts of Nancy Harrowtiz's book, *Anti-Semitism, Misogyny, and the Logic of Cultural Difference*. Finally, I would like to thank Professor Ray Fleming for reading the volume and offering cogent and helpful criticism.

# Introduction

*Maria Ornella Marotti*

There are undeniable signs of positive change in the Italian literary environment, changes signaled and probably brought about by the flowering of publications and films by women during the last decade. In Italy, during the last few years prestigious literary prizes have been awarded to women writers. Two examples: the 1991 Premio Campiello went for the fourth consecutive time to a woman writer, Isabella Bossi Fedrigotti, for her novel, *Di Buona Famiglia* (From a good family); and again in 1993, the Strega prize was awarded to Dacia Maraini, for *Bagheria*. However, while we have every reason to rejoice for the well-earned success of talented and accomplished writers and filmmakers, we should not forget that many illustrious Italian women writers are still not part of the official canon of Italian literature. Very few are mentioned in the histories of Italian literature used in Italian high schools and universities, and those few that have gained a mention are described as minor writers. Moreover, even contemporary women writers who achieved recognition during the past decades did so to limited acclaim by both critics and readers. In an interview, Lalla Romano complained: "To be a woman in the literary environment of our country still weighs heavily against you. [The critics] treat you with a sort of patronizing and condescending attitude."[1]

In her poem, "Le poesie della donne," Dacia Maraini, denounces literary critics' prejudice against women's writing. In the poem, a literary critic, while discussing poetry with the author, strongly resists any gendered reading of women's texts. In his initial statement he lumps together most women's poetry under one category which he rejects in the name of male-centered aesthetic criteria: "Poems by women are frequently / flat, naive, realistic and obsessive." However, after the author's rebuttal ("It may be true, I reply. But you don't know / what being a woman means"), the critic resorts to what he

considers a universal aesthetic principle based on the erasure of difference
and gender:

> I don't care
> whether or not I'm a woman. I want to see the poetic
> results. There are those who can make donuts
> with holes: Does it matter whether they're men or women?

In her final rebuttal the poet stresses the need for a gendered reading that
would take into account women's bodies and experiences:

> It matters, my green-eyed friend, it matters;
> because a woman is unable to pretend
> that she's not a woman. And to be a woman
> means to know her own state of subjection,
> it means to live and breathe the humiliation
> and self-contempt that can be overcome
> only by painful toil with black tears.[2]

Maraini's poem provides a possible explanation for the exclusion of women
writers from the literary scene and of critics' "condescending attitude" toward
women's writing. By not recognizing the gender bias of his own critical
method, the critic (in the poem, and outside the poem) fails to understand
the gender specificity of women's writings and ends up by excluding them
from the canon.

Inclusion in the official canon is still an uphill battle for most talented and
well-published Italian women writers. However, one cannot ignore the recent proliferation, both in Italy and in the United States, of anthologies of
women's writings and of critical works illustrating the literary achievements
of Italian women writers of the past and present. The importance of these
publications lies in their documentation of a paradoxical reality: a rich, although basically submerged, tradition of women's literature in a deeply patriarchal society. This centuries-long literary corpus (which is not always the
expression of female protest) documents the persistence of female subjectivity.[3]

Critical works dealing with women's literary achievements in Italy could
be divided in two broad categories. One group traces an epistemology of a
given culture and epoch; the second tries to establish a history of women's
memory. Although the aims and theoretical premises of these two groups of

works diverge, both attempt to add works by women to the already established official canon.

The goal of the first group of works is to contribute to the study of the culture of a specific area by providing the missing element, that is, the presence of literary women.[4] The purpose of these epistemological works is neither to challenge the existence of the canon, nor to question the well-established literary reputation of the writers who have always inhabited it. Their scope is more precise, if more limited: to deepen and broaden the canon by enriching it with the contributions of forgotten, neglected, or submerged writers who happen to be women. The complementarity of man and woman, and therefore of literary texts produced by both genders, is shown to be essential for a well-balanced appraisal of a region and its culture. Although these works might not have direct political impact, they serve two purposes: they provide data for further study of women's literary history; they also point out the inadequacy of the canon.

The second group of critical works are more explicitly feminist and its authors sometimes work at the fringes of academia. In addition to anthologies of writings and critical works, this group includes journals such as *Donna/Woman/Femme*, the more scholarly (now defunct) *Memoria*, and many more quarterly publications. These works establish theories of knowledge based on gender and difference: if their purposes are similar, the scope and methods of research of these publications are diverse and so are the aspects of feminist theory that inspire them.

One concern of contemporary women's scholarship is the study of social conditions of women (including women writers) in various epochs; particular attention has been paid to the publishing world in which women writers operated.[5] The impetus for such studies is given by the conspicuous absence or scarcity of published women writings during the long period from the end of the Renaissance to the end of the nineteenth century. The results achieved through a work of careful recovery often contradict common assumptions.[6] Instead of finding a paucity of writings by women, scholars recover a rich literature that had rapidly disappeared after publication. Another important area of recovery is the Renaissance itself. Contemporary scholarship has discovered and reevaluated a long-lost tradition of female thought and has shown the active presence of talented women who carved a viable, although limited, social space for themselves as scholars, poets, stateswomen, courtesans, and actresses. They also contributed to an elaboration of theories about women that we can well claim as part of the feminist tradition.[7]

Despite interruptions in the development of feminist thought in Italian

culture, anthologies of women writings have shown the persistence of a female voice that articulates feminine identity. At times, the voice is faint; at
others, very audible in its protest. Anthologies of poetry, one of the preferred
genres for women, document this tradition of female literary protest and trace
the literary presence of women in Italy.[8] It may also be noted that the development of themes in contemporary novels by women often parallels the theoretical development of literary feminism. Novels often document a work of
recovery that invests both women's memory and the very roots of female
identity.[9]

Italian scholarship dealing with women writers in the United States is also
a fertile field of investigation. The relative distance from the target culture
and archives has enhanced rather than discouraged scholarly interest and directed it toward a theoretical elaboration and critical analysis of women's
texts and Italian feminisms in their diverse expressions. Just as in Italy, feminism has attracted anthropologists such as Ida Magli, philosophers such as
Luisa Muraro and Adriana Cavarero, and historians such as Anna Rossi
Doria, Gianna Pomata, and Annarita Buttafuoco; in the United States the
boundaries of Italian women's studies have been expanded by scholars of film,
the English Renaissance, and American feminist studies.

One should not forget, however, that in the United States the dissemina-
tion of knowledge concerning the field is blocked by many obstacles. One in
particular: the scarcity of translated texts in a country where the knowledge
of Italian is limited greatly affects both critical and textual analyses and the
diffusion of writings. Books of criticism, dealing with texts unknown to
the general public, are unlikely to be published, especially if they take non-
thematic approaches to the material and address a wider academic audience.
Moreover, strange choices by publishers and translators have created a distorted vision of the field by excluding important writers who present linguistic difficulties due to the complexities of their prose: an example is Gianna
Manzini, one of the most distinct and refined female voices of our century,
whose work has never been translated into English. A partial antidote to this
situation have been anthologies of women's writings, such as *The Defiant
Muse*, and *New Italian Women*. They have been particularly beneficial in
reaching a wider audience and in making pedagogical material available for
college teachers. The impact of such anthologies is still limited, but they
create viable models to be followed.

The scarcity of translated texts has also affected the response and expectations of a more generally educated audience. An article on Natalia Ginzburg,
which appeared a few years ago in the *New York Times Magazine*, sums up

these attitudes. Its author, Mary Gordon, starts with the assumption that women writers are nonexistent in Italy, thus denying literary achievements by women and perpetuating the misconceptions created by the official literary establishment. This allows her to shape the myth of Ginzburg's exceptional achievements given what she imagines to be her intellectual isolation as a woman in a social context in which women apparently don't write. I am afraid that Mary Gordon and the readers of the *New York Times Magazine* are not the only ones to have these misconceptions. Only a greater familiarity with the actual writings of Italian women could change the situation. This needs to happen not only through translations of texts, but also through critical readings and works of recovery that would in turn stimulate interest and, therefore, create a demand for translations. There are signs that such a process is under way: publications have recently appeared or are being published, in the United States, dealing with contemporary Italian women writers, Renaissance women's thought, and feminism in Italian culture.[10]

This present volume, too, is a collection of essays dealing with Italian women writers from the Renaissance to the present. However, it differs from previous works on this topic, which have appeared in the United States and in Italy as well, in that it is not primarily an introduction to women's literary achievements in Italy and it is not restricted to a specific area of study or historical period. Although the authors' aims and methods of research are diverse, as are the areas and epochs they deal with, the unifying theme of the work is the complex relation, throughout the centuries, between women writers and the Italian literary canon. The authors revise this prejudice-laden canon and suggest and implement strategies for such a revision. Although not all the writers examined in the essays are self-proclaimed feminists, the authors' readings are informed by feminist thought. The volume is not meant to be a systematic history of women's writings; it does, nonetheless, encompass several centuries. Indeed, it begins with the Renaissance, the first time that Italian women writers achieved significant literary status—a status soon to be lost, and not regained during the two following centuries.

Part I explores the relation between women writers and the official canon. The essays discuss the present literary status of women writers, and consider the possible expansion, feminist revision, and radical restructuring of the existing literary canon. Part II traces feminist thought and the origin of women's writings in Italy in the Renaissance. The essays focus upon treatises defending women and letters by courtesans. These texts contain clear indications of the narrow, yet vital, space conquered by women in the literary and social life of their time, and of their aspirations for a radical revision of gender relations.

Part III is devoted to writers in the nineteenth century and at the turn of the century. After centuries of absence women writers gained again some acceptance in the Italian literary establishment. The essays in the section study the contradictory aspects of the texts: acceptance into the canon meant, for some writers, compromising their ideas and feminine identity, while, for others, it allowed deviation from the well-established literary conventions of the time. Part IV deals with contemporary writers. It comprises essays on writers of the older generation such as Elsa Morante and Fausta Cialente, and new writers such as Fabrizia Ramondino, and neo-avant-garde poets, such as Amelia Rosselli. The authors of this section also contemplate the impact of feminist thought on contemporary women writers and attempt to define female writing. Part V deals with women filmmakers and includes essays on Monica Vitti as screenwriter and Liliana Cavani's *Portiere di Notte*. Here again, the authors point out the novelty of women's contribution to Italian cinema either in proposing to movie-goers a female perspective on gender relations, or in redefining and expanding the idea of femaleness, and therefore of feminism.

Although Italian scholars are almost unanimously aware of the exclusion of women writers from the official Italian canon, they are still debating how such a situation should be corrected. The groups of works that I have briefly discussed in this introduction have as their goal the inclusion in the official canon of larger numbers of women writers. As commendable as this additive activity appears to be, the authors of this volume intend to move one step further by fostering a thorough revision and reformulation of the canon rather than a mere addition of a few more female writers to its lists. For the revision and reformulation to occur one needs to change the critical subject and the aesthetic criteria that have supported the formation of the canon as it stands. One must embrace a theoretical approach that places women at the center of both the production and the reception of the literary work.

In their essays the authors have pursued several avenues. First, they have reclaimed literary foremothers. They have found Renaissance thinkers who have anticipated aspects of modern feminist thought (Jordan) and first-wave feminists who have grappled with the complex issue of female subjectivity (Luciano). In studying writers from the past they have observed the effect of oppression in shaping a female language of marginalization (Bassanese, Magistro). Second, they have revaluated lesser known texts that are excluded from the canon, either because of critical prejudice (Harrowitz) or because of the authors' social marginalization (Magistro). Third, they have studied deviations by women writers from literary conventions and thematic developments established by their contemporaries who inhabit the canon (Cottino-Jones, Holub, Magistro, Marotti, Parati). Fourth, in their critical discourse they have espoused methods and aesthetic criteria that go beyond the boundaries of traditional Italian criticism and that are meant to explore and redefine female language, and addressee in women's works (Allen, Cannon, Cottino-Jones, Re, Waller). Fifth, they have studied authors and film-makers who foster in their work the creation of a new feminine symbolic order either through mythic revisionism (Holub, Re) or the redefinition and expansion of the concept of femininity (Boscagli, Marotti, Parati, Waller).

The diversity of the authors' areas of study, methods of research, and critical approaches represents the spectrum of critical debate that on both sides of the Atlantic has developed in Italian Studies. It must be added, however, that, in exploring the female language and imagination, the authors of the volume have expanded beyond the boundaries of a more traditional Italian critical discourse. Critical methodologies employed in the volume range from New Historicism to philology, from deconstruction to psychoanalysis; most important, however, all these methodologies are informed by feminist thought. In their revisionary activity the authors have been inspired by equally revisionary works done by both European and American theorists who have redefined critical theories in feminist terms. One of the novelties of this volume is the use of critical strategies inspired by the theoretical elaborations of the Diotima group of women philosophers. In particular, Adriana Cavarero's and Luisa Muraro's recent publications, which propose a deconstruction of myth in Western civilization and a reconstruction of a feminine symbolic order, call for a redefinition of aesthetic perspective. French and American feminist theories are also widely represented in the volume. Autobiographical theories play an important role in some of the essays exploring women's genealogies. Feminist re-readings of Freudian psychoanalysis have an equally strong impact on essays dealing with a re-definition of the female textual imagination and symbolism. Historical and psychological studies of women's social and literary marginalization also inform some of the essays. The chief distinction of this volume, of course, lies in the original textual interpretations offered by all the authors. It is indeed through a fresh and creative approach to well-known and less well-known women's texts that a thorough revision of the canon will occur.

## Notes

1. This is my translation from Sandra Petrignani, *Le Signore della scrittura*, 17. The original reads as follows: "Essere donna, poi, nell'ambiente letterario del nostro paese pesa ancora molto. Ti trattano con una sorta di condiscendenza, di concessione."

2. Dacia Maraini, "Le poesie delle donne," in *Donne mie*. The English translation of the poem is from Beverly Allen, Muriel Kittel, and Keala Jane Jewell, eds., *The Defiant Muse*. The original reads as follows: "Le poesie delle donne sono spesso / piatte, ingenue, realistiche e ossessive" "Ma tu non sai / cosa vuol dire essere donna." "A me non importa / se sia donna o meno. Voglio vedere i risultati / poetici. C'e chi riesce a fare la ciambella / con il buco. Se è donna o uomo cosa cambia?" / "Cambia, amico dagli occhi verdi, cambia; / perche una donna non può fare finta di non essere donna. Ed essere donna / significa conoscere la propria soggezione, / significa vivere e respirare la degradazione / e il disprezzo di sè che si puo superare / solo con fatiche dolorose e lagrime nere" (94–96).

3. On 2 November 1991, in my opening remarks at the conference, "Italian Women Writers," the University of California, at Santa Barbara, I observed that "the situation of the Italian woman writer often resembles that of the muse Clio in a painting by Rosalba Carriera. Carriera has the muse face her audience in the apparently conventional posture of the object of a portrait. Yet, within the framework of the portrait, Clio unveils her breasts. While exerting her erotic power over her audience, she suggests a link between creativity and gender, and between literary expression and the language of the body."

4. A typical example of this kind of scholarship is Antonia Arslan, Adriana Chemello, and Gilberto Pizzamiglio, eds., *Le stanze ritrovate: Antologia di scrittrici venete dal quattrocento al novecento*, a study and anthology of writings by women writers of the Veneto region.

5. Examples of works of recovery are: Mariarosaria Olivieri, *Tra libertà e solitudine. Saggi su letteratura e giornalismo femminile: Matilde Serao Sibilla Aleramo, Clotilde Marghieri* and Olivieri, "Per un'analisi dello stato socio-economico delle scrittrici italiane (dalle origini della stampa al 1860) appunti su una produzione femminile, stampa, mercato."

6. For example, studies have revealed the existence in Italy of numerous works by women throughout the nineteenth century: both published and unpublished works of quite extraordinary literary quality that later disappeared from publication. Anna Santoro has worked in particular in this field. Anna Santoro, ed. and introd., *Narratrici Italiane dell'Ottocento*. See Neria De Giovanni's *Artemide sulla soglia. Donne e letteratura in Italia*; Elisabetta Rasy's *Ritratti di signora*; and Nancy Harrowitz's *Anti-Semitism and Misogyny and the Logic of Cultural Difference. Cesare Lombroso and Matilde Serao*, which are also noteworthy.

7. Some works on Renaissance women that have appeared in the United States are Constance Jordan, *Renaissance Feminism*; and Marilyn Migiel and Juliana Schiesari, eds., *Refiguring Woman*. The following works have appeared in Italy: Christine Klapisch-Zuber, *La famiglia e le donne nel Rinascimento a Firenze*; Romeo De Majo, *Donne e Rinascimento*; Marina Zancan, ed., *Nel cerchio della luna*; Maria Luisa Lenzi, *Donne e madonne*; Antonio Barzaghi, *Donne o cortigiane?*; Georgina Masson, *Cortigiane Italiane del Rinascimento*; Ginevra Conti Odorisio, *Donna e società nel Seicento*.

8. Agata Curra, Giuseppe Vettori, and Rosalba Vinci, eds., *Canti della Protesta Femminile*.

9. Works such as *La Murata* by Toni Maraini and *La lunga vita di Marianna Ucria* by Dacia Maraini recover figures of the past—both a historical and imaginary past. In a New Historical mode, instead of dealing with the major and most prominent figures, as in past decades Maria Bellonci had done, authors concentrate on those who were erased by official history and yet resisted annihilation. On the other hand, works by Bossi Fedrigotti, Cerati, Morandini, Morante, Ramondino, Romano, Sanvitale, Sereni, Tamaro, and many more explore those personal relations and that world of connections and continuities that make up the female world.

10. In recent years, besides the above-cited volumes on women in the Renaissance, the following volumes have been published: Santo Aricò, ed., *Contemporary Women Writers in Italy*; and Carol Lazzaro-Weis, *From the Margins to the Mainstream*.

# Works Cited

Allen, Beverly, Muriel Kittel, and Keala Jane Jewell, eds. *The Defiant Muse*. New York: Feminist Press, 1986.

Aricò, Santo, ed. *Contemporary Women Writers in Italy*. Amherst: University of Massachusetts Press, 1990.

Arslan, Antonia, Adriana Chemello, and Gilberto Pizzamiglio, eds. *Le Stanze Ritrovate*. Venice: Editrice Eidos, 1991.

Barzaghi, Antonio. *Donne o cortigiane?* Verona: Bertani, 1980.

Bossi Fedrigotti, Isabella. *Di Buona Famiglia*. Milan: Longanesi, 1991.

Cavarero, Adriana. *Nonostante Platone*. Rome: Editori Riuniti, 1990.

Conti Odorisio, Ginevra. *Donna e Società nel Seicento*. Rome: Bulzoni Editore, 1979.

Curra, Agata, Giuseppe Vettori, and Rosalba Vinci, eds. *Canti della protesta femminile*. Rome: Newton Compton, 1977.

De Giovanni, Neria. *Artemide sulla Soglia. Donne e Letteratura in Italia*. Rome: Demian Edizioni, 1994.

De Majo, Romeo. *Donne e Rinascimento*. Milan: Mondadori, 1987.

Gordon, Mary. "Surviving History: Natalia Ginzburg." *New York Times Magazine* 139 (25 March 1990), col. 1.

Harrowitz, Nancy. *Anti-Semitism, Misogyny and the Logic of Cultural Difference. Cesare Lombroso and Matilde Serao*. Lincoln: University of Nebraska Press, 1994.

Jordan, Costance. *Renaissance Feminism*. Ithaca: Cornell University Press, 1990.

Klapisch-Zuber, Christine. *La famiglia e le donne nel Rinascimento a Firenze*. Bari: Laterza, 1988.

Lazzaro-Weis, Carol. *From the Margins to the Mainstream*. Philadelphia: University of Pennsylvania Press, 1993.

Lenzi, Maria Luisa. *Donne e madonne. L'educazione femminile nel primo Rinascimento italiano*. Turin: Loescher, 1982.

Maraini, Dacia. *Bagheria*. Milan: Rizzoli, 1993.

———. *La lunga vita di Marianna Ucria*. Milan: Rizzoli, 1990.

———. "Le poesie delle donne." In *Donne mie*. Turin: Giulio Einaudi Editore, 1974.

Maraini, Toni. *La Murata*. Introduction by Alberto Moravia. Palermo: La Luna Edizioni, 1991.

Masson, Georgina. *Cortigiane Italiane del Rinascimento*. Milan: Rizzoli, 1981.

Migiel, Marilyn, and Juliana Schiesari, eds. *Refiguring Woman*. Ithaca: Cornell University Press, 1991.

Muraro, Luisa. *L'ordine simbolico della madre*. Rome: Editori Riuniti, 1991.

Olivieri, Mariarosa. "Per un'analisi dello stato socio-economico delle scrittrici italiane (dalle origini della stampa al 1860) appunti su una produzione femminile, stampa, mercato." *Prospettive Settanta*, no. 1 (1984).

———. *Tra libertà e solitudine. Saggi su letteratura e giornalismo femminile: Matilde Serao, Sibilla Aleramo, Clotilde Marghieri*. Rome: Edizioni dell'ateneo, 1990.

Petrignani, Sandra. *Le Signore della scrittura*. Milan: La Tartaruga, 1984.

Rasy, Elisabetta. *Ritratti di Signora. Tre Storie di Fine Secolo*. Milan: Rizzoli, 1995.

Santoro, Anna, ed. and intro. *Narratrici Italiane dell'Ottocento*. Naples: Federico and Ardia, 1987.

Zancan, Marina, ed. *Nel cerchio della luna*. Venice: Marsilio Editore, 1983.

# Part I

---

## Canon Formation/Canon Revision

# 1

---

# Women Writers and the Canon in Contemporary Italy

*JoAnn Cannon*

In certain American academic circles when one speaks of the canonized or canonical writers as Dead White Males, the emphasis is on the last term—male—as that which excludes the "others." In Italy, by contrast, the first of these qualifiers seems to be equally important in gaining canonical status. There has been a tendency until recently in Italy to dismiss contemporary authors as objects unworthy of serious scholarly inquiry. Thus the very notion of a canon in the sense of an agreed-upon list of classics when applied to contemporary Italian writers seems to be a contradiction in terms. To clarify the matter of canons in speaking of contemporary Italian literature I borrow from a recent article on "canonicity."[1] The author defines as the diachronic canon those authors whose works have endured over centuries. In Italy, of course, the works of Dante, Petrarch, Boccaccio, Ariosto, Macchiavelli, Leopardi, and Manzoni constitute the diachronic canon. This "glacially changing core" is to be distinguished from certain contemporary authors who have a high visibility and whose works are part of a "nonce canon." Only a very few of these writers will ever become part of the diachronic canon. The object of this essay, then, can only be the "nonce canon" in Italy. Critics cannot foresee which contemporary writers will stand the test of time and enter the diachronic canon. One thing, however, is certain: whether women writers will become candidates for the diachronic canon depends not only on their intrinsic "worth" but also on the diligence of their readers and critics in promoting their candidacy.[2] In other words, a canon is intimately and necessarily linked to an interpretive community.[3]

There are a number of ways in which one might approach the question of Italian women writers and the canon in contemporary Italy. One of the easiest is to chronicle the exclusion of Italian women writers from the canon. Works by Italian women writers have attained quite large sales and still been neglected in general studies of Italian literature, anthologies, monograph series, and scholarly journals. The most influential studies of modern Italian literature, from Gianfranco Contini's *Letteratura dell'Italia unita: 1861–1968* to Dominque Fernandez's *Roman italien et la crise de la conscience moderne* focus only on works by male writers.[4] In the Il Castoro series published monthly by La Nuova Italia and devoted to the "great" contemporary Italian writers the first ninety-four volumes are dedicated to male writers. Of sixty-five Italian writers featured in a similar series published by Mursia (*Invito all lettura*) up to about 1980, only four women were included: Grazia Deledda, Gianna Manzini, Elsa Morante, and Natalia Ginzburg. (By 1989 that number had increased slightly to include Lalla Romano, Anna Maria Ortese, and Matilde Serao. At present seven of the ninety-two writers featured in the series are women.)

Women writers have fared somewhat better in the pedagogical canon than in the critical canon. One sure measure of acceptance in the pedagogical canon is inclusion in Einaudi's influential Letture per la Scuola Media series. Books included in this series are read by large numbers of Italian school-children. The first forty-eight titles in this series include five titles by Italian women: Natalia Ginzburg's *Lessico famigliare*, Lalla Romano's *Maria* and *L'ospite*, Renata Viganò's *L'Agnese va a morire*, and Gianna Manzini's *Una vita operaia*. Some of these books have taken the form of "adolescent classics," like *The Diary of Anne Frank* or Primo Levi's *Se questo è un uomo*. They do not, however, figure prominently in the critical canon. In an article on contemporary U.S. fiction Richard Ohmann has noted that neither acceptance in the pedagogical canon nor large sales necessarily leads to acceptance in the critical canon.[5] This lack of complementarity seems to hold true for all contemporary literatures as texts move from "precanonical" to "canonical" status. To enter the canon, to endure over time and to become even a contemporary classic, texts need "the right kind of critical attention."[6] Canon formation takes place "in the interaction between large audiences and gate-keeper intellectuals."[7] Although many works by "serious" Italian women writers typically enjoy large audiences, they have only rarely captured the attention of key gatekeeper intellectuals (the vast majority of whom are of course male).

There is another form of neglect of Italian women writers that should be addressed. In feminist literary criticism outside of Italy, particularly in the United States, *Italian* women writers do not figure prominently. At least one critic has lamented the narrow focus of "the founding texts in feminist literary criticism," which deal almost exclusively with British and American writers.[8] Even those transnational studies that provide an overview of "representative" women writers from a Eurocentric perspective virtually ignore Italian women. For example, Ellen Moers's 1976 *Literary Women: The Great Writers* discusses more than one hundred women writers, only two of which are Italian: Natalia Ginzburg and Vittoria Colonna.

In short, Italian women writers have been excluded from the critical canon both in Italy and in the United States. There are, however, a number of promising signs on the horizon: there is a greater tendency than in the past to include women writers in general studies of contemporary Italian literature like Marco Forti's *Prosatori e narratori nel Novecento italiano*[9] and Stefano Tani's *Il romanzo di ritorno: Dal romanzo medio degli anni sessanta alla giovane narrativa degli anni ottanta*.[10] There are also important studies dedicated exclusively to Italian women writers, studies such as Anna Nozzoli's *Tabu e coscienza: La condizione femminile nella letteratura italiana del Novecento*,[11] Sandra Petrignani's *Firmato donna: Una donna un secolo 1986*, [12] and, in English, *Contemporary Women Writers in Italy* and *From Margins to Mainstream: Feminism and Fictional Modes in Italian Women's Writing, 1968–1990*.[13] And special issues of academic journals have been devoted to Italian women writers.[14]

The emergence of Italian women's fiction as a new field of study is both welcome and long overdue. It is not surprising that the study of Italian women's fiction is emerging with particular strength in the United States. The American academy provides a unique context in which to study women writers of all nationalities. The vitality and excitement of feminist literary studies in the American academy has produced original and provocative results, from Sandra Gilbert's 1979 *Madwoman in the Attic: The Woman Writer and the Nineteenth-Century Literary Imagination* to Nancy K. Miller's 1988 *Subject to Change: Reading Feminist Writing* (1988). The American academy seems to be more conducive to innovative work on Italian women writers than its Italian counterpart. (There is nothing comparable to women's studies programs in the Italian university. The closest equivalent, the Centro di Documentazione sulla donna in such cities as Bologna, is generally supported by the local government, not by the academy.) This is not to suggest that important work is not being done in Italy. Much of the interesting work in feminist literary criticism is, however, emerging outside of the academy. The fact that several of the best studies of women writers in Italy are authored not by academics but by journalists (Sandra Petrignani and Elisabetta Rasy, for example) testifies to the difficulty Italian women have had in entering the ranks of the professoriat and the constraints imposed upon their scholarly activity by the male-dominated profession.

With the emergence of the new field of Italian women's fiction comes a need for new critical tools and approaches. As Nancy Miller has pointed out in the introduction to *Subject to Change*, the interest in reading women writers has created the need for a poetics of women's writing. Miller's work is characteristic of feminist literary scholarship as it attempts "to find working metaphors for the problems involved in creating a critical discourse in which to talk about women's writing both within the field of feminist studies, and within the critical debates that have dominated literary studies." [15] How to construct such a discourse has been the subject of intense debate. In *Le donne e la letteratura* Elisabetta Rasy surveys many of the key points in that debate. Rasy takes as her point of departure the question of whether a feminine language exists. [16] Rasy argues against the position of French thinkers like Hélène Cixous, who hold that such a language does exist. Rasy suggests that we should ask instead whether there exists a particularly female position with respect to language. She turns not to the theorists but to women writers for the answer and cites in particular the positions of Yourcenar, Wittig, and Woolf. As distinct as those positions are, they have in common a certain uneasiness with respect to language that Rasy sees as a characteristic feature of women's writing. Rasy argues vigorously against the notion of a "linguaggio femmino." At the same time she defends the validity of a critical approach based on the sex of the author. "Literary texts by women should not be read with the intent of discovering the traces of the eternal feminine, but with particular attention to the material condition of the women who produced them." [17] According to Rasy, what links such very diverse writers as Yourcenar, Wittig, and Woolf is the anomalous position that they, as women writers, occupy in society.

The emergence of Italian women's fiction as a new field of study raises frequently debated questions: To what extent is it important to study women writers as a group? And to what extent do we by so doing risk ghettoizing women writers?[18] As Lillian Robinson has pointed out, there are both advantages and disadvantages to feminist literary criticism's construction of a female countercanon. "In one sense, the more coherent our sense of the female tradition is, the stronger will be our eventual case. Yet the longer we wait, the more comfortable the women's literature—ghetto-separate, apparently autonomous, and far from equal—may begin to feel."[19] Feminist or female literary criticism obviously runs the risk of marginalizing women writers in the women's studies ghetto. Yet at the same time it is apparent that the label *women's fiction*, like other labels, may have its uses. In order for "canon revision" to take place, in order for unappreciated writers to be recognized and assimilated into the critical canon, it may be useful for them to be situated in a context, a cohort of "like" writers. This does not necessarily have to take the form of a countercanon (which implicitly rejects the traditional canon) but may simply be a subgenre within a canon.

One might consider as anecdotal evidence for the need for contexts and categories the example of Primo Levi's *Se questo è un uomo*. This is perhaps one of the prime examples of an unjustly neglected book. It can be argued that having a context—Holocaust literature—in which to read this novel helped it finally attract the attention it deserved in Italy.[20] *Se questo è un uomo* is now considered a classic of Holocaust literature. One wonders too whether the good fortune of Renata Viganò's *L'agnese va a morire* relative to works by other women writers had to do with the existence of a convenient category— neorealism—in which to place her work. It seems clear that such categories help us to receive and make sense of literary works. The label of Holocaust literature has helped the fortunes of *Se questo è un uomo* at the same time that it has to some extent ghettoized the book. Similarly we will both help and hinder women writers as we study them and anthologize them as women writers.

If we do not want to ghettoize Italian women writers, do we want to incorporate them into the almost exclusively male canon of Italy? One of the first acts of feminist literary criticism in all countries seems to be that of insinuating greater numbers of women writers into a male-dominated tradition. The rediscovery of "lost" writers is certainly a valuable and important first step. But there has also more recently been a growing awareness that "to talk of the female tradition of writing can reinforce the canonical view, which looks upon literary history as a continuum of significant names."[21] Some of the most interesting feminist literary theory in the United States has called into question "the individualistic values by which the mainstream canon has been created." Many feminist critics have begun to problematize the notion of "greatness" and to suggest that literary value is not universal but historically specific.[22] Efforts to replace a few "great" Italian male writers by a few "great" Italian female writers may smack too much of tokenism.[23] More important, such efforts mask a deeper issue: the contingent nature of literary "value."

The exclusion of women writers from the male-dominated canon was perhaps most acutely felt by Elsa Morante's generation of Italian women writers. This is the generation of women featured in Sandra Petrignani's 1984 *Le signore della scrittura*.[24] The frustration of these writers, who seem to have been convinced of the desirability of gaining membership in the "club," testifies above all to the uselessness of competition with the male tradition.[25] The women in Petrignani's study tended to define themselves as far as one can discern from these interviews vis-à-vis male writers. Lalla Romano cites strong ties to Pavese, Vittorini, and Montale and identifies Flaubert as her "greatest love." Fausta Cialente mentions Conrad, Stevenson, Dessì, and Sciascia. Anna Banti laments: "I am cited in encyclopedias, I am present in the anthologies. But a woman writer, even if successful, is, nonetheless marginalized. They will call her a great woman writer, but they won't compare her to male writers. It is a common practice."[26] Banti's lament is revealing. On the one hand it is understandable that she does not want to be ghettoized. Yet one wonders why she objects so strongly to being grouped with other women writers. The objection is particularly striking from a writer who seems to understand the importance of solidarity among female artists. In her historical novel based on the life of the Renaissance painter Artemisia Gentileschi, Anna Banti deals with this issue with unique sensitivity. In an essay on Banti's *Artemisia* Deborah Heller has shown how the author departs from the historical record in order to make a statement about the relationships between female artists. Heller shows how a painting that was in reality a self-portrait of the artist is transformed by Banti into a portrait of a fellow female artist, Annella.[27] In Banti's rewriting of history, Artemisia's overtures of friendship are rejected by Annella. Despite this rejection, Artemisia pays tribute to Annella in her portrait of the artist and explains: "That a woman achieves honor, honors her as well." As Heller points out, just as Artemisia finds honor for herself in Annella's achievement, so Anna Banti, "in celebrating and resuscitating Artemisia, finds honor for herself in another woman's creative achievement" (57). It is interesting that, despite Banti's sensitive fictional tribute to the importance of female solidarity, the author objects so strenuously to being considered a great *woman* writer.

Banti's rejection of the label "scrittrice" seems to be characteristic of her generation of women writers. Elsa Morante's response to this designation is the most vitriolic. When asked by Petrignani: "You are a writer, not a woman writer. Why so much disdain for your own sex?" Morante responds: "I must have been unfortunate but I have never known a truly intelligent woman."[28] It is difficult to decide how to account for Morante's antipathy for women and women writers. Perhaps we should read it as Artemisia reads her rejection by a fellow artist, as a sign of "the impossibility of friendships between women in a world created by men."[29]

The rejection of the label "scrittrice" and the desire to be admitted into the ranks of the "scrittori" might also be considered in the light of Italian feminism and its critique of equal rights. This critique has been articulated with particular vehemence by the feminists of the Milan Women's Bookstore Collective whose work *Non credere di avere dei diritti* has recently been published under the title *Sexual Difference*.[30] The feminists of the Milan Women's Bookstore Collective are sharply critical of the idea of equal rights: "the ideal of equality did not, and does not, have anything to do with the history and the present state of relations among women. So much so that the equality meant when speaking of women is the equality of women to men" (121). The critique of equal rights for women might also be leveled at the proponents of equal rights for women writers, including those writers featured in Petrignani's study. Rather than call for equal rights a more productive strategy would follow the lead of the Milan feminists who have attempted to "counter the rights-oriented, sociological arguments of much Italian feminism" by assuming as their project the reconstruction of a female symbolic or a female genealogy. The women of the Bookstore Collective espouse:

> a freedom for women that is not made possible by adherence to the liberal concept of rights . . . but is generated, indeed engendered, by taking up a position in a symbolic community, a "genealogy of women," that is at once discovered, invented, and constructed through feminist practices of reference and address. Those practices . . . include the reading or rereading of women's writings; taking other women's words, thoughts, knowledges, and insights as frame of reference for one's analyses, understanding, and self-definition; and trusting them to provide a symbolic mediation between oneself and others, one's subjectivity and the world. (2)

This construction of a female genealogy and of new reading practices grounded in the works of women writers is at least as important as adding women writers to the male-dominated canon of exclusions. There are signs that contemporary Italian women writers (Dacia Maraini for example) are beginning to entrust themselves to their literary foremothers for this kind of symbolic mediation.[31]

The discovery of or construction of a female genealogy or female symbolic represents an important step in the effort to gain women writers the recognition they deserve. The importance of identifying a uniquely female literary tradition in support of contemporary women writers has been widely recognized by American feminist critics.[32] One interesting feature of the female genealogy being constructed by Italian feminists of the Milan collective and by some Italian feminist critics is its international or transnational character. There is an attempt to cross national boundaries and to construct a female genealogy that is not limited to Italian women. The last chapter of *Sexual Difference* tells of the decision of the women of the Milan bookstore collective to read their favorites, or "le madri di tutte noi." These include Jane Austen, Emily Brontë, Charlotte Brontë, Elsa Morante, Gertude Stein, Sylvia Plath, Ingeborg Bachmann, Anna Kavan, Virginia Woolf, and Ivy Compton-Burnett. Similarly Elisabetta Rasy in *Le donne e la letteratura* singles out as "historic mothers" Jane Austen, the Brontë sisters, George Eliot, Harriet Martineau, George Sand, Mary Wollstonecraft, Virginia Woolf, Simone de Beauvoir, Dacia Maraini. Indeed, Rasy goes so far as to suggest that the tendency of women writers to look to the works of other women writers as a natural point of reference is one of the two common threads linking all women writers (35). Whether contemporary Italian women writers will embrace this notion and explicitly define themselves vis-à-vis other women writers remains to be seen. It remains important that we read women writers not only in the context of the male-dominated canon but also in the company of other women writers. It is not enough simply to assimilate women's writing into the list of great Italian works. A more interesting approach would also study the anxiety of influence subtending the male-dominated Italian literary canon and contrast this to the dynamic that subtends the emerging female literary tradition.

In short, the practice of reading Italian women writers as part of a female literary tradition or a "female symbolic" is useful for strategic reasons. What one discovers in this exercise is not, however, some essence of feminine writing. Without summarizing all the arguments in the essentialism/anti-essentialism debate, I would prefer to second de Lauretis's defense of Silvia Bovenschen's article "Is There a Feminine Aesthetic?"[33] Summarizing Bovenschen's argument, de Lauretis suggests:

there is no such thing as an ever-present female counterculture as such, or a "female nature" outside of historical development.... Since it is the specifics of feminine experience and perception that determine the form the work takes, we must not accept a priori categories and should look for evidence of feminine sensitivity in concrete tests. It is good, Bovenschen claims, that no formal criteria for 'feminine art' can be definitively laid down.... It is not a question of what or how women write, but of how women produce (as makers) and reproduce (as receivers) the aesthetic object, the text; in other words, we need a theory of culture with women as subjects—not commodities but social beings producing and reproducing cultural products, transmitting and transforming cultural values.[34]

If canon revision is to entail something other than an "additive" approach, then women must not only become the producers of aesthetic objects but also the receivers. What must be studied is not only the importance of certain Italian women writers but also the production, reception, and circulation of women's writing. It is the work of what Nancy Miller calls "female critical subjects" not only to call into question the "canon of exclusions"[35] but also to shape an understanding of the conditions in which certain literary works are preserved and circulated. As women constitute themselves as new social subjects both inside and outside the academy, they will necessarily contribute to the reshaping of our cultural heritage.

# Notes

1. Wendell Harris, "Canonicity," *PMLA* 106 (January 1991): 110–21. See particularly 112–14 for the distinction between diachronic and nonce canon.
2. See Barbara Herrnstein Smith, "Contingencies of Value," *Critical Inquiry* (spring 1983): 11, on the notion that all value, even literary value, is "radically contingent."
3. See Harris, 116, for a discussion of that link.
4. For a more complete survey of the neglect of Italian women writers, see *Contemporary Women Writers in Italy: A Modern Renaissance*, ed. Santo Aricò (Amherst: University of Massachusetts Press, 1990), 3–7.
5. Richard Ohmann, "The Shaping of a Canon: U.S. Fiction, 1960–1975," in *Canons*, ed. R. von Hallberg (Chicago: University of Chicago Press, 1984), first published in *Critical Inquiry* (1983).
6. Ohmann, 206.
7. Ohmann, 207.

8. *Feminist Literary Theory: A Reader*, ed. Mary Eagleton (Oxford: Basil Blackwell, 1986), 2.

9. Forti studies seven Italian women writers: Banti, Romano, Manzini, Bellonci, Ginzburg, Morante, and Cialente.

10. Stefano Tani, *Il Romanzo di ritorno: Dal romanzo medio degli anni sessanta alla giovane narrativa degli anni ottanta* (Milan: Mursia, 1990).

11. Anna Nozzoli, *Tabu e coscienza: La Condizione femminile nella letteratura italiana del Novecento* (Florence: La Nuova Italia, 1978).

12. *Firmato donna: Una donna. Un secolo*, ed. Sandra Petrignani (Roma: Il ventaglio, 1986).

13. Carol Lazzaro-Weis, *From Margins to Mainstream: Feminism and Fictional Modes in Italian Women's Writing, 1968–1990* (Philadelphia: University of Pennsylvania Press, 1993).

14. See *Italica* 65 (winter 1988), a special issue entitled "Women's Voices," and *Annali d'italianistica* 7 (1989), ed. by Rebecca West (includes Italian women writers throughout the centuries).

15. Nancy K. Miller, *Subject to Change: Reading Feminist Writing* (New York: Columbia University Press, 1988), 3.

16. Elisabetta Rasy, *Le donne e la letteratura* (Rome: Editori Riuniti, 1984). "Esiste un linguaggio specifico femminino?" Rasy summarizes the debate on this issue and her own response from pp. 26 to 36.

17. Rasy, 34. "I testi letterari femminili dunque non vanno letti con il pregiudizio di rintracciarvi i tratti dell'eterno femminino, ma con lo sguardo attento anche alla condizione materiale di donne delle loro autrici." Rasy cites Ellen Moers's *Literary Women: The Great Writers* (New York: Doubleday, 1976) extensively in making this point.

18. See Carol Lazzaro-Weis, "From Margins to Mainstream: Some Perspectives on Women and Literature in Italy in the 1980's," in *Contemporary Women Writers in Italy*, 197–217.

19. Lillian S. Robinson, "Treason Our Text: Feminist Challenges to the Literary Canon," in *The New Feminist Criticism: Essays on Women, Literature and Theory*, ed. Elaine Showalter (New York: Pantheon Books, 1985), 118.

20. I have made this argument in an article entitled "Canon-formation and Reception in Contemporary Italy: The Case of Primo Levi," *Italica* 69 (spring 1992): 30–44.

21. Eagleton, 3.

22. See Susan Stanford Friedman, "Post/Poststructuralist Feminist Criticism: The Politics of Recuperation and Negotiation," *New Literary History* 92 (spring 1991): 465–90, for a discussion of Nancy K. Miller's work as the epitome of this view.

23. See Lillian S. Robinson, 109, for a discussion of this issue.

24. Sandra Petrignani, *Le signore della scrittura* (Milan: La tartaruga, 1984).

25. Michele Barrett, as summarized in Eagleton, 4.

26. Petrignani, 106, as quoted in Aricò, 5. "Sono citata nelle enciclopedie, sono presente nelle antologie. Ma una scrittrice, anche se di successo, è comunque emarginata. La diranno grande fra le altre scrittrici, ma non la equipereranno agli scrittori. E un'usanza diffusa."

27. Deborah Heller, "History, Art, and Fiction in Banti's *Artemisia*," in *Contemporary Italian Women Writers*, 45–62. See notes 4 and 18 above.

28. Sandra Petrignani, 119. "Lei è scrittore non scrittrice. Perchè tanto disprezzo per il suo sesso?" "Sarò stata sfortunata ma non ho mai conosciuto una donna veramente intelligente."

29. Heller, 57.

30. *Sexual Difference*, ed. Teresa de Lauretis (Bloomington: Indiana University Press, 1990).

31. In a conference at the Italian Cultural Institute in San Francisco in 1990, Dacia Maraini traced her "foremothers" at least as far back as Isabella de Morra.

32. See Eagleton, 1–6, for a summary of the positions of Tillie Olsen, Elaine Showalter, Ellen Moers, and others regarding the importance of a female literary tradition.

33. Silvia Bovenschen, "Is There a Feminine Aesthetic?" *New German Critique*, no. 10 (winter 1977): 111–137.

34. Teresa De Lauretis, *Technologies of Gender* (Bloomington: Indiana University Press, 1987), 92–93.

35. See Nancy K. Miller, *Subject to Change*, particularly the introduction, for a discussion of the female critical subject and the questioning of the "canon of exclusions."

# 2

---

# From One Closet to Another?
# Feminism, Literary Archaeology,
# and the Canon

*Beverly Allen*

A few years ago, I heard a lecture by a successful middle-aged female Italianist regarding some of the female figures in a major canonical text of the national Italian literary tradition. I recall that this scholar attributed a great deal of importance to these female figures and suggested that they constituted symbolic dynamics in the well-known work which would be unavailable in any interpretive act that failed to recognize the specific significance of the feminine gender of the figures in question.

After the lecture, which had been given in the privileged surroundings of a research center at a major university, I went to offer my congratulations on the clarity and precision of the talk. The speaker responded by affirming most heartily, "Well, I finally came out of the closet!" At a bit of a loss as to her meaning, since I had not found her talk to be particularly revealing in the way that phrase generally implies, I asked her "As a feminist, you mean?" "No," she replied. "As a *woman*."

The radical aspect of her statement, if not her lecture, has lately become clear to me. I have realized that our field traditionally bears a great patch of darkness that it seeks constantly to avoid, a black hole it names only to

demonize as the site of the (always negative) irrational. The name that patch
of darkness bears in Italian studies, I would suggest, is one so telling that
Jacques Lacan could use it as signifier—in *Italian*—of all that is mysterious,
unknowable, and yet somehow indicative of the presence of a body: *odor di
femmina* (Lacan, 46).[1]

Not surprisingly, the placement of the feminine in a dark patch in the field
of contemporary U.S. Italian studies echoes that found in canonical Italian
literature, its main *body* of study. There, women are repeatedly represented as
irrevocably other, as objects of desire and/or derision, as that which is lacking,
as a necessary absence/abscess where male dominance risks losing its reason,
allots to women only a symbolic role, where symbol is manipulated in the
service of male privilege, or phallogocentrism. Constantly objectified by the
masterworks of the national literary canon and by other discourses of Italian
national "identity," women's bodies serve the signifying practices of such
male-male literary communications as the poetry of the Sicilians at Federico's
late medieval court, the "chivalric" Tuscan *stilnovisti* (Allen, "Nietzsche"),
Dante, and Petrarch; and of the relatively more expansive communications
of Boccaccio, Ariosto, Tasso (Schiesari), Leopardi, D'Annunzio (Spackman),
Montale, and Zanzotto (Allen, *Andrea Zanzotto*), to name a few. Furthermore, gender effects play a major role, along with other classificatory discourses such as "race" and class, in cultural constitutions of Italian "identity,"
in peninsular life as well as beyond it (Allen and Russo).[2]

Alessandra Bocchetti of the Centro di Cultura Virginia Woolf in Rome
reminded us in 1982 that "Freud discovered the unconscious through the
bodies of women" and, in so doing, guaranteed the coaxial notion that "the
unconscious is the first great discovery of the female body" (Bono and Kemp,
150). Similarly, male scholars during the eighteenth and nineteenth centuries in Italy and during the twentieth century in Italy and elsewhere including
the United States invented a national literary canon through, among other
things, the symbolic objectification of women's bodies, from before Beatrice
to after Sylvia. In so doing, they guaranteed the once-again coaxial suggestion that canonic Italian literature enables its readers to discover women.
What actually happens, however, is that this canonical "body" of Italian literature obfuscates the experiential bodies of women, *beginning with the bodies of
the women who engage in the writing and the study of Italian literature*.

Much contemporary literary archaeology that sees itself as woman-
oriented if not "exactly" feminist works to correct the picture provided by the
Italian national literary canon. In particular, it seeks to add women to the list

of writers centrally privileged by that canon. Unfortunately, however, not enough of our recent work (and I include my *Defiant Muse* here) recognizes the ways in which this additive activity can mimic the male-determined nature of the canon itself and thus postpone the kind of change that would recognize women as subjects of literary production. The institutionalization of Italian literary studies has enabled the almost entirely male older generations of tenured full professors to trivialize the work of younger feminists, female or male. Even as younger Italianists feel impelled to widen the scope of Italian literary and cultural studies, their efforts are often cloaked in the mantle of traditionalism. While the forces that constitute the career apparently encourage such scholars to include in the canon ever more women writers, they simultaneously conspire to accommodate such additions only in the context of traditional critical discourse such as monographs and anthologies. Such modes, however, mimic the existing canon and thereby tend to neglect cultural specificity and the gendered subject both in the works studied and in the subject positions of the scholars themselves. In many cases, therefore, our anthological and monographic activities, which aim at taking women writers out of the closet of obscurity and silence, do so only to enclose them once again, this time in the closet of the canon.

Since the authors in this volume are gathered not as a group of Italian writers but rather as a group of scholars of Italian literature and culture, let me speak about the effects of canonicity and its related guarantee of male dominance in our own field of literary studies, on the bodies of those of us who are women working as Italianists in the United States.

Italian literary studies in the United States demonstrate a chiastic gender switch from the lowest ranks to the highest. In a field that makes its bread and butter from a vast majority of undergraduate students who are female, the privilege accorded to maleness is glaringly evident in the simple fact that the vast majority of tenured full professors, editors, board members of journals, and presidents of professional associations are male. From the lowest level, where there are many women, to the highest, where there are few, the stepping stones of status in our field are determined to an extent we never acknowledge quite enough by gender; and the scholarly seriousness and even the accomplishments of women are no guarantee of our full participation. In U.S. Italian studies, therefore, the dominant discourse goes something like this: It's wonderful for women to major in Italian, okay for them to do graduate degrees, appropriate for them to use these degrees to work in insecure positions such as lecturer, and threatening for them to publish seriously and be admitted on a permanent basis to the realms of institutional authority. In fact, those allowed to accede to such realms have often paid the price of conformity to the very norms of their own oppression.

The figures in a study Bettina Huber did in 1991, "Women in the Modern Languages, 1970–1990," show that this situation is not limited to Italian. In 1987, women in all "foreign" language fields holding faculty positions were divided as follows: 35.1 percent of women in faculty positions were assistant professors, 37.8 percent were associate professors, and 27.1 percent were full professors. In 1985–86, women were 58.7 percent of the Ph.D. recipients in the three largest languages, Spanish, French and German. The following year, only 27.1 percent of full professors in all languages other than English were women. This was the case only one year after 72.4 percent of the recipients of bachelor's degrees in the three largest languages other than English were women. The distance from a 74 percent female participation at the undergraduate level to a 27.1 percent female participation at the level of full professor is not accounted for by such simple considerations as, say, the professional sacrifices involved in raising a family (still mainly the burden of women). In fact, it spells out quite eloquently the infamous but widespread phenomenon known as the glass ceiling, that invisible (or at least unacknowledged) barrier to upward mobility in the academy. An institution can gain an attractive affirmative action profile by hiring women and so-called minorities at entry-level positions while protecting the male privilege of the upper strata simply by making the promotion of female or so-called minority persons an impossible or at least highly unlikely event.

While the figures in Huber's analysis do not speak directly to Italian Studies, I believe that the gender reversal from lowest to highest levels in the academic hierarchies represented there will resonate with what we notice in our own classrooms and in our own careers. Further, we may also be noticing a resounding silence about this gender reality, a silence made of our own reticence to speak about the significance of these figures and in particular about their effects on the kinds of work we who are women are allowed to do and the ways in which our work is received by male colleagues. Our silence is understandable, if regrettable. We are keyed into a rigid male hierarchy, first, simply by being in the university (historically a medieval, monastic male institution), and then by situating ourselves in a field where, as in many others, careers are almost entirely controlled by men—a field, moreover, that takes as its object of study one patriarchal culture and pursues that study in the context of another one. In particular, I would add, the subject positions of those of us who are women in Italian studies are keyed into the notion of canonical national literature and resonate with the values—I would call them phallogocentric—promulgated by that particular cultural production. Therefore, when we intervene in the formation of the canon, we are engaging in some high-risk labor.

Let me elaborate on this. I see our professional intellectual and methodological heritage as Italianists to be a bipartite legacy that is strongly phallogocentric but that also contains the possibilities of feminist methodologies. This bipartite legacy is positivism and philology. Positivism in Italian literary studies is a phallogocentric discourse par excellence. Promulgating the notion that a national literary history predates the nation-state (and therefore that a kind of "master plan" for the nation-state is legible in Dante and Petrarch, say, just as Dante finds a prophecy for the world order he would have preferred in Virgil's fourth eclogue), the positivist philosophy underlying canonical national literary history sees that history as chronologically progressive and simultaneously dependent on diachronic intertextual "influence." The dynamic of this nationalist literary reproduction resembles nothing so much as paternity and the unsexed birthing of sons. In fact, standard versions of the national Italian literary canon (Sapegno's, for example) imply that Italian national literature is almost exclusively a matter of male lineage with now and then a deviant female twig, a genealogy in which what women there are must always fill the role of daughter and never that of mother. Just as it is difficult to imagine Beatrice, Laura, Angelica, or Silvia as mothers and grandmothers, so it is not given us to see literary matrilineage in any canonical form. In contemporary literary production, this master narrative of the woman as receiver but never progenitrix is exemplified by Maria Luisa Spaziani, who is depicted as being "influenced by" Montale in the very fiber of her *endecasillabi* but who never "mothers" Patrizia Cavalli or Dacia Maraini or even—and especially not—Valerio Magrelli, despite these poets' own evident wranglings with the very same metric skeletons Spaziani privileges, and despite their mutual Roman provenance and similar themes. According to the positivist discourse of Italian national literature, women writers may be depicted only in filial roles, although they are cast in quotidian time as mistresses and wives (Spaziani again, and of course Maraini, who spent years with Alberto Moravia). In any case, they never accede to maternity, are never allowed the powerful status of originatrix, or "influencer."

The limited female role allowed in the formation of the canon is echoed by that allowed in the profession of Italian literary scholarship, where women, as perennial students, are cast time and again as the *creature* of the significant male professor who sends us out into the world where we will implicitly be barren ourselves. This daughterly status is often contradicted by other modes of relating—not all of them free of misogyny, not all of them even ethical or legal—in the daily experience of faculty interactions, but none of these enters the symbolic discourse, thus leaving female Italianists to spend our careers under the authoritative shadow of the possessive father to a greater extent than is suffered by male colleagues who can hope to aspire to that paternal status themselves.

When I see positivism and its resultant discourse of national literary canons in this light, I must recognize that the potentials it holds for feminist revision are risky, if unavoidable, and even to some degree historically necessary. Such potentials for feminist revision, I believe, lie in the practice of addition. While finding and promulgating texts by women that have previously gone unnoticed or dismissed is clearly part of feminist literary archaeology, I would suggest that such activities do not require a feminist commitment on the part of scholars. In fact, at times it seems to me that some of the additive work now going on has hints of opportunism rather than any sort of feminist consciousness as its strongest motivating factor (Allen, Review). The bandwagon, unfortunately, may be an ideologically ambiguous place.

The second part of our intellectual and methodological legacy as Italianists is philology. To the extent that it posits the notion of a chronological line or even a synchronic dynamic of influence that organizes words (and hence *referentiality, meaning, and cognition*) around clearly definable principles and practices of such influence, philology reveals itself to be at least as phallogocentric as positivism. Nonetheless, philology differentiates itself from positivism by its necessary methodological emphasis on such variables as regional specificity (in its recognition of dialectal differences, for example) and demographic fluctuation. Less abstract, therefore, and less idealist than positivist "literary history," philology emphasizes the quotidian place contexts of human experience on the Italic peninsula and in immigrant or postcolonial communities elsewhere: place contexts that lend "identity" to those who speak dialects, place contexts that contradict the phallogocentrism of nation-state "identity" that positivism, in the guise of national literary history, preaches. The emphases on group specificity, or difference, and on multiplicity that philology provides offer models for feminist thinking about literary texts precisely because they challenge any model of supreme centrality such as that of a canon. Furthermore, philology insists on the independent and interwoven significance of particular situations such as that, I would suggest, of subject positions, or even of the kind of dual subjectivity we find in much Italian feminist theory (Bono and Kemp, 1).

In this context of the gender chiasmus and the double intellectual legacy of contemporary U.S. Italian studies, what I would propose as feminist literary archaeology differs from both traditional canon revision and traditional philological research. As I see it, feminist literary archaeology would include not only the discovery and bringing to light of neglected or previously unknown texts by women and other marginalized persons but also a constant critical recognition of the effects of canonicity itself.

One goal, therefore, of such archaeology would be not to limit the study of texts according to the gender of the author. A literary archaeology inspired by a recognition of the significance of gender in cultural power dynamics would be sensitive to other categories that may be used to marginalize texts unjustly. For example, such feminist literary archaeology would seek to discover and analyze texts by men as well as women who by virtue of their sexuality, ethnicity, regionality, so-called race, or the simple fact that they write in dialect, are nudged away from positions of centrality, persons who, by virtue of these subject positions and regardless of their sex, are gendered as feminine.

Another, trickier, goal of a feminist literary archaeology would be to devise modes of textual availability and promulgation that would not imply canonical status. They would not, that is, be organized as a foundational discourse for national "identity" or any other phallogocentric ideology that builds symbolic and lived experiential power on the bodies of women while it leaves women (and any men whose subject positions are gendered as feminine) in silence, effectively cutting out our tongues, allowing us to bang our heads on glass ceilings, and reducing us to objects of adoration or contempt—which amount, as far as power is concerned, to the same thing.

I advocate, therefore, as feminist literary archaeology, a cultural practice that would hover somewhere between utopianism and *Realpolitik*. It is difficult to find an appropriate paradigm for the utopianism I suggest. As a weak model for it, I would perhaps evoke some aspects of Monique Wittig's 1969 novel, *Les guerillères*, including the creative undermining, to whatever extent possible, of phallogocentric writing, which, in her novel, exists as an institutionalization of female literature in nonlinear, impermanent, authorless books called "feminaries." Another aspect I would evoke is the novel's insistence on the desirability of forgetting traditional modes of literary history. While not without its appeal (and it is this appeal that I want to hold on to), the model holds dangers that are all too evident. First of all, Wittig's women warriors, in spite of all their literary acumen and refusal to engage in traditional master narratives, at least in writing, reproduce by gender substitution in experiential life the master narrative they seek to destroy. By establishing a matriarchy, they do no more than substitute one gender for another, a gyno-cracy for a phallocracy, a substitution that never challenges the notion of logocentricity. In so doing, they warn us against the risks of even historically necessary additive literary archaeology, which, because its aim is to get more women into the canon, posits the ideal situation of a canon made entirely of women writers. The temporary co-optation or repressive tolerance we experi-ence at present in our profession, therefore, might lead to gender substitution. But none of these strategies promotes a critique of canonicity.

Another evident danger in Wittig's novelistic model is that its utopian forgetfulness, if applied to literary production, could easily subvert any pos-sible foundational discourse, either the instrumentally essentialist one sug-gested by Gayatry Spivak or an experientially essentialist one, as suggested by Diana Fuss, for literary production by women. Forgetfulness, in the Wittigian sense, would risk erasing experience, and hence any eventual nonessentialist, or culturalist, basis for scholarly and political practice. With these notable and perhaps unsurmountable drawbacks, Wittig's novel nonetheless provides some initial version of utopian revision.

I would draw the second, *Realpolitik*, model for feminist literary archaeol-ogy from Dacia Maraini's novel, *Donna in guerra*, where Maraini emphasizes the specificity of individual subjects and the negotiations those subjects en-gage in within particular contexts such as class, region, sexuality, and physical capacity. Put into practice, this model would encourage reform within the most hierarchical, feudal, phallocentric institution outside organized religion: the university. This model would advocate literary archaeology from any given subject position in any given context without overt concern for the projected status of the found texts. It would, therefore, advocate the desirabil-ity of remembering and harken to the ways in which canonicity constitutes a kind of ideological memory, but it would claim the right to remember free of the injunction to remember in a particular way. The dangers of this *Realpolitik* model lie, I think, in the ways creative practices of remembering might im-pede an ongoing critique of canonicity.

Given these difficulties, then, I finally suggest as models for a feminist liter-ary archaeology neither Wittig's *guerillères*, who practice only gender substi-tution (or revision of the canon) without challenging logocentrism, nor *The Defiant Muse*, which did not yet recognize the implications of its additive stance. Rather, I hold to Maraini's novel, or to poems like her "Le poesie delle donne" or Marta Fabiani's "The Poetess," or especially perhaps Livia Candiani's "La morte della poesia" (in Allen, Jewell, and Kittel), because these poems remind me how normative models of Italian literature contradict the reality of my body, and how my body can be the grounding for a new literature. Like many others before, contemporary with, and after them, these Italian women writers advocate an assault not only on traditional notions of authorial propriety, but also on traditional notions of style. I believe that feminist literary scholarship now must take up a similar undoing of traditional notions, not simply of the canon, but of canonicity itself.

Those of us who engage in this critical project will be inventing new modes of discourse much in the way Luce Irigaray invents her modes of *écriture féminine*. We may, that is, adopt a technique of unraveling, of pulling the threads out of traditional phallogocentric discourse, by writing between the lines, as Irigaray does in *Speculum de l'autre femme*, or by proposing new symbolic images of ourselves, as she does in *Ce sexe qui n'en est pas un*. We may adopt the value given to lived experience, say, by the thinkers at the Libreria Collettiva della Donne in Milan. We may take from *Donna Woman Femme* a concern with situating individual subject positions and determining the relation between subject and action in order both "to affirm the self and to make it problematic" (Bono and Kemp, 197). In our individual practices, we may follow the anti-style of Dacia Maraini, and in our collective actions, we may adopt the political lesbianism of *Psych et Po* in Paris in the 1960s, thereby valorizing the community of women—or, as I would put it, the communality of all those who inhabit subject positions gendered as feminine—in our career management, our choice of scholarly projects, and our handling of the results of our literary archaeology. We might benefit as scholars, that is, as *scientists*, from Adrienne Rich's notion of a "common world of women." This would be a community based not on an essential femininity but on the communality of gendered subject positions I just mentioned. Thus, as I suggested earlier, a feminist literary archaeology would investigate the literary production of all persons whose "identities" the status quo determines are marginal. Such an archaeology would also investigate the forgotten appearance of women and other feminine subjects for the last two and a half centuries in the phallogocentric discourses of nationalism and fascism and, long before that, in the male discourse that perhaps most has touched our Western or Westernized bodies: Italian courtly love.

In all this, a feminist literary archaeology that aims simultaneously at radical canon revision and a clear critique of canonicity must recognize that it is operating from within the system it seeks utterly to undo. It thus resembles a Deriddian critique of language, a Marxist critique of class, and, perhaps most closely, the reevaluations of subject positionality that are taking place at present in ethnographic practical theory. The song accompanying all this is the song that says there is no subject position not already traversed by ideology, and that the body is the final site of ideology. As long as I keep humming this song, I shall be able, I believe, to understand the intellectual and scholarly implications of my own subject position and my own feminism. And if I do that, I shall avoid the fearful silencing that would occur were I to pull some texts out of the closet of obscurity only to lock them up once again in the closet of canonicity.

The need for a critique not only of the canon but of canonicity itself in contemporary Italian studies was brought home to me the other day when, after spending a month reading Irigaray for my course on "Comparative Feminisms: France and Italy," a male student from the Ivory Coast raised his hand to complain. "I'm troubled by all this talk about phallogocentrism," he said. He went on, "These French feminists blame everything on male power: everything powerful is phallogocentric; all women are oppressed. But it just isn't true. I know two matriarchal cultures, one in Dahomey and one in the Ivory Coast, where the men are still struggling, *struggling really hard*, for equal rights, and the women are incredibly cruel rulers."

Precisely. The most fruitful feminist scholarly interventions now are clearly about the culturally specific dynamics of gendered power relations, about not only *who* gets to have power, but *how* power is constituted. This is why I must begin my critique with an analysis of my own field and my position within that field, as gendered subject, as feminist, as Italianist.

## Notes

1. Lacan's writings contain a good number of moments where, surprisingly, all languages other than Italian seem to fail him. It is time for a study of what these moments reveal, particularly in their implications for gender and cultural difference.

2. See in particular the essays in *Designing Italy*, by Allen, Chang, Miller, Pinkus, and Russo.

## Works Cited and/or Consulted

Allen, Beverly. *Andrea Zanzotto: The Language of Beauty's Apprentice*. Berkeley and Los Angeles: University of California Press, 1988.
———. "Nietzsche's Italian Decline: The Poets." *Stanford Italian Review* 6, nos. 1–2 (1986): 333–42.

————. Review of Santo L. Aricò, ed., *Contemporary Women Writers in Italy: A Modern Renaissance*. *Modern Philology*, 1993.

Allen, Beverly, and Mary Russo, eds. *Designing Italy: "Italy" in Europe, Africa, Asia, and the Americas*. Minneapolis: University of Minnesota Press, forthcoming 1996.

Allen, Beverly, Keala Jewell, and Muriel Kittell, eds. *The Defiant Muse: Italian Feminist Poems from the Middle Ages to the Present*. New York: Feminist Press, 1986.

Bono, Paola, and Sandra Kemp, eds. *Italian Feminist Thought: A Reader*. Oxford: Blackwell, 1991.

Clifford, James. *The Predicament of Culture*. Cambridge: Harvard University Press, 1988.

Fuss, Diana. *Essentially Speaking: Feminism, Nature, and Difference*. New York: Routledge, 1989.

Huber, Bettina. "Women in the Modern Languages, 1970–1990." Manuscript. New York: Modern Language Association, 1991.

Irigaray, Luce. *Ce sexe qui n'en est pas un*. Paris: Editions de Minuit, 1977.

————. *Speculum de l'autre femme*. Paris: Editions de Minuit, 1974.

Lacan, Jacques. *Le Séminaire sur "La lettre volée." Écrits I*. Paris: Le Seuil, 1966.

Maraini, Dacia. *Donna in guerra*. Turin: Einaudi, 1975.

Miceli Jeffries, Giovanna, ed. *Feminine Feminists: Cultural Practices in Italy*. Minneapolis: University of Minnesota Press, 1994.

Rich, Adrienne Cecile. *The Dream of a Common Language*. New York: Norton, 1978.

Rosaldo, Renato. *Culture and Truth*. Boston: Beacon, 1989.

Schiesari, Juliana. *Appropriating the Work of Women's Mourning: The Legacy of Renaissance Melancholia*. Milwaukee: University of Wisconsin, Center for Twentieth-Century Studies, 1990–91.

Spackman, Barbara. *Decadent Genealogies*. Ithaca: Cornell University Press, 1989.

Wittig, Monique. *Les guerillères*. Paris: Editions de Minuit, 1969.

## Italian Philology

Balduino, Armando. *Manuale di filologia italiana*. 3d ed. Florence: Sansoni, 1989.

Bessi, Rossella. *Guida alla filologia italiana*. Florence: Sansoni, 1984.

Castellani, Arrigo Ettore. *Saggi di linguistica e filologia italiana e romanza (1946–1976)*. Rome: Salerno editrice, 1980.

*Chroniques italiennes*. Paris: Université de la Sorbonne nouvelle–Paris III.

Contini, Gianfranco. *Altri esercizi (1942–1971)*. Turin: Einaudi, 1972.

————. *Letteratura dell'Italia unita. 1868–1968*. Florence: Sansoni, 1968.

————. *Letteratura italiana del Risorgimento, 1789–1861*. Florence: Sansoni, 1986.

————. *Ultimi esercizi ed elzeviri (1968–1987)*. Turin: Einaudi, 1989.

————. *Varianti e altra linguistica*. 3d ed. Florence: Sansoni, 1989.

*Documents de travail et prepublications du S.L.P.T. (Nanterre)*: Université de Paris X, Nanterre, Centre de recherches de langue et littérature italiennes.

*Forschungsstand und Perspektiven der Italianistik*. Erlangen: Universitätsbund Erlangen–Nurnberg, 1988.

Migliorini, Bruno. *The Contribution of the Individual to Language*. Oxford: Clarendon, 1952.

————. *Dal nome proprio al nome comune*. Geneva: L. S. Olschki, 1927.

————. *Lingua contemporanea*. 2d rev. ed. Florence: Sansoni, 1939.

————. *Lingua d'oggi e di ieri*. Caltanissetta-Rome: S. Sciascia, 1973.

————. *Parole e storia*. Milan: Rizzoli, 1975.

————. *Storia della lingua italiana*. 3d ed. Florence: Sansoni, 1961.

Nencioni, Giovanni. *Di scritto e di parlato*. Bologna: Zanichelli, 1983.

————. *Fra grammatica e rettorica*. Florence: Olschki, 1953.

————. *Francesco De Sanctis e la questione della lingua.* Naples: Bibliopolis, 1984.
————. *Intorno alla linguistica.* Milan: Feltrinelli, 1983.
————. *La lingua dei "Malavoglia."* Naples: Morano, 1988.
Schiaffini, Alfredo. *Italiano antico e moderno.* Milan: Ricciardi, 1975.
Stussi, Alfredo. *Nuovo avviamento agli studi di filologia italiana.* Bologna: Il Mulino, 1988.

## Italian Literary History

Allodoli, Ettore. *Storia della letteratura italiana ad uso dei licei classici e delle persone colte.* Palermo: R. Sandron, 1929.
Asor Rosa, Alberto. *Sintesi di storia della letteratura italiana.* Florence: La Nuova Italia, 1972.
————. *Storia della letteratura italiana.* Florence: La Nuova Italia, 1985.
Barberi-Squarotti, Giorgio. *Storia della civiltà letteraria italiana.* Turin: UTET, 1990.
Cecchi, Emilio. *Storia della letteratura italiana.* Milan: Garzanti, 1965.
D'Ancona, Alessandro. *Studi sulla letteratura italiana dei primi secoli.* Ancona: Morelli, 1884.
De Sanctis, Francesco. *Storia della letteratura italiana.* Naples: Fratelli Morano, 1913.
————. *Storia della letteratura italiana dai primi secoli agli albori del trecento corredata con una ampia antologia dalle origini a Iacopone da Todi.* Milan: Hoepli, 1950.
Donadoni, Eugenio. *Breve storia della letteratura italiana dalle origini ai nostri giorni.* Milan: Signorelli, 1924.
————. *A History of Italian Literature.* New York: New York University Press, 1969.
Flora, Francesco. *Storia della letteratura italiana.* 12th ed. Milan: Mondadori, 1961.
Getto, Giovanni. *Poeti del Novecento e altre cose.* Milan: Mursia, 1977.
————. *Storia della letteratura italiana.* Milan: Rizzoli, 1972.
Mengaldo, Pier Vincenzo. *La tradizione del Novecento.* Milan: Feltrinelli, 1975.
Momigliano, Attilio. *Storia della letteratura italiana dalle origini ai nostri giorni.* 8th ed. Milan: G. Principato, 1963.
Pacifici, Sergio. *A Guide to Contemporary Italian Literature, from Futurism to Neorealism.* Cleveland: World, 1962.
Sapegno, Natalino. *Compendio di storia della letteratura italiana.* Florence: La Nuova Italia, 1960–61.
————, ed. *Storia della letteratura italiana.* Milan: Garzanti, 1988.

# 3

# Italian "Difference Theory": A New Canon?

*Renate Holub*

In 1987, two volumes appeared on the Italian publishing market that were to leave a decidedly distinct mark on the feminist public sphere in Italy, one that persists to this day. The first one, entitled *Diotima: Il pensiero della differenza sessuale*, was authored by a group of twelve individually mentioned women philosophers from Verona, and the second one, entitled *Il Filo di Arianna: Letture della differenza sessuale*, was authored by three feminist scholars, and again by women philosophers from Verona, this time representing themselves under the single name tag of "Gruppo di filosofia Diotima."[1] What both volumes squarely signal—*pace* this somewhat confusing interchange between Diotima qua concept and Diotima qua collective authors—is a relation of Diotima to the concept of "differenza sessuale," which, as a version of Western essentialist feminist theory, is perhaps best rendered for the purposes of this essay as "Italian difference theory." Known all over Italy, Diotima has turned into a controversial point of reference. Women's groups from Lecce to Turin or from Bari to Pisa follow the "Diotima phenomenon," observe the group's dynamics, comment on its publications in reviews and articles, and reject, modify, or incorporate Diotima's perspectives into their own political and cultural programs. No doubt, the advent of Diotima is one of the most important developments of Italian neofeminism in the eighties. Indeed, some foreign observers go so far as to suggest that Diotima's program could revolutionize the state of the Western feminist arts.[2]

For readers unfamiliar with the salient developments of Italian neofeminism, readings of Diotima's texts evince no immediately apparent analytical, topical, or methodological significance. Their textual goals are those of ordinary Western feminist fashion. For one, as *Il Filo di Arianna* discloses, they attempt to construct a canon of literary and philosophical writings that focuses on women rather than on men figures, that emphasizes continuities (*filo*) rather than ruptures, thereby legitimating feminine, rather than masculine, genealogies and point of references. In this, they parallel the efforts of countless women's studies courses in the United States over the last twenty years, attentive to reconstructing, and consequently to legitimizing, literary and cultural traditions of and for women. For another, and as *Pensiero della differenza sessuale* notes, they develop a body of philosophical knowledge based on the principle of "sexual difference." In this, they also parallel the efforts of countless Western neofeminist essentialist theorists to construct a philosophical system from a perspective that not only questions the gendered or embodied nature of traditional knowledge systems but that also surveys the possibility of ontological, epistemological, and ethical structures based not on masculine but on feminine fundamentals. Moreover, by evoking the tradition of Greek mythology and philosophy with figures such as Arianna or Diotima and by adhering to the concept of "pensiero" or "thought," the Verona group Diotima chooses to juggle a value-laden symbolics that, by privileging Western philosophical traditions at the expense of non-Western ways of seeing and doing, chooses not to exceed the limits of that worldview. So in cleaving to Greek philosophy as the preferred point of reference—*Nonostante Platone: Figure femminili nella filosofia antica* is a recent publication of Adriana Cavarero, a member of the Diotima group—they legitimize the institutional, disciplinary, and geographic hegemony of classical philosophy.[3] In this, they offer no alternative to most Western philosophical texts. They also offer few feminist research advances when not expressly moving within the referential and topical orbit of classical philosophy. In *Mettere al mondo il mondo: Oggetto e oggettività alla luce della differenza sessuale*, where they exclusively target women philosophers and theologians such as Saint Teresa d'Avila, Simone Weil, and Hannah Arendt, they likewise engage in a research program typical of some branches of Western feminist theory: that which chooses feminine models in order to subvert, detour, replace, or even nullify masculine authority.[4] In short, in the context of Western intellectual feminism, there seems to be nothing particularly inordinate or advanced in Diotima's textual practice of the feminist arts.

Why then would Diotima so conspicuously command the Italian feminist spotlight, cash in on cultural windfall profits, enjoy tabloid and genteel culture popularity alike, if all they do is participate in the standard neofeminist liberal practice of textually instituting feminine philosophical canons? Is it because Italian women, unheeding feminist canon output of other cultural contexts, lay claim to undue indigenous substance? Alas, a brief look at the reception history of Western feminist thought in Italy will *tout de suite* make it obvious to anyone that Italian feminists have made it their province to be and to remain adept in Western feminist theorems, radical, conservative, liberal, and neoliberal alike.[5] Italian feminists are well versed in feminist trajectories in the United States; U.S. feminists have far less reciprocal knowledge. So if Italy's peripheral position in the Western hegemonic feminist discourse does not propel plausible explanatory powers, what then accounts for Diotima's dynamite performance on the Italian feminist pulpit? In order to provide some answers, I will have to turn my attention to another book that also appeared in 1987: *Non credere di avere dei diritti: La generazione della libertà femminile nell'idea e nelle vicende di un gruppo di donne*. Its author is again a collective, this time not Diotima, but women from the "Liberia delle donne di Milan," from the Milan Woman's Bookstore Collective.[6]

I should say from the outset that in the Italian feminist public sphere, *Non credere* met with strikingly momentous resonance. Again from Lecce to Turin and from Bari to Pisa, women's groups are dramatically familiar with this publication, comment on its grounds, polemicize against or for it, and offer unbridled opinions of it. Indeed, *Non credere*'s embattled discursive journey throughout the peninsula seems clouded only by the prevailing radiance of an equally embattled discourse, that of the already mentioned Verona Diotima group. What constitutes the relation between Verona and Milan, between a group of women philosophers, Diotima, and the Women's Bookstore of Milan? Does Milan sustain the efforts of Verona, or is it the other way around? What or who is their common denominator, what constitutes their weaknesses, and what their strengths? To begin with, similar to other Diotima publications, *Non credere* evidences no inordinate feminist knowledge to readers unfamiliar with the intellectual history of Italian neofeminism, and the way in which feminist problematics are played out in the dialectic between media representation and everyday life. This is probably the reason why the English/American translation of this text, compared to the German

translation, received a rather modest reception.[7] In spite of publishing efforts
on the topic by numerous scholars, Italian neofeminism and its conceptual
innovations in the area of political, social, and cultural theory, are still largely
unknown to an American intellectual audience. So on the surface, there
seems nothing particularly thematically novel in the text of *Non credere*. The
book narrates a story of the Italian neofeminist liberational struggles, beginning with the well-known feminist manifesto of the mid-sixties and continu-
ing with many nationally known feminist meetings in the seventies, while
simultaneously painstakingly tracing the evolution of a "sexual difference"
perspective that in English is perhaps best rendered as the Italian version of
essentialist, fundamentalist, and in any event separatist, feminism. This "sexual difference" perspective, informing a rigorously pursued separatist con-
structivist politics, is the upshot, so the narrative asserts, of reflecting on almost twenty years of collective experiences in the neofeminist movement.
Indeed, practicing separatist politics, based on the principle of "sexual difference," is viewed as a historical necessity. While deconstructing male privilege
and power, circumscribing women's victimization in current societies, challenging women's marginal status in the political and social spheres, and mili-
tantly participating in political organizations had yielded some emancipatory
proceeds for women—changes in family and abortion law; advanced research
programs in victimization mechanisms—such feminist campaigns have not,
however, so the book reasons, secured women's authentic freedom. Juridical
emancipation and advanced knowledge of victimization are thus conditions
of, but no substitutes for, authentic liberation. When women neither legitimize each other, nor ascribe authority to each other by way of referential
systems indifferent to the law-of-the-father, to use a Lacanian formulation,
then women's social legitimation, their acquisition of status and authority,
necessarily takes place within a symbolic and social framework that denies
women their fundamental difference: the fact that they are essentially different from men, and, moreover, that that difference remained unnamed in the
"neutral," abstract, and disembodied knowledge and value structures sustaining Western thought as they contribute to the subordination of women.[8]
The knowledge of sexual difference, that women are both the other of men
and the other from each other, leads not only to the recognition of women's
victimization. It also leads, so the book argues, to the recognition that women
are not equal but unequal to each other, insofar as some women enjoy more
economic and social advantages than other women, and insofar as some
women are endowed with more will and determination than other women.
However, since recognition of a "more" in other women, or of a "less" in

oneself, can easily lead to envy and to a static position of powerlessness, the volume suggests that it is preferable to develop a positive practice that transforms stasis into dynamics: the practice of sexual difference. This is what the history of the Italian neofeminist movement, as experienced and narrated by the authors of the volume, indubitably implies. A crucial document for arriving at this position is the famous "Sottosopra Verde" of 1983, a collectively authored document of the Women's Bookstore of Milan entitled "Piu donne che uomini."[9] In this document as well as in *Non credere*, the success of women's liberation, or women's individual realization as social and human beings, hinges not on solidarity between women together striving for equality in the public sphere, nor on attempting to wrest fair and equitable treatment of women from existing social, juridical, and political systems, as the hegemonic ideology of Western neofeminism propounded throughout the sixties and seventies. What that feminist history urges instead is that women's authentic freedom hinges on practicing a separatist politics of nonsolidarity that by stressing an acknowledgement not of equalities but of disparities between women, calls for activating these disparities in a process in which women entrust themselves to other women for the immediate purpose of delimiting the limits—social, economic, cultural, symbolic—imposed on women's actual lives. In short, a system of mentoring between women, called "affidamento" or the entrusting of a woman of less authority to one of more authority, will contribute, so postulates *Non credere*, to women's liberation from less power in real and symbolic terms, which is synonymous with women's access to more social status and power in real and symbolic realms.

If the important message of *Non credere* resides in the relation of "affidamento" or "matronage" system to women's liberation, a reader on this side of the ocean might appropriately cite a series of political objections or wonder whether he/she was being offered a dated feminist hat. After all, "affidamento," can be easily interpreted as belonging to the register of basic common sense in antidiscrimination discourses. Most liberational struggles, conservative or progressive alike, include a concept of mentoring or patronage. A member of a minority, as Anita Hill recently phrased it, stays at the outside of power as long as he/she has no access to power via a patron or an authority who enjoys status and power within the inside.[10] Moreover, we are used to the demands of so-called minorities to be represented by a member of their community, or to have a member of their community function as an authority or role model for reasons that are as political as they are symbolic and social. Multicultural student organizations regularly ask for multicultural representation and curricula at educational institutions. In addition, a critic of *Non credere* might also point out that the institution of patronage has been a fundamental structure in power management and maintenance systems in one thousand years of bourgeois political history of which the "old boys' network," among other institutions, identified but not dismantled by neofeminist analysis, is still a vestige, and in which the "old girls' network," constructed by women without structurally transforming its sustaining liberal bourgeois value-system, functions in ways commensurate with the "old boys' network:" some are part of the network, at the expense of those who are not. In other words, a reader might object to the desirability of the structure of "matronage," if that structure indeed differs little from patronage, thereby facilitating the social access of some, albeit women, at the expense of the social negligence of others, possibly again women? Furthermore, when *Non credere* contends that the "matronage" system of constructive politics, as the quid pro quo of women's access to authentic freedom, reflects the ineffectiveness of exclusively deconstructionist techniques in the project of women's liberation, then a reader might again point out that separatist constructionist solutions, including various forms of "matronage" systems, have been the by-product of many Western feminisms since the inception of neofeminism. In the United States, for instance, separatist constructionist feminist politics inspired the vision of feminist institutions, women's studies and women's centers, women's bookstores and houses for battered women; and this vision continues, albeit more in the interstices than in the mainstream of civil society, to this day. What also continues to this day is the inexorable connectedness of a political will to that vision. If that political will centers on individual rather than on collective social proceeds, the vision often turns into a callous neoliberal free-for-all. So separatist constructionist feminist politics provided not only the basis for attempting to transform institutions and for building new organizations in the United States; they also shaped research programs in the social sciences and the humanities. "Standpoint theory," as elaborated by Nancy Hartsock, and Patricia Collins's *Black Feminist Thought*, are examples of attempts at separatist knowledge systems, and so are the various philosophical propositions based on an ethics of care, motherhood, and mother-daughter relations.[11] And finally, when *Non credere* adds to the conceptual scheme of "matronage" system and liberation the term "authority," recommending that women accept and seek the authority of other women, then such a term also does not ring an unfamiliar bell. In a hierarchically structured society, such as in a class society, there are always women of more authority and women of less authority. While it is surely true that that authority often or always was and still is contingent on women's relation to a man of authority, and while, for this reason, women's male-contingent authority has often been rejected by feminists, we can still raise the question as to why the new authority should consist of superior qualities. Simply because this time this new authority is presumably autonomous (unrelated to male authority, that is)?[12] From the point of view of nonauthority position, both authority positions, the feminine-autonomous authority and the male-contingent authority are still authorities, positions of more power in relation to positions of less. What *Non credere* fosters is an acceptance of "authority," or rather a submission to it, not dissimilar from assumptions that sustain neoliberal pragmatic policies in the new world order: some will have access to social proceeds; a third, let us say, at the expense of two-thirds, who do not, and the latter are expected to ascribe a state of normalcy to that relation.

No doubt, *Non credere* is fraught with an entire series of political liabilities if one works from the philosophical premise that nonhierarchical relations are preferable to unequal relations of power between human beings, and also between women, or if one postulates that women's struggle for political and juridical equality cannot be left to destiny as new developments in transnational capitalism and their effects on existing welfare state systems affects women's relation to the household, to work, to state policy (women's status as private or public citizens, that is).[13] "Difference theory" surely has been criticized from such perspectives, and I do not intend to discuss these and other objections here.[14] The question I pursue instead concerns the conditions of possibility of the book's resonance. Has the Italian feminist community, once a paradigm of leftist militancy in European feminism, renewed an interest in liberal political thought by turning neoliberal with their adherence to "difference theory," which does not challenge but rather legitimates social, economic, and cultural inequities between women? Or should the "affidamento" principle, sanctioning "natural" hierarchies and unequal relations of power, be understood as part not only of a short-term, but also of a long-term political strategy, one that views women's liberation as a complex historical process inexorably extending over many generations? Was feminism not, as Sheila Rowbotham phrased it as early as the sixties, the longest revolution? Plausible responses to such questions, it seems to me, would have to take into account the complex shifts in Western democracies and formerly socialist countries alike affecting the makeup of social and intellectual movements and apparently encouraging the recurrence of belief systems based on antiegalitarian rather than egalitarian philosophies. Again, it is obviously not the place here to approach such problems, which involve sophisticated interdisciplinary studies of prejudice production structures ranging from social mem-

ory and the role of language to the structuration and reproduction of symbolic, belief-, and value-systems. The reemergence of prejudice, ethnic strife,
racism and anti-enlightenment social beliefs, particularly, but not only in the
formerly socialist countries, has brought home the need for rigorous study of
the structures of what Gramsci called civil society, the site of anti-egalitarian
prejudice production and reproduction and their social effects. While many
comparative social studies research programs focusing on these issues are under way, tangible results are still outstanding.[15] And so are the range of the
applicability of methods and analysis to other forms of prejudice production.
Above all, there is as of yet no dependable body of knowledge that would go
beyond offering tools for detection and analysis of nonegalitarian belief systems and their social and cultural representation by suggesting ways for
implementing transformatory processes from prejudice to antiprejudice and
nonprejudice. Given such enormous conceptual, methodological, and analytical difficulties, let it suffice to say here while Italian "difference theory,"
with its submission to nonegalitarian figures of thought, plausibly reflects a
"neoliberal" shift of large parts of the Italian feminist community in the era
of renewed interest in free-market economies and its concomitant espousal of
an end-of-history ideology, it is nonetheless equally plausible that the Italian
version of "difference theory" understands itself as what we might call not a
"neoliberal" but a "pre-liberal" social and political policy, a pre-phase and
preface to authentic liberation of sorts, precisely because authentic liberation
is not only, as Hegel thought, a matter of consciousness propelling itself
through the various historical and conceptual stages of the master-slave dialectic. Rather, liberation is also a matter of the unconscious, as one of the
major models of Italian "difference theory," Luce Irigaray, had proposed when
she problematized the absence of freedom in women's lives in its relation to
the Lacanian four-dimensional dynamic fields—symptom, real, imaginary,
and symbolic—propelling the unconscious.[16] The texts of Milan and Verona
reflect, to various degrees, a desire to find ways of cleansing the unconscious,
which they understand in a Lacanian-Irigarayan way as the site of mathema-
tized patriarchal orders of linguistically structured imaginaries and symbolics.
They are searching for ways, contrary to Lacan, yet still partially with Hegel,
of structuring both consciousness and the unconscious with a presumably liberatory matriarchal or feminine symbolics of which there is no order as of yet.
Some brief observations on the latter contention are in order.

   While there is not much evidence to sustain that the Milan Women's
Bookstore Collective and the Verona Diotima group have expressly opted for
a long-term rather than a short-term political strategy in their struggle for

women's liberation, there is evidence—textual and otherwise—to sustain that both groups engage in painstakingly structured linguistic and conceptual operations. For what is striking about the texts of both Milan and Verona is the dextrous use of language, syntax, and rhetorics, resulting in an intricate web of present and absent textual relations, of informant, invocatory, and silenced information, a shifting interchange of intentionalities and meaning in textual self-representation, a feminist cabala of sorts. *Non credere*, for instance, on the surface, deploys a simple, straightforward, jargonless prose, perhaps designed to reach the largest possible language. (As ardent followers of Luce Irigaray, as many of the feminists under consideration are, their stylistic discipline might come as a surprise.)[17] Historians of Italian feminism could point out that the conscious use of an accessible language is not new to Italian feminist rhetoric. The texts of many second-wave Italian feminists, from the most diverse fields of knowledge, are marked by rhetorical discipline. Let me mention the sociologist and political theorists Mariarosa Dalla Costa *The Power of Women and the Subversion of the Community*, written in conjunction with Selma James (1972), or the work of the philosopher Carla Lonzi, *Sputiamo su Hegel: La Donna clitoridea e la donna vaginale* (1974). The work of the psychoanalyst Lea Melandri, *L'infamia originaria: Facciamola finita col cuore e con la politica* (1977) can also be cited.[18] To this list, we can easily add internationally known intellectuals such as Rossana Rossanda, Maria Antonietta Macciocchi, or Dacia Maraini, feminists who made it their explicit business to wisely use disseminatory technologies for feminist purposes.[19] What all of these women have in common is their politicized sensibility for rhetorical matters, which manifests itself in their self-imposed stylistic constraint in spite of the complexity of the theoretical matters they propose. This is also a striking feature of earlier Italian feminist writings, such as the work of the most outstanding Italian emancipationist, Anna Maria Mozzoni.[20] That *Non credere* observes the rules of accessibility is thus not without historical precedence in Italy. What is unprecedented is that it subsumes its linguistic accessibility into a complex theory of liberation by way of a rhetorical process that downplays the complexity of the theory by syntactical choices and by studiously omitting any reference to major philosophical systems or models as it evokes, due to conceptual and terminological choices, massive registers of political, social, philosophical, and psychoanalytical bodies of knowledge with which it indubitably entertains relations. The fact that Marx, Hegel, Freud, Nietzsche, Lacan, Irigaray, Cixous and other major modern philosophers are not by name mentioned in connection with "difference theory" is neither indicative of the philosophical depth informing this theory, nor reflective of the extensive philosophical and political debates that "difference" theorists engaged in over many years. A dialectic between simplicity and complexity is thus the trademark of "difference theory," and the full title *Non credere di avere dei diritti: La generazione della libertà femminile nell'idea e nelle vicende di un gruppo di donne*, is a good case in point.

The first sentence links the history of Italian neofeminism to a woman philosopher, Simone Weil, whose "non credere di avere dei diritti" functions as the informing introductory quote of the text. The second sentence implies that feminine freedom, and its generation, the practice of "difference theory," was the upshot of women's experiences, and their reflection thereof, during the period of neofeminism. What these two titular phrases also signal, however, is the impact of ideas on the interpretation of facts, and the impact of ideas, therefore, in the evolution of "difference theory." Indeed, key concepts of modern political and social theory as they have been developed in the context of materialist and idealist philosophical systems are constitutive of the title. Terms such as "diritti," "generazione della liberta," and "idea" and "vicende" evoke the complex discourses of political rights and duties, (*diritti*), the autopoetic generation of freedom (*generazione della libertà*), and the dialetic of theory and practice (*vicende, idea*), thereby moving the argument into a series of knowledge fields ranging from the history of natural-rights philosophy to debates on women's private and public citizenship relation to state, society, and culture, and from the philosophical problem of the essence and origin of true freedom (guarantee of individual rights and will to freedom) to the practical problem of how to achieve it in a society without reducing these rights to mere duties or without reducing the rights of others. Moreover, these key terms also move the argument into the embattled arena of materialism and idealism. "Non credere di avere dei diritti" alludes to women's nominal possession of *political rights* in a modern democratic state, which is no guarantee for "having rights," for exercising full *social rights* in everyday life: you are off when you think you have any rights. As citizens, women entertain a certain relation with the state, or with political and juridical society, which guarantees the political right to vote as well as legal rights and duties. Yet this political relation of women to the state defining their subjecthood is mediated by civil and cultural society, the site of the production and reproduction of nonequality relations between the sexes, and the site of nonequality relations between social groups. As a result, women's political rights do not deter the absence of social rights for women. This lack of social rights is a limitation or even a lack of freedom. In order to "generate freedom" for women, "difference theory" promotes a process in which they attempt to work out the pernicious problem of gaining social rights as corollaries of political rights.[21] Insofar as the lack of social and cultural rights is linked to both the presence of a patriarchal language of power and to the absence of a feminine or mother-based language of power, the process of women's liberation involves not only a liberational phenomenological practice inspired by the relation of Hegel's philosophy of right, or his "filosofia del diritto," to his phenomenology, or his "generation of freedom." It also involves going beyond Hegel when the feminine unconscious joins feminine consciousness in its dialectical march toward freedom by erasing the patriarchal data from the feminine unconscious and consciousness, by devaluing all values in the validation of new symbolic orders: that of the mother as point of departure and point of arrival of the feminine subject. Radical linguistic and conceptual defiguration refigures the figures of consciousness and the unconscious housed in a female body. *Nonostante Platone: Figure femminili nella filosofia antica* is Adriana Cavarero's latest book, and *L'ordine simbolico della madre* belongs to Luisa Muraro.[22]

So "difference theory" promotes the notion of an authentic liberation contingent on a dialectical process in which an entirely novel symbolic and imaginary system, a woman's autonomous language, painstakingly attempts to withdraw the conscious and unconscious grounds of patriarchal referents in order to stake the sites with the symbolic order of the mother.[23] Yet "difference theory" also promotes the notion that the restructuring of texts includes not only the texts of mind and body, or written texts of women writers and philosophers. It also includes the restructuring of social texts. Indeed, Diotima in writing their texts, restructure, by way of the specific form of their production process, the social text within which they function. Their model is not a women's studies program, but a program of studies of women based on a radical feminine principle in the context of a traditional university. So without naming it in their texts, Diotima executes, what "difference theory" proposes, the practice of a theory of sexual difference, the practice of establishing a tradition of practitioners of "difference theory." In this sense Diotima is the most immediate and visible implementation of a long-term political strategy, and as such perhaps the most important political asset of Milan's "difference theory."

There is no doubt that this unusual symbiosis of Verona and Milan has played a role in the prestige, however embattled, that "difference theory" enjoys all over Italy. There is also no doubt, however, that "difference theory" did not simply evolve out of Italian neofeminism, as *Non credere* would have it. Powerful women orchestrated the organization of the practice of "difference theory," and Luisa Muraro is perhaps the best example of such women. She indefatigably shuttles "difference theory" among Milan, Verona, and the rest of Italy, directs disciples from city to city, organizes monumental seminars, translates all of Luce Irigaray into Italian, relentlessly intervenes in the mainstream press, and composes her own scholarly and theoretical books while practicing the art of "sexual practice," the art of socially advancing women. While hundreds, perhaps thousands of women facilitated and participated in the advent of Italian "difference theory," there is also no doubt that the leadership of women such as Luisa Muraro was decisive for the success of the operation and that women like her directed the implementation of theory into practice or of practice into a theory.

That Luisa Muraro is probably the top manager of the "difference" corporation is fascinating insofar as it suggests that a business, in order to yield profits, needs leadership, vision, energy, and force. The feminist business is no exception. What will also be fascinating is seeing whether "difference theory," the practice of which depends on a hierarchical principle of nonegalitarianism, will be able to sustain its current diffusional power as Italian culture experiences, next to other cultures, the effects of momentous political and social transformations in Europe. While feminists in the Italian south have in general cautiously reacted to a proposal from the north that stresses nonegalitarian practices as a key to feminist liberation, recent recurrences of discriminatory political agendas, such as the Lega Lombarda, should intensify the skepticism of southern feminists with respect to Lombardian "difference theory."[24] Political circumstances, such as the relentless intensification of the New Right, may not constitute the only obstacle, however, in the path of a theory whose long-term strategy is as intriguing as its short-term practice is problematical. Sooner or later "difference theory" will have to settle with the problem it inherited by choosing to settle with a resettlement—however radical—of the grounds of social-symbolic canonical sets. So far there are no indications that wresting social-symbolic power, with its inherent nonegalitarian structures, from the canon of the father will turn into egalitarian social-symbolic powers of the canon of the mother. Momentous credit is still due to "difference" theorists for having tried.

# Notes

1. Adriana Cavarero, Cristiana Fischer, Elvia Franco, Giannina Longobardi, Veronica Mariaux, Luisa Muraro, Anna Maria Piussi, Wanda Tommasi, Anita Sanvitto, Betty Zamarchi, Chiara Zamboni, Gloria Zanardo, *Diotima: Il pensiero della differnza sessuale* (Milan: La Tar-

taruga, 1987); and Franca Bimbi, Laura Grasso, Marina Zancan, Gruppo di filosofia Diotima, *Il Filo di Arianna: Letture della differenza sessuale* (Rome: Cooperativa Utopia, 1987).

2. See Rosi Braidotti, *Patterns of Dissonance: A Study of Women in Contemporary Philosophy* (New York: Routledge, 1991), 261; also Renate Holub, "For the Record: The Non-Language of Italian Feminist Philosophy," *Romance Language Annual* 1 (1990): 133–40; as well as Renate Holub, "The Politics of 'Diotima,'" *Differentia* 6 (1990): 161–72; and Renate Holub, "Weak Thought and Strong Ethics: The 'Postmodern' and Feminist Theory in Italy," *Annali d'Italianistica* 9 (1991): 124–41.

3. Adriana Cavarero, *Nonostante Platone: Figure femminili nella filosofia antica* (Rome: Editori Riuniti, 1991).

4. Diotima. *Mettere al mondo il mondo: Oggetto e oggettività alla luce della differenza sessuale* (Milan: La Tartaruga, 1990).

5. Most of the classics of Western feminism have been translated into Italian. The journals *Memoria* as well as *Donna Woman Femme* produced many issues focusing on international feminism, and many figures such as Virginia Woolf, Adrienne Rich, and Simone de Beauvoir are as well known as they are admired by Italian feminists. The important women centers in Rome are Virginia Woolf A, and Virginia Woolf B, respectively, another comment on the figures of importance to Italian feminists. For an introductory essay on Italian feminist theory, see Renate Holub, "Towards a New Rationality: Notes on Feminism and Current Discursive Practices in Italy," *Discourse* 4 (1981–82): 89–107. For a detailed account of Italian feminism, see Lucia Chiavola Birnbaum, *Liberazione della donna: Feminism in Italy* (Middletown: Wesleyan University Press, 1986).

6. Librerie delle donne di Milano. *Non credere di avere dei diritti: La generazione della libertà femminile nell'idea e nelle vicende di un gruppo di donne* (Turin: Rosenberg and Sellier, 1987).

7. The Milan's Women Bookstore Collective. *Sexual Difference: A Theory of Social-Symbolic Practice* (trans. Patrizia Cicogna and Teresa de Lauretis) was published by Indiana University Press in 1990. Discussions on "difference theory" here in the United States in general make no reference, however, to the Indiana University edition. On the other hand, Libreria delle donne di Milano. *Wie weibliche Freiheit entsteht: Eine neue politische Praxis* (Berlin: Orlanda Frauenverlag, 1988) received a good deal of attention soon after its publication throughout Germany, and women's groups have formed in order to practice "difference theory." See Dorit Werner, *Theorie und Praxis der "Differenza Sessuale," und das Konzept "Weibliches Arbeitsvermögen"—Kulturelle Übersetzung als Möglichkeit, die italienische Theorie und Praxis darzustellen und ins Deutsche zu übertragen.* Diplomarbeit im Fach Politikwissenschaften und der Universität Bremen, 1991. See also Dorit Werner, "In der PCI zu sein ist eine Synthese. Frauenpolitik in der PCI—eine Politik der Differenz," in *Kommune* 10 (1988): 36–38.

8. See Adriana Cavarero's essay "The Need for Sexed Thought," in Paola Bono and Sandra Kemp, eds., *Italian Feminist Thought: A Reader* (Oxford: Basil Blackwell, 1991), 181–86.

9. Libreria delle Donne di Milano, "More women than men," in Paola Bono and Sandra Kemp, eds., *Italian Feminist Thought: A Reader*, 110–23. This piece is known as *Sottosopra Verde* in Italy, where it has been published in many editions. Lia Cigarini, a lawyer, key theorist of "difference theory" and one of the authors of this piece, informed me during my visit to the Milan Bookstore on 9 November 1992 that the Bookstore Collective worked six years on the content and wording of this piece.

10. Anita Hill, speaking at Georgetown University in November 1992, as reproduced on Channel 9, San Francisco, 2 January 1993.

11. For Nancy M. Hartsock, see "The Feminist Standpoint: Developing the Ground for a Specifically Feminist Historical Materialism," in *Discovering Reality*, ed. Sandra Harding and Merrill B. Hintikka (Boston: D. Reidel, 1983), 283–310; as well as her *Money, Sex, and Power* (Boston: Northeastern University Press, 1983). For Patricia Collins, see her *Black Feminist Thought: Knowledge, Consciousness, and the Politics of Empowerment* (Routledge: New York, 1990). For discussions of U.S. difference theory, see Claudia Card, ed. *Feminist Ethics* (Law-

rence: University Press of Kansas, 1991); Sarah Lucia Hoagland, *Lesbian Ethics: Toward New Value* (Palo Alto, Calif.: Institute of Lesbian Studies, 1988); Eva Feder Kittay and Diana T. Meyers, eds., *Women and Moral Theory* (Savage, Md.: Rowman and Littlefield, 1987); Sara Ruddick, *Maternal Thinking: Toward a Politics of Peace* (New York: Ballantine Books, 1989).

12. It would be interesting to study the problematic nature of such a position in relation to the development of gender theory in the early eighties here in the United States.

13. See Anne Showstack Sassoon, "Equality and Difference: The Emergence of a New Concept of Citizenship," in *Socialism and Democracy*, ed. David McLellan and Sean Sayers (London: MacMillan, 1991): 87–105, who discusses new developments in women's complex relation to the state.

14. For Italian critics see Teresa de Lauretis, "The Practice of Sexual Difference and Feminist Thought in Italy: An Introductory Essay," in *Sexual Difference: A Theory of Social-Symbolic Practice*, by the Milan Women's Bookstore Collective, trans. Patricia Cigogna and Teresa de Lauretis (Bloomington: Indiana University Press, 1990): 2–19 (original Italian edition 1987). See also Renate Holub, "Il pensiero della differenza sessuale in un mondo multiculturale," *Iride* 10 (1992–93): 116–28.

15. Since the fall of the Berlin Wall in 1989, many research groups have attempted to study the social conditions as well as the social effects of this phenomenon by way of an elaboration of Gramsci's concept of "civil society," long unexamined by mainstream Marxist political science and sociology. International research groups such as the Berliner Institut für Vergleichende Sozialforschung or the IRAS, International Italian Research and Study Group at the Center for German and European Studies, University of California at Berkeley, have focused on the effects of shifting political societies on civil societies in the area of migration and attitudes toward race.

16. For a discussion of feminist appropriations of Lacan see Renate Holub, "Reviewing Shoshana Felman, *Jacques Lacan and the Adventure of Insight*, Jane Gallop *Reading Lacan*, Juliet Flower MacCannell, *Figuring Lacan: Criticism and the Cultural Unconscious*, and Ellie Ragland-Sullivan, *Jacques Lacan and the Philosophy of Psychoanalysis*," in *Textual Practice* 7, no. 1 (spring 1993): 117–32.

17. Luce Irigaray is possibly the most important point of reference of "difference theory." See Luisa Muraro, "Bonding and Freedom," in Bono, *Italian Feminist Thought*, 123–26. See also Renate Holub, "Irigaray in Italy," paper presented at the Santa Barbara Conference on Italian Feminism, organized by Maria Marotti, May 1992.

18. Mariarosa Dalla Costa, *The Power of Women and the Subversion of the Community* (London: Falling Wall, 1972; 3d ed., 1975); Lea Melandri, *L'Infamia originaria: Facciamola finita col cuore e con la politica* (Milan: L'Erba Voglio, 1977); Carla Lonzi, *Sputiamo su Hegel: La Donna clitoridea e la donna vaginale* (Milan: Gammalibri, 1982 and Milan: Rivolta Femminile, 1974).

19. The work of these three internationally known Italian feminists is far too extensive to give it adequate representation here. Let me cite the following: Maria Antonietta Macciocchi, *Lettere dall'interno del PCI* (Milan: Feltrinelli, 1969); *Le Donne e i loro padroni* (Milan: Arnoldo Mondadori, 1980); *Duemila Anni Di Felicitè* (Milan: Mondadori, 1983). For Rossana Rossanda see *Anche per me: Donna, persona, memoria dal 1973 al 1986* (Milan: Feltrinelli, 1987); *Le altre: Conversazioni sulle parole della politica* (Milan: Feltrinelli, 1989). For Dacia Maraini see *Woman at War*, trans. Mara Benetti and Elspeth Spottiswood (New York: Italica Press, 1988 [original Italian edition 1975]); *Letters to Marina*, trans. Dick Kitto and Elspeth Spottiswood (London: Camden, 1987); and the most recent *La lunga vita di Marianna Ucria* (1991), also translated into English *The Silent Duchess* (London: Flamingo, 1993).

20. Anna Maria Mozzoni, *La Liberazione della donna*, ed. Franca Pieroni Bortolotti (Milan: Mazzotta, 1975).

21. The connection between legal rights and social rights in "difference theory" is reflected in the fact that "difference theory" played an important role in the public debates on sexual

violence. See Elisabetta Addis, "Women's Liberation and the Law on Sexual Violence: The Italian Feminist Debate." *Socialist Review* 19, no. 4 (1989): 114–15.

22. Luisa Muraro, *L'Ordine simbolico della madre* (Rome: Editori Riuniti, 1991); for a detailed account of the place of Hegel's phenomenology in Italian "difference theory," see Renate Holub, "Between the United States and Italy: Critical Reflections on Diotima's Feminine/Feminist Ethics," in *Feminine Feminists: Cultural Practices in Italy,* ed. Giovanna Miceli Jeffries, 233–61 (Minneapolis: University of Minnesota Press, 1994).

23. A good example of their textual rhetorics is Adriana Cavarero's oft-cited essay "L'Elaborazione filosofica della differenza sessuale," in *La Ricerca delle donne: Studi femministi in Italia,* ed. Cristina Marcuzzo and Anna Rossi-Doria, 173–88 (Turin: Rosenberg and Sellier, 1987). See also her "Per una teoria della differenza sessuale," in *Diotima: Il pensiero della differenza sessuale,* 42–77. Yet many other Diotima texts should be mentioned, such as Wanda Tommasi's "La Tentazione del Neutro," in the same volume, 82–103.

24. For this insight I am indebted to Marisa Forcina (Lecce), Patrizia Calefato (Bari), Paola Zaccaria (Bari), and many other women of the Women's Group of Lecce and the Women's Group of Bari, who have generously shared their ideas and work with me during my visit in October–November 1992. Their work on this issue is forthcoming.

# Works Cited

Addis, Elisabetta. "Women's Liberation and the Law on Sexual Violence: The Italian Feminist Debate." *Socialist Review* 19, no. 4 (1989): 114–15.

Bimbi, Franca, Laura Grasso, Marina Zancan, Gruppo di filosofia Diotima. *Il Filo di Arianna. Letture della differenza sessuale.* Rome: Cooperativa Utopia, 1987.

Birnbaum, Lucia Chiavola. *Liberazione della donna: Feminism in Italy.* Middletown: Wesleyan University Press, 1986.

Bono, Paola, and Sandra Kemp, eds. *Italian Feminist Thought: A Reader.* Oxford: Basil Blackwell, 1991.

Braidotti, Rosi. *Patterns of Dissonance: A Study of Women in Contemporary Philosophy.* New York: Routledge, 1991.

Cavarero, Adriana. "L'Elaborazione filosofica della differenza sessuale." In *La Ricerca delle donne: Studi femministi in Italia,* edited by Cristina Marcuzzo and Anna Rossi-Doria, 173–88. Turin: Rosenberg and Sellier, 1987.

———. "The Need for Sexed Thought." In *Italian Feminist Thought: A Reader,* edited by Paola Bono and Sandra Kemp, 181–86. Oxford: Basil Blackwell, 1991.

———. *Nonostante Platone: Figure femminili nella filosofia antica.* Rome: Editori Riuniti, 1991.

———. "Per una teoria della differenza sessuale." In *Diotima: Il pensiero della differenza sessuale,* by Adriana Cavarero et al., 42–77. Milan: La Tartaruga, 1987.

Cavarero, Adriana, Cristiana Fischer, Elvia Franco, Giannina Longobardi, Veronica Mariaux, Luisa Muraro, Anna Maria Piussi, Wanda Tommasi, Anita Sanvitto, Betty Zamarchi, Chiara Zamboni, and Gloria Zanardo. *Diotima: Il pensiero della differenza sessuale.* Milan: La Tartaruga, 1987.

Collins, Patricia Hill. *Black Feminist Thought: Knowledge, Consciousness, and the Politics of Empowerment.* New York: Routledge, 1990.

de Lauretis, Teresa. "The Practice of Sexual Difference and Feminist Thought in Italy: An Introductory Essay." In *Sexual Difference: A Theory of Social-Symbolic Practice,* by the Milan Women's Bookstore Collective, translated by Patricia Cigogna and Teresa de Lauretis, 2–19. Bloomington, Indiana University Press, 1990. (Original Italian edition 1987)

Diotima. *Mettere al mondo il mondo: Oggetto e oggettività alla luce della differenza sessuale.* Milan: La Tartaruga, 1990.

Hartsock, Nancy M. "The Feminist Standpoint: Developing the Ground for a Specifically Feminist Historical Materialism," in *Discovering Reality,* ed. Sandra Harding and Merrill B. Hintikka, 283–310. Boston: D. Reidel, 1983.

———. *Money, Sex, and Power.* Boston: Northeastern University Press, 1983.

Holub, Renate. "Between the United States and Italy: Critical Reflections on Diotima's Feminist/Feminine Ethics." In *Feminist/Feminine: Cultural Practices in Italy,* ed. Giovanna Miceli-Jeffries, 232–59. Minneapolis: University of Minnesota Press, 1994.

———. "For the Record: The Non-Language of Italian Feminist Philosophy." *Romance Language Annual* 1 (1990): 133–40.

———. "Irigaray in Italy." Paper presented at the Santa Barbara Conference on Italian Feminism, May 1992.

———. "Il pensiero della differenza sessuale in un mondo multiculturale." *Iride: Filosofia e Discussione Pubblica* 10 (1992–93): 116–28.

———. "La politica economica di un'aristocratica femminista italiana: Cristina di Belgiojoso (1808–1871)." *Note: Bollettino del Centro "Charles Péguy," Dipartimento di Filosofia Università degli Studi di Lecce* 12, nos. 23–24 (1991–92): 35–57.

———. "The Politics of 'Diotima,'" *Differentia* 6 (1990): 161–72.

———. "Reviewing Shoshana Felman, *Jacques Lacan and the Adventure of Insight,* Jane Gallop, *Reading Lacan,* Juliet Flower MacCannell, *Figuring Lacan: Criticism and the Cultural Unconscious,* and Ellie Ragland-Sullivan, *Jacques Lacan and the Philosophy of Psychoanalysis.*" *Textual Practice* 7, no. 1 (spring 1993): 117–32.

———. "Towards a New Rationality: Notes on Feminism and Current Discursive Practices in Italy." *Discourse* 4 (1981–82): 89–107.

———. "Weak Thought and Strong Ethics: The 'Postmodern' and Feminist Theory in Italy." *Annali d'Italianistica* 9 (1991): 124–41.

Libreria delle Donne di Milano. "More women than men." In *Italian Feminist Thought: A Reader,* ed. Paola Bono and Sandra Kemp, 110–23. Oxford: Basil Blackwell, 1991.

———. *Non credere di avere dei diritti: La Generazione della libertà femminile nell'idea e nelle vicende di un gruppo di donne.* Turin: Rosenberg and Sellier, 1987.

———. *Wie weibliche Freiheit entsteht: Eine neue politische Praxis.* Berlin: Orlanda Frauenverlag, 1988.

Marcuzzi, Cristina, and Anna Rossi-Doria. *La Ricerca delle donne.* Studi femministi in Italia. Turin: Rosenberg and Sellier, 1987.

Muraro, Luisa. "Bonding and Freedom." In *Italian Feminist Thought: A Reader,* ed. Paola Bono and Sandra Kemp, 123–26. Oxford: Basil Blackwell, 1991.

———. *L'Ordine simbolico della madre.* Rome: Editori Riuniti, 1991.

Sassoon, Anne Showstack. "Equality and Difference: The Emergence of a New Concept of Citizenship." In *Socialism and Democracy,* ed. David McLellan and Sean Sayers, 87–105. London: MacMillan, 1991.

Tommasi, Wanda. "La Tentazione del Neutro." In *Diotima: Il Pensiero della differenza sessuale,* 82–103. Milan: La Tartaruga, 1987.

Werner, Dorit. "In der PCI zu sein ist eine Synthese. Frauenpolitik in der PCI—eine Politik der Differenz." *Kommune* 10 (1988): 36–38.

———. *Theorie und Praxis der "Differenza Sessuale," und das Konzept "Weibliches Arbeitsvermögen"—Kulturelle "Übersetzung als Möglichkeit, die italienische Theorie und Praxis darzustellen und ins Deutsche zu übertragen.* Diplomarbeit im Fach Politikwissenschaften an der Universität Bremen, 1991.

# Part II

---

# Renaissance Women

## Rethinking the Canon

# 4

# Renaissance Women Defending Women: Arguments Against Patriarchy

*Constance Jordan*

The real myth of Sisyphus is this on the condition of women: to carry a boulder to the top of a mountain and to witness its descent to the base, to discover what every generation forgets and revives.

(È questo il vero mito di Sisifo della condizione femminile: trasportare un macigno fino in cima a una montagna e assistere al suo precipitare in basso, scoprire ciò che ogni generazione dimentica e rinnova.)
— Ginevra Conti Odorisio

To explore the terms of a pro-woman argument as it took place in early modern Europe is to discover the first formulations of many of the positions now fundamental to twentieth-century feminist thought. The terms of this pro-woman argument are obviously those of the discourses of the period: the humanist debates of post-Reformation Europe, with their considerable investment in settling the kinds of issues raised by the Council of Trent; the languages of commerce, with their characteristic emphasis on questions involving property rights and trade; and finally the exchange of ideas in matters of natural philosophy and law—or what many cultural critics now describe as the discourse of the subject. To recognize that these discourses shaped the terms of pro-woman argument and to understand precisely how these determinations were effected are essential for any understanding of the history of feminist thought. Yet it is this history that we also must see and write in our own terms.

To speak of the positions *fundamental* to twentieth-century feminist thought as already expressed and adopted by early modern social critics is not, I think, to entertain presentism, to romanticize the past. It is to identify

a certain kind of interest that such pro-woman argument can have for
twentieth-century feminist historians. Of course, any study of the past will be
inflected with the biases of the student, the historian. And while the evidence itself—those samples of reality left over for us to examine—must not
be tampered with, the meanings it suggests to later readers may well be ones
that could not have been in the minds of contemporaries, those whose past
is under review.

In her study of feminist thought in Italy, Ginevra Conti Odorisio distinguishes the period prior to the French Revolution as one in which social
critics could express a "theoretical feminism" (*femminismo teorico*); this period contrasts with what follows, which is one of "modern feminism" (*femminismo moderno*), characterized by political agendas and agitation.[1] The feminist thought of early modern Europe, the treatises of defenders of women
voicing pro-woman argument, are clearly in the category of the "theoretical";
what this thought expresses are the ideational models upon which might be
constructed a different and essentially nonpatriarchal social order, to be sustained by a different and essentially nonauthoritarian intellectual order. This
essay will examine two treatises that address the challenge of fashioning such
critical models: Moderata Fonte's *Il Merito delle donne* (1600); and Lucretia
Marinelli's *La Nobiltà et l'eccellenza delle donne* (1601). The conceptual basis
for the position of each of these critics differs: Fonte's "new society" is organized with reference to the principle of *amicitia*; Marinelli's understanding of
"science" reflects a novel way to think about *auctoritas*.


Feminist scholarship to date has now made it abundantly clear that historical
evidence supports the thesis of Joan Kelly, announced so many years ago,
that women did not have a Renaissance, at least in the ways that men did.
Urbanization and the codification of procedures regulating commerce, trade,
and all kinds of market relations restricted the activities of women in ways
unknown in previous centuries. The forms of protest in reaction to this development are many but in general they can be reduced to two: protests against
a misogyny based on assumptions derived from natural and divine law
(woman is an inferior creature and prone to sin); and protests against social
practices, specifically those involving education, courtship, marriage, and inheritance. Most of the protests that appeared in print are signed by men; in
western Europe (including England) the great bulk of their production is
from Venetian presses, and comes before the reading public in the years between 1530 and 1560, with a second and lesser wave just at the turn of the
next century. Notable in this Italian work are the subjects of this essay, the

defenses of Fonte and Marinelli. Fonte's construction of a feminized society may suggest to twentieth-century readers a separatist consciousness: she describes a society of women that excludes men. Yet the principle upon which this society rests is one that is applicable to the general order of humankind—Fonte refers to the notion of *libertà* as the guarantee of both law and individual autonomy. Marinelli, by contrast, is clearly a revisionist: she is concerned with examining the ideological bases for patriarchy in the work of canonical *auctores*, principally Aristotle. Her analysis implicitly deconstructs the idea of natural law: hence, it can be argued, it constitutes an attack of what twentieth-century feminists have termed phallogocentrist thought.

Fonte's entire treatise is predicated on a paradox that goes to the very heart of contemporary discussions on the nature of a civil society: that is, that a society in which law prevails over the individual will to power is a society in which all its citizens can have a public voice and standing. Her city, Venice, exemplifies this civil society, at least potentially: it is a microcosm of the globe: "in it are people from all countries" (in lei sono persone de tutti i paesi);[2] and in its multiplicitous character it resembles the sea. Like the sea, Venice fosters commerce among its citizens and the world; itself fluid, multiform, and the seat of liberty, it gives laws to others: "it is a city as free as the sea, and without laws, it gives laws to others."[3] That is, I take it, not only does Venice control the sea by commerce—doubtless Fonte's bid to situate Venice among those states whose imperialism is benign because bloodless—but the commerce she controls is also regulated by her law.

The image itself suggests that Fonte has in mind some vaster point of reference, that she sees Venice as responsible for an international system of exchange based on fluid and constantly shifting but nevertheless actionable agreements, regulated by a common consent to certain rules. In itself an enterprise fraught with uncertainty, international trade in early modern Europe was in fact characterized by the kind of mentality Fonte may be alluding to here. Commerce was both entrepreneurial and regulated, a matter of individual negotiation, and also of contracts that were, however, honored as much by a concern for reputation as by a fear of litigation. Commerce was thus both free and in a sense legalized, if not actually then virtually bound by the kind of law that might have been upheld in a court were a court serving commercial interests to have existed.[4] What is surprising in Fonte's treatment of this idea of a Venetian commerce is that she associates it with the society of Venetian women. As she goes on to claim, civility—true civility—is the product not of a female society per se, but rather of a society sustained by those principles typically informing exchanges between women. Criticized here are not only the relations of patriarchy but the systems of value that make them re-spectable. For Fonte, patriarchal society is essentially uncivilized; her femi-nist argument implies it may be instructed by a feminized social practice.

One has now to ask by what concept does Fonte ground her vision of a civil society—best realized in the society of women—as both free and law-abiding? It is by the concept of friendship, rendered more telling by contrast to the practice of patriarchy and especially marriage, which require the en-forced contact of an inferior (a woman) with her superior (a man). Escaping households dominated by a father or husband, the women she describes con-stitute a new order that allows for a self-expression controlled only by the terms of friendship: "for many gather together having developed a dear and discrete friendship among themselves, . . . they talk among themselves about those things that are most to their liking."[5] As Fonte notes later, the friend-ship of women is also a contrast to the rivalry characterizing relations among men, who habitually see each other in competitive, hierarchical relations.

Friendship, as Fonte proceeds to represent it in her text, exists to sustain the relations among seven women, each of whom represents a stage or an office in a woman's life—a woman betrothed, one recently married, one long-married; then, a young widow, an old widow, and finally a spinster or "woman scorned." Privileged before all others is the spinster Corinna, who has been abandoned by her lover; this is because she is most able to exercise those virtues so prominently featured in moralistic and especially humanist dis-course. As the married woman Lucretia, addressing Corinna, observes: "you and whoever follows your way of life are most blessed, and the more so be-cause God gave you such a superb intelligence that you display and put to work in virtuous actions."[6] The attribution to woman of a wit or intelligence that leads them to virtuous action is of course commonplace in the literature of defense; it is a response to misogynist assertions that a woman's intelligence is inherently defective. Fonte's formulation is notable because she makes it part of a social argument by insisting on Corinna's good fortune; in other words, she implies that a woman's virtue is not as traditionalists would have it, to be restricted to domesticity; rather, it is most fully realized in activities that fall outside the household. That the household she has in mind is the site of servitude, oppression, and exploitation is clear from the conversation that follows.

Fonte's society of women assembles to claim the kind of freedom they can-not have in society at large; a specific project they all endorse is to speak whatever evil is true of men "liberamente" (C2). They find a suitable (and highly symbolic) locus for this activity in the garden of Leonora, in which its centerpiece—a fountain created by the water flowing from the breasts of six statues of women, each of a particular allegorical character—conveys in figurative form the paradoxical "libertà" alluded to at the opening of the treatise. Most obviously, the statues provide visual analogues to the conditions of women in the society outside the garden. As explicated by Leonora, they suggest the range of possibilities open to women in patriarchy. These extend from chastity at one end of the spectrum, symbolized by the statue whose "imprese" is an ermine, to solitude and freedom as (relatively) beneficent dispensations; and then move to the progressively more negative positions of naïveté, deception, and death-dealing cruelty, the horrible fate of gullible girls: "the miserable women who to marry believe too much in the false vows and lying tricks of men."[7] Were these statues not also fountains, their collective meaning would remain merely monitory; as it is, the water from them, "abundantly clear, fresh, and sweet" (abbondantissime acque chiare, fresche, e dolci) recalls the water of the Venetian sea, both a sign of and a means to secure a free people (B4v). Read as a whole, Fonte's garden image suggests an internalization of the principle of a maritime libertà in a separatist and feminine body politic, in whose material conditions are registered various effects of patriarchal power. The fact that statues are united by a third attribute— each is crowned with laurel and bears an olive branch—suggests that even the worst of these effects carries with it a certain kind of honor and is susceptible to understanding.

A good part of Fonte's defense is taken up with her characters' relation of the abuses of patriarchy: this begins with a simple question posed by Verginia: Why are men generally acknowledged to be the superiors of women? In other words, what set of attitudes and assumptions, ideology if you will, continues to sanction the social, economic, and politic preeminence of the male? In its origins, Verginia surmises, it is supported by no more than a kind of fiat, exercised in the interest of obtaining a kind of disgraceful service: "this preeminence they themselves have assigned to themselves . . . in order that we remain their subjects." But she goes on to point out that while women must serve men "with Christian charity" (con carità christiana), the particular arrogance of the male has transformed this concept to one justifying tyranny: "they wish to tyrannize over us" (ci vogliono tiranneggiare). They are driven by jealousy: "envying our virtue, they seek to destroy us."[8] And—most important—the tyranny of men over women is absolutely and utterly ensured by economic power, the systematic exclusion of women from all forms of property ownership and control.

As Corinna then declares, this tyranny begins in infancy: no feasts, no celebrations, no gifts are given for and to the female infant (contrast what happens to males). Nor is anything spent on their education; indeed, as children they are required to do housework while their brothers are instructed in schools and by tutors. This state of affairs continues into adulthood in the houses of their husbands, or if unmarried their brothers, in which women are treated as slaves: "they keep us housebound like slaves . . . against every form of justice" (tenute in case per ischiave . . . contra ogni giustizia; C4). Their work is unrewarded; indeed, as Corinna later points out, the dowry a woman brings to a marriage is spent on the necessities of family life, on children, on clothes, food, and other worries, "fastidii." Unmarried, a woman's dowry would allow her to live like a queen: "remaining single without a husband, she could live on her dowry like a queen according her station in life." Married, she loses the power that comes with having property: "enslaved and losing her liberty, she also loses power over her goods and she places everything at the disposal of the person who has bought her."[9] The irony here is striking. The nature and extent of a woman's servitude are especially apparent at the time of marriage: as Leonora remarks, "how great was the cruelty of a father who sells his own daughter for his own benefit."[10]

What then is the answer of Fonte and her women characters to the problem of patriarchy? I think it is quite simply in the fact of their association as women, and more particularly as women without men. As I have noted, their conversation takes place in Leonora's garden; notably, it is a garden to which the married women resort as a kind of escape from domesticity: as Helena says of her husband, "he is a good enough companion, but one thing displeases me: he does not wish me to leave the house and I want nothing more than to do so."[11] It is, moreover, a place designed for self-reflection; its decor is emblematic of the very condition and choices these women must confront and make. Its centerpiece, the fountain produced by the individual statues, would appear to image the transgressive nature of this feminine assembly by recalling the sea surrounding Venice, "without laws" (senza leggi). But the statues themselves also convey the kinds of real social and psychological constraints that condition the energy and shape the lives of women. They represent in essence the element of difference as it is instanced by women as opposed to men, as well as that difference which is revealed among individual women, the difference between one woman and another. It is important, I think, that the fountain's water of change flows *through* these statues, which are themselves rigid forms. In fact, I suggest that this paradoxical and complex image conveys the essence of Fonte's notion of liberty, a state of political being publicly signaled by the voices of individuals who speak from positions of difference that are not created by a limitless freedom or license but shaped by the constraints that follow particular choices or, if you will, a particular fate. Most important, Fonte's liberty permits different voices to sound not in isolation, as in a desert, or cacophanously, as in a jungle, but in a communal setting and social order.

Fonte concludes her defense pessimistically. As Cornelia observes, the benefits of friendship are not to be experienced outside Leonora's garden world of women because patriarchal society functions differently: "through the malignity of men . . . they rarely find these very rare and close friendships among themselves or between themselves and us." Men are typically vain and proud: "they are so committed to this stupidity of wanting to make themselves esteemed and to be considered of repute by everyone that they use certain nasty practices, pretending to do through courtesy what they really do by artifice, so that instead of honoring friends they dishonor friendship and its sacred laws."[12]

Nevertheless, Fonte suggests that the concept of *amicitia* with its attendant benefit of *libertà*, will continue to serve the interests of a civil society fashioned by feminist principles. Here Corinna has the final word: "true friendship is the cause of all goodness; through friendship the world is maintained, marriages are made by which we preserve the individual in the species, through friendship the union of elements within our bodies maintains health."[13] Corinna refers to the body of woman, but also to the body politic, both the defensive and highly constructed "body" assembled in Leonora's garden and, more generally, the body politic as constituted by the republic itself, comprising the private world of marriage and the public world of the city.

Marinelli's defense focuses on the concept of authority, *auctoritas;* in a sense, she attacks the basis by which men claim superiority over women, a claim questioned earlier by Fonte's women. To make her feminist argument Marinelli resorts to an examination of contradiction, and most interestingly, of historical relativism. Unlike Fonte's persuasive and poetic prose, Marinelli's argument is intellectual, abstract, and logical. She begins by drawing the reader's attention to rhetoric; that is, not to the writer's subject but how it is presented. How does one discover the truth? she asks. Some writers search diligently for evidence and present it in a straightforward manner: "they use every care not only in the choice of a subject but also in representing it in a polished manner of speech, one clear and open to discerning readers." Others spurn truth: "and by a facile wit they seek with every possible means to make the world believe that the true is false . . . and with deceptive reasoning they often attain much of what they have desired."[14] Marinelli's own text is a lesson in interpretation. Having declared her own purpose in writing her treatise—to destroy the credibility of Boccaccio, both Tassi, Sperone, Passi, and especially Aristotle—she directs the reader to the question of intentionality.

Her initial object of attack is Aristotle—the authority above all others establishing the inferiority of women. She deals with several texts: *The History of Animals*, in which the female is said to be a defective male; and the *Politics* and the *Nichomachean Ethics* in which woman is said to possess a moral nature that is less developed than that of man and therefore to be naturally subject to him. These were views Marinelli's contemporaries associated with Aristotle and reproduced in various ways in texts justifying a patriarchal social order. She demonstrates that because Aristotle contradicts himself in these very texts, he can neither be considered authoritative, nor, by extension, are his views to be taken as natural law, as they so often were (B5, B5v). Why he has written with such inconsistency about a topic so important to him, Marinelli concludes, is "because he loved his own sex too much" (percioche amava con troppo fervore il proprio sesso; B5v). His intentions are more particularly subject to criticism, she later explains, because they reflect his dislike of his wife, and hence of women in general! (G7).

Aristotle's self-contradictions, which call his status as *auctor* into question, are matched by a second level of contradiction that engages more directly the whole question of natural law as it was understood in contemporary social debate. Natural-law arguments frequently followed the line of argument developed by Aristotle in his *Nichomachean Ethics*, in which the "law" was defined as a norm from which some variation was always to be expected. The example Aristotle gives is of handedness: most human beings are naturally right-handed but some are left-handed (V.vii.4). Strictly speaking, left-handed people violate no law, they merely depart from a norm. Natural-law advocates sought to demonstrate that human societies conformed to certain standards of organization and behavior that could be understood as normative; their reasoning is similar to that supporting arguments from custom.[15] But as defenders of women had discovered, natural-law arguments defining the position of women in patriarchy were far more legalistic than those addressing other social concerns. Linked to the divine law that appears in Scripture, natural-law arguments voiced by advocates of patriarchy sought to establish nature not as constitutive of a norm from which particular exceptions as well as customary practices might depart without violating a "law," but rather as constitutive of a law in the ordinary sense of that term. Departures from the natural law of woman's inferiority transformed the woman into a monster; no longer merely different, the woman who rejected subordination could appear to be lawless and unnatural.

The second line of Marinelli's defense argues against such a rigid concept of natural law. Here she extrapolates the familiar argument from custom, which typically runs as follows: women in Italy are treated in one way, women in other countries are treated in other ways, hence Italian practice is no more than customary; and she makes cultural practice the basis for an attack on the notions of an absolutely fixed gender system characterizing all human society. Like other feminists of the period, she cites Herodotus, Plato, and others, who reveal that women are treated differently in different societies. There is therefore no natural law that applies to women; it is all custom.

There was, of course, a sense in which the nature to which Aristotle and his Renaissance readers referred was associated not only with social life, or the polis, but also with biological life. In this discourse, nature was *physis*. Here too Marinelli argues against the concept of law. She addresses the common belief that woman is inherently cool and moist, man warm and dry.[16] But even if this is generally the case (and Marinelli does not admit that it is), it does not fail to admit exceptions:

> for there are many provinces and not only towns or castles in which the women are naturally hotter than the men of another province, as those [women] of Spain and Africa are hotter than the men who live in the cold north and in Germany. And how many [women] do we believe were and may be naturally hotter than Aristotle and Plato, and so nobler in the works of the soul?[17]

Her objection here would appear to be addressing, at least in theory, difficulties in interpreting statistical evidence. The importance of her reasoning exceeds the obvious silliness of the case (which was not, of course, a silly one in 1601). What she shows is that even when natural law appears to be derived from biological nature, it establishes norms not laws. In the case of the physical "temperaments" of male and female (assuming a distinction is valid), she says, one is not talking about absolute differences but relative distributions. This leaves the door open for an infinite number of exceptions to a pattern that indicates no more than what is probable.

Marinelli extends her inquiry into the meaning of nature as physis when she addresses the question of physical strength. Unlike the distinction between cool woman and warm man, the physical strength of the man relative to the woman was far more susceptible to general proof. But Marinelli limits the conclusions that can be drawn from this difference. It does not mean that strength confers knowledge, "scienza"; otherwise, laborers would be wiser than doctors. Nor, more tellingly, does might confer right; otherwise, those elections to the Roman Senate that were guaranteed by military force would be as "just" as those reflecting the will of the people (H4v). In all her reasoning with respect to fact and opinion, Marinelli is dealing with the effects of what we would call ideology. The merit of her work is in part that it draws the reader's attention to the formation of ideology in structures of power.

Her argument as to why the kind of analysis she engages in has yet to be recognized is illustrative, chiefly because it raises the question of ideology: What is the source of the real power of men over women? Natural-law arguments against women continue to prevail in the public consciousness, Marinelli says, because men have the power to suppress all evidence to the contrary, evidence that women would be in a position to record were they taught and encouraged to read and write. This statement is part of her argument for recognition of women's accomplishments in arms and the arts, the traditional areas of humanist endeavor: "since men, afraid of losing authority over women and becoming their servants, often forbid them to learn to read and write." She points once more to pure self-interest: a man who disparages the intelligence of a woman does so because, "being a man is reason enough to desire the importance and superiority of men and not of women."[18] This is, of course, a point stressed by many defending women: they insist that women be educated—women must write history.

Marinelli's last argument is perhaps the most telling in that it deals with the conditions in which we write intellectual history, bound up as it is with the interests of particular authors, situated as it is (somewhat less obviously) in the ideologically grounded programs and projects of institutions and social classes. To expose history in this way, Marinelli has to analyse what is commonly understood as a "fact," and "the factual." These, too, in her view, are no more objective than is natural law. A "fact" is merely what is held to be true, objectively. But like history itself, "facts" change. Citing Aristotle on the biology of the female as a defective male ("factual" information to many of her contemporaries), she compares its epistemological status with the "facts" of astronomy:

> It could also easily be that Aristotle was mistaken about the nature and essence of women . . . just as we see that many thought that the earth and the heaven were unmoving, others that there were an infinite number of worlds, and yet others that there was only one . . . and

so everyone defends his opinion with many unshakeable reasons. Such are the answers that should be given to those who disparage the female sex.[19]

Here "facts" are reconceived as opinion. As subject to historical change as any human artifact, the "facts" of nature, as human beings determine them, are subject to infinite reconception. Marinelli's point—a strong one—implicitly deconstructs the notion that woman "is" generically, and for all time, a certain kind of human being.

In the subjects broached and the analyses offered, the defenses of Fonte and Marinelli are not unrepresentative of feminist debate, "il femminismo teorico," in early modern Europe. The debate itself was carried on with determination and ingenuity through the first half of the seventeenth century, and then, associated more or less directly with political agitation, through the eighteenth and nineteenth centuries. It was vigorously revived in the 1880s and we hear its continuation today. The epigraph that begins this essay alludes to the way in which the history of the condition of women has a mythic character. Like the strength of Sisyphus, feminist thought works against the reversals it provokes. Utopian and analytical, the treatises of Fonte and Marinelli allow the twentieth-century reader some understanding of this problematic history.

# Notes

1. Odorisio, 77.
2. Fonte, sig. B.
3. "è città libera pur come è il mare e senza leggi dà leggi ad altri" (Bv).
4. For an overview of this complicated development, see "International Enterprise in Trade and Finance," in *The Cambridge Economic History*, 5:407–23.
5. "percioche molto si confacevano insieme havendo tra loro contratto una cara e discreta amicitia, . . . tra esse ragionavano di quelle cose che più loro à gusto venivano" (Bv).
6. "[è] beatissima dunque voi e chi segue il vostro stile e molto più poiche vi ha Dio dato cosi sublime ingegno che vi dilettate e essercitate nelle virtuose attioni . . ." (B3).
7. "le misere Donne che sono per maritarsi tropo credono a i falsi vezzi e alle finte lusinghe de gli huomini" (B4v).
8. "questa preminenza si hanno essi arrogata da loro . . . che dovemo star loro suggette"; "invidendo al merito nostro, cercano di distruggerci" (C2v).
9. "stando sola senza marito, con la sua dote può viver da Regina secondo la sua conditione"; "diventi schiava e perdendo la sua libertà perda insieme il Dominio della sua robba e ponga tutto in preda e in arbitrio di colui che ella ha comprato" (H2).

10. "quanto fu gran crudeltà d'un padre mercantar la propria figliuola per sua utilità" (G4v).

11. "mi fa assai buona compagnia, ma una cosa sola mi dispiace, che egli non vole chi io mi vada fuor di casa e io per me non desidero altro" (B2).

12. "per la malignità de gli huomini . . . di raro si trovano queste cosi rare e inseparabili amicitie tra essi medesimi, e tra essi e noi" . . . "stanno tanto su queste sciochezza di voler farsi stimar e esser riputati da ognuno con usar certi costumi schifi, mostrando far per cortesia quel, che fanno per arte, che in vece di honorar gli amici dishonorano l'amicitia e le sue sante leggi" (I2).

13. "la vera amicitia è cagio d'ogni bene, per l'amicitia si mantiene il mondo, si fanno i matrimonii, con cui si conserva l'individuo nelle spetie, per l'amicitia, e union de gli elementi ne i nostri corpi si mantien la sanità" (I3).

14. "ogni diligenza usano non solamente nella inventione della materia; ma anchora di ren-derla con polito modo di dire chiara e aperta a' diligenti lettori . . . et da prontezza d'ingegno cercano con ogni studio possibile di far credere al mondo che il vero sia falso . . . e con ragioni apparenti bene spesso attengono il tanto da loro desiato fine"; Marinelli, sig. A.

15. On the concept of natural law as it was considered by political philosophers seeking a basis for establishing normative states, see Kelley, 307–36, especially 313.

16. See Maclean, 28–46; Laqueur, 98–113.

17. "e percioche si ritrovano molte provincie non dirò ville, ò castella, ove le Donne sono più calde di natura, che non sono gli huomini di un'altra provincia, come quelle di Spagna e di Africa sono più calde de gli huomini che habitano il freddo settentrione e l'Alamagna a quanti credemo noi che fossero e sieno più caldi di natura di Aristo. e di Platone adunque più nobili nelle operationi dell'anima?" (H4).

18. "percioche gli huomini, temendo di non perdere la signoria et di divenir servi delle donne, vietano a quelle ben spesso ancho ill saper leggere e scrivere . . . essendo egli huomo era cosa conveniente che desiderasse la grandezza e la superiorità de gli huomini e non delle donne" (B8v).

19. "Potrebbe anco esser di leggiero che si havesse ingannato [i.e. Aristotle] intorno alla natura e all'essenza della donna . . . si come anco si vede che molti hanno creduto che la terra e che il cielo stia ferma, altri che si sieno infiniti mondi, e acuni altri un solo . . . e cosi ogn'uno difende la sue opinione, con molte ragioni e ostinatamente e queste sono le risposte che si danno à coloro che vituperano il femenil sesso" (G7).

# Works Cited

## Primary Sources

Aristotle. *Nichomachean Ethics* Loeb Classical Library. Cambridge: Harvard University Press, 1990.

Fonte, Moderata. *Il Merito delle donne*. Venice, 1600.

Marinelli, Lucretia. *Il Nobiltà et l'eccellenza delle donne*. Venice, 1601.

## Secondary Sources

*The Cambridge Economic History of Europe*. Vol. 5. Edited by E. E. Rich and C. H. Wilson. Cambridge: Cambridge University Press, 1977.

Kelley, Donald. *The Beginning of Ideology: Consciousness and Society in the French Reforma-tion*. Cambridge: Cambridge University Press, 1983.

Laqueur, Thomas. *Making Sex: Body and Gender from the Greeks to Freud*. Cambridge: Harvard University Press, 1990.

Maclean, Ian. *The Renaissance Notion of Woman*. Cambridge: Cambridge University Press, 1980.

Odorisio, Ginevra Conti. *Storia dell'idea femminista in Italia*. Turin: ERI, 1980.

# 5

# Selling the Self; or, the Epistolary Production of Renaissance Courtesans

*Fiora A. Bassanese*

In the first-century tract on style *De elocutione*, author Demetrius stated that the letter "should abound in glimpses of character. It may be said that everybody reveals his own soul in his letters. In every other form of composition it is possible to discern the writer's character, but in none so clearly as in the epistolary."[1] As an autobiographical act, a letter reflects the life, thoughts, and personality of its sender. The writer communicates part of herself in words, but her words also communicate a panoply of established formulas originating in social and literary discourse: to write is to enter the rhetorical realm, where letters become instruments for persuasion and self-fashioning according to culturally defined criteria. To quote feminist critic Domna Stanton, autobiographical writing "assumes and reworks literary conventions for writing and reading. And its texture is ultimately determined by the ways in which meaning can be signified in a particular discursive context, an (ideo)-logical boundary that always already confines the speaking subject" (9). Understood in this way, a cinquecento letter is equally a significant exercise in conventional eloquence and an instrument for personal exchange. This essay will explore the manner in which courtesans responded to canonical standards and attempted to imitate them, concurrently evincing their dependent position as women at the margins of both society and culture.

Regrettably, limited examples of Renaissance female epistolary writing survive, due in large measure to gender restrictions on literacy. All Renaissance women encountered boundaries formed by class, station, economics, instruction, and sex. However, prostitution was one sixteenth-century path to upward mobility for ambitious women born poor, illegitimate, or untitled. At its summit, the courtesan possessed celebrity, status, wealth, and considerable respect, albeit precariously. To please her clientele and achieve professional distinction, she was also required to obtain, or at least feign, an education equal to that of her aristocratic contemporaries as part of her public image, thereby filling a social demand for cultivation as well as sexual availability. "Italy's elite of rulers, professionals, and humanists shared the language of classical Latin. They shared a common rhetoric. And they drew from the same storehouse of moral attitudes and life examples learned in school."[2] To appeal to this predominantly male elite who controlled political and economic power, the courtesan found it necessary to infiltrate the rhetorical and intellectual background influential men shared and imitate them in her own discourse.

Men monopolized access to education and pupils were predominantly boys, particularly in the lower classes. As historian Paul Grendler notes, "girls learned vernacular reading and writing almost exclusively. They did not study the Latin curriculum, because most males judged Latin learning to be impractical and unsuitable for girls" (410). At the center of the *studia humanitatis*, or Latin curriculum, imparted to the elite stood rhetoric, generally accepted as the most important of all studies, central to life itself.[3] While rhetoric had been viewed classically as an orator's craft, its tenets had transferred to the written word, including epistolary prose, during the Middle Ages. From the eleventh century on, a whole methodology of rhetorical letter-writing emerged. Known as the *ars dictaminis*,[4] it was based on the rules governing the structure of classical orations. The *ars* influenced letter-writing throughout the Renaissance, as did direct contact with texts from antiquity.[5] Few sixteenth-century women were fortunate enough to be versed in either the Latin or the vernacular curriculum. While boys were taught Latin prose style by imitating Cicero's familiar letters or by practicing useful epistolary formulas derived from the *ars dictaminis*, most girls were relegated to the kitchen, learning to wield spoons rather than pens. A cultivated woman was a clear exception in a society with a female literacy rate approaching 12 percent in urban centers and far less in the countryside. This historical reality makes the literacy of courtesans all the more extraordinary and illuminates their achievement. Among the few surviving examples of courtesan epistolary writing are a small collection of letters composed by housemates Camilla Pisana and Alessandra Fiorentina, discovered in Florentine archives among the papers of their patron Filippo Strozzi; a handful of Tullia D'Aragona's communications to her lover Benedetto Varchi; and Veronica Franco's *Lettere familiari*, published in 1580. In addition, dedicatory letters preface other writings by D'Aragona and Franco.[6] Although these women's lives spanned the entire sixteenth century, they shared similar concerns for convention and linguistic propriety, purposely adhering to an epistolary style that was inherently orthodox and rhetorically established by the educational curriculum of the day.[7]

The era's epistolary models were Cicero and Ciceronian imitations, including the Latin collections of Francesco Petrarca and other early humanists. However, by the mid-sixteenth century, vernacular Italian was supplanting Latin as the accepted medium for epistolary exchange, particularly following the sensational publication of Pietro Aretino's first book of letters in 1537.[8] Therefore, women like Camilla Pisana and Alessandra Fiorentina, who did not master Latin, still possessed adequate tools for correspondence: the letter was an open genre that did not require serious classical preparation. Nevertheless, some letters composed by courtesans were conceived as public, not private, messages, appearing as dedications to their works. Rhetorically, these letters favor the oratorical models of antiquity, emphasizing stylistic embellishment and persuasion over simplicity and communication.[9] Tullia D'Aragona's and Veronica Franco's acknowledged addressees are powerful individuals whose patronage would benefit the courtesan's status and whose benevolence could become protection. By adopting a tone of humility in the face of a superior being, the courtesan receives validation through the merits of her addressee, who, in turn, gilds her reputation through the literary association. Attached to a public document—the book—the dedication contributes to the fame of the person named and praised. But it also adds to the author's name and fame. Such an odd coupling is sanctioned by the shared belief in the eternal power of the word, as Tullia D'Aragona explains to Eleonora di Toledo, wife of Cosimo De'Medici, in the dedication to her *Rime* (1547): "becoming bold, I finally determined not to fail myself, remembering that the compositions of all writers in all languages, especially those of poets, have always had such grace and prominence that no one, however great, has ever refused them, but has always held them dear."[10]

Such dedicatory letters can easily be assigned to the Ciceronian rhetorical

category most imitated in the Renaissance: the epideictic, used for praising
or blaming an individual.[11] While the period's Ciceronianism created a stum-
bling block for most female correspondents, untrained in the linguistic sub-
tleties of Latin, there is nevertheless an elective pattern of vernacular "Latinity" in the courtesans' discourse of flattery: complex syntactic structures; an
attempt to reproduce the rhythms of the *cursus*,[12] or metric prose of the *ars
dictaminis*; amplification; and stylistic embellishment. These abound in both
public and private correspondence, as in the examples below. The first is
taken from Veronica Franco's dedication of the *Lettere familiari* to Cardinal
Luigi D'Este; the second, from a letter written by Camilla Pisana to her lover
Filippo Strozzi, echoes the blandishments and stylistic ornateness found in
Franco's manifestly public statement in a private communication:[13]

> In a time of greater opportunity, more prosperous fortune, and more
> practiced style, with the aid of your divine humaneness, I may well
> dare an enterprise that better expresses my soul and my obligations
> than does the consignment [of] this slight book at the feet of your
> lofty worthiness; by extending the arms of your kindness from the sub-
> lime throne of your immense graces to appreciate and receive this
> small token of mine, proceeding from my most fervent desire to ren-
> der you that sign of devotion which best suits me, you will acquire
> much esteem for your benignity, all the greater in that I am far from
> deserving anything from your most illustrious Excellency . . .

> My most unique Filippo; if my repentence were equal to the desired in-
> dulgence, I would have already achieved forgiveness a thousand times
> over for the fault committed; but since I have too unjustly offended your
> eminence, I have doubts of my worthiness to receive that coveted boon
> that my defects deserve. I confess to having erred in my haste and hav-
> ing wrongly complained about so much good, which occurred because
> I wrote so angrily without reading all your letter: so, genuflecting at your
> most sacred feet, with every humility I am asking your forgiveness, pray-
> ing you by that true and unrestrained love I bear you, to return to me
> appeased and gentle, not maintaining any indignation against me, for,
> dear heart, I neither adore nor recognize any other God except you: let
> me see you, to my greatest solace, and keep you in sight, without which
> I cannot possibly live any longer. (XVIII)[14]

David Wagner notes that rhetoric's "place within the complete system of the
verbal arts was defined by the concern for correct expression (or, alterna-

tively, persuasion)" (96). Franco's and Camilla Pisana's letters seek to persuade their readers of the writer's self-worth by employing the culturally designated language of courtly compliment, suitably phrased. The courtesan's letter flatters, cajoles, ingratiates, and adulates the male addressed; yet its function is intrinsically practical, notwithstanding its rhetorical stance. Veronica Franco curries favor in high places. Camilla Pisana must persuade a capricious Strozzi of her devotion or risk losing his support; her insistence on stylistic propriety serves to disguise the mercenary relationship between mistress and master. Nor is it incidental that Camilla's vernacular takes on Latinate spellings and approximates religious discourse, transforming her protector into an almighty idol as a method of intellectual seduction.

Rhetorically, Veronica Franco and Camilla Pisana are stretching the functions of the *benevolentiae captatio*, the section of the formal letter devoted to securing the goodwill of the recipient or to persuasively influencing his attitude toward the sender. Both elevate the enthroned male patron, at whose feet they genuflect, indicating female homage. Such affected style and obsequiousness is taken to excess by Camilla's housemate, Alessandra Fiorentina,[15] whose flattery translates into a naive hodgepodge of Latinized and improper vernacular, somewhat lost in translation, as in this example:

> My glorious and edexcellent lord my infinite salutem.
> Yours received this day past has been most welcome to me, and as for the thanks you refer me to a small thing sent to you, I am most astonished by your words. *Cum sit* just as my heart was bestowed on you, so also my goods and all my exsiguous riches, are conceded and placed in your most precious hands, so that Your Lordship can dispose of them, I say, as though they were your very own, not searching for any other prize from your kindness, nor any other reward save reciprocal love, even though the obligations we have with you yourself are infinite, nonetheless your grace in all other matters made me most hobliged to you, and I esteem it and hold it dearer than if all the precious threasures of the world were bestowed on me. (XXVIII; 1967)[16]

Alessandra's linguistic choices are a measure of her desire to present the appearance of proper *elocutio*, albeit at a very primitive level. Like Camilla Pisana, she associates elegance with Latinisms, eloquence with excess, praise with sycophancy. Yet popular rhetorical texts, such as *Rhetorica ad Herennium*, taught that "the means of lending distinction (*dignitas*) to style [was] by rendering it ornate."[17] Not only does Alessandra take such advice to heart but she also borrows the approved Neoplatonic terminology of the day, equating herself and her protector to the lover and beloved of philosophical discourse. Marginally educated, Alessandra's confusion of excess and ornament underscores the nature of her relationship to the addressee and, by extension, the relationship of courtesans to their clients. Such women depended on the goodwill of the men celebrated thus; their letters have a social and economic genesis in a "political" relationship founded on subordination and gender.

Most addressees remain undesignated in Veronica Franco's *Lettere familiari*; this anonymity offers intriguing clues about a courtesan's attitude toward style and, quite possibly, about society's attitude toward courtesans. Amedeo Quondam assigns this lack to a literary function: Franco's book "first of all intends showing the completely rhetorical-linguistic exemplariness of the letter, its entirely tautological and self-reproducing pertinence (an exemplary letter for correctly writing a letter: proper names do not count, nor do dates, or places . . .)."[18] Lack of specificity suggests the possibility that these letters may be inventions, literary exercises composed for the purpose of persuading the reading public of Franco's worthiness, both as a writer and as a woman. However, if these letters are true autobiographical documents, Franco's reticence would well indicate the courtesan's marginality and the sociopolitical desirability of concealing a direct relationship with her. Equally suggestive is Franco's identification of a mere handful of addressees, namely: a cardinal, a king, a great artist, and a patrician family. The individuals named are highly connotative, as is the rhetorical communication with which they are addressed. Symbols of achievement and power, they cannot be diminished but illuminate the writer, who shines through her words.

As Franco's letters suggest, the success of a courtesan was dependent on male desire and male approval: sexually and culturally. Among the highest-ranking professionals of her generation, Tullia D'Aragona was celebrated as the intellectual courtesan, thanks to her superior education and brilliance.[19] Notwithstanding general acclaim, D'Aragona's correspondence abounds in a lexicon of subordination. In the letters addressed to the duke and duchess of Florence, social condition and political expediency would require the employment of a submissive, flattering tone. However, in private exchanges with Benedetto Varchi, her lover and friend, the language of humility and deference suggests other motivations, related to gender difference and social inferiority. On the one hand, D'Aragona uses Varchi to lend credence to her scholarly image, his friendship being a testimonial to her intellectuality. On the other hand, he represents the cultural establishment as a keeper of the literary keys. In this role, he must constantly be courted and seduced.

D'Aragona's attitude is synthesized in her habitual salutation: "caro patrone." Varchi is her mentor, intellectual father-figure, patron saint, benefactor, and master: *padre, padrone, patrone* (father, owner, patron). As such, she subordinates herself to him: "if I am good enough to be of service here, command me, for I have no greater desire than to be of service to you."[20] This submission to male superiority is seconded by D'Aragona's use of the *Lei* mode of address. In only one letter does D'Aragona employ the semiformal *voi* with Varchi, never the informal *tu*. Introduced in the sixteenth century, the *Lei* purposely distances writer and addressee, placing the latter on a semantic pedistal in keeping with an environment that assumes social differences.[21] D'Aragona's letters do not, and cannot, reflect her existential situation but intentionally serve to mask it through linguistic propriety. The courtesan's public facade of seemliness extends to decorous language, a code of verbal behavior as significant as actual deed.

D'Aragona's perception of inferiority is predicated on the intellectual superiority of her *patrone*. Therefore, in all her letters, she turns to Varchi for help in editing, polishing, and correcting her own work. While the request for rhetorical assistance was hardly unusual in the cinquecento, it does infer the gendered notion that men had mastery of the written word. Given limited female access to education, this view is not surprising. Camilla Pisana makes a similar editorial request of a friend, Francesco Del Nero, while Alessandra Fiorentina openly declares her epistolary shortcomings: "My writing is ill-arranged and idiotic [uneducated], my letter totally deformed . . . but I pray your kindness exchuse my insufficiency."[22] In the dedicatory letter to the *Lettere familiari*, Veronica Franco defines herself "a woman inexperienced in the disciplines and poor in invention and in language."[23] Sex—the female sex—is equated with stylistic inadequacy. It is an intellectual evaluation, founded on an absence of knowledge ("the disciplines"), a paucity of eloquence ("poor in language"), and a lack of the most critical rhetorical measurement: "invention," or creativity. The author's self-justification is itself a trope: youthful inexperience, or literary immaturity, as she clearly defines her pieces "lettere giovenili" (youthful letters). All four courtesans employ similar protestations of shortcomings to describe the deficiencies of their intellectual formation, emerging rhetorically inadequate in their own estimation. As a result, their communications suffer from internal censorship. Reading these letters, it is evident that the classicism of the times invited conformity, codifying it in the prevalent theories of imitation to such a degree that only the mastery of the accepted curriculum was deemed satisfactory. Courtesans understood the function of language as "a sensitive indicator of social relationships such as deference, familiarity, solidarity" and as "an active force in society, a vehicle for social mobility [or] for the assimilation of new recruits to a group" (Burke, 79).

Speaking of Renaissance rhetorical attitudes, Richard Lanham notes that all language "was naturally premeditated. Attention would fall, first and last if not always, on the verbal surface, on words not ideas" (3). The importance of this rhetorical attitude prevails in the most formal writing of courtesans.[24] Their verbal surface is an instrument for creating a constructed self in a socially endorsed voice, underscoring their awareness that established knowledge has social value and that learning is empowering. Late in the century, Veronica Franco demonstrates full realization of the importance and power of words in her society, finding pride in her work and the image it projected of herself to the world. The *Lettere Familiari* were her intellectual calling card, distributed to suitable recipients, like Montaigne, who records in his travel journal: "On Monday, November 7th, at supper, Signora Veronica Franca, a Venetian gentlewoman, sent a man to present him with a little book of letters that she had composed" (920). Franco's self-awareness is exemplified in the first letter of her collection, addressed to the "most invincible and very Christian King Henry III of France and Poland." Filled with the flowery and ornate embellishments of cinquecento compliment, this missive flatters its recipient while diminishing the sender, reverently bowed "to embrace your sacred knees." However, beyond the obligatory ingratiation of the *captatio benevolentiae*, Franco enacts some amusing and none-too-subtle image-building, begun in the very first sentence of the text:

> I could never adequately repay, either by thought or desire, the sublime favor that Your Majesty deigned show me, coming to my humble residence and taking away my portrait. In exchange you left me the shining image of your heroic virtues and divine valor deep in my heart—a blessed and fortunate exchange for me.[25]

Since this letter has a dual addressee—the king and the book's readers—it can be interpreted both on its surface and between the lines. Even the uninformed reader must question the innate humility and unworthiness of the writer and her abode, since both have been visited by royalty. Moreover, regal magnanimity is transferred from king to courtesan. She has generously given to the monarch: her words, her accompanying poems, her portrait. King Henry himself can add "body" to this list, having tasted the courtesan's hidden beauties during his regal visit. Understanding the concealed aspect of the rapport, the text can be re-read as sexual innuendo. The king's "virtú eroiche" (heroic virtues) and "divino valore" (divine valor) acquire new virile meaning; her memories are privatized; her desire and his image de-platonized. Either reading forces a reevaluation of Franco, aiding her in her self-fashioning.

By producing a self central to her own published work, Franco becomes a literary subject as well as an author: she becomes her own creator. Unlike other courtesan letters, Franco's collection is intended as an artistic undertaking. As a work of art, its very nature and title challenge the Ciceronian model, courageously inviting direct comparison with the *primum*, or best, Cicero's *Epistulae ad familiares*, the primary instructional text of the entire Latin curriculum. As a woman of letters, Franco develops a literary presence, a powerful authority that challenges preconceptions about both women writers and courtesans. She defies gender stereotyping, stretches the female boundaries, revises preconceptions about her sex and profession. As an *auctor*, she also presents herself as an authority in a culture that believed literature held lessons and writers were moralists. On occasion, Franco offers herself as a moral philosopher of sorts. Putting aside the traditional *salutatio*, since addressees are unacknowledged, her letters offer an *exordium* instead. Cicero's *De Inventione* elaborates on the characteristics of an *exordium* (beginning) of an oration, which "ought to be sententious to a marked degree, and of a high seriousness, and . . . should contain everything which contributes to dignity" (Murphy, *Rhetoric*, 12). The following epistolary openings clarify this aspect of Franco's *Lettere*:

> Since the travails of the soul cannot be purged with medicinal concoctions . . . (III)

> Since true love principally consists of the union of the soul and the will of the person who loves with that of the person loved, and since the obligation of false love is unworthy of the correspondence of true love, it is to your benefit that I manifest the truth, which is itself an effect of loving. (XIV)

> The administration of a family is harmed as much by great severity as it is by too much indulgence . . . (XV)[26]

The attempt to persuade the reader or listener to act morally or adopt a pattern of good behavior is central to classical rhetoric's function. The messenger, not the message, is unexpected: courtesan as moralist. Franco's self-authored "I" is a revisionist who carefully produces an attractive female subject in contrast to the negative representation of courtesans painted by the pulpit and the press. Veronica Franco's letters, clearly derived from classical epistolography, function as instruments for self-fashioning and persuasion, according to her society's expectations. As Margaret Rosenthal has noted: "Franco redefines the courtesan's profession as contrary to mercenary and duplicitous love; she portrays herself as a devoted friend and mother uninterested in financial gain, a faithful companion and partner in love, and a professional writer and editor engrossed in literary projects" (4). As projections of a constructed self-image, Franco's letters are rhetorical instruments, meant to persuade readers of her intrinsic worth both as a woman and an artist.

Having recognized established cultural codes, courtesan letters reflect the literary and ideological systems in force, taken at face value and put to practical purpose. Needing to express herself in acceptable and recognizable forms to her correspondent, the courtesan seeks to please her clients by reproducing a facsimile of the code and referents of his world and attempting to transform herself into his feminine vision. In short, she physically and intellectually becomes the product she sells in a Renaissance version of gender correctness, similar to the standard[27] proposed in the third book of the *Cortegiano*, itself a manual for suitable behavior among the elite: "it seems to me that a certain pleasing affability is highly suited to the woman living at court, so that she can courteously entertain every sort of man with welcome and honest conversation, adapted to the time, place, and quality of the individual with whom she speaks."[28] The fundamental transgression of the courtesan must be recognized. She appropriates the language, thereby the essence, of a social class and intellectual group to which she does not belong. Whether it be her dress, manners, jewelry, or rhetoric, the courtesan imitates the lady, which she is not. Predestined to ignorance, she educates herself. Relegated to the bedroom, she affirms herself in the salon. Educated to feminine silence, she speaks and writes herself into existence. By pursuing communication and exchange with her clients, she seeks entrance into the world of knowledge, the male world. By writing to him in his own idiom, she gains control of the very act that distinguishes her social superior. By addressing the elite, the woman writer necessarily addresses the canon itself and, at a profound level, her own place within it, which she sold to them and to posterity.

# Notes

1. Quoted in Clark, 105.
2. Grendler, 410. Grendler states that roughly a quarter of the Italian urban population was literate, based on data for Venice in 1587 (403).
3. In the Middle Ages, the nucleus of a humanist education had been instruction in the

trivium, namely, grammar, rhetoric, and dialectic. For an extensive discussion of rhetoric in the Renaissance, see the essays contained in Murphy's *Renaissance Eloquence*.

4. See Murphy's *"Ars dictaminis:* The Art of Letter-Writing" and Faulhaber's article. The *ars* was used predominantly, but not exclusively, for legal and ecclesiastical correspondence.

5. According to Grendler, "the humanists of the fifteenth century changed the Latin curriculum, a major academic revolution. In . . . place [of the late medieval Latin curriculum] they substituted grammar, rhetoric, poetry, and history based on Latin classical authors and texts just discovered or newly appreciated. Above all, they inserted the letters of Cicero as the Latin prose model" whereas the vernacular education retained a more medieval character (404–5).

6. D'Aragona's letters to Varchi are quoted in Biagi. Her dedicatory letters to the duke and duchess of Florence appear in her *Le Rime* (ed. Enrico Celani) and in her *Dialogo della Infinità d'Amore*. These letters all date from 1545 to 1548. Franco's *Terze Rime* (1575) are dedicated to Guglielmo Gonzaga, duke of Mantua. Camilla Pisana and Alessandra Fiorentina's private letters were most recently printed in *Cortigiane del Secolo XVI: Lettere Curiosità Notizie Aneddoti*, *etc.*, originally published in Florence by Il Giornale di Erudizione Ed., no date, but somewhat posterior to Luigi Alberto Ferrai's edition of *Lettere di cortigiane del secolo XVI*. These letters date c. 1515.

7. Not all letters by Camilla Pisana, Alessandra Fiorentina, Tullia D'Aragona, and Veronica Franco are formal compositions. This essay focuses on the courtesans' most rhetorical pieces.

8. Publication date for the first of six books of letters. The first volume contains some three hundred selections.

9. According to Lechner, "These literary forms provided multiple occasions for the Renaissance orator [or writer] to open the fonts and treasuries of his learning . . . and to let the flood of his eloquence amplify, embellish, and enrich his speech to the delight and persuasion of his audience" (120).

10. "mi risolsi finalmente di non mancare a me medesima, ricordandomi che i componimenti di tutti gli scrittori hanno in tutte le lingue, e massimamente quegli de' poeti, avuto sempre cotal grazia e preminenza, che niuno quantunque grande, non solo non gli ha rifiutati mai, ma sempre tenuti carissimi." All unattributed translations are my own.

11. See *De inventione*. The three classes of subjects are the epideictic, deliberative, and judicial.

12. Used in the *ars dictaminis*, the *cursus* is a style based on proper employment of accents; syllabic stresses result in a noticeable sound pattern. "The prose rhythms known as *cursus* were to become a constant medieval adjunct to the theory of epistolary compositions" (Murphy, *"Ars dictaminis,"* 210). A rhythm akin to the *cursus* was part of Latin prose, notably used by Cicero. For a discussion of the *cursus*, consult Murphy, 248–53.

13. The differentiation of private and public spheres of epistolary exchange were somewhat blurred in the sixteenth century, when letters were often read aloud and shared with friends. A letter such as this had a clearly public encomniastic function.

14. "Forse che a tempo di maggior occasione e di più prospera fortuna e di più essercitato stile, ardirò con l'aiuto della vostra divina umanità tentar impresa di maggior espressione dell'animo e dell'obligo mio, che non è mandar questo poco libro a piè del vostro eccelso valore, col quale stendendo voi dal sublime trono delle vostre immense grazie le braccia della vostra gentilezza a gradire e ricevere questa mia picciola dimostrazione, proceduta de ferventissimo desiderio di rendervi quella recognizione d'osservanza, che mi si conviene, acquisterete a voi preggio di benignità tanto più alta quanto io sono più lontana da poter meritare alcuna cosa con Vostra Signoria illustrissima" (Franco). "Filippo mio singhularissimo; s'el pentir mio fussi valido alla desiderata indulgentia, già mille fiate arei conseghuito perdono del fallo commesso; ma perchè ho obfeso troppo ingiustamente vostra prestantia, dubito non esser degna di ricever da voi quella concupita venia che il mio defecto merita. Io confesso per troppa subitezza aver errato, et a torto lamentomi di troppo bene, ma perchè non lessi tucta la lettera achadde che scrissi così alterato: di che genuflexa a' vostri sacratissimi piedi con ogni humiltà vi domando

perdono, pregandovi per quel vero et immoderato amore qual vi porto, vi piaccia rendermivi placato et mite, non riservando alcun sdegno ad presso di voi contra di me, che altro Dio che solo voi, anima mia, non adoro nè conoscho, et lasciatemi per mio sommon refligerio vedere et posseder la vista vostra, senza la quale più non m'è possibile poter vivere" (Camilla Pisana, xvIII).

15. Alessandra Fiorentina's and Camilla Pisana's surnames presumably derive from their native cities, Florence and Pisa. This was typical usage for designating courtesans and prostitutes in the Middle Ages and Renaissance and generally indicates lowly class origins. Tullia D'Aragona declared herself the daughter of a cardinal of the house of Aragon while Veronica Franco was a minor Venetian patrician.

16. "Inclito et edexcelso signor mio infinite salutem. Gratissima m'è stata la tua nel passato giorno riceuta, et quanto alle gratie mi referisci d'una pichola cosa a te mandata, mi maraviglio assai delle tue parole. *Cum sit* che avendoti largito el core, così anchora la roba et d'ogni mia exighua facultà, et concepso et posta nelle tue pretiosissime mani, potendo la Signoria tua di quella disporre non altrimenti, dico, che della tua medesima, non ricercando della gentileçça tua altro premio, nè altra ricompensa che un reciproco amore, quantunque infiniti sieno gli obrighi abbiamo con esso teco, non di manco la gratia tua sopra tucte l'altre cose mi ti facesse hobligatissima et quella stimo et tengo cara più che se mi fussi largito tucti li pretiosi thesori del mondo" (xxvIII; 1967).

17. Martin Camargo, "Rhetoric," in Wagner, 99.

18. Quondam 57: "intende mostrare in primo luogo l'esemplarità tutta retorico-linguistica della lettera, la sua pertinenza interamente tautologica, auto-riproduttiva (una lettera esemplare per scrivere una lettera correttamente: i nomi propri non contano, né le date, né i luoghi . . .)."

19. With a clever pun on names, Jacopo Nardi, a humanist, saluted D'Aragona's gifts and learning in the dedication of his translation of Cicero's *De oratore* (1536): "che per sè stessa oggi dirittamente da ogni uomo è giudicata unica e vera erede cosí del nome e di tutta la tulliana eloquenza." The pun derives from the correspondence of names: Tullio Cicero and Tullia D'Aragona. The *De oratore* was considered Cicero's most significant work on rhetoric.

20. "se io sono quaggiù buona per suo servigio, mi comandi, ché non è in me maggior desio che di fargli servizio" (in Biagi, 696).

21. Burke, 88: "one of the most striking, and indeed alien features of the texts of this period is the language of hierarchy, the formality of modes of address, the elaborate vocabulary of deference . . . [which] need to be placed in their social context, that of a society where it was natural to perceive others as one's superiors or inferiors and behave accordingly." Italian, like other Romance languages, distinguishes between formal and informal address. The introduction of the *Lei* mode resulted in three ways of addressing a singular "you."

22. "El mio scrivere è incomposito ed idioto, la lettera al tucto deforme . . . ma priegho vostra gentileçça abbia per ischusata la mia insufficientia" (xxix).

23. "donna inesperta delle discipline e povera d'invenzione e di lingua."

24. In other letters, Camilla Pisana and Alessandra Fiorentina find spontaneous voices, cleansed of Latinity and mimicry, but not in their premeditated rhetorical correspondence. These letters are generally inspired by emotional states such as affection, anger, and despair. D'Aragona's letters to Varchi are personal communications but reflect her rhetorical preparation, retaining a patina of propriety and encomnium. This essay is focusing on the most formal aspects of courtesan epistolary writing.

25. "All'altissimo favor che la Vostra Maestà s'è degnata di farmi, venendo all'umile abitazione mia, di portarne seco il mio ritratto, in cambio di quella viva imagine, che nel mezo del mio cuore Ella ha lasciato delle sue virtù eroiche e del suo divino valore—cambio per me troppo aventuroso e felice, —io non sono bastevole di corrispondere né pur col pensiero, né col desiderio . . ."

26. "Poiché i travagli dell'animo non si purgano con beveraggi medicinali" (III); "Poi che 'l

verace amore principalmente consiste nell'unione dell'animo e della volontà della persona ch'ama con quello della persona amata, e che l'obbligo dell'amor finto non merita corrispondenza d'amor vero, siavi davantaggio ch'io vi manifesti la verità, ch'è pur l'effetto d'amorevolezza" (xiv); "Nel governo della famiglia nuoce la molta severità non meno che la troppa indulgenzia" (xv).

27. The lady of the court had to be lexically differentiated from the *cortegiana* or courtesan, the feminization of *cortegiano*, or courtier. On the surface, the main distinction between these women focused on the issue of chastity and womanly honor, understood sexually.

28. Castiglione, 212: "a quella che vive in corte parmi convenirsi sopra ogni altra cosa una certa affabilità piacevole, per la quale sappia gentilmente intertenere ogni sorte d'omo con ragionamenti grati ed onesti, ed accommodati al tempo e loco ed alla qualità di quella persona con cui parlerà."

# Works Cited

Aragona, Tullia D'. *Dialogo della Infinità d'Amore: Trattati d'amore del '500*. Edited by Mario Pozzi. Reprint, Bari: Laterza, 1975.

———. *Le Rime*. Edited by Enrico Celani. Reprint, Bologna: Commissione per i testi di lingua, 1968.

Biagi, Guido. "Un'etera romana: Tullia D'Aragona." *La Nuova Antologia* 88, no. 4 (1886): 655–711.

Burke, Peter. *The Historical Anthropology of Early Modern Italy: Essays on Perception and Communication*. Cambridge: Cambridge University Press, 1987.

Castiglione, Baldassarre. *Il libro del cortegiano*. Edited by Ettore Bonora. 2d ed. Milan: Mursia, 1976.

Clark, Donald Lemen. *Rhetoric in Greco-Roman Education*. New York: Columbia University Press, 1957.

Faulhaber, Charles B. "The Summa dictaminis of Guido Faba." In *Medieval Eloquence: Studies in the Theory and Practice of Medieval Rhetoric*, edited by James J. Murphy, 85–111. Berkeley and Los Angeles: University of California Press, 1978.

Ferrai, Luigi Alberto, ed. *Lettere di cortigiane del secolo XVI*. Florence: Libreria Dante, 1884. Reprint, *Cortigiane del Secolo XVI: Lettere Curiosità Notizie Aneddoti, etc*. Bologna: Forni, 1967.

Franco, Veronica. *Lettere*. Edited by Benedetto Croce. Naples: Ricciardi, 1949.

Grendler, Paul F. *Schooling in Renaissance Italy: Literacy and Learning, 1300–1600*. Baltimore: Johns Hopkins University Press, 1989.

Lanham, Richard A. *The Motives of Eloquence: Literary Rhetoric in the Renaissance*. New Haven: Yale University Press, 1976.

Lechner, Sister Joan Marie, O.S.U. *Renaissance Concepts of the Commonplaces*. New York: Pageant, 1962.

Montaigne, Michel. *The Complete Works of Montaigne*. Translated by Donald M. Frame. Stanford: Stanford University Press, 1948–1957.

Murphy, James J. "Ars dictaminis: The Art of Letter-Writing." In *Rhetoric in the Middle Ages: A History of Rhetorical Theory from Saint Augustine to the Renaissance*, edited by James J. Murphy, 194–268. Berkeley and Los Angeles: University of California Press, 1974.

———. *Renaissance Eloquence: Studies in the Theory and Practice of Renaissance Rhetoric*. Berkeley and Los Angeles: University of California Press, 1983.

Quondam, Amedeo, ed. Le "carte messaggiere": Retorica e modelli di comunicazione epistolare: per un indice dei libri di lettere del Cinquecento. Rome: Bulzoni, 1981.

Rosenthal, Margaret F. "Epistolary Self-portraiture in Veronica Franco's Terze Rime." In Writing the Female Voice: Essays on Epistolary Literature, edited by Elizabeth C. Goldsmith, 3–23. Boston: Northeastern University Press, 1989.

Stanton, Domna C. "Autogynography: Is the Subject Different?" In The Female Autograph: Theory and Practice of Autobiography from the Tenth to the Twentieth Century, 3–20. Chicago: University of Chicago Press, 1984.

Wagner, David L., ed. The Seven Liberal Arts in the Middle Ages. Bloomington: Indiana University Press, 1983.

# Part III

## At the Turn of the Century

### Women Writers at the Margins of the Canon

# 6

# Double Marginality: Matilde Serao and the Politics of Ambiguity

*Nancy Harrowitz*

A well-known and respected journalist for over forty years, Matilde Serao's literary and journalistic reputation during her lifetime was in high regard. The variety and abundance of her literary and journalistic production is interesting in itself, as she wrote many front-page editorials on political and social issues, wrote fashion and travel columns, and was the author of more than sixty novels. Serao's literary work often concentrated on the *bassifondi* of Naples, her place of birth. Other novels of hers center on the lives of working-class and aristocratic women whose lives are affected by their passions and whose fate in the society of the time is dictated by their gender. Her novelistic efforts were acclaimed not only for the works of *verismo*, as we today might expect, but for some of her sentimental novels as well, which were considered unusual, interesting, and daring.

The critical prejudices about the worth of popular fiction that have grown up in the past fifty years have largely obfuscated the interest of Serao's work for the modern reader. Together with this critical prejudice, Serao's pluralistic literary production has served to marginalize her as a writer of interest almost exclusively to feminist scholars who are re-examining the work of women writers and their place in the canon. The ironies and contradictions that surround the creation and subsequent loss of Serao's literary reputation do not end here. For when we examine the renewed interest in Serao's work within the critical community and then compare her journalistic production with her novels, the theme of contradiction itself stands out when it comes to Serao's views about her own sex. And it is precisely the effects of marginalization, both critical and political, that has resulted in Serao's estrangement from the canon and, as we shall see, highly problematic categorization as a woman writer of interest for the political and social issues of feminism.

The issues surrounding any analysis of Serao's work are complex indeed. There have been debates regarding the possibility of reading Serao as a feminist, or at the least a woman writer who perhaps had hidden feminist leanings. Some critics point out that since some of her novels and editorials concentrate on the lives of working women and their deplorable working conditions, Serao provides if not a feminist perspective on women's work, at least a viewpoint sympathetic to women's autonomy outside the home.[1] Other critics devote themselves to situating Serao within a tradition of women writers and so they address a specific set of feminist concerns, reevaluating her work from within this perspective. For example, the complicated and interesting set of female protagonists found in Serao's popular novels lends itself well to this type of analysis. Furthermore, the characters' relationship to themselves as female and their identity within the fictive society of the novel furnishes interest.

One critic has found a way of articulating what can be called feminist tensions in Serao's work while at the same time understanding the difference between the raising of such issues and any claim to a specific political position. Ursula Fanning, in an article entitled, "Sentimental Subversion: Representations of Female Friendships in the Work of Matilde Serao," presents a convincing argument regarding the important role of friendship between female protagonists.[2] Fanning draws out these protagonists' intricate friendships and relationships with other female characters. In the texts that Fanning analyzes, friendship between women either supplants or enriches heterosexual relations, seen as unfulfilling or unsatisfactory. Fanning claims at the end of her article that "Serao's presentation of female friendship must ultimately be recognized as undeniably political, *in spite of herself.* It functions as a challenge to specific institutions, including heterosexual marriage and patriarchal society as a whole" (285; my emphasis). Through this statement Fanning makes a crucial distinction between the effect of these friendships; in other words, how they can be read and understood, especially by readers today, and authorial intent. She also points to a set of contradictions and paradoxes within Serao's work regarding her views on women, since this purported affirmation of female friendship occurs "in spite of herself."

What could the phrase "in spite of herself" mean for an author like Serao? How does the position of political and personal ambivalence that this phrase suggests manifest itself within the complex opus of Serao's multifaceted literary and journalistic production? A look at Serao's declared political stance on issues important to women is a good way to begin the challenge of understanding the complexity of Serao's work. Her newspaper editorials concerning the lives of women are unabashedly prescriptive as she advises women to stay home and avoid most professions. She states openly and clearly that woman should be the center of the home, the mother, the wife, perhaps even the woman writer, but never the divorcee, the voter, the lawyer, the professional. Serao's own life reflects an extraordinary level of paradox and ambivalence: her editorials speak out against divorce and against spinsterhood, yet she left her husband and then lived with another man. She spoke out against women's suffrage and advised women to stay home, yet she built a career for herself as one of Italy's foremost journalists and the first woman to found a newspaper. Her empowerment of herself and her continued support of the disenfranchisement of women is a puzzle whose pieces can be discovered only through a reading of both her journalistic and fictive works.[3]

In her editorials, Serao is not content with merely dictating the place of women as passive, nonvoting homemakers. Her disdain and contempt for women comes across clearly in her writings concerning women's suffrage and feminism. The following passage, taken from an editorial she published in her own newspaper, *Il Giorno*, in 1925 shows clearly why it is hard to conceive of Serao as any kind of feminist at all. The article, entitled "Ma che fanno le femministe?" (But what are feminists doing?), mocks women's intellectual capacity and jeers at the constituency for whom the feminists are attempting to obtain the vote:

> Have you ever considered, o suffragists, that the majority of women is crassly ignorant? Have you ever considered that this large number of ignorant women do nothing to diminish their ignorance; they don't read a newspaper, open a book; they are only interested in conversations that come out of gossip? Have you ever considered that this feminine mass is impermeable to ideas and to knowledge, that they flee from thinking, from reflecting and from judging? Look out, suffragists, if you want to explain to them local and statewide law . . . as they do

in the kindergartens, with children, teach them a little summarizing lesson, and then make them repeat it. A kind of catechism, tit for tat.[4]

In this editorial, Serao sets up a devastatingly misogynist argument. She forestalls potential objections and explanations for what she calls the ignorance of women as she destroys any possible "lack of opportunity" explanation, claiming that women do not *want* to alleviate their lack of knowledge, even with the tools of education laid out before them. Resorting to an old favorite in the arsenal of misogynist weapons, she asserts the incapacity of women to think and to reflect. This theoretical remark is followed up by a recipe for practice as she claims that the teaching of laws to women by repetition is the only way to teach them. She ends her remarks with an explicit and disturbing comparison of women to small children, the latter taught by the same repetitive method.

The story regarding Serao's views toward her own sex does not end here; in fact, it becomes curiously equivocal. In other editorials she condemns the working conditions of the telegraph operators, a job she herself held briefly as a young girl. She is a staunch supporter of women writers, but not of most other professions for women. In an editorial entitled "La politica femminile" (*Corriera di Roma*, 6 April 1887) Serao outlines the reasons why women should avoid the taking of political positions and uses as examples two woman doctors. One is the socialist Anna Kulischioff who is refused the right to practice medicine at the hospital in Padua. Serao approves of this expulsion and explains that Kulischioff's "defect," as Serao calls it, is that she speaks her mind about politics. Serao compares her to another doctor, a "medichessa," who is described as tranquil and apolitical and who is esteemed in her profession. The message here, and in other Serao editorials regarding professions for women, is that if women are going to engage in professions, they should be quiet, meek, and nonthreatening (emphasized here by the use of the diminutive term "medichessa" for the second doctor).[5]

Looking at both Serao's journalistic writings about women as real subjects in the world and her imaginary treatment of them brings up some interesting questions of what the world of fiction held for a writer like Serao. In Serao's first novel, *Cuore infermo*, published in 1883, we already see a pattern of ambivalence toward female protagonists that will continue through other later novels. In this novel, Beatrice marries Marcello but keeps her distance from him emotionally, fearing that a passionate attachment will prove her undoing. Her own mother had died from a weak heart that could not take the knowledge of her husband's infidelities, and Beatrice fears that she has inherited this weak heart. Because he feels rejected and hurt by Beatrice's seeming indifference, Marcello begins an affair with Lalla, described as a sickly and masochistic convalescent. Lalla is interested in Marcello both because he is married and because he can function as an agent to bring her closer to Beatrice, who is most likely the actual, though unstated, object of her love. This triangle, described by Anna Banti in her biography of Serao as a "morbosa attrazione" (sick attraction) continues until Marcello decides to leave Beatrice completely, at which point she breaks down and confesses her love for him. They embark on a whirlwind of intense passionate love that lasts for a few months until Beatrice's heart, as she feared, literally gives out from the strain of love and she collapses and dies. Lalla, the sickly yet empowered widow who does precisely as she pleases, survives in the end, although chastened by the loss of Marcello and the death of Beatrice. Beatrice, the "good" woman whose only failing is, in mid-twentieth-century rhetoric, to love too much, literally dies from love—as do several of Serao's other female protagonists in other novels.

Who "wins" in this novel? Is it the strange character Lalla, who leads a highly unconventional life and causes such discord but somehow gets away with it? Is the novel designed to elicit sympathy for the beautiful, but doomed—through a physiologically weak female genealogy—Beatrice? Are we to understand that woman's highest achievement and goal in this world is to die of love? To put it more bluntly, what is Serao's point? The assumption, either implicit or explicit, that any work of fiction or nonfiction has a deliberate "point" that the author is in control of making is dangerous and misleading. Nonetheless, this question makes itself heard often after reading a Serao novel. Or at least a more limited version of the question What is Serao's point about women?

In other Serao novels, for example, *Addio amore!* and its sequel *Castigo*, there is a rather utopian manipulation of some of the female characters as they enjoy a partial but ambiguous empowerment within the "safe" world of fiction. Others are condemned, like Beatrice, to die for love. All this holds endless and fascinating possibilities of interpretation, especially when considered against the backdrop of one of the statements Serao has made regarding real women's lives in her present society. As she declares: "I know, as do many other women, that as the laws of modern society are written, there is no happiness possible for woman, in whatever condition she finds herself: neither in marriage, nor in free love, nor in illicit love . . . and I also know, as do many other women, that everything should be changed in society, in the hearts of men and in human actions . . . and I know that no one will change everything and so thus it is not worth changing anything."[6]

This bitter and defeatist attitude betrays at the same time Serao's ability to be brutally honest about what women in her time faced in their lives and what their possibilities were. Is this the statement of a woman who thought that men and women were treated equally? Obviously not. It is certainly not the statement of a woman willing to fight for better conditions for women— but only, it would seem, because she doesn't feel it would do any good, so stacked are the odds against women. Does this recognition of the difficulties for women and her simultaneous resignation to accepting this fate make her a "feminist manquée"? Or, to use a highly charged word in our post-Holocaust era, a collaborator? Does the self-hatred apparent in the citation above regarding women's inability to handle the vote intelligently mean that she believes in the intrinsic inferiority of women—or is it rather that she is angered by what she sees as a betrayal by women who don't try harder to raise themselves above the level of ignorance in which their society has left them? Where does one draw the line between what could easily and perhaps too simplistically be categorized as self-hatred or misogyny and an embittered but honest reckoning of precisely those conditions generated by inequality?[7]

If we are indeed willing to call this misogyny, it must be immediately recognized that the question of a misogynist woman writer, especially one who concentrates on the situation of women in society, is an issue that has not been adequately addressed.[8] Andrea Dworkin discusses the appeal that the Right holds for some women in her text *Right-Wing Women*, but does not discuss female misogyny as such; in fact, there is a kind of apology made for figures like Anita Bryant and Marabel Morgan through an analysis of the emotional and physical security the Right holds for them.[9] This is not to imply that there is always or necessarily a connection between female misogyny and right-wing or conservative politics. We can see, however, that what was at stake in a feminist position at the end of the nineteenth century when battles about women's suffrage were heating up, is hardly in line with the kind of political conservatism that Serao demonstrated throughout her career, especially in regard to the role of women. A notable exception to this conservatism is her antifascist position taken early on in the fascist regime, which literary historians agree cost her the Nobel Prize for Literature at the same time that fascist censorship was ruining the newspaper that she founded. Some of the criteria that Dworkin applies to these right-wing women in order to understand their political allegiances can, I believe, be applied to Serao as well. As the lone woman figure on the journalistic front in Italy at the end of the century, she was surrounded by domineering male figures such as Gabriele D'Annunzio and her husband and harshest critic, Edoardo Scarfoglio. It seems possible to speculate that it was easier for Serao to pretend she was one of this male-dominated literary circle than to explore in depth her allegiance to other women and her own connection to the female condition.[10] As Dworkin remarks about a contemporary right-wing figure: "Phyllis Schafly, the Right's not-born-again philosopher of the absurd, is apparently not having a hard time. She seems possessed by Machiavelli, not Jesus. It appears that she wants to be The Prince. She might be viewed as that rare woman of any ideological persuasion who really does see herself as one of the boys, even as she claims to be one of the girls" (29). To speculate once again is tempting: if Phyllis Schafly were to become a novelist, what would *her* female characters be like?

The issue of female misogyny, in general and in particular in the case of Serao, is not easy to discuss or to accept, and so each case must be considered individually and with a great deal of care. Was it self-hatred that motivated Serao to make such condemning journalistic statements about women? Or perhaps despair at women's condition, aggravated from Serao's perspective by the ignorance of many women themselves? The issue is best examined at the point in which we see the most tension erupt concerning women in Serao's work: that is, when she appears to contradict herself. Contradiction as a category through which ambivalence can be understood and even appreciated is demonstrated by the following assessment of another woman writer's text, Mary Shelley's *Frankenstein*. Barbara Johnson demonstrates how the story can be read as one of deep ambivalence toward parenting, and then addresses the issue of contradictions in a woman's life. As she discusses Shelley's attitudes toward the creation of the monster, Johnson highlights an interesting aspect of this ambivalence, applicable I believe to Serao as well: "While the story of a man who is haunted by his own contradictions is representable as an allegory of monstrous doubles, how indeed would it have been possible for Mary to represent feminine contradiction from the point of view of its repression otherwise than precisely in the gap between angels of domesticity and an uncompleted monsteress, between the murdered Elizabeth and the dismembered Eve?"[11] Johnson claims that the "power of feminine contradiction," as she calls it, provides a solution for the problem of female authority in the text. Contradiction is thus a vehicle for this authority and at the same time becomes an analysis of the source of its power.

Contradiction sums up very well the situation in which we find Serao. She is both the threatening monsteress who questions the status of women, *in spite of herself*, and the would-be angel of domesticity, who feels that women had better just quietly make the most of their fate, doomed nonetheless to unhappiness in a society not set up in their favor. Accusing Serao of outright misogyny or self-hatred is to miss the point: the very ambivalences that lead to her highly problematic and contradictory stance on women in society also provide a bitter condemnation of that society. From this perspective hers is a subtly feminist viewpoint after all, but tinged with bitterness and defeat.

Just as her many female characters express different responses to their entrapment within society, critics of Serao have often fallen into a trap themselves as they attempt to over categorize her work, insist on consistency, and do not allow her the play and tension of contradiction. Seeing contradiction as a positive attribute as Johnson does allows us to more fully understand and appreciate the rich complexity of Serao's work. It further suggests that the dramatic lack of consistency we see in the kinds of fates she hands out to her female characters can be read as a statement in itself, and a telling one at that.

Serao as a novelist is both marginalized by criticism, and self-marginalizing as she problematizes the position of women in her work, adopting a difficult, contradictory and highly ambivalent stance toward her sex. She is caught between categories as she wrote both journalism and fiction, both popular novels and works of *verismo*. The bind of double and even triple marginality in which we find Serao is a complex and critically puzzling one, characterized by a great deal of ambivalence generated by her critics and by her works themselves. Rather than struggling further to make Serao fit any narrow categorization, we might find it more fruitful to understand that Serao has written an entirely different kind of text, one that explores the politics of ambiguity. And it is precisely through an understanding of what is involved in the politics of ambiguity that light is shed on the dangers of any critical analysis that seeks to assign one simplistic political spot to a writer as complex and as divided as Serao. Her very divisions reflect, after all, the complexity of the political world in which we still live. Serao's ambivalences and contradictions about the role of women and society and how women can best adjust to their lot speaks to the lives of many women today, as they struggle to incorporate personal freedoms while at the same time walking the tightrope of relationships, career, and family in an unequal world divided by difference.

# Notes

Some of the material in this article is reprinted from my *Anti-Semitism, Misogyny, and the Logic of Cultural Difference: Cesare Lombroso and Matilde Serao* (Lincoln: University of Nebraska Press, 1994), by permission of the University of Nebraska Press. © 1994. All translations of Serao are by the author.

1. For example, see Umberto Eco, Maria Federzoni, Isabella Pezzini, and Maria Pia Pozzato, *Carolina Invernizio, Matilde Serao, Liala: Tre donne attorno al cuore* (Florence: La Nuova Italia, 1979). Ursula Fanning's article, "Angel vs. Monster: Serao's Use of the Female Double," *The Italianist* 7 (1987): 63–88, positions Serao's work within the tradition of the double, usually analyzed in works by male authors. Through her analysis of the primacy of female relationships in Serao, Fanning is situating Serao as an author whose interests lie at the edge of feminist concerns.

2. Ursula Fanning, "Sentimental Subversion: Representations of Female Friendships in the Work of Matilde Serao," in *Annali d'Italianistica* 7 (1989): 273–86.

3. For an analysis of many of Serao's newspaper editorials and a summary of her journalistic career, see Wanda De Nunzio Schilardi, *Maltilde Serao giornalista* (Lecce: Milella Editore, 1986).

4. Ma che fanno le femministe?" from "Il Giorno" (20 June 1925). Reprinted in Wanda De Nunzio Schilardi's *Matilde Serao giornalista*, 223. "Avete mai pensato, o suffragette, che la massa delle donne è di una ignoranza veramente crassa? Avete mai pensato che questa massa di donne ignoranti, non fa nulla per diminuire la propria ignoranza, non legge un giornale, non apre un libro, non si interessa [che] alle conversazioni che escano dal piccolo pettegolezzo? Avete mai pensato che questa massa femminile è impermeabile alle idee e alle conoscenze, che essa rifugge dal pensare, dal riflettere e dal giudicare? . . . Guardatevi bene, suffragette, dal voler spiegare loro la legge comunale e provinciale . . . così come si fa negli asili, coi bimbi, fate imparare loro una lezioncina sommaria, e poi, fatevela ripetere. Una specie di catechismo a botta e risposta."

5. For further discussion, see Wanda De Nunzio Schilardi, "L'antifemminismo di Matilde Serao," in *La parabola della donna* (Bari: Adriatica Editrice, 1983), 277–305.

6. Reprinted in Wanda De Nunzio Schilardi, "L'antifemminismo di Matilde Serao," in *La parabola della donna* (Bari, 1983), 272–305. "Io so, come tante altre donne sanno, che, come sono composte le leggi nella società moderna, non v'è felicità possible per la donna, in qualunque condizione essa si trovi: nè nel matrimonio, nè nell'amore libero, nè nell'amore illegale . . . e so anche, come tante altre donne sanno, che tutto si dovrebbe mutare nella societá, nel cuore degli uomini e nei fatti umani . . . e so che nessuno muterà tutto e che, allora non vale la pena di mutare niente" (277).

7. For an excellent discussion of the problems inherent in the label "self-hatred," albeit in a different context, that of "Jewish self-hatred," see Paul Marcus and Alan Rosenberg, "Another Look at Jewish Self-Hatred," *Journal of Reform Judaism* 36, no. 3 (summer 1989): 37–59.

8. One critic who does discuss the issue of female misogyny, albeit in a different context, is Juliana Schiesari in *The Gendering of Melancholia: Feminism, Psychoanalysis, and the Symbolics of Loss in Renaissance Culture* (Ithaca: Cornell University Press, 1992).

9. Andrea Dworkin, "The Promise of the Ultra-Right," in *Right-Wing Women* (New York: Putnam, 1983), 13–36.

10. Dworkin reports that a technique of religious displacement of Jesus onto the figure of the insufferable husband is suggested in order to "help" women live through a difficult marriage. Dworkin reports the following example:

In *The Gift of Inner Healing*, Ruth Carter Stapleton counsels a young woman who is in a desperately unhappy marriage: "Try to spend a little time each day visualizing Jesus coming in the door from work. Then see yourself walking up to him, embracing him. Say to Jesus, 'It's good to have you home Nick.'" (23)

The issue of difficult marriage is relevant to Serao as well, as her husband and critic Edoardo Scarfoglio used to say publicly about her, "Matilde non sa scrivere" (Matilde doesn't know how to write).

    11. Barbara Johnson, *A World of Difference* (Baltimore: Johns Hopkins University Press, 1987), 153.

# Works Cited

Dworkin, Andrea. *Right-Wing Women*. New York: Putnam, 1983.

Eco, Umberto, Maria Federzoni, Isabella Pezzini, and Maria Pia Pozzato. *Carolina Inverzinio, Matilde Serao, Liala: Tre donne attorno al cuore*. Florence: La Nuova Italia, 1979.

Fanning, Ursula. "Angel vs. Monster: Serao's Use of the Female Double." *The Italianist* 7 (1987): 63–88.

———. "Sentimental Subversion: Representations of Female Friendship in the Work of Matilde Serao." *Annali d'Italianistica* 7 (1989): 273–86.

Harrowitz, Nancy. *Antisemitism, Misogyny, and the Logic of Cultural Difference: Cesare Lombroso and Matilde Serao*. Lincoln: University of Nebraska Press, 1994.

Johnson, Barbara. *A World of Difference*. Baltimore: Johns Hopkins University Press, 1987.

Marcus, Paul, and Alan Rosenberg. "Another Look at Jewish Self-Hatred." *Journal of Reform Judaism* 36, no. 3 (summer 1989): 37–59.

Schiesari, Juliana. *The Gendering of Melancholia: Feminism, Psychoanalysis, and the Symbolics of Loss in Renaissance Culture*. Ithaca: Cornell University Press, 1992.

Schilardi, Wanda De Nunzio. "L'Antifemminismo di Matilde Serao." *La parabola della donna*, 277–305. Bari: Adriatica Editrice, 1983.

———. *Matilde Serao giornalista*. Lecce: Milella Editore, 1986.

# 7

## The Diaries of Sibilla Aleramo: Constructing Female Subjectivity

*Bernadette Luciano*

In the preface to *Orsa minore*, a 1938 collection of personal observations and reminiscences, Sibilla Aleramo states that in her thirty years of writing she had been obsessed by the search for the autonomy of the female spirit[1]—a female subjectivity. In fact, the beliefs that history has been written from a position of male subjectivity, and that there exists a profound spiritual and expressive difference between men and women that needs to be explored date back to her essay "Apologia dello spirito femminile" in 1911[2] and to her 1906 autobiographical novel, *Una donna*.[3] Hence, from the beginning of the twentieth century Aleramo had been prescribing what the Italian women's liberation movement of the seventies dictated: that women must not define themselves in relation to man but rather must recognize their difference.[4] As the *Manifesto* of the Rivolta Femminile advocates: "Liberation for woman does not mean accepting the life man leads, on the contrary, it means expressing her own sense of existence."[5] The question of difference is further defined by the founder of Rivolta Femminile, Carla Lonzi in her seminal book *Let's Spit on Hegel:*

> Difference is an existential principle which concerns the modes of
> being human, the peculiarity of one's own experience, goals, possibili-
> ties, and one's sense of existence in a given situation and in the situa-
> tion one would want to create for oneself. The difference between
> woman and man is the basic difference of human kind. . . . Woman's
> difference is her millennial absence from history.[6]

Finally, as feminist philosopher Adriana Cavarero warns, the female subject
does not emerge from history by simply investigating her existence but must,
rather, actively decide to be her own subject, to take herself as her starting
point. The assertion of sexual difference through symbolic self-representation
is necessary in order for a woman to recognize her image, and thus find and
recognize herself.[7] Since subjectivity is linked to the symbolic order, women
writers need to create their own discourse; they have long been repressed by
male-authored texts and denied a voice within the existing framework of
male subjectivity. Aleramo, in adherence to such a concept of a female discourse, maintained that a woman writer should express her own distinct experience of life rather than feel obligated to write like a man.[8] Writing became for her a form of "autocoscienza," a process of discovery and of
constructing and reconstructing the self, the female subject.[9]

It was this staunch sense of feminist integrity and artistic obligation that
drove Aleramo to write her second autobiographical novel, *Il Passaggio*. Her
first attempt at autobiography, the 1906 novel, *Una donna*, published when
she was thirty-one years old, reveals the events and psychological process that
led Aleramo to escape her abusive and oppressive marriage, a decision that
cost her her son. Shocking as this was for the era, it is a story that fails to
tell the entire truth. Absent from the account is any mention of Aleramo's
extramarital relationship which, though by no means the main reason for her
leaving her husband, was a contributing factor. Initially, Aleramo omitted
this information as a concession to her then-lover and literary consultant,
the writer Giovanni Cena, who insisted that the suggestion of adultery would
compromise the moral force of the novel. Later, however, she came to believe
that what the deliberate omission had really compromised was the woman
writer's definition of self. An element of the complex, multifaceted reality
had been left out to favor circumstances more appealing to the male literary
tradition. Therefore, thirteen years after the publication of *Una donna*, Aleramo retold her story in *Il Passaggio*. For her, the later work was a revisionary
struggle, what Adrienne Rich would call "the act of looking back, of seeing
with fresh eyes, of entering an old text from a new critical direction."[10] The

act of rewriting was a revolt against patriarchal literary authority, an affirmation of female subjectivity, and established a pattern of revision based on re-reading that would repeat itself frequently in Aleramo's work.

That women should in essence "write themselves" is the overarching moral standard that explains the autobiographical nature of Aleramo's entire body of work. For Aleramo, such a poetic construct allows for virtually no dichotomy between life and art, causing many critics to question the "literariness" of her work. She was accused of reproducing her experiences in a literal fashion rather than imaginatively transforming them into "literature," of lacking the modesty to separate the private from the public. Her honesty embarrassed a literary culture that saw in her books only base matter that did not transcend human nature to rise to the level of "art" in the classic male tradition. Rather, the welding together of fiction and reality was evident, and this break with literary tradition disturbed and alarmed her early critics.[11]

This constant osmosis across the permeable boundary separating the literal and the invented realms leads inevitably to a blurring of the boundaries of genre as well. Under the guise of novels, her fictions become untransformed accounts of a life; conversely, pages of her diaries and private letters are copied and inserted into fictional works. Aleramo was an avid recorder of her own experiences. Her diaries offer perhaps the most representative example of how she merged various genres. In this paper, I examine these works both in terms of the diaristic genre itself and of certain recurring female themes that Judy Simons discusses in her book *Diaries and Journals of Literary Women from Fanny Burney to Virginia Woolf*. Simons examines the connections between the writer's life and literature and the insight diaries provide into literary production. She also addresses the question of readership, the diary's connection to texts specifically meant for publication, and the status the woman writer herself attributes to this most marginalized of genres.[12]

I preface my discussion of Sibilla Aleramo's diaries with some observations on the diaristic genre itself. The diary is a form of personal writing differing from autobiography in both formal features and organization. Rather than providing a retrospective view of the self with the distance of time and the benefit of hindsight, the diary is composed of daily entries that often give equal weight to events of extremely different importance. Rather than being a concluded work, having achieved through linear production the goal of self-realization, the diary is always a work in progress, demonstrating the fluctuating and often contradictory elements of the human personality.

That Aleramo never considered her diaries serious literature is not surprising. Diaries as texts have been traditionally considered extraliterary. They

are, in essence, twice marginalized texts—first within autobiographical criticism and second through their typical gender association—their definition
as female texts.[13] They reflect women's position in a patriarchal system. Just
as women have historically been relegated to the private realm and men to
the theoretically more important public domain, so private writings are diminished in status while public writings, composed for others to read (novels,
poetry) are deemed more "male" forms and therefore more important. And
even for men who venture into the private literary realm, writing in a diary
remains distinctly secondary to "real" writing. It is something one does when
one lacks the artistic inspiration to transcend life and transform it into art.

Two volumes of Sibilla Aleramo's diaries were published: *Un amore insolito*
(a later version of *Dal mio diario* [Tuminelli: Rome, 1945]), which covers the
years 1940–44, and *Diario di una donna* (1945–60). These pages were written
in the final twenty years of her life. The pages of the earlier work overflow
with accounts of Aleramo's stormy relationship with Franco Matacotta, a
young poet forty years her junior, and the last great love of her life. However,
the focus of the diary does occasionally turn outward to provide factual quasi-
documentary reports of World War II conditions and events.

In *Diario di una donna*, Aleramo turns her attention from personal love to
social obligation: her conversion to communism, her heartfelt dedication to
the movement, and the trips and conferences she attends. She even expresses
guilt at having been so self-absorbed in her younger years that she underval-
ued major world events. In many ways this volume is also a memoir of her
life, weaving recollections of past experiences into the fabric of her final
years. The two diaries provide the forum for self-expression for the "real" Aleramo, the Aleramo who did not consider herself a narrator, who insisted that
she would never sacrifice love for poetry, and who unleashed in unstructured
form the vitality of her existence and of her womanhood. Her own self-
reading defines the nature of these diaries which represent her life. In one
entry she writes: "I reread between yesterday and today the five bundles of
the unedited diary, 1945 to 1949, about 1200 large sheets of paper. So much
life, so little literature and none or at most very little art, but an unrestrain-
able flow of life."[14]

One of the means by which the diary reveals the connection between literature and life is in its daily record of routine personal activity, recalling both
the individual's encounters with others as well as moments of self-
introspection. Aleramo's diaries are filled with the usual accounts of meals,
parties, and visits to and from friends, students, and family members; as well
as allusions to articles of clothing, to physical appearance, to books she has

read or plans to read and to material necessities. Aleramo's diaries, like many women's diaries, repeatedly document her loneliness, highlighting the lack of comfort and understanding available to her in her daily lives. While Aleramo's diaries discuss her numerous encounters with other people, the overwhelming effect remains one of loneliness and solitude. One of the causes of this, of course, is the fact that writing in itself is a task undertaken in a solitary state. In *Un amore insolito*, for example, Aleramo writes almost exclusively at times when Matacotta is not present. As Rich suggests "to be a female human being trying to fulfill traditional female functions in a traditional way *is* in direct conflict with the subversive function of the imagination."[15] And in fact, when Matacotta is with her, she falls automatically into a traditional female role, becoming occupied with domestic tasks such as shopping and the preparation of meals—activities that interfere with and in essence preempt her writing. And though she does return to her writing when he leaves, the pages of her diary reflect the recognizable female discourse of absence, expressing her sadness that Matacotta is not with her, speculation as to when he might return, and disappointment when he repeatedly postpones visits to her. In *Diario di una donna*, written for the most part after there are no longer any significant romantic interests in her life, Aleramo expresses a different sort of loneliness—that which accompanies old age. Alone in her attic of Via Margutta she feels ancient, alone, and forgotten, particularly when she spends significant occasions (birthdays, Christmases, and New Years) in unwelcome solitude.

The diaries also offer insights into Aleramo's actual methods of literary production. In them, she discusses the conditions under which she wrote as well as the relationship between her life and her works. In terms of her methods of operation she reveals: "I write in a halting fashion, often at great intervals at whatever hour of the day or night, but preferably in the afternoon or late at night, in any place and climate always with a tormenting slowness, correcting each sentence in turn and not proceeding until I think I have achieved the most suitable, most fitting form for the idea and the intimate rhythm."[16] She rarely wrote more than two or three hours a day, with countless breaks, often painfully trapped by a word or expression. She also draws a distinction between her prose writing and her poetry. "There is a difference in the composition of verse and of prose. But for novels as well as for dramatic and critical writing and poetry, passion and meditation are twin-godmothers, always in sync with each other, and without which nothing good and vital can result."[17]

She defines her writing (the pages she wrote to narrate her life, to explain

herself) as "an unceasing madness of self-creation."[18] In spite of the clear relationship between her life and her art visible in the autobiographical nature
of her work, Sibilla does draw a distinction between writing and living. While
she wrote only of her life, she did not sacrifice living for writing, refusing
what Rich calls "the myth of the masculine artist and thinker—that to write
well it is necessary to become unavailable to others."[19] In her diaries she be-
rates herself for not having written more and yet excuses herself because it is
more important to live. In comparing herself to Emily Dickinson she says:
"Thirty years and not even two hundred poems . . . Emily Dickinson left two
thousand. It's true that she didn't write anything else. It's true that in her
entire life she expressed herself only through her poetry, without outside activity of any kind."[20] Indeed, one cannot find a woman writer more different
from Aleramo than Emily Dickinson: How can one begin to compare Dickinson's years in self-imposed isolation to Aleramo's cosmopolitan travels to
Paris, her temporary residence in various cities of the Italian peninsula, and
the avalanche of romances with men whose names constitute the annals of
early twentieth-century Italian literature? Dickinson removed herself from
the world; Aleramo immersed herself in it, and accordingly, her writing becomes her gift to the living, a remedy for the suffering: "The other day, I was
writing that the writing of poetry is something inhuman. And yet what has
been most human for me this year has been the echo of my poetry in so many
simple hearts. May the coming year allow me to write more, and may some
lines at least be worthy of outliving me."[21]

Her diaries do not confine themselves to her present. An event or a reread-
ing of past letters sparks the memory of a different time, place, or person, and
the period or individual recalled enters the diary in the form of a letter or
poem composed in the historically distant time. For example, in April 1957
Aleramo writes of re-reading the emotion-filled pages written in 1928–29
during the time of her love affair with Giulio Parise. The relationship became
the basis for the 1947 epistolary novel, *Amo dunque sono*, with Giulio being
transformed into the fictional character, Luciano. The 1957 diary achieves a
certain nonlinearity that diverges from the traditional linear production of
male-authored autobiography as Aleramo interrupts the flow of the new text
with copied entries of the earlier diary. Furthermore, it is interesting that
when she first refers to Giulio in her diary, she calls him the Luciano of *Amo
dunque sono*, reminding the reader that the fictional character is one and the
same as her real lover. Ironically, however, through his appearance in a public
text, the flesh-and-blood lover has in fact become more recognizable in the
form of the fictional character.

A further example of this juxtaposition of a present and past time is seen in Aleramo's diary entry of 16 September 1959. Here she speaks of extracting Umberto Boccioni's letters (1913–14) from her trunk of two-way correspondences, which date back to her first letter to her father when she was five years old. Boccioni, she claims, was her most passionate love at the most brilliant point in her life, the time she was writing the first pages of *Il Passaggio* and was acquiring a consciousness of her own individuality. Among the letters, she discovers the manuscript of a poem, "Ancor oggi," written for Boccioni, and later published in her collection of poems, *Momenti*. The unpublished version is a more complete and uncut rendition of the poem, and Aleramo in fact does not now understand why she chose to publish only part of it. The published portion suggests an existential desire to die, and the first person narrator is the only character: a lonely soul walking through a crowd in a clamoring city on a sunny day and denying any sense of being alive. The published version ends with the verb "andavo" ("I was going"), a verb in the imperfect tense, followed by an ellipsis rendering a definite sense of incompleteness. That sense disappears in the original poem, where the narrator subsequently reveals where she was going—in search of a man, obviously Boccioni, the only person who she felt could affirm her existence. In 1959, Aleramo decided to copy the entire poem as originally written into her diary, her private writing thus providing, ironically, a forum for the revision of a published work.

This episode raises the question of the value of self-readership to both the woman and the writer. Aleramo recognizes the poem as her own, but re-reading it after the passing of time and distance from Boccioni allows her to judge it more objectively. As a woman seeking "autocoscienza" her early editing was an affirmation of female subjectivity through the intentional omission of the male subject. However, she later realizes that the poem was in fact written with an intended male subject without whom the edited version is rendered incomplete. Such awareness can only occur from re-reading and reevaluating with the benefit of a certain objectivity resulting from the passage of time that distances her from the experience.

The effect of re-reading one's own material can be noted once again in Aleramo's entries of June 1950. A return to Sorrento reminds her that it was a place where her spirit had lived intensely while she was writing the first chapters of *Il Passaggio*. As a result, she takes out a bundle of letters marked 1912–13, Gerace. Re-reading them, she is struck by the intensity of life emanating from those pages; she wants someone to read them, but who? The question reminds her of her spiritual solitude, a theme often found in women's diaries. She has no one of whom to ask advice nor to confide in. Not only does she fear for herself as a woman, but as a writer, for how is a writer to be remembered if not through her writing? And Aleramo wonders who is going to organize and save all her manuscripts. Her loneliness and fear that these particular letters will go lost provokes her to glue them physically to the pages of her diary, for she is too tired to recopy them. These letters become what she calls a "singular parenthesis of eighteen pages for the eventual readers of the future."[22] These actions also reflect her hope, and indeed, her assumption that her diaries, while private at present, will eventually become public documents. It is to these presumably private pages that she turns to assure that her letters will not be destined to obscurity.

Although the diary is typically considered a private document, a written text by definition presupposes a reader. As Umberto Eco suggests "a text is produced for someone who might actualize it—even if one may not hope (or may not want) that someone to concretely and empirically exist" ("un testo viene emesso per qualcuno che lo attualizzi-anche se non si spera [o non si vuole] che questo qualcuno concretamente ed empiricamente esista").[23] The assumption of an eventual reader is especially true in the case of published writers, many of whom (Aleramo included) assume that their most personal thoughts will eventually reach an audience since they are already public figures subject to public scrutiny. Furthermore, Aleramo's consent to the publication of *Un amore insolito* seems to presuppose the eventual publication of future diaries. Her obvious awareness of the fate of these texts should naturally affect our reading of *Diario di una donna*. That this text is more public in its concerns than the earlier diary is not simply due to Aleramo's devotion to public causes as she grew older, but also to her cognizance of the diary's inevitable public destiny. As we mentioned earlier, what fills many pages of her second diary are accounts of her involvement with the Communist party and her close connection with Palmiro Togliatti to whom she was indebted for the financial backing of her trips to Russia, Hungary, and Czechoslovakia. Her desire to publicly acknowledge her debt to him is thereby fulfilled in the diary.

The rather problematic relationship between writer and reader is never far from Aleramo's thoughts. Early on in *Un amore insolito*, she expresses concern as to how her work will be judged by her readers: "It's so difficult to establish an understanding relationship between reader and author. The writer never really comes to know what s/he has given to the reader. Just as our voice and appearance are reflected differently in each person who sees us and hears us given the different way we are perceived in their eyes and ears, so the sense of worth of our work will appear differently depending on the soul that confronts it."[24]

Since a diary is a written text, and an eventual audience is inevitable, who is it that Aleramo is writing for? Who is her model reader? I think it is safe to say that just as the writer evolves over the years, so the intended reader also changes. Certainly her first diary, centering around her relationship with Franco Matacotta, becomes an extension of the dialogue between them: "In the evening he wanted to read what I had done since he had left, I had accomplished so little, that I didn't want to give him these poor pages. Instead he told me that they were exactly what he wanted from me, that they are the beginning of the great book that I will write in five or six years."[25] Not only does he read her work but he becomes co-author: "Franco left again today, and so I, reopening the pages of the diary, find at the top of the new page words written by him."[26] And later: "The previous page where I had written the date and the first word, 'Franco,' was continued by Franco himself who, on arriving home that night, found the word suspended. I wouldn't have written it much differently except that I would have omitted the last sentence, and I would have spoken perhaps a little bit of the pain that I had felt that New Year's day on account of my darling's gloominess."[27]

These words bespeak the lovers' unity of spirit but also reveal a certain male presumption. Franco assumes the right to impose his voice, to speak for her (as men have traditionally spoken for women in the public arena and in books) despite his obvious inability to comprehend her emotional state. While Franco is the primary intended reader, a third-party reader, a sort of confidante, is implied and indeed desired. By inserting into the diary letters that Franco wrote her as well as her reactions and responses to them, Aleramo is in essence asking her reader to both judge and validate her sentiments. An example can be seen in her reaction to his letter of 11 September 1947: "The letter I received today from Franco is one of the most extraordinary I have ever received and it's worthwhile copying it."[28] The copying is interrupted by an aside to the third party: "And here is the good part."[29] "The good part" informs the reader that what strikes Aleramo is the fact that he has something important to tell her, but he is afraid to do so, and suggests rather that she guesses what it is. She finishes recopying the letter, and then asks both Franco and the confidante "What should I guess?"[30]

Furthermore, the audience is fundamental to the construction of the particular self that Aleramo is striving to portray in her diaries. Aleramo is attempting to dispel her public image as a self-absorbed individual and the lover of great writers of the century, an image diffused in the Italian press. The desire to erase that image explains Aleramo's repeated insistence on her public actions, roles, and commitments in the second published diary. It is not enough for Aleramo to write of this self, but she must choose her material carefully in order to convince her audience; only then can this construction be complete. As Margo Culley observes in her study of the diaries of American women: "The presence of a sense of audience, in this form of writing as in all others, has a crucial influence over what is said and how it is said. It shapes the selection and arrangement of detail within the journal and determines more than anything else the kind of self-construction the diarist presents."[31] Hence the self that Aleramo portrays finally is not a total self but a construction or a reconstruction of reality, a fictional persona, a version of the self that she wishes to perfect, however unconsciously.[32]

In Aleramo's work one finds a close relationship between personal writings and texts originally meant for publication. It is no surprise that in her writings, in which fiction and life are so closely connected, the relationship between the diaries and letters and the novels and poems is a close one. As we have already seen in the case of the poem "Ancor oggi," not only does she discuss her other works in her diaries; she actually revives them in the diary itself. The diary thereby becomes a compendium of other genres. The autobiographical nature of her fictional works allows her to insert pages from these texts into her diaries to provide descriptions of past events. Aleramo also uses the pages of her diary to cast critical judgment on her own works as well as to express her personal feelings about them. She reveals the maternal affection she has for her books as a function of having produced them: "I loved every one of my books . . . because each one, more or less successful from an artistic point of view, expressed the profound truth of my soul."[33] Furthermore she uses her diary as a sort of belated marketing device for the less critically acclaimed texts such as *Il Frustino,* as if her promotion would boost its new popularity. Revising her own earlier negative judgment of the book, she writes: "I had almost disowned it, judging it as the worst of my works. Why? It has a constant tone, authentic in its grace, purity, and vivacity. And yet, like all of my books, it is not literature—it blossomed from a profound humanity. Closing it after the last page, I found myself happy to have written it."[34] And later, she boasts of the merits of the work both in the value it holds as a biographical account of a certain period of her life and in its literary qualities:

> In certain ways, *Il Frustino* is among my most significant works, the most revealing of certain sides of my biography, even though I appear under the name of Caris di Rosia. I don't know how I could, in these twenty years since I wrote the book have considered it among my

minor works and loved it so little. It has, above all narrative and dialogue qualities that aren't found in the other novels. And also, many
moments of stylistic excellence which are superior even to *Il Passaggio*
. . . and finally a unique spirituality, revealing of my secret soul.[35]

While she feels obliged to discuss the book's literariness in order to attract a
conventional market, Aleramo's true pride stems from having reproduced life
rather than having succeeded in the conventions of literature.

In the case of *Il Passaggio*, Aleramo promoted the critically unsuccessful
text through name-dropping. That an acclaimed writer such as Cesare Pavese
would appreciate the work suggests approval within traditional literary convention and might convince prospective readers to buy her book:

> Visit from Pavese who returned to me the two books I had lent him.
> He had read *Una donna* and *Il Passaggio*. He had never read anything
> of mine before. He spoke to me of them at length and with profound
> respect. In comparing the two works, he saw the former as being moral
> in content, and the latter as exclusively lyrical and stated that the
> second had greater potential for survival. He finds that *Il Passaggio* is
> already to be considered a classic.[36]

The diary entry reveals Aleramo's attempt to raise *Il Passaggio* to the popular
stature of *Una donna*, a book that had already gained international acclaim.

Finally, the status that women assign their diaries is critical to the approach
they take to the medium. As mentioned previously, Aleramo did not consider
diary-writing serious work. She begins writing *Un amore insolito* on 3 November 1940 at Capri under the suggestion of her then-lover Franco Matacotta,
who believes that it can serve as a substitute for "work." At first she is uncertain about what should be included in it. The fact that she feels she must
abide by some standard of selectivity moves the diary closer to the realm of
literary text and distances it from being simply spontaneous writing: "What
to write in this diary? Notations of the arrival of some rare letter of his, of the
uniform passing of my days of solitude in the attic, of the invitations received
from the few friends remaining in the city, of my readings."[37] While it seems
selective in content, it still frees her from any structural or technical limitation that "public" writing demands. The seriousness with which Sibilla re-
gards her diary increases with the passage of time and the accumulation of
pages. In fact, when Matacotta suggests that she abandon the diary altogether
and write an autobiography instead, she is at a loss. A tone of bereavement

and desperation accompanies the suggestion: "And all these pages then?"[38]
By the time Aleramo must decide whether to allow the publication of the
diary in her own lifetime, she finds herself facing problematic issues concerning both the nature of the work and her position as woman/writer with personal and public obligations:

> I ask myself if I will give in to Debenedetti and give him my diary to
> publish. I wrote it entirely for myself while I didn't have the energy
> for creation: for my liberation, and maybe a little bit in order to leave
> an almost daily account of my soul, to leave to future generations a
> souvenir of what was the intimate life of a woman-poet, in years
> which were cruel to the world.[39]

This passage, while divulging the extremely intimate nature of the diary, also
affirms its inevitable publication.

Ironically, once *Amore Insolito* has been published, Aleramo's concerns for
its private content are replaced by her outrage at its unfair treatment as a
public text. In *Diario di una donna*, she discloses her disappointment that her
first published diary cannot be considered in a competition for best novel
because it does not pertain to a narrative genre (DD, 88). Its relevance as
text remains paramount to her because of the connection it bears to her life:
it is after all "the most charged with life of all my books!"[40] And in her discussion of the reviews of critics Falqui (DD, 79) and Belloni (DD, 97), she expresses her disillusion at the lukewarm reception by critics who judge her
work by the prevailing literary standards. She is pleased that Falqui and Belloni recognize the poetic value of her work. Their endorsement was a high
literary compliment to a writer who defined herself primarily as a poet: "I am
not what you would call a 'born narrator.' I am irreparably lyrical."[41]

Sibilla Aleramo's diaries served as a continuous narrative of her life and
permitted her formal flexibility as she recorded daily fluctuations of tempera-
ment. While such an exercise does not enjoy the benefit of hindsight, it is an
evolving process toward self-definition, toward "autocoscienza." The diaries
are also, to a greater extent than any other of Aleramo's work, a reflection of
her search for female subjectivity: female subjectivity (as defined by Teresa
de Lauretis) as a process that is "continuous, its achievement unending or
daily renewed. For each person, therefore subjectivity is an ongoing construction, not a fixed point of departure or arrival."[42] Aleramo's diaries certainly
reveal the unseverable link between her life and her art. They are anthologies
of literary genres alternating between the personal memoir, the letter, the

poem, the document of the political and social history of a war-torn country. In these works she writes and rewrites herself in a unending quest for self-definition; "Am I not perhaps trying to unveil myself to myself?"[43] she asks. The process involves using the diaries to juxtapose accounts of her private life, present and past, and to edit and critique her published works. Finally we are left with the sense that despite Sibilla Aleramo's claim that writing played a secondary role to living, her identity is constructed, reconstructed, and valorized precisely through her writing, through the pages of narrative fiction and poetry that are reassessed in the diaries. The woman/writer is both re-formed and reformed (into a socially responsible individual). The thousands of pages of diaries, and letters, and unfinished manuscripts, of intimate and public writing left behind in her attic closet are the legacy of this woman/writer, and the most faithful account possible of a life lived to its fullest:

> I have felt the enormous amount of life that is expressed in those thousands and thousands of pages, expressed chaotically, helter-skelter, often in almost indecipherable ways, but constituting a testimony the force of which no woman has ever left, so full of herself and with such faith in her thirsty soul. I feel that after my death this inheritance of words will assume a profound value if it finds someone who has enough devotion and strength to organize and publish it.[44]

Her ultimate desire, acknowledged in these words, is to be read; the completion of her construction lies in the reader. The legacy she offers us represents this writer's conscious and constant effort to reveal to her potential readers that which is spontaneous, natural, and above all personal. To accept it is to re-read Aleramo forgoing traditional definitions of genre and to struggle with her through this process of *autocoscienza:* "a process of the discovery and (re-)construction of the self, both the self of the individual woman and a collective sense of self: the search for the subject-woman,"[45] the search that dominates Aleramo's sixty years of autobiographical writing.

# Notes

1. "Chi mi ha seguita nella lenta mia opera d'un trentennio, sa che una delle mie "fissazioni" è quella dell'autonomia dello spirito femminile; quella di voler che la scrittrice, la poetessa si differenzi nettamente dallo scrittore, dal poeta; sia se stessa, esprima la sua realtà e il suo mistero, di là da ogni maschia suggestione." Sibilla Aleramo, preface, *Orsa Minore* (Mondadori: Milan, 1938), 14–15.

2. "Se siamo persuasi d'una profonda differenziazione spirituale fra l'uomo e la donna dobbiamo persuaderci che essa implica una profonda diversità espressive; che un autoctono modo di sentire e di pensare ha necessariamente uno stile proprio e nessun altro." Sibilla Aleramo, "Apologia dello spirito femminile" (1911), reprinted in *Gioie d'Occasione e altre ancora* (Milan: Mondadori, 1954), 165.

3. Sibilla Aleramo, *A Woman*, trans. Rosalind Delmar (Berkeley and Los Angeles: University of California Press, 1980). The novel is dedicated to the spirit of "autocoscienza." See in particular pages 114, 122, 138, 218 among others.

4. From the *Manifesto* of the Rivolta Femminile, 1970, translated and reprinted in Paola Bono and Sandra Kemp, eds., *Italian Feminist Thought: A Reader* (Oxford: Basil Blackwell, 1991), 37.

5. Bono and Kemp, 37.

6. Carla Lonzi, *Let's Spit on Hegel*, 1979, excerpted, translated, and reprinted in Bono and Kemp, 41.

7. Adriana Cavarero, "The Need for a Sexed Thought" (1986), translated and reprinted in Bono and Kemp, 185.

8. Aleramo, *Orsa minore*, 14–15.

9. The term "autocoscienza" was first introduced by Carla Lonzi. See Bono and Kemp, 9.

10. Adrienne Rich, "When We Dead Awaken: Writing as Re-Vision," in *Adrienne Rich's Poetry*, ed. Barbara Charlesworth Gelpi and Albert Gelpi (New York: Norton, 1975), 90.

11. An extensive list of articles published in the Italian press critical of Sibilla Aleramo's writing and lifestyle are provided by Adriana Chemello in "Lo specchio opaco. Sibilla nella critica del suo tempo," *Svelamento*, ed. Annarita Buttafuoco and Marina Zancan (Milan: Feltrinelli, 1988). See in particular 256 nn. 6 and 7.

12. Judy Simons, *Diaries and Journals of Literary Women from Fanny Burney to Virginia Woolf* (Iowa City: University of Iowa Press, 1990), 14.

13. Cynthia Huff, rev. of *Centuries of Female Days: Englishwomen's Private Diaries* by Harriet Blodgett in *a/b: Auto/Biography Studies* 5 (1990): 164.

14. "Ho riletto tra ieri e oggi i cinque fascicoli del diario inedito, dal 1945 al 1949, circa milleduecento cartelle grandi. Quanta vita, quanta! Niente letteratura, e niente anche, o pochissima arte. Ma un flusso irrefrenabile di vita." Sibilla Aleramo, *Diario di una donna* (Milan: Feltrinelli, 1978), 266. All translations in this paper are my own with the Italian original appearing in the footnotes. All future references to this edition will be indicated by the abbreviation DD followed by the page number.

15. Rich, 96.

16. "Scrivo saltuariamente, spesso a grandi intervalli, in qualsiasi ora del giorno o della notte (ma preferibilmente nel pomeriggio, oppure a tarda sera), e in qualsiasi luogo e clima; sempre con tormentosa lentezza, correggendo frase per frase, non procedendo sin che non creda aver raggiunta la forma più adeguata, più aderente all'idea e all'intimo ritmo." DD, 253.

17. "Beninteso, c'è differenza tra la composizione in versi e quella in prosa. E ciò richiederebbe un lungo discorso. Però, tanto per i romanzi come per il teatro e le pagine critiche e le poesie, sempre passione e meditazione insieme sono le madrine, in singolare accordo: ché se questo non s'avvera, nulla di buono e vitale risulta." DD, 253.

18. "Un furore di autocreazione, incessante." Sibilla Aleramo, *Un amore insolito* (Milan: Feltrinelli, 1979), 21. All future references to this edition will be indicated by the abbreviation AI followed by the page number.

19. Rich, 96.

20. "Trent'anni e neppure duecento liriche . . . Emily Dickinson ne lasciò duemila. E' vero che lei non scrisse altro. E' vero pure che tutta intera la sua vita si espresse unicamente nella sua poesie, senza eventi esteriori di nessuna specie." AI, 439.

21. "L'altro giorno scrivevo che far poesie è cosa davvero inumana. Eppure, eppure, ecco che

in questo mio bilancio dell'anno che finisce, ciò che risulta di più 'umano' per me è proprio l'eco che in tanti cuori semplici ha avuto la mia poesia.

Possa l'anno nuovo condedermi di scriverne ancora, e che qualche verso almeno sia degno di sopravvivermi un poco." DD, 163.

22. "una parentesi singolare per gli eventuali lettori dell'avvenire." DD, 283.

23. Umberto Eco, *Lector in Fabula* (Milan: Bompiani, 1979), 52.

24. "Ma com'è difficile stabilir un rapporto di comprensione fra lettore e autore. Chi scrive non arriva mai a sapere quel che veramente ha dato a chi legge. Nello stesso modo che la nostra voce e il nostro aspetto si riflettono diversamente in ciascuno di quelli che ci odono o ci guardano, per la diversa conformazione del loro orecchio e del loro occhio, così il senso e il valore della nostra opera appare differente a seconda dell'animo che l'affronta." AI, 47.

25. "Alla sera, ha voluto a sua volta leggere quel che ho fatto io dacchè era partito. Così poco, che non volevo dargli i poveri foglietti. Invece, m'ha detto che sono proprio quello che lui voleva da me, che sono l'inizio del grande libro che scriverò, sia pure in cinque, sei anni." AI, 96.

26. "Franco è ripartito stamane, ed ecco riaprendo le cartelle del diario, trovo in cima alla pagina nuova le righe da lui trascritte." AI, 161.

27. "La pagina precedente, ov'è di mia mano la data e la prima parola, 'Franco,' è stata continuata e per intero vergata da Franco stesso, che rincasando a sera la trovò sospesa. . . . Poco diversamente l'avrei scritta io, se non che avrei omessa l'ultima frase, e avrei forse, parlato un poco del dolore da me patito, quel dì di Capodanno, dinanzi all'accesso di tenebra del mio caro." AI, 234.

28. "La lettera di Franco è veramente una delle più straordinarie ch'io abbia mai ricevuto, e vale la pena di proseguire a copiarla." DD, 155.

29. "E qui viene il bello." DD, 156.

30. "Che cosa debbo indovinare?" DD, 156.

31. Margo Culley, *A Day at a Time* (New York: Feminist Press, 1985), 11.

32. Culley, 12.

33. "Ho voluto bene ad ogni mio libro . . . perchè in ciascuno, più o meno riuscito dal punto di vista dell'arte, ho sempre trovata espressa la verità profonda dell'anima mia." DD, 230.

34. "l'avevo quasi rinnegato, giudicandolo come la cosa mia più scadente. Perchè? Ha un suo tono costante, una grazia e una purezza e anche, sì una vivacità, autentiche. . . . E invece neppure questo libro, come nessun altro mio, è 'letteratura' . . . è fiorito da una fonda umanità." DD, 191.

35. "Sotto certi aspetti ho trovato che il *Frustino* è fra le opere mie più significative, più rivelatrici di alcuni lati della mia biografia, sebbene lì io appaia sotto le spoglie di Caris di Rosia. Non mi rendo conto di come abbia potuto, in questi vent'anni dacchè il libro vide la luce, sempre considerarlo fra i miei minori e pochissimo amarlo. Anzitutto, ha qualità narrative e di dialogo che non si trovano negli altri romanzi. Poi, moltissimi momenti, moltissimi incisi d'una eccellenza stilistica che forse supera quella del *Passaggio* . . . e infine una spiritualità singolarissima, rivelatrice della mia più segreta anima." DD, 262–63.

36. "Visita di Pavese, che mi ha riportato i due miei libri che gli avevo prestati, *Una donna* e *Il Passaggio*. Non aveva mai letto nulla prima di mio. Me ne ha parlato diffusamente e acutamente, con profonda stima. Fatta la distinzione fra le due opere, l'una di contenuto morale, l'altra esclusivamente lirica, ha affermato che la seconda ha maggior forza di sopravvivenza. Tuttavia egli trova che questo *Passaggio* è ormai da considerarsi come un classico." DD, 96.

37. "Allora, che cosa scrivere in questo diario? Notare l'arrivo di qualche sua rara lettera, notare lo scorrere uguale delle mie giornate nella solitudine della soffitta, qualche invito dai pochi amici rimasti in città, qualche lettura." AI, 83.

38. "E tutte queste pagine allora?" AI, 38.

39. "Mi chiedo ancora se cederò all'istanza di Debenedetti e gli darò a pubblicare questo

Diario. L'ho scritto talmente per me, mentre non mi sentivo il vigore della creazione: per me, a liberazione, e forse, un poco anche per lasciare una testimonianza quasi quotidiana della mia anima, per consegnare all'avvenire il ricordo di quel ch'è stata la vita intima di una donna-poeta, in anni crudeli per il mondo." AI, 436.

40. "Forse il più carico di vita di tutti i miei libri!" DD, 354.

41. "Certo io non sono quella che si chiamerebbe 'narratrice nata.' Sono irrimediabilmente lirica." DD, 273.

42. Teresa de Lauretis, *Alice Doesn't: Feminism, Semiotics, Cinema* (Bloomington: Indiana University Press, 1984), 159.

43. "Non sto forse tentando di svelare me a me stessa?" AI, 444.

44. "ho sentito la somma enorme di vita ch'è espressa in quelle migliaia e migliaia di foglietti: espressa caoticamente, alla rinfusa, spesso in maniera quasi indecifrabile, ma costituente una testimonianza quale forse nessuna donna ha mai lasciato tanto ampia di se' e con tanta fedeltà alla propria anima assetata. Ho sentito che, dopo la mia morte, quest'eredità di parole assumerà un valore profondo, se troverà chi avrà devozione e forza sufficiente ad ordinarla e pubblicarla." DD, 33.

45. Bono and Kemp, 9.

# Works Cited

Aleramo, Sibilla. *Amo dunque sono*. Verona: Mondadori, 1947.

———. *Una amore insolito*. Milan: Feltrinelli, 1979.

———. *Diario di una donna*. Milan: Feltrinelli, 1978.

———. *Il Frustino*. Verona: Mondadori, 1932.

———. *Gioie d'Occasione e altre ancora*. Milan: Mondadori, 1954.

———. *Momenti*. Florence: Bemporad, 1920.

———. *Orsa Minore*. Milan: Mondadori, 1938.

———. *Il passaggio*. Milan: Treves, 1919.

———. *A Woman*. Translated by Rosalind Delmar. Berkeley and Los Angeles: University of California Press, 1980.

Bono, Paola, and Sandra Kemp, eds. *Italian Feminist Thought: A Reader*. Oxford: Basil Blackwell, 1991.

Buttafuoco, Annarita, and Marina Zancan, eds. *Svelamento*. Milan: Feltrinelli, 1988.

Culley, Margo. *A Day at a Time*. New York: Feminist Press, 1985.

de Lauretis, Teresa. *Alice Doesn't: Feminism, Semiotics, Cinema*. Bloomington: Indiana University Press, 1984.

Eco, Umberto. *Lector in Fabula*. Milan: Bompiani, 1979.

Huff, Cynthia. Review of *Centuries of Female Days: Englishwomen's Private Diaries*, by Harriet Blodgett. *a/b: Auto/Biography Studies* 5 (1990): 164.

Rich, Adrienne. "When We Dead Awaken: Writing as Re-Vision." In *Adrienne Rich's Poetry*, ed. Barbara Charlesworth Gelpi and Albert Gelpi, 90–106. New York: Norton, 1975.

Simons, Judy. *Diaries and Journals of Literary Women from Fanny Burney to Virginia Woolf*. Iowa City: University of Iowa Press, 1990.

# 8

# Narrative Voice and the Regional Experience: Redefining Female Images in the Works of Maria Messina

*Elise Magistro*

The works of the Sicilian Maria Messina (1887–1944), were rediscovered in the mid-1980s by her compatriot and fellow author, the late Leonardo Sciascia. In his afterword to a selection of Messina's stories republished under the title *Casa paterna* (My father's house), Sciascia expresses surprise that in this era of reexamining feminine texts, Messina has yet to attain the recognition accorded her better known contemporaries (59). Certainly, a review of Messina's substantial opus reveals a writer of considerable talent and one who should rank alongside Deledda, Serao, and other enigmatic women writers who attempted to break into the male-dominated tradition of fiction writing in Italy at the turn of the last century. What, if any, were Messina's particular contributions to Italian regional narrative? Did she succeed in expanding the perimeters of the veristic canon or "art rooted in the study of life" as defined by that school's most celebrated figures Giovanni Verga and Luigi Capuana? Finally, to what extent did the writer's gender determine the deviations in themes and imagery found in her mature work?

Though the details of Messina's life are at best sketchy, what little we do know about this obscure writer comes to us from letters penned in her own hand to Giovanni Verga between 1909 and 1919.[1] The picture that emerges from this scant epistolary is one of a determined yet retiring woman wholly dedicated to her art. To a great degree self-educated, unmarried, and a product of provincial Sicilian life, Messina was the first to recognize that her solitary existence was as uneventful as those of the characters she portrays (Agosta, 33–34). The correspondence with Verga—initiated by Messina when she was just twenty-two—was a source of deep pride for the aspiring young writer and clearly one of the most influential factors in her literary career.

What permeates Messina's letters is both a tremendous admiration for her mentor ("Illustrious, most beloved teacher" [*Illustre amatissimo Maestro!*]) and an unfaltering commitment to the principles of fiction writing he expounded. In 1910 Messina dedicated *Piccoli gorghi* (Small vortexes), her second collection of stories to Verga while the Catanian writer reciprocated the honor with a letter of introduction for the publication of Messina's *Luciuzza* in "Nuova Antologia" (Agosta, 30). With Verga's encouragement, Messina continued to publish sporadically until 1921. Growing frustration, however, with both her failing health and a literary market that had long tired of *verismo*'s dire portrayals of life, is evident in the author's last letters. Oddly, this disillusionment coincided with that of Verga himself, some fifty years her senior. By the time of Verga's death in 1922, Messina had all but fallen into literary obscurity, felled by a debilitating sclerosis that rendered writing impossible.

Though *verismo* had all but exhausted itself during the first decade of this century, comparisons with Verga and his style of writing seemed inevitable from the outset for Messina, if only by virtue of her commitment to describing life within the Sicilian provinces. That Messina's contemporary, Giuseppe Antonio Borgese, referred to the young Sicilian writer as "a scholar of Verga" (164) is hardly surprising when one considers both the content and style of the stories contained in *Pettini fini* (Fine combs) (1909) and *Piccoli gorghi* (1910), many of which are admirable attempts at reproducing in a true Verghian fashion the regional world of Sicily at the turn of the last century: a linguistically and culturally diverse locality, plagued by poverty, governed by religious attitudes and enslaved by centuries of tradition.

Stylistically, Messina is most reminiscent of Verga when she alters standard Italian syntax or incorporates Sicilian expressions into her texts. Certain titles—"Ti-nesciu" ("Ti faccio uscire"), "Ciancianedda" ("Campanellino") and "La Merica" ("L'America")—also reflect this use of dialect as the primary vehicle for authenticating her narrative. Consider the following excerpt from the short story, "Janni The Cripple" ("Janni lo storpio"):

"Hey Janni," said gna' 'Ntonia one morning with a mysterious air. "How'd you like Maralucia for a wife?"

"Me?" said Janni narrowing his dark eyes.

"Me? Maralucia? Don't kid me like that, it's not Christian."

"I'm telling you the truth! Can't you see how she waits around for you?"

"And can't you see me?"

She saw him all right, just like everyone else saw him, but gna' 'Ntonia was an old matchmaker who had sensed a match to be made: after all, Janni earned enough to get by and Maralucia hadn't had any offers. (*Piccoli gorghi*, 24–25)[2]

Passages such as these abound in Messina's early works. Proverbial sayings and a distinctly choral perspective also bring the drama of daily events to life and further enhance the *tranche de vie* character of these first stories. The absence of an intrusive narrator completes the veristic canvas executed by an artistically deft yet "invisible" hand. Here, as in Verga, the rift with French naturalism is apparent, and ambience supersedes heredity as a determining factor in the lives of the many vanquished (*vinti*) Messina sought to portray.

Judging from both the content and style of these short stories, there is little reason to believe that Messina questioned the validity of her literary paternity in the early stages of her career; rather, she embraced it. Like Verga, the author belonged to the Sicilian middle class and the inspiration for these first stories was similarly rooted in personal observations of the poor in her society (*Piccoli gorghi*, 11–15). Furthermore, the choice of a subject matter so dear to the *veristi*, that of the economically and socially disenfranchised, as well as a particular emphasis on the mythic as opposed to the historic reality of Sicilian lives, would also indicate that Messina shared many of Verga's philosophical ideas on social destiny, including the Darwin-inspired "struggle for existence." Consider the musings of the protagonist in "Caterina's Loom" ("Il telaio di Caterina"): "She thought how time passes quickly; passes quickly and always seems the same. And people hurry too. And some stop; fall; others overtake them, never looking back" (*Gente che passa*, 158).[3]

The passage is strikingly similar in tone to the preface of Verga's *I Malavoglia* (51–53), and indeed such unabashed imitation of her mentor might well have relegated Messina to the status of a lesser Verga of sorts, if not for the fact that amongst these portraits in miniature of individuals who populated the lower strata of Messina's society, is to be found a nucleus of stories that revolve around the lives of very middle-class subjects. The impetus in these works is clearly more personal and less dispassionate than in Verga, as Messina ventures out of the preferred terrain of the *veristi* and reveals an authorial predilection for a psychological reality more representative of her own stifling provincial existence.

Borgese was the first to identify this tentative direction in Messina's writing: "I sense there, however awkward and uncertain, a spirit of freedom" (Mi pare di sentirvi ancora impacciato ed incerto, uno spirito di libertà). He recognized its potential for success; a success, however, contingent upon Messina's ability to liberate herself "from the dry and somewhat cautious narrative method to which she [has] limited herself up to this point in time" (dal metodo narrativo un po' troppo secco e prudente che finora s'è imposto [169]).

In the most exemplary of these stories, the reader is no longer immersed in the colorful and tragic world of I *Malavoglia*, but in that of *Mastro don Gesualdo*, one generation removed. It is a stagnant and dismal provincial setting that, as Sciascia aptly notes, is closer in makeup to the Girgenti of Pirandello's L'*esclusa* (*The outcast*) (*Casa paterna*, 62). Undoubtedly, the struggle for economic survival is still at the heart of the narrative and, as in Verga, the quest for financial security has exacted a predictable price: the forgoing of meaningful human relationships in exchange for monetary security. Yet in these works Messina sets her artistic lens not only on the unrelenting penury of this struggling bourgeoisie but on the destructive and amoral nature of what she perceives to be its underlying cause: patriarchal social structures whose necessary sacrificial victims are most often women.

That women are protagonists and no longer marginal figures in a number of these works, suggests that the new direction in Messina's writing was accompanied if not spurred by, a crisis of consciousness regarding her own inferior status as a female in her society. Unmarried, and as such relegated to a life of solitude, Messina in essence became the prototype for a more realistic female character fashioned directly out of her own experience. As her niece, Annie Messina, would write nearly half a century after her aunt's death:

> In those days in Sicily, the male child could escape suffocating provincial life if he wanted. He could study, go out with his friends; then there was the university and ultimately a career. But for a young girl, condemned to embroidery and piano lessons, there was no other hope than that of marriage arranged by relatives, or if she was lucky, one that materialized amid family reunions and parties which were rigidly monitered by her parents. (*Piccoli gorghi*, 12)[4]

Certainly, the preeminent question posed by Gilbert and Gubar—What does it mean to be a woman writer in a culture whose fundamental definitions of literary authority are overtly and covertly male? (45–46)—is even more compelling when one considers the repurcussions for Messina, an aspiring writer in a society that severely restricted the activities of women and subjected them to rigorous codes of social behavior.[5] Furthermore, to the degree that Messina was influenced by Verga and his style of writing, the new thematic focus on the plight of women, while clearly a literary response to a personal situation for Messina, was also a cautious attempt at expanding the tenets of *verismo* as outlined by Capuana (263) and applied by Verga ("L'amante," 200–201).[6]

In consciously creating introspective female protagonists, many of whose provincial lives were similar to that of the author herself, Messina was no longer a casual observer but an active participant in the dramas she sought to portray. And functioning in this novel role of both the observer and the observed was a phenomenon that necessarily brought into question the most fundamental of all veristic maxims: authorial impartiality. What Messina opts for in these colorless and heartwrenching stories is a blueprint for *verismo* more in keeping with that of Federico De Roberto, outlined in the preface to his 1890 *Documenti umani*. In this work, De Roberto carries the veristic principle of observation one step further by proposing as a possible subject of observation the author's own psychological process:

> Psychological analysis is, in fact, a product of a particular kind of imagination: the imagination of states of mind. In only one case can it be the true product of immediate observation, and that is *when the author makes himself the object of his analysis*. By putting himself directly on stage, or *by lending his own consciousness to one of his actors*, an author is able to dissect the rarest, most complex, most delicate states of mind which form within his conscience and under his own direct perceptions. (317)[7]

Though we find no references to De Roberto in her letters, Messina (an astute critic in her own right) was most likely familiar with his work. But whether or not Messina consciously adopted this more flexible design, what remains indisputable is that by tailoring Verga's express goal of "putting himself under the skin of his characters, trying to see with their eyes and speak in their words," Messina expanded the perimeters of the *veristic* canon to include a point of view that was distinctly female and thus by its very nature biased. As Gilbert and Gubar note regarding the nineteenth-century woman writer in general:

> Her battle . . . is not against her (male) precursor's reading of the world but against his reading of *her*. In order to define herself as an author she must redefine the terms of her socialization. Her revisionary struggle therefore often becomes . . . the act of looking back, of seeing with fresh eyes, of entering an old text from a new critical direction. (49)

Messina's implicit rejection of impartiality as the primary prerequisite for truly realistic fiction not only challenged the validity of this concept as envisioned by Verga and Capuana, but exposed in a broader context, the legacy and amorality of patriarchal socialization so often reinforced in Verghian texts.

With Verga's focus on popular culture, for example, and his explicit aim at retaining as closely as possible the features of popular narration in his writing (*L'amante*, 199–200), it was inevitable that he create characters that embodied female cultural extremes. Mena Malavoglia is nothing less than a domestic angel at her loom (*I Malavoglia*, 67); La Lupa, a female aberration (however fascinating) who asserts her sexuality and wreaks destruction on Christian men (*Tutte le novelle*, 145).

Certainly these types of fictional creations raised disturbing doubts for Messina, caught between admiration for the underlying literary principles of *verismo* and her own experience, which invalidated such stereotypical portrayals of women. As a consequence of this ambivalence, what emerges from Messina's critical exposés is a dramatic persona who is outwardly submissive yet whose motivations and behavior lay bare the damaging psychological effects of social conditioning and of subsequent internalized rebellion against it.

It is this unsavory reality, no less brutal or real than the harsh world depicted by the *veristi*, that Messina confronts in three representative short stories: "The Guests" ("Gli ospiti"), "The Passing Hour" ("L'ora che passa"), and "My Father's House" ("Casa paterna"). The introspective, middle-class Vanna of "Casa paterna" is more reminiscent of Pirandello's outcast Marta Ayala than Verga's Mena Malavoglia. Though all may be said to be victims of societal prejudice and cultural norms regarding the proper role of women in traditional Sicilian society, Messina—much like Pirandello and unlike Verga—strips away the mask of a united family to reveal the disharmony and moral decadence within a house divided. Far from the nurturing refuge envisioned by Verga, the family unit is here a powerful instrument of coercion and retaliation that preys on rebellious individuals such as Vanna, who leaves her husband in Rome to return to her father's house in Sicily. The potential scandal caused by such actions unites the family in an effort to force her return. Social decorum and economic constraints demand as much in that Vanna's subversive actions undermine male authority and threaten the economic stability of the family. At stake are not only the honor of her husband but the future marital prospects for her younger sister (22).

All this might appear too Verghian in tone if not for the fact that Messina persistently focuses on Vanna's betrayal by the family, that cultural icon so revered by Verga. In underscoring the protagonist's rejection and subsequent suffering at the hands of her family, Messina exposes with painful accuracy the moral contradictions of this economically struggling society; one in which the patriarchal family structure had surpassed in importance the ancient values that inspired its formation.

Though Vanna ultimately submits to the will of her family (and here we see the influence of Verga's cyclical vision of life; the futility of trying to change one's lot), the author's covert anger and subtle cynicism are not lost on the reader. Indirectly challenging the maternal ideal put forth by Verga in the person of Mena Malavoglia's mother, La Longa, "who had known how to raise her daughter" (che aveva saputo educarla la figliuola [67]), Messina presents us with Vanna's mother, a woman who clearly comprehends the reasons behind her daughter's rebelliousness yet who is nonetheless torn by guilt "[because] she had failed to inculcate in her daughter the most essential of all female virtues: sacrifice and submission" ([perché] non aveva saputo inculcare alla sua Vanna quei sentimenti di sottomissione e di sacrificio, che sono le virtù principali di una donna [22]).

And behind the facade of the nest (il nido), one of the Verghian myths systematically dismantled by Messina throughout this and other works, self-interest and antagonism reign, transforming the beloved casa paterna into the place of Vanna's destruction. The protagonist's imminent death by suicide is both a silent protest against the debilitating alternatives she faces, as well as a symbolic gesture: the choice of death over life when life has become nothing more than a deathlike existence.

Messina also explored the destructive nature of this provincialism and its accompanying moral decadence in explicit symbolic terms. In "Gli ospiti," the natural landscape and youth of the protagonist, Lucia, contrast sharply with images of ruin and decay: the dilapidated family home, its ailing patriarch and the physical and psychological inertia that paralyzes this family and negates any hope of future regeneration: "How long had her father been like this? She could barely remember him healthy and standing tall" (Da quanti anni era così suo padre? Quasi non lo rammentava piu sano e diritto ["Casa paterna," 33]).[8]

More often, however, the outside world is curiously absent from Messina's mature prose, which relies instead on a spare, linear plot and few dramatics to communicate the feminine condition. That Messina had settled on a definitive narrative structure that complemented the bleak content of her stories is evident in two noteworthy collections, *Sicilian Girls* (*Ragazze siciliane*) and *The Leash* (*Il guinzaglio*), both originally published in 1921. As their titles aptly suggest, the collections underscore the lack of social identity accorded unmarried women in Messina's society. Here the author narrates as one who has lived from within the dismal alternatives facing young Sicilian women: arranged marriages, lonely spinsterhood, or immigration to the Americas. What dominates in these works is atmosphere: the steady, monotonous flow of life and the inability of characters to interact openly with one another. In keeping with a narrative that seeks to portray as accurately as possible the female experience, Messina almost wholly eliminates the exterior world from view. Instead, the imagery of confinement is fully developed with a characteristic emphasis on restricted inner spaces and the ruthless self-suppression of women that manifests itself in claustrophobia, agoraphobia and retreat from the real world (Gilbert and Gubar, 53–59, 64, 83–86).

In the disturbing and more complex "Caterina's Loom" ("Il telaio di Caterina") Messina explores with remarkable psychological accuracy for her day, the underlying causes of agoraphobia, which afflicted females schooled in reticence and strict compliance to social customs. As a backdrop for this work, Messina chooses bereavement or *il lutto*, one of the cruelest modes of confinement imposed on women in her society well into this century. Here, as in "Gli ospiti" (23), the author reveals how the debilitating physical and psychological effects of prolonged lack of exposure to the light of day, coupled with emotional grief, trigger a deterioration process whose end result is, as Gilbert and Gubar note, the acceptance of sickness over wellness as the norm of female existence. Women who demonstrate all the classic symptoms of claustrophobia (Messina's heroines complain constantly of suffocating atmospheres) inevitably take refuge behind those very walls that have obstructed personal fulfillment. When hope for a better life gives way to fear of the unknown, an ingrained sense of inferiority prevails and they embrace their fate accordingly.

In "Il telaio di Caterina," two sisters are inseparable after the death of their mother, so much so that they walk in one another's shadow, fearing the light of day and open-air spaces their bodies and spirits so desperately crave: "One would not leave the room if the other felt poorly; one would cease talking if the other knit her brow, assailed by painful memories. They slept together, in two small white beds" (148).[9]

More than two kindred spirits, however, the sisters are complementary sides of a single paradigm of female perfection, both of which embody the "dis-ease" of female provincial existence: Marietta the more delicate and physically pleasing; Caterina a model of virtue and selflessness:

> They even resembled one another. Only Caterina seemed stronger; Marietta more delicate. For this reason, Aunt Vanna took great care with her favorite. At home there was general agreement: no jealousies arose if at breakfast Marietta sipped an egg or two while the other contented herself with a bit of fruit or cheese. Or, if when stepping out into the courtyard, Aunt Vanna followed Marietta with a shawl ready in her hands. She had developed a cough that refused to go away. (148)[10]

When the weaker Marietta succumbs to a lingering tuberculosis, Caterina—true to character as the repressed, more psychologically ill half of the duo—sets about in transforming the *casa paterna* into a veritable crypt, embroidering testaments of devotion to her deceased sister. When an out-of-town guest arrives to meet Caterina for the first time, she is "ushered into [a] small living room, shut off in semi-darkness and filled with the heavy scent of must and wilted flowers" (La condusse nel salottino tutto chiuso mezzo al buio, dove si respirava un pesante odore di muffa e di fiori appassiti [154]). Strangely, the protagonist has neither the desire nor strength of will to break the chain of this morbid existence that, ironically, is slowly killing her as well:

> Caterina, absorbed in her work and assailed by vague passing thoughts, was reluctant to break the lethargic silence that enveloped her soul. She embroidered, even in the evenings, pictures to offer her sister.
>
> At dawn she set to work and, no sooner had she dined, would return to judge the effect of a bud or a leaf sketched in the morning. Perfecting her embroidery of strange flowers in various hues of grey and ash, she lived for these sad, silent works, loved as though they were living things.

> Observing her niece curved over the loom, Aunt Fifi whispered to
> Vanna: "She's going to go, just the way the other one did . . ." (151–
> 52)[11]

Messina's point here is clear. Not only would physical death be preferable
to figurative dying or virtual entombment behind the walls of a domestic
prison, but women doomed to such a fate unconsciously live out a death wish,
unable to break free of the psychological chains that bind them. Thus when
a suitor is found for the passive protagonist:

> Caterina was frightened. She had never gone out except for a few
> times, in the evenings with Mrs. Teta; she hadn't met anyone new in
> so long. . . . And now, to have to go to her uncle's house to meet a
> man . . . to meet him, then, to . . . (158)[12]

Fate, as Caterina sees it, offers only one alternative for escape: marriage to
a man she has never met. When the plan fails miserably, the cause appears to
be none other than Caterina herself who remains obstinately silent in the
presence of her prospective suitor. Messina would have us believe otherwise,
however, for in this tale riddled with psychological ambiguities she presents
us with a woman filled with self-loathing yet desperate to salvage the last
vestiges of her integrity. The anxiety Caterina experiences at her own inferiority is reflected in intensely distorted perceptions of her body, while the
physical repercussions of repression manifest themselves in the excruciating
migraines from which she suffers:

> She thought about the purpose of the meeting and reddened. Seeing
> her arms so long in sleeves too short; it seemed to her that her bust
> was enormous, her body enormous. She experienced a kind of shame
> just being there in that room, on display for a complete stranger who
> scrutinized her, only then to make his observations known to Mrs.
> Teta's husband.
>      . . . She felt a sharp pang of disgust for herself and for those who
> surrounded her.
>      . . . She must have seemed awkward indeed in that insignificant
> corner of the sofa. Could she ever interest that man? No, never. She
> would never interest anyone.
>      Her head pounded.
>      How long had she been suffering like this? (160–61)[13]

Rebellion finally surfaces, but only in the guise of silent refusal, the sole manner in which Caterina allows herself to exercise free will. When the suitor predictably rejects her in favor of a gregarious younger cousin, Caterina seems unfazed, preferring to live out her days embroidering and reminiscing about the deaths of her mother, Marietta, and her own dreams.

This type of imagery and passive female character are also employed in Messina's short novel, *The House in the Alley* (*La casa nel vicolo*). Though the external world looms large and inviting, it is rarely seen by the female protagonists cloistered within the walls of their joyless and shadowy home. Indeed the opening paragraph of the novel is replete with the spatial imagery Messina so often used to reflect the sickening psychological effects of confinement on females:

> Nicolina sewed on the *balcony*, hurrying to add the finishing touches in the *dying* light of dusk. The view from the high balcony was *blocked*, practically *suffocated* between the *narrow* street which at that hour appeared deep and *dark* as an empty well, and the great stretch of reddish moss covered roofs upon which weighed a *low and colorless* sky. Nicolina sewed quickly, never raising her eyes; she felt, as though she were breathing it in with the air, the *monotony of the confining landscape*. (9)[14]

The oppressive tone of the passage sets the stage for a work that draws its momentum as much from the psychological dread of the female protagonists as from the subdued plot of familial incest. The patriarchal home is here a fitting metaphor for the desolate interior world of two sisters whose deep bond of attachment and dreams of marriage are shattered when the husband of the elder, Antonietta, takes as his paramour the younger Nicolina. Within a tightly structured narrative, Messina expands upon the *veristic* idea of allowing characters to narrate themselves via the objects and ambience with which they most closely identify. The psychological association of men with the animal world so effectively employed by Verga in "Jeli il pastore" and "Rosso malpelo" is here carried one step further as Messina develops a static imagery of objects wholly in sync with provincial female existence.

When alone in a room containing Lucio's most prized objects, Nicolina experiences a masochistic and perverse sense of well-being as if she senses, but is unable to fully comprehend, Lucio's perception of her and she of herself as little more than one of his possessions. Consequently, though she is repelled by the brother-in-law who forcibly seduces her, Nicolina nonetheless fiercely defends this amoral being on whom her self-image and survival depend (57). And certainly the brutish Lucio—who prefers his women malleable, "to be molded like fresh clay" (30)—reinforces this lack of self-esteem in the women whose lives he totally dominates:

> Don Lucio savored the smoke [from his pipe] with an almost voluptuous satisfaction. With his eyes half-closed he followed even the slightest movements of the two sisters. Both had, in their expression, in their way of moving and looking, the same awkwardness, the same clumsiness, which arose from their continual fear of disturbing him. Each time he realized the depth of the fear he instilled in them, he experienced a renewed sense of satisfaction. (12)[15]

There is little doubt that Messina expresses the psychological corollary to the confinement of females much in the same manner as had her English nineteenth-century predecessors in their symbolic depictions of claustrophobic interiors, suffocating clothing, and domestic furnishings. Yet Messina's characters are not prone to romantic spleen, that most emblematic of all female diseases found in nineteenth-century texts. Rather, they are individuals without self-image or hope who have so wholly internalized the strictures of patriarchy that overt rebellion against the exhausting physical and emotional demands placed upon them appears all but impossible ("La casa nel vicolo," 16–19).

Interestingly, though Nicolina and Antonietta tend to perceive themselves as middle-class and thus less susceptible to actual physical abuse, the author makes it clear that social rank has little bearing on the psychological suffering that most women in this society are forced to endure. As the following passage exemplifies, Nicolina sees no connection between her own pathetic condition and that of a woman considered far less fortunate than she:

> From the narrow street arose the lament of La Rosa who had been beaten and cast out by her lover. . . . Even Nicolina glanced at her for a moment, more with surprise than pity. She was dirty, filthy, disheveled. Why did she continue to suffer? Why didn't she flee and break the chain which kept her tied to that closed door? Nicolina blushed, thinking that behind that door was her lover, the man who had beaten her and who would later allow her to reenter, as always. But was that really love? (52)[16]

Nicolina's sister, the passive Antonietta, fares little better. A woman who in the presence of her husband "dares have neither desires nor hopes" (in presenza del marito non osava avere desideri, o speranze [35]), she is unable to cope with the sordid reality that confronts her or to rebel openly against her nightmarish condition. She thus retreats from life first by taking refuge in the sickbed of childbirth and ultimately in mental breakdown when the death of her son strips her of the will to live.

One may suggest at this point that Messina simply perpetrates a morality that she herself despised in creating characters whose staid acceptance of "destino" negates any meaningful possibility of change. Yet beneath the apparent stoicism and Christian resignation of Messina's heroines is the bitter realization that the primary cause of their suffering is having been born female. As Nicolina muses after the birth of Antonietta's third child, a baby girl: "Had it only been a boy. . . . Fate would have been easier. Women were born to serve and suffer. For this and nothing more" (Fosse almeno un maschietto. . . . La sorte sarebbe più facile. Le donne sono nate per servire per soffrire. Non per altro [64]).

Clearly Messina's aim in this and other works is to focus on the rupture of close female bonds—sister versus sister, mother versus daughter, cousin versus cousin—in order to underscore the debilitating effects of patriarchy on women. Competing for men and marriages in a society already rent assunder by greed and economic struggle, victimized women all too often exploit others of their own sex, and sadly those whom they should most protect. Though the author's voice can be cynical in this regard ("The Shattered Ideal" ["L'ideale infranto"] in Gente che passa, 164–70), more often it strives to expose the devastation that occurs as a result of entrenched cultural norms.

The poignant tale "Red Roses" ("Rose rosse") recounts the story of a young woman cheated out of her dowry by the calculated actions of a jealous sister-in-law. Without a substantial dowry, the protagonist Liboria loses her fiancé and is forced to live out her life as little more than a servant in her brother's home. Years later when Liboria's niece is to be wed, she finally relinquishes all hope for her own happiness, symbolized by the gift of her beloved trousseau to her niece. Included within is the exquisite coverlette of red roses whose flowers were "still as vivid and fresh as her own heart" (ancora vivide e fresche come il suo cuore [Gente che passa, 110–15]).

A story with a more sustained psychological twist, "The Young Girl" ("La bimba") pits a beautiful, aristocratic mother against her adoring adolescent daughter in a fierce yet subtle sexual rivalry. If in "Rose rosse," "Casa paterna," and La casa nel vicolo, Messina decreed that more meaningful female bonding is undermined by economic exigency and cultural forces at work in her Sicilian society, here she goes to great lengths to demonstrate that even that most basic rapport between mother and daughter has been poisoned by the inculcation of patriarchal aesthetic ideals (Gilbert and Gubar, 3–44).

The refined Signora Giulia frequents the most celebrated salons of the day, yet she is bored and strangely ill at ease in the presence of her daughter, Titina. The physical resemblance between the two is striking, and the dark truth that the mother must confront in the face of her waning vitality and youthful beauty is not only her own mortality but her inevitable uselessness once she ceases to be an object of desire: "While her child blossomed like a beautiful flower, she felt her limbs less agile; as the child's eyes grew more luminous and her complexion brighter, her own eyes were losing their splendor. And on her cheeks there appeared the first wrinkles, ably hidden by a layer of powder. In order for the child to grow in beauty, it was necessary that she grow old" (48).[17] The depth of moral erosion in this society is layed bare with Titina's discovery that the soldier who stirs her heart is in fact her mother's lover.

If in these stories of failed human relationships Messina casts a critical eye on her complaisant society's harsh treatment of women, she is nonetheless keenly aware that men, and particularly those who exhibit "feminine" traits, also stand little chance of survival in such a preordained structure. That most female and sensitive male characters are afflicted by similar ills is movingly exemplified in La casa nel vicolo, a novel that is as much the tragedy of Alessio, Antonietta's emotionally fragile and physically delicate son, as it is that of his vanquished mother and aunt. Never does Messina so effectively challenge gender stereotypes, blurring the line of distinction between male and female as in the creation of this introspective romantic youth who reads Jacopo Ortis and dreams of escape for himself and those he loves. Depicted as weak by nature and psychologically so by virtue of his close ties to his mother and aunt, Alessio is doubly feminized much in the same manner as Grazia Deledda's Elias Portolu, who also fails to measure up to prescribed societal codes of male behavior (Opere scelte, 136).

In the microcosm of Messina's provincial world, Alessio's fate is sealed from the outset. Emotionally and economically dependent on a father who views his interest in academic pursuits as a personal affront to paternal authority, Alessio eventually surrenders to the hopelessness of his condition. Rationalism—the idea that life should and could be different—ultimately fails to save him. Feelings of ineptitude for failing to better his own lot as well as that of his mother and aunt make death the only viable option in Alessio's eyes. Particularly disturbing and equally as telling of Alessio's final act of desperation, is the title of the open book found alongside his lifeless body: *Life is Folly* (*La vita è una sciocchezza*).

The novel's final, sad irony is quite simply that the most positive male character is by nature also the most feminine. Those very qualities of depth of feeling and blind optimism in the face of defeat that render Alessio contemptible in the eyes of his authoritarian father are those that represent the only hope for this society's spiritual regeneration. Lucio's cruel yet frank assessment of his dead son—"He was a weakling" (Era un debole)—aptly reflects his indifference to the fragility of human nature. Hardly a literary device of authorial impartiality, however, this deep-rooted indifference is rather a defining human characteristic and one that ultimately reigns supreme in Messina's vision of the universe. Life's flow remains unarrested by the tragedies of ordinary people who are swallowed up by the small vortexes or "piccoli gorghi" of everyday existence.

In conclusion, what might then on the surface be viewed as a Verghian vision of the human struggle, must also be considered a forthright attempt on Messina's part at deconstructing female paradigms found in the established veristic canon. Furthermore, in virtually all Messina's stories one senses the author's participation in a larger, well-defined Sicilian narrative tradition in which authors as diverse as Verga, Pirandello, Lampadusa, and Sciascia explore a negative (one might say characteristically *Sicilian*) view of history. Cyclic or mythic as opposed to linear in nature, this underlying current—which implies that the more things change the more they remain the same—finds a consistent if not always efficacious vein throughout the whole of Messina's opus.

Since the author gives little indication that she believed this vicious cycle of existence could be broken, some may argue that her works cannot be considered feminist in any real polemical sense. Yet Messina's portrayals of women are in themselves a powerful statement of defiance; a sobering recognition of the degree to which entrenched values in her Sicilian society determined the destiny of women even more so than that of men. In her revision of the canon or the veristic "human document," Messina thus bridges the gap between *verismo* and more modern literary trends. In doing so she narrows the separation between literature and life that was to become the hallmark of Italian neorealism.

# Notes

1. Messina's letters as well as her signed photograph were discovered among Verga's papers in 1977. See Agosta, 7–11.

2. —O Janni, —disse la gna' 'Ntonia un mattino con aria misteriosa—la vuoi per moglie la Maralucia? —Io? —fece Janni, sgranando gli occhi scuri. —Io la Maralucia? Non mi prendete in giro così, che non è opera da cristiani. —Ti dico da vero. Non vedi come t'aspetta? —E voi non mi vedete, me? Lo vedeva come lo vedevan tutti; ma la gna' 'Ntonia era una vecchia ruffiana che aveva sentito esserci per aria qualche cosa da combinare, già che Janni alla fin fine guadagnava tanto da sbarcar la giornata, e a Maralucia non s'era ancora presentato un partito. (Unless otherwise noted, all emphases and translations are my own).

3. "Pensava che il tempo scorre; scorre e pare sempre lo stesso. E anche la gente s'affretta. E qualcuno si arresta sul più bello; cade; altra gente sopraggiunge e va, senza guardarsi indietro."

4. "A quei tempi, in Sicilia, *il figlio maschio* poteva evadere, volendo, dalla chiusa vita di provincia: c'erano gli studi, le scappatelle con i compagni, poi l'università e infine una carriera e l'indipendenza. Ma per una ragazza, condannata al ricamo e alle lezioni di pianoforte, non c'era altra speranza che un matrimonio combinato dai parenti, o per le piu fortunate fiorito tra le riunioni e le festicciole in famiglia, rigidamente sorvegliate dai genitori."

5. Though Gilbert and Gubar focus primarily on the literary works of English and French women writers at the turn of the last century, their arguments are particularly applicable to Messina, a writer whose gender and social conditioning had great impact on the theme of female repression in her novels and short stories.

6. Luigi Capuana's 1885 essay, *Per l'arte* is generally considered to be the manifesto of Italian *verismo*. See Capuana, in Bertacchini (263).

7. "L'analasi psicologica è infatti il prodotto d'un particolar genere d'immaginazione: l'immaginazione degli stati d'animo. In un solo caso puo essere il prodotto reale dell'osservazione immediata, *cioè quando lo scrittore fa oggetto della propria analisi se stesso.* Mettendosi direttamente in iscena, o *prestando la propia coscienza a uno dei suoi attori*, egli potrà sviscerare gli stati d'animo più complessi, rari e delicati che nel campo di questa coscienza e sotto la propria diretta percezione si formano."

8. The "decadent" tone of "Gli ospiti" recalls that found in Grazia Deledda's *L'Edera* of the same period. Both Deledda and Messina chronicled the moral decline of their respective Sardinian and Sicilian societies, though landscape plays a far more significant role in Deledda's fiction. See Magistro.

9. "L'una non usciva dalla camera se l'altra si sentiva poco bene, l'una smetteva di parlare se l'altra corrugava un po' la fronte, afferrata dai dolorosi ricordi. Dormivano insieme in due bianchi lettini . . ."

10. "Si somigliavano anche. Solo, Caterina pareva più forte; Marietta era più gracile. Per questo zia Vanna aveva molte cure per la sua prediletta. In casa era convenuto, e non nascevano gelosie se a colazione Mariettina sorbiva un paio di ova mentre l'altra si contentava d'una frutta o d'un pezzetto di cacio fresco; o se, uscendo nel cortile zia Vanna seguiva Marietta con uno scialle pronto fra le mani. Aveva preso un po' di tosse, che non se ne voleva andare." On the concept of female disease see also "The Queen's Looking Glass," in Gilbert and Gubar.

11. "Caterina, assorta nel lavoro, presa dal vago fluttuare di vari pensieri, non desiderava rompere il letargico silenzio che le circondava l'anima. Ricamava, anche di sera, quadri da offrire alla sorella. . . . All'alba si metteva al lavoro, e a pena desinato andava a vedere l'effetto di un boccio o di una foglia abbozzata nel mattino. Perfezionandosi a ricamare strani fiori con tutte le sfumature del grigio e del cenere, viveva per i tristi pazienti lavori, amati come cose vive. Zia Fifi osservava la nipote curva sul telaio: —Se ne va come l'altra! —diceva a zia Vanna—"

12. "Caterina si sgomentò. Non era mai uscita—fuori che poche volte, di sera, per i campi, con la signora Teta; non vedeva gente nuova da tanto tempo. . . . E ora doveva andare in casa dello zio per conoscere un uomo. . . . E conoscerlo, poi, per. . . . Pensava allo scopo dell'incontro e arrossiva. Si vide le braccia lunghe nelle maniche troppo corte; le parve di avere un petto enorme, un corpo enorme. Provò una specie di vergogna nel sentirsi li, in quel salotto, esposta allo sguardo di uno sconosciuto che l'osservava per poi fare le sue considerazioni col marito della signora Teta. . . . Sentì un acuto disgusto di se e di coloro che la circondavano. . . . Doveva

essere ben goffa in quel cantuccio di divano. Poteva mai interessare quell'uomo? No, non l'avrebbe mai interessato. Non avrebbe mai interessato qualcuno. . . . La testa le martellava. . . . Da quanto tempo soffriva cosi?"

13. Strikingly similar to Caterina is the protagonist of Borgese's "La siracusana" who also suffers from migraines as a result of domestic confinement. For a thorough discussion on anxiety and agoraphobia in feminine texts see Gilbert and Gubar, 45–93.

14. "Nicolina cuciva sul *balcone*, affrettandosi a dar gli ultimi punti nella *smorta luce del crepuscolo*. La vista che offriva l'alto *balcone* era *chiusa*, quasi *soffocata*, fra il vicoletto, che a quell'ora pareva fondo e *cupo* come un pozzo vuoto, e la gran distesa di tetti rossicci e borraccini su cui gravava *un cielo basso e scolorato*. Nicolina cuciva in fretta, senza alzare gli occhi: sentiva, *come se la respirasse* con l'aria, *la monotonia del limitato paesaggio*" (my emphasis).

15. "Don Lucio assaporava la sua fumata con soddisfazione quasi voluttuosa. Tenendo gli occhi socchiusi seguiva ogni piccolo movimento delle due sorelle. L'una e l'altra avevano nell'espressione, nella maniera di muoversi, di guardare, lo stesso impaccio, la stessa goffaggine che nascevano dal continuo misterioso timore di recargli fastidio. Egli provava una compiacenza sempre nuova ogni qual volta si avvedeva come fosse profonda la soggezione che ispirava alle due donne . . ."

16. "Dal vicolo saliva il lagno della Rossa, che era stata battuta e scacciata dall'amante. . . . Anche Nicolina la guardò un momento, più sorpresa che impietosita. Era sudicia, laida, scarmigliata. Perche continuava a soffrire, e non fuggiva, e non si liberava dalla catena che la teneva legata a quell'uscio chiuso? Nicolina arrossì, pensando che dietro l'uscio doveva esservi l'amante, l'uomo che l'aveva battuta e che piu tardi l'avrebbe lasciata rientrare, come sempre. . . . Ma era quello l'amore?"

17. "Mentre la bimba sbocciava come un bel fiore, essa sentiva le membra meno agili; mentre gli occhi della bimba si facevano più luminosi e la carnagione più chiara, i suoi occhi perdevano lo splendore, e sulle gote appariva qualche ruga, abilmente nascosta da uno strato di cipria grassa. Perché la bimba si facesse bella, era necessario che lei invecchiasse."

# Works Cited

Agosta, Giovanni Garra. *Un Idillio letterario inedito verghiano: Lettere inedite di Maria Messina a Giovanni Verga*. Catania: Greco, 1979.

Borgese, Giuseppe Antonio. "Una scolara di Verga." In *La vita e il libro*, 3 vols., 3:164–69. Bologna: Zanichelli, 1923.

Capuana, Luigi. "Per l'arte" (1885). Reprinted in *Documenti e prefazioni del romanzo italiano dell'Ottocento*. A cura di Renato Bertacchini, 254–66. Rome: Studium, 1969.

Deledda, Grazia. *L'Edera*. 1906. De Michelis. *Opere scelte*. 2 vols. Vol. 1.

———. *Elias Portolu* (1900). *Opere scelte*. A cura di Eurialo De Michelis. 2 vols., 1:61–226. Milan: Mondadori, 1964.

De Roberto, Federico. *Documenti umani* (1880). Reprinted in Bertachini, *Documenti e prefazioni*, 292–303.

Gilbert, Sandra M., and Susan Gubar. *The Madwoman in the Attic: The Woman Writer and the Nineteenth-Century Literary Imagination*. New Haven: Yale University Press, 1979.

Magistro, Elise. "Beyond Regionalism: The Evolution of the Deleddian Novel 1896–1936." Diss., University of California at Los Angeles, 1988.

Messina, Maria. *Casa paterna*. Edited by Sellerio. Afterword by Leonardo Sciascia. Palermo: Sellerio, 1986.

————. *Il guinzaglio*. Milan: n.p., 1921. *Ragazze siciliane*. Florence: n.p., 1921. Reprinted as *Gente che passa*. Edited by Sellerio. Palermo: Sellerio, 1989.

————. *Piccoli gorghi*. Palermo: n.p., 1911. *Pettini-fini*. Palermo: n.p, 1909. *Le briciole del destino*. Milan: n.p., 1918. Reprinted as *Piccoli gorghi*. Edited by Sellerio. Palermo: Sellerio, 1988.

Moers, Ellen. *Literary Women*. 1976. New York: Oxford University Press. 1977.

————. *I Malavoglia* (1881). Milan: Oscar-Mondadori, 1973.

Verga, Giovanni. "L'Amante di Gramigna." *Vita dei campi* (1880). Reprinted in *Tutte le novelle*. Milan: Oscar-Mondadori, 1974.

# Part IV

---

# Contemporary Women Writers

## Toward a New Canon

# 9

---

# Brushing Benjamin Against the Grain: Elsa Morante and the *Jetztzeit* of Marginal History

*Maurizia Boscagli*

In a letter of March 1937 to Walter Benjamin, Max Horkheimer comments upon a passage from "Edward Fuchs, Collector and Historian," which Benjamin had written for the *Zeitschrift für Sozialforschung:* "I have long been thinking about the question whether the work of history is complete. Your formulation can certainly stand as it is. I have but one personal reservation: that I think this is a relationship only to be perceived dialectically. The pronouncement of incompleteness is idealistic if it does not incorporate completeness as well. Past injustice is done and finished. Those who have been beaten to death are truly dead. Ultimately you are making a theological statement. If one takes incompleteness absolutely seriously, then one must believe in the Last Judgement. My thinking is too contaminated with materialism for that." [1]

The question of the "incompleteness of the past" is further elaborated by Benjamin in the *Theses on The Philosophy of History*, a text of 1940. In the *Theses*, by opposing the work of historical materialism to that of historicism, Benjamin presents a theory of the real course of history, as well as a theory of materialist historiography. This new historiographical practice inaugurated by Benjamin is at work in Elsa Morante's novel *History* (1974),[2] where the "incompleteness of the past" is foregrounded (and compensated for) by confronting the "objective" narration of the history book (realism) with the rich language of fiction, this time in a tone that could be defined as magic realism or perhaps, "hyperhistoricism." Both Benjamin's and Morante's writings are critiques (and in the case of the latter a real *J'accuse*) of the supposedly scientific and disinterested character of history in Western culture. History, in their thinking, is a form of representation. With a move that anticipates the perspective of Michel Foucault and of Hayden White,[3] both Benjamin and Morante show that history is first of all narration, a cultural practice that takes shape in the always already colonized territory of language: that is, history is a form of knowledge produced and governed by power. In turn, power proceeds through the logic of the same: the victor, he who survives and has the means of formulating and managing the *representation* of the "facts," will pose himself at the center of history, and will delete any memory of his victims. Both Benjamin and Morante establish their deconstructive notion of historiography by questioning the privileged discourse of rationalism with "irrationality": through Jewish messianism Benjamin exposes the fallacy of Western philosophy (both idealism and marxism), while Morante deploys *and* debunks realism as a bourgeois narrative mode through an unorthodox religious discourse.

The *Theses* constitute a critique of historicism, the dominant, teleological vision of history in both its Hegelian and orthodox Marxist interpretation. Benjamin rejects the historicist view of the past as an uninterrupted flow of events and linear development, together with the notion of history as progress, founded on the belief of the perfectibility of man and of the social formation. While the historicist critic believes that "the truth will never run away from us," the historical materialist (as Benjamin himself) knows that history is a history of loss: "The true picture of history flits by. The past can be seized only as an image which flashes up at an instant when it can be recognized and is never seen again. . . . Every image of the past that is not recognized by the present as one of its concerns threatens to disappear irretrievably" (Benjamin, *Theses*, thesis 5, 255). If the past is not completed, if history is not retrieved from the representation provided by the victor, "even the dead will not be safe" (Benjamin, 255).

It must be made clear that for Benjamin the historical flow of facts, what is remembered of the past, is the history of the victor. This particular version of history ("And all the rulers are the heirs of those who conquered before them" [thesis 7, 256]) makes invisible the history of the oppressed, in Benjamin's instance, the working class. While "historicism sympathizes with the victor," reproducing the lie of history as the all-encompassing flow of a "completed" past, the task of the historical materialist is to redeem what is, or could become, irretrievably lost: the "anonymous toil" of those who guarantee power its course. In particular, the task of the historian is to make visible the barbarism inscribed in any document of civilization, to use Benjamin's own words.

The lost past flashes up, intermittently, at moments of danger, of emergency. Fascism, the historical conjuncture that Benjamin experienced personally, constitutes this moment of danger, a danger that the historicist does not recognize as such, and rather poses as the norm: "One reason why fascism has a chance is that in the name of progress its opponents treat it as historical norm" (275). To fight fascism, therefore, "it is our task to bring about a real state of emergency." Yet revolution ("the real state of emergency") is not posed by Benjamin as inevitable. It is exactly on the question of history and the revolution that Benjamin's theory takes distance from the assumptions of orthodox Marxism. In Marx's vision, the conflict between the forces of production inevitably leads to the blowing-apart of the property relations, and then produces a new social formation. Instead, Benjamin sees the proletariat of his own times as the blinded subject of history, reduced to conformism and complicity with capitalist power, and no longer the promoter of an inexorable historical development. If the revolution is no longer the necessary telos of history, how can historical movement itself be theorized? What can inject a new revolutionary stimulus in the calcified theory of historical materialism is not philosophy but theology. The "leap into the open air of history," what will interrupt and change the course of history, takes place not through an act of will, but through an act of faith.

In order to do away with the notion of historical progress purported by the historicist, Benjamin needs a new notion of time: "The concept of the historical progress of mankind cannot be sundered from the concept of its progression through a homogeneous, empty time" (thesis 13, 261). This homogeneous, empty time (*Das Immergleiche*, the always-the-same) is what produces the illusion of the completeness of the past. It is by focusing on rupture, intermittence, interruption that the "other history," the history of the oppressed can be made visible: "History is subject of a structure whose site is not homogeneous, empty time, but filled with the presence of the now [*Jetztzeit*] (thesis 5, 261). In order to grasp the movement of history, its flow must be brought to a halt. The *Jetztzeit* is exactly the moment that cuts through history, the "now" that blasts its continuum open, thus disrupting and contradicting his-

tory's claimed completeness: "In this structure [the historical materialist] recognizes the sign of a messianic cessation of happening—or, put differently, a
revolutionary chance in the fight for the oppressed past" (263). Here there
are two Benjamins speaking: one is the younger man who begins his reflection on the incompleteness of history through the images and the concepts
of Jewish mysticism; the other is Benjamin the unorthodox marxist, enlisting
his theology in the service of historical materialism in order to denounce its
insidious participation in the logic of oppression, ultimately in fascism. In the
*Theses*, the "politicians" that have reduced the proletarian to passivity and
conformity with the capitalist norm, are not only the German social demo-
crats, but, even more, Stalin. The *Theses* were written during and in the immediate aftermath of the Hitler-Stalin Pact, in the summer of 1939, and represent Benjamin's attempt to dissociate himself from a "thinking," and a
political practice (orthodox Marxism), that at that moment was compromising with fascism: more precisely, from Marxism as a science that legitimized
the politics of Stalin.

This is the historical state of emergency that prompts Benjamin to revise
historical materialism's faith in progress through theology, and particularly
through the discourse of Jewish mysticism. The messianic idea of redemption,
central in the *Theses*, the suspension of the continuum of history through the
*Jetztzeit*, relies upon the antithetical distinction (and the possibility of a
clash) between historical and Messianic time. In the Kabbalah, the access to
the realm of redemption is depicted as a violent and dangerous process: the
transformation of historical time into the messianic era takes place through
a series of future natural disasters and catastrophes. However painful and
costly this process may be, the historical materialist must exercise his "weak
messianic power"; that is, he must enact, even provoke the same catastrophe
and ruptures, in order to redeem the past. Only a disrupted and disruptive
historiography can properly signify the catastrophic character of history: the
*Jetztzeit* becomes then the focal point of historiography, as the moment that
reveals and reintegrates what has been canceled from the records.

This same moment of disruption, denunciation and, finally, reintegration
of the "other history" from the "space off,"[4] the realm of invisibility to which
the history of the oppressed has been reduced, is at the core of Elsa Morante's
narrative in *History*. In this essay I read her novel as an enactment of Benjamin's theory of history and historiographical praxis, and at the same time as
a revision and a manipulation of the literary conventions of sentimentality
and of realism from a materialist and, more problematically, feminist point
of view.

Benjamin's and Morante's intentions and methods of analysis overlap more than once: both are concerned with the same historical period, a period whose "historicity" they experienced in person; both consider fascism as a historically specific embodiment of power, of the logic of the victors (the bourgeoisie); both write under a desperate pressure, precisely with the intent of "reawakening" the dead, as well as the conformist subject of history. In her *L'Unita* article "Censorship in Spain" (15 May 1976), Morante affirms: "Now, almost an old woman, I felt that I couldn't depart from this life without leaving the others a testimonial memory of the crucial epoch in which I was born. Besides being a work of poetry (which, thank God, it is!) my novel *History* wants to be an accusation of all the fascisms of the world. And at the same time, it represents an urgent and desperate demand—addressed to everybody—for a possible, communal awakening."

Morante shares with Benjamin the awareness that marginal history is a flash that could never be seen again, depending on who constructs and manages the circulation of this memory. Like Benjamin, she starts by deploying a materialist analysis of the past, and at the same time—thus showing the shortcomings of the orthodox Marxist interpretation of history—she too moves into the realm of theology, this time that of the Gospel. These points of juxtaposition between Morante's and Benjamin's texts are what makes the exploration of their writing interesting to me. By no means, however, do the similarities imply identity. As an analysis of Morante's novel in the light of Benjamin's theory, this essay illustrates the particular strategies through which *History* enacts, and simultaneously modifies, Benjamin's concept of history. At the same time, I show how Morante makes Benjamin's theory of oppression more specific in terms of gender and race, and, last but not least, how her writing questions Benjamin's theory. Although both writers deploy the same method of inquiry (a marxist view "theologically" revised) each comes to a different conclusion about history and its redemptive possibilities.

Morante's novel is constituted by a series of intermittent *Jetztzeiten*, moments of historical rupture when the Other of history is made visible. Benjamin's imperative of interrupting, the "messianic" cessation of happening he describes in the *Theses*, is visible at the level of the narrative, precisely in the way the plot is constantly articulated and disarticulated. The book, and later each chapter, begins with a sequence of dates, each listing a number of political, "public," national, and international events: "1918. World War I ends with the victory of the Entente . . . ten million dead." A long period of Italian, as well as world history, from 1900 to 1967, is remembered year by year and "fact by fact": the death of Lenin, the march of Mao, the Spanish civil war, Mussolini's ratification of racial laws, the rise of Nazism, and then the German occupation of Italy in 1941. At this point we have the first Benjaminic rupture: the flow of history is interrupted and the novel begins. Later, the narrative action will be interrupted over and over again in order to introduce another set of "dates and facts," now reaching to our times.

Through her weaving in and out of history, through this movement across macro- and microtemporal structures, Morante shows us that the private and the public are not opposites: history directly shapes the lives of its individual subjects, and conversely, the apparently meaningless individual is really part of history. The continual exchange between the general and the particular, the "official" and the banal, is signified and anticipated by the title: *History: A Novel* (in Italian, *La storia*, a semiotically ambiguous term, meaning both "story, narrative" and "history"). History, as Morante implies, is a piece of fiction, artificial because narrated. Already at the opening of the book, the author posits the nature of history as "interested" narrative, structured by power and deploying specific rhetorical strategies to persuade the audience of the "truth" about a certain event. Yet the traffic between historiography and fiction writing suggested by the title points to a further interpretation of Morante's intentions: the history of the excluded, of the marginal, is necessarily made of stories. Since no documentation, no records have been kept, how can the historian fix the traces, register the presence of those who have been silenced and deleted from history except through an act of imagination? The existence of those who did not, who could not speak, who could not bear witness to their own existence on earth, can only be reconstructed through an act of fiction. Their history needs to be a novel.

Morante's narrative opens with an act of violence that symbolically refers to the logic of oppression informing historical "progress": in 1941, during the German occupation of Rome, Ida Ramundo is raped in her own house by a young German soldier. Ida is an elementary school teacher, half-Jewish by birth and the widowed mother of a child, Nino. She is a subjected figure, bowing down and bearing the yoke of any form of constituted authority: men, the family, her superiors at school, the state and its racism. As a consequence of the rape, she becomes pregnant, and gives birth to Useppe, who will die of epilepsy in his sixth year. Ida is a survivor, and not only of rape: she literally survives the hunger, the homelessness, and the deprivations of war. Although she could be considered the heroine of the novel, Morante inserts her story in a larger narrative frame, thus inextricably mixing it with the stories of other marginal characters with whom Ida comes in contact: her petit bourgeois family, the Jews in the ghetto of Rome, the refugees of Pietralata, the partisans whom Nino, her eldest son joins, and Davide Levi, another key figure in the novel. The stories Morante tells and the detailed account of the lives of the figures she introduces invariably end with their irretrievable eclipse, their death. Ultimately, Ida's own family will be destroyed: Nino dies in a car accident, Useppe dies of a violent epileptic crisis; Ida will survive him only for nine years, dying alone in a mental hospital.

Gender is the crucial element through which Morante complicates Benjamin's historiographical method. The subject of history is defined as genderless by Benjamin: the proletariat have only a class determination in his writing. Although Morante does not exclusively privilege women as the depositories of historical knowledge, she shows interest in the way in which women's oppression and deletion from history is produced: the "struggling, oppressed class" of which Benjamin writes in the *Theses,* is individualized and gendered in Morante's text.[5] Women in *History* are exploited and oppressed *as women,* through sexuality and the body, and in the name of "femininity"; that is, by a specifically patriarchal construction of femininity. Mariulina and her mother are raped; Santina, the prostitute, is exploited and then murdered by Nello, her pimp; Ida herself (without ever complaining) is literally a servant to men. She is the Althusserian subject, working "all by herself," successfully interpellated by a sexist ideology of femininity: as a daughter, bride, mother, widow and unaware propagator of fascist knowledge for her students, she blindly respects authority, thus reproducing the internalized LAW (of capital, of racism, of gender, of the state), without recognizing its effects on herself.

At the same time, gender is not the only (not even the main) category that defines oppression in *History.* Although Morante recognizes the specificity of female oppression, she does not fetishize women as the only subject of history; rather, she closely looks at the ways in which their victimization intersects with the victimization of other marginalized groups: the ill, the old, the insane, the poor, for instance.[6] By focusing on the historical juxtaposition of different oppressions, Morante avoids an easy, manichaean division between good and bad, a superficial reading of who the victors and who the victims are. In this perspective the German soldier Gunther is recognizable both as Ida's rapist and as a childlike being "caught in the war" and actually looking for maternal shelter. He is sentimental; before leaving Ida, he gives her his penknife, while taking a flower as a souvenir ("gravely placing it among some papers of his wallet he said, "Mein ganzes Leben lang!" "for all my life!" [62]). This contradictory representation of Gunther as defenseless oppressor, shows that even characters who seem to occupy a position of power, are actually only power's subjects. In this sense, through Morante's endless work of revealing what history and historical progress leaves unsaid, the tables are continually turned in the novel.

The detailed inquiry into the individual life of each of her characters is perhaps the most effective strategy the author deploys to open up the continuum of history. Through what could be defined as a technique of "re-familiarization," Morante "identifies" both the victim and the enemy one by one, thus giving them a face, a voice, a story. In other words, she tries to unmake what history does: depersonalizing human beings, equating difference, reducing everybody to numbers, flattening individuality and differences to a common denominator. While history says "fifty thousand dead," Morante tells the story of one of those fifty thousand in detail, thus taking a leap from the general, impersonal macrostructure of history into the particular, the everyday.

By giving these "numbers" a face, she turns them into recognizable individuals. By telescoping from the public (impersonal) to the private (the personal) with what could be called a photographic zoom technique, she is able to show what the reader could never detect and recognize with the naked eye. Through her novelistic close-ups, Morante pushes to the limit the conventions of realism to produce an effect of closeness and familiarity. Nothing is left out of her text: both the lives and the deaths of her characters are told, and not even the most atrocious details of their suffering are passed under silence. One of the most unforgettable and painful passages of the book describes the tortured body of the partisan and ex-refugee Moscow, left on the streets of Marino by the Germans for days, and kicked by the passers-by. The unbearable horror is almost unreadable. And yet, what this passage represents is exactly what we don't want to see, what goes untold in history books. This is a moment when pain is made material on the page, the moment when we are reminded that our blindness, our choice of not seeing is impossible, only a false choice.

This moment of strident contradiction between "brute reality" and the particular rhetorical strategies through which history discursifies events (the strategies through which we are constructed as an anesthetized audience) is repeated throughout the novel by Morante, to the aim of defamiliarizing our commonsensical view of history. This time, we are asked to see and experience the horror of murder through the eyes of a child: Useppe at the kiosk, looking at the photographs of hung and tortured partisans in an illustrated magazine; Useppe at the Tiburtina station, zooming in on the cattle cars in which the Jews have been imprisoned, while Ida tries to spare him the view

by covering his eyes. Another example of the contradictory relationship between "raw reality" and ways of explaining it, is Davide's speech on power:
"Power . . . is degrading for those who submit to it, for those who administer
it and for those who control it. Power is the leprosy of the world" (306). This
speech is delivered to Santina the prostitute, whose injured and exploited
female body is subjected to the inevitability of the power that Davide depre-
cates and, at the same time, embodies as her client. This contradiction is
again perceptible in Giovannino's letters from Russia. The tragic irony of the
letters lies in their clashing discourses: Giovannino's ungrammatical writing,
full of pain and fear, appears under the word "CONQUER," heading the official
stationary of the Italian army. The linguistic and discursive clash, as in the
case of Gunther, reveals the duplicity of Giovannino as "conquered con-
queror," sharing both in the arrogance of fascism and in the submission of
the wretched.

Morante's narrative is centered upon the contradictory relationship of History to "stories": her aim is to make visible and audible what otherwise could
not be seen and heard. In its work of interrupting, denouncing, and reinteg-
rating, the novel addresses three major concerns: the inadequacy of language
(the impossibility to translate human suffering into language; the automatic
exclusion of those whose language is not understandable to the rationality of
history); the question of visibility and of "vision" (here Morante is concerned
not with sensory vision, but with the visionary capability of the marginal);
and the question of self-recognition, that is, the consciousness of one's position in history as the necessary, or perhaps not so necessary, condition for
self-redemption. While the first two concerns are dealt with through the logic
of Benjamin's theory, the question of self-recognition is another crucial point
in which Morante's writing distances itself from Benjamin's.

According to Benjamin, redemption is not transcendental: "It's our own
task," he says. "Our coming was expected on earth. Like every generation
that preceded us, we have been endowed with a weak messianic power, a
power to which the past has a claim" (254). Endowed with such "weak messianic power," the oppressed themselves are capable of interrupting the continuum of history. As thesis 15 reads, "The awareness that they are about to
make the continuum of history explode is characteristic of the revolutionary
classes at the moment of their action" (255). For Benjamin the *Jetztzeit* is a
moment of revelation that produces consciousness *and* praxis: it becomes, in
Benjamin's page, both the necessary condition to operate the revolution *and*
the beginning of a messianic era inaugurated through a violent interruption
of history through praxis (revolution). In other words, in order to change the

course of history, Benjamin's system implies the presence of a self-aware subject, a subject capable of *seeing* his oppression. Perhaps, we could add, the realization of this oppression is corroborated by vision, "theology enlisted in the service of historical materialism." Yet for Benjamin the oppressed, through their awareness of their real conditions of existence, can become active agents of history. The irruption of messianic time into historical time will at least question and jeopardize bourgeois history and bring a yet unknown, new temporality that will see the proletariat as its subject.

Morante finds herself in a quite different position, because her subject is not so automatically capable of self-awareness and of self-recognition. In fact, the novel presents a series of characters "invested" by history, figures at the margins upon whose anonymous toil the edifice of power is erected. But these figures understand neither the logic of power nor their own part in making the machine of history function. Ida herself is totally blind to her own complicity with the social and political structures that oppress her: "she knew how to do nothing except transmit to her elementary pupils those ordinary notions that to her, as an elementary pupil, had been passed on by her teachers, who in turn had received them from their teachers. On occasion, obeying the dictates of the Authorities, she introduced into their themes and dictations the king, Duce, Fatherland, glory, battles that History imposed; however she did it in all mental innocence, unsuspecting, because History, no more than God, had never been an object of her thoughts" (402). Morante often underlines the innocence of these figures by sympathetically comparing them to animals. It is their lack of self-awareness that redeems them, and not their class consciousness. In *History* the working class is not the depository of a higher historical knowledge: the workers to whom Davide tries to get close in the factory in Mantua are completely blind to their own oppression, and forgetfully spend Sundays listening to the radio and talking of "women, music and sport."

Morante's choice of an omniscent narrator speaks exactly of the characters' incapability to know and to see. Nonetheless, at a certain point of the narration, the omniscent narrator shares the power of vision with Davide, both counterfigures of Morante the historian. While the narrator can see through a stroke of narrative artifice, Davide is made aware of oppression exactly because he simultaneously lives in two worlds: he belongs to the class that administers power and at the same time subjects himself to that very power. As a bourgeois, a Jew, and an anarchist intellectual, his subjectivity is constructed through a series of contradictions, of ideological and material clashes that make him acutely aware of other people's oppression. His passionate denunciation of the "pornography of history" in the speech he delivers in the bar, represents the culmination of his process of self-awareness as historical subject. Yet, notwithstanding his "enlightened" condition, Davide is helpless and totally unable to change things (in the end, he will commit suicide). In this instance, he seems to play the role of Benjamin's *Angelus Novus*, the Angel of History, whose clarity of vision—"where we perceive a chain of events, he sees a single catastrophe, which keeps piling wreckage upon wreckage and hurls it in front of its feet" (243)—cannot prevent the storm and the disaster. All he can do, like Davide, is to express despair at the obscenity of history.

Nonetheless, in Morante's tale, the angel's desperation grows in stages into a visionary hope. In another part of his speech Davide counterposes to the irredeemable historical time the "oneness" of a catastrophic time outside the progression of history: "existence is one, the same, in all living human things. And the day consciousness knows this, what is left to death? In the 'all-one' death is nothing. Does the light suffer, if you or I close our eyelids? Death is nothing. Unity of consciousness: this is the victory of the revolution over death, the end of History, and the birth of God" (484). Morante proposes here her own version of materialist theology; the end of History for Benjamin brings the birth of the oppressed; for Morante instead, it brings the birth of God as a *Jetztzeit*, a moment of historical suspension. The past is "completed" not through the revolution, but through the recourse to an eternal time, a cyclical time in which life and death unceasingly partake of each other and are no longer opposites. It is Morante's faith in this space of ahistorical present that redeems the horror of history in her novel. As we have seen, even its narrative structure, made of ruptures and separations, reproduces this horror. The novel respects the formal conventions of the realist novel only apparently: neither the narrator's omniscience, nor the deployment of the fictional plot can guarantee final reconciliation, solution, or happy ending. In fact, the narrative proceeds through a series of frustrating disconnections and losses that divide the characters, instead of bringing them together. The characters Morante introduces are not a function of the plot, they are both created so that the plot can come to completion and any conflict can be resolved. Human beings are not partaking in the progress of history; rather, they are wiped off its scene. Things as well as people disappear silently: in the first chapter, the soldier Gunther, Ida's parents and husband. Objects, affectively associated to people are lost as well: for instance, Gunther's penknife, and the African mask that Alfio gives Nino. The story develops through a series of painful separations, made even more painful by the familiarity Morante is able to establish between reader and fictional character. All of them exit as characters in a play, until the stage—at the moment of Ida's death—is totally empty. This emptiness can be redeemed, but only outside history and outside the realm of rational, sensorial experience. In this sense, a key moment of the narration is Ida's visit to the Jewish ghetto after the Jews have been departed. The scene is totally silent and deserted: "They are all dead," Ida says to herself. The silence of the ghetto is filled only within Ida's mind, through a state of "auditive hallucination" that re-creates the quotidian prattle of female voices, the everyday life she once had witnessed: "I'm on the roof collecting the laundry. . . . If you are not finishing your homework you are not leaving the house. . . . Put the light out, electricity costs money" (290). In this same mnemonic and semi-oneiric dimension opposites lose their contradictory nature, so that even the laments and the desperate cries of the Jewish people in the cattle cars in the scene witnessed by Ida at the Tiburtina train station, sound to her as familiar voices, "a place of repose that drew her down into the promiscuous den of a single, endless family" (209). Here the materiality of history is transfigured into a different order of existence, and historical materialism as a method of inquiry, on which Morante's social and individual analysis was founded is ultimately abandoned.

Orthodox historical materialism is rejected also by Benjamin, but not abandoned. He deploys theology to revise and correct the Marxist interpretation of history and to give "a new stimulus to revolution." Even though for some of his critics the *Theses* are nothing more than "a handbook of urban guerrilla" (Tiedemann, 202), bearing witness to the less materialist and most anarchist and mystical moments of Benjamin's critical activity, even though the new historical realm opened by the irruption of messianic time into the linearity of events is an unknown, apocalyptic time, for Benjamin the revolution is possible, and the oppressed will be redeemed *in history*.

For Morante, history must be completed and the *Jetztzeit* constitutes the moment of premonition and revelation that precedes its completion. Yet, for the writer the injustice, the "pornography" of history can be exposed, but not redeemed, at least within the time of human experience. No revolution is possible, nor perhaps even desirable; not even in Benjamin's unorthodox formulation ("a leap in the open air of history"). The course of history does not, cannot change, as the conclusion of the novel indicates: after Ida's death, the sequence of dates that had opened the novel reappears, ". . . and History continues" (555). Redemption for Morante is possible at a different level, on another plane of existence, signified exactly by what history does not have the tools to deal with, the many other marginal textualities, voices, and language Morante includes in her writing.

For the historical materialist this is utopia: he cannot accept that humanity can be redeemed in the absence of history. Yet the spheres of messianic and historical time are for Morante unreconcilable; her redeemed subject is an Oedipus whose power of vision is acquired only through historical blindness. In *History* as readers and subjects of history ourselves, we are asked to take a very wide jump: from Benjamin's "leap into the open air of history," to a leap into a necessary blindness, a leap into what is to date, unspeakeable and unknowable ("the unity of consciousness"). Morante's leap can be taken only through an act of faith, and it is this very moment of faith that closes the book. The real conclusion, the only conclusion that for Morante can allow the words "the end" to be written, is a further rupture in the frustrating and unredeemed continuity of history, a moment of unstable hope that replaces the optimism of the historical materialist. The real conclusion is another marginal text, another marginal and transitory inscription, this time written on the walls of a prison:

> All the seeds failed except one.
> I don't know what it is but it is
> probably a flower and not a weed.

> (Prisoner 7047 in the penitentiary or Turi)

# Notes

1. Max Horkheimer, *Letters*, quoted in Tiedemann, 181.

2. Elsa Morante, *History: A Novel* (New York: Vintage, 1984), translated from the Italian by William Weaver. Future references to the novel quote the page number of this edition.

3. Michel Foucault elaborates the theoretical grounding of his critique of history in *The Archaeology of Knowledge*; see also Hayden White's seminal work on the rhetorical value of the language of history, *Metahistory*.

4. In film theory the space off is that part of the screen, of the image, that is not made visible to the viewer, but that can only be inferred and desired by the audience. Teresa de Lauretis uses the phrase in *Technologies of Gender* to hypothesize not-yet articulated formulations of gender.

5. "No man or men but the struggling oppressed class itself is the depository of historical knowledge," Walter Benjamin, *Theses on the Philosophy of History*, thesis 12, 260.

6. Ettore Scola's film A *Special Day* (*Una giornata particolare*) offers another interesting dramatization of Morante's operation, this time presenting and debating the analogy and the impossible solidarity between a woman and a gay man during fascism.

# Works Cited

Benjamin, Walter. "Theses on the Philosophy of History, in *Illuminations.*" Edited and with an introduction by Hannah Arendt. Translated by Harry Zohn. New York: Schocken, 1987.

de Lauretis, Teresa. *Technologies of Gender: Essays on Theory, Film, and Fiction.* Bloomington: University of Indiana Press, 1987.

Foucault, Michel. *The Archaeology of Knowledge.* Translated by A. M. Sheridan Smith. New York: Pantheon, 1972.

Morante, Elsa. *History: A Novel.* New York: Vintage, 1984. (Originally published 1974).

Smith, Gary, ed. *Walter Benjamin: Philosophy, Aesthetics, History.* Chicago: University of Chicago Press, 1988.

Tiedemann, Rolf. "Historical Materialism or Political Messianism? An Interpretation of the Theses 'On the Concept of History.'" In *Walter Benjamin,* ed. Gary Smith. Chicago: University of Chicago Press, 1988.

White, Hayden. *The Content of the Form: Narrative Discourse and Historical Representation.* Baltimore: Johns Hopkins University Press, 1973.

———. *Metahistory: The Historical Imagination in Nineteenth-Century Europe.* Baltimore: Johns Hopkins University Press, 1973.

# 10

# From Genealogy to Gynealogy and Beyond: Fausta Cialente's *Le Quattro Ragazze Wieselberger*

*Graziella Parati*

Fausta Cialente's *Le Quattro Ragazze Wieselberger* (1976) (The four Wieselberger girls) is an autobiographical act that contributes to the definition of the autobiography as a malleable space within literature, as a genre that partakes of other genres. Cialente's work contains at first glance a biography of the main character's mother and, at the same time, an autobiographical construction of a female self. Cialente attempts to revise the autobiographical space in order to create a context in which she can construct a woman's past; such a creation is based on the destruction of traditional dichotomies that separate male and female traces and identities. In this essay I analyze Cialente's personalization of the autobiographical space intended as a hybrid sphere where the construction of her past is transformed into the creation of, what I have named, gynealogy and later transformed into a braided genealogy. Gynealogy is a form of matrilinearism that develops into an interwoven genealogy containing at the same time the traditional opposite of matrilinearism: the inheritance from the father(s). My interest in the construction of gynealogies, a genealogy in which female traces are privileged, foregrounds the construction of a concept of hybrid genealogy that partakes of both the paternal and the maternal. The articulation of a gynealogy is not only a mediating element that allows for the construction of hybrid genealogies. Gynealogy is the necessary component in the elaboration of a woman's genealogy, firmly grounded in a female past that cannot be silenced any more. The process of creating braided genealogies echoes François Lionnet's work on *métissage* among cultures. Lionnet uses the concept of *métis* in a postcolonial context to talk about the destruction of cultural and racial dichotomies in order to privilege a "transcultural," linguistic hybridity: literary *métissage*.[1] I construct a minimal translation of her techniques of *métissage* in my analysis of an autobiographical narrative. In such a context the female character becomes a *métis*, a hybrid, the result of an intertwining of paternal and maternal traces. Such a character is the protagonist of a gynealogy that allows a woman to find the silenced voices of her mothers. From such a newly discovered maternal plot she can articulate her past as a braided genealogy a hybrid entity that defies the rigid separation between male and female, paternal (i.e., dominant) and maternal (i.e., secondary) traces. Gynealogy is a space where the "company of women" is privileged, but it is also the context in which it is possible to begin the rewriting of male identities and paternal influence in order to transform difference into a dialectic based on the opposite of separatism.

An opposition between male identity and unidentified female plurality is the starting point for Fausta Cialente's construction of a self in an autobiographical work. It is a fragmented interweaving of official history and personal "life/lines."[2] *Le Quattro Ragazze Wieselberger* contains autobiographies of both a mother and a daughter. In my analysis of the text, I have divided the autobiography into two parts: the first includes the initial seventy-five pages of the narration and is the author's attempt to write another person's autobiography. This is not a contradiction in terms, but rather an attempt to write one's own life starting from another woman's "life/lines."[3] The author attaches the daughter's life to the mother's past in order to create a continuum between generations, a link between mother and daughter that has been called matrilinearism.[4] The second part of *Le Quattro Ragazze Wieselberger* is the narrative of Fausta's own life, starting from the first memories of childhood to the years after the Second World War. Together the first and second sections of Cialente's autobiographical act construct both a female self and a revisionary concept of femininity that take into account past and present—the identity of mothers and daughters throughout most of the twentieth century.

Fausta Cialente's autobiographical act initially presents binary opposition between female and male identities. The reader is, in fact, confronted with the title of the autobiography, which introduces four female characters who are identified by the name of their father, Wieselberger. The male characters dominate the beginning of the book and the female characters represent the unimportant and plural female presence ("the girls") within the household. The author looks back on her family's past (the bourgeois life of the four sisters) and on official history (i.e., the "irresponsible" *irredentismo* of Trieste's middle class) in order to re-read the past. The private story of her family is therefore brought into the public sphere and, in a reverse movement, public history is reflected within the nuclear familial sphere. From the initial discourse of oppositions in the autobiographical act, the author's text creates a unity between Memory—that is, official history—and personal memories where the fragmented inheritance from the father and the mother can co-exist.

In the first part of the autobiography, Fausta Cialente, as narrator, has the role of reader and writer of her mother's life. Elsa, Fausta's mother, only exists as a character in metonymic relation to her sisters: Alice, Alba, Adele. The Wieselbergers are a "giudiziosa, benestante famiglia" (a discreet and well-off family) living in Trieste toward the end of the last century.[5] The father's presence is accompanied by a female plurality, a generic entity that includes the sisters and the mother. He is a well-known composer, while the mother and the daughters fulfill their duties in the familial sphere. The relationship between the sisters is already implicit in their names; the father has decided to give them all names beginning with the same vowel. Only the youngest escapes this fate, because he chooses instead the name of an opera heroine he liked, Elsa. The process of naming is repeatedly presented as the act of limiting a person's identity. All of the women in the house are called *babe*, by the father.[6] In a private sphere inhabited by the generic identity of *babe*, his male creativity is a priority. His orchestra rehearsals, which totally disrupt the domestic life, are commented upon by the narrator:

> Those evenings when the orchestra came to the house to play, the family had to have dinner rather earlier than usual so that the lady and the girls . . . had enough time to clear the table in the dining room . . . the big glass door that separated them from the entrance had to stay open. All the doors leading to the kitchen and the servant's areas had instead to be kept closed because, during the performance, the father did not want to hear the loud noises from the washing up and the chatter, the *ciacole*, of the women servants. (15)[7]

The two doors, one open and one closed, define the difference between the two spheres: one inhabited by the father and the other by the *babe*. The open door through which music—that is, male creativity—penetrates is the passage to the outside world. It is the "public door" that connects the paternal creativity to the male logos of creativity which can be disturbed by the nonsensical *ciacole* of women. The closed door between the rehearsal and the domestic activities defines the private world of the *babe* as the sphere that "disturbs" man's creativity. Some of the women are allowed to listen to the music and they have a very strange role. The two oldest sisters, Alice and Alba, sit in front of the brass section of the orchestra and eat lemons so that the players salivate more and perform better. It is a funny anecdote that underlines the fact, however, that the daughters can acquire only a marginal role in relation to the father's creativity. They are never isolated behind the closed door, but neither are they allowed to play in the father's beloved orchestra. Their education is carried out within the domestic sphere, and only Elsa will have the opportunity to pass through the open door toward a public, creative role. Named after an opera heroine, Elsa becomes an opera singer. However, her stay in the public realm will not last long.

The sisters are "same and different"; the relationship between them is expressed through their silence as women and as characters in the narrative: together they absorb the father's inheritance, his love for music, and their mother's passive acceptance of the father's will. The mother only desires tranquillity and is disturbed by the daughters' talk which she calls *sempieze*, nonsense. The connotative value of two words, *ciacole* (chatter) and *sempieze*, shows the real nature of the relationship between Gustavo Adolfo Wieselberger and his meek wife. The peaceful atmosphere in the house is the result of the absolute compliance with the demands of patriarchy. Linguistically the mother's definition of women's talk, *sempieze*, is a direct echo of the husband's derogatory approach to the female voices, *ciacole*, in the house. The mother, who mirrors the father's tongue and has no independent voice, makes no demands beyond the limits established for a middle-class wife. The boundaries of the private sphere are explored only by the daughters; however, to leave the private and enter the public realm is, for them, impossible. The "girls" become characters who represent the transition between their mother's total acceptance of her role and the granddaughter's, Fausta's, pioneering role in the public sphere. The character who best symbolizes this transition is Adele, the "girl" who dies young: "Only faded photographs are left of her which show her wearing a ball gown and looking like a fairy. But she also wears a harsh expression on her bitterly turned-down mouth, as if she already knew that she had to die, at about twenty-seven years of age, of a disease that was mysterious in those times" (23).[8] Adele is better known in the family as "la Bella" (the Beauty), who has had an incredible number of suitors. Yet, what is left for posterity is a picture of her as a mysterious woman with a bitter expression. Adele loves to recite poetry, yet never seems to write it. She reads it in many languages as if she had stepped into a world of creativity, but somehow could not be a part of it; she cannot create, but can only echo the poetry that she admires. "La Bella" refuses marriage and dies at an age when women were considered "spinsters." She refuses to be enclosed within the private sphere of wifehood and maternity, and yet remains suspended in a no-man's-land where, if no man can penetrate, she cannot acquire a creative role other than the mythical Echo's relationship to language. She cannot establish a personal signifying system through which she can survive. She seems, in fact, to fade away because of her lack of creativity. Her bitter expression in the portrait is both the sign of her knowledge that she is going to die and the mirror of the other girls' future unhappiness. Through memory Adele is transformed by Alba into a mythical woman: Alba remains throughout her life the keeper of her sister's memory since they have shared a common refusal of marriage. However, Alba becomes identified with stereotypical negative connotations of spinsterhood: she is aggressive and moody. If Adele escapes through death and acquires a new dimension in memories, Alba is still enclosed, trapped within the private sphere. After the first few pages of the text no character seems to remember that Alba was considered the "intellectual" and not just the introverted and lonely spinster, who is the father's faithful companion and nurse.

The father's Law conditions the daughters' approach to reality and reveals an embedded sense of social class and of the position created for them by the patriarchal order. The static atmosphere that characterizes this middle-class family is described by the narrator as a protective environment that secludes the sisters and gives them the illusion of living in a personal golden age, of being part of an elite, which has the holy historical role of uniting Trieste to the Italian kingdom. The Trieste of the time is an international city where several nationalities coexist. However, the "girls" belong to that social caste of people who blindly consider themselves superior to the large population of Slovenians, the "s'ciavi" (Slave/slovenians).[9] From their golden peaceful cage the sisters are able to look at reality only through the eyes of the father. As daughters of the father, they look at other women without being able to read a different story from the one they have been told. Fausta Cialente calls the Wieselberger women "autentiche borghesi" (68) (authentic bourgeois women), who, from the privileged position assigned to them by the name of the father, distance themselves from other women and become "honorary members" of the patriarchy through their silent acceptance of the unwritten rules of domination.[10]

The narrator's intervention in the text comments on the comfortable life the Weiselbergers have in Trieste and also stresses the shortsightedness of the father's, and consequently the girls', vision of history since they are not aware that "a greedy and reactionary middle class was already fattening its ranks; a class that he, a naive musician, could neither judge nor even less condemn. Furthermore, from those heterogeneous ranks, came the castes that filled the theatres, concert halls and his beloved Philharmonic" (32).[11] The concept of "liberation" from the Austrians, still portrayed in history books as the "natural" desire of all the Triestini to join their blood brothers, is rejected by Cialente as historical fallacy. She stresses the presence of a large number of Triestini still faithful to the Austrian empire and, above all, of existence in the city of a large number of Slovenians—who occupied key positions in public offices as the Triestini often refused to learn German. The narrator adds that "it was with disdainful envy that the *irredentisti* would even utter: these bumpkins [*cafoni*]! who become lawyers, doctors, and managers!—as if they considered unacceptable the [Slovenians'] right to study in order to improve themselves without even realizing how racist instead their contempt was" (49).[12] The nationalistic fanaticism of the *irredentisti*, which the father expresses with goliardic eloquence by farting at the name of the emperor whenever he reads it in a newspaper, is exposed by Fausta Cialente as a mixture of bigotry, racism, and historical shortsightedness.

The first part of the narrative also strives to introduce alterity as a subject of the discourse: it is the otherness of both the mother, described only as an extension of the collective feminine entity in the house, and of the Slovenians, who are seen as victims of history and blind nationalism. Public history and the personal, familial story become unified in the concepts of otherness and difference. The mother is described as a polyvalent character: she is a woman, and therefore, "other," and she is a complacent victim, an accomplice of the establishment—and, more specifically, of Gustavo Adolfo Wieselberger's *Weltanschauung*. On her way to reconstruct a new genealogy, Cialente must reject the mother in order subsequently to reconstruct and reclaim the maternal message for which she is searching. Elsa, the acquiescent mother, is the fictional incarnation of femininity viewed as passivity and complete compliance with the demands of her extended patriarchal "family." It is the *irredentisti* who look at the Slovenians as inferior, as intruders in a territory they have arbitrarily claimed as their own. The outcome of such fanaticism is the First World War which, as catalyst, helps Fausta, the grand-daughter, to acquire a clear perspective on the bigotry involved in the family's *irredentismo*. Elsa is blind to the common characteristics that link her to the oppressed Slovenians. Cialente, however, as interpreter of the mother's, Elsa's, life, reveals that

> the war that I witnessed did not only make me feel sick, but it inspired in me a hatred that I felt could not be healed: a hatred against any form of nationalism or racism ("these damn *s'ciavi*, these damn aus-trophiles, these damn Jews), against any form of abuse, therefore; in addition I had already learnt that the first ones to pay and be subju-gated are always poor people. Wars seem to be invented for them, because it is poverty that better teaches how to resist and endure. (208)[13]

When the narrator's "I" becomes the subject of the autobiography, the moth-er(s)' oppression is voiced through Cialente's analysis of all oppressions with which Elsa came in contact, but never attempted to understand. Elsa is an *irredentista* and later becomes a fascist. However, in her personal life, Elsa succeeds in acquiring independence as she leaves her husband and an abusive marriage. It is a dialectical creation of matrilinearism that does not rely on a diachronic structure. The chronological progression from the grandmother to Elsa and finally to Fausta does not reflect a progressive inheritance of female "wisdom." A mythical woman is not portrayed in this autobiography: knowl-edge is acquired by gradually transgressing both the rules established by patri-archy and the traditional feminine models supplied by the mothers. Fausta succeeds in creating an independent identity that is not inherited from the mothers but is obtained by disobeying the rigid impositions to which the grandmother had completely acquiesced and that Elsa had timidly challenged before accepting a traditional role as wife and mother.

Alice marries a rich Jew in 1886 and becomes an unhappy wife and mother. Elsa's fate seems different from her sister's; Elsa temporarily acquires indepen-dence from the family. She starts her career as a singer in Bologna and has considerable success, which is interrupted by her engagement and then by marriage. However, the handsome young officer who falls in love with the gifted singer has the power to disrupt, to forbid, to separate his acquired wife from her comfortable relationship with her sisters. The collective maternal image is destroyed by the male intervention that kills the creative component

of the close *quartetto* of sisters. The death of creativity is symbolically represented in the text by the disappearance of the most beautiful among the sisters. She is described in the narration as the poet whose death is negated by
the survival of the "word" in the hands of another woman, the writer and
narrator whose sameness and, at the same time, otherness from the dead an-
cestor creates a connection between the two main parts of the book. Man
has, in *Le Quattro Ragazze Wieselberger*, the power to silence women's independent creativity, but his ability to "interrupt" a female discourse is only
temporary. The silenced poet, Adele, and the silenced singer, Elsa, constitute
a rediscovered text for Fausta. In this autobiographical act, the construction
of the self by the narrator is also the search for the voice of the mother or for
the collective maternal creativity of the sisters.

Elsa and Alice share a common destiny, but once they belong to husbands,
they appear unable to confess their unhappiness to each other. Within the
narrative their changed life is scrutinized by looking at pictures from the family album: "[Alice] is a stately woman; . . . in a snapshot, certainly taken at
home, she wears a gloomy and dark dress, she wears an enormous and threatening hat on top of her blond head and she leans against a three-legged coffee
table on which an incomprehensibly unsettling small statue is exhibited. The
statue seems to foretell something fatal to the immobile, dignified, and sad
lady: maybe her own destiny" (65–66).[14] Alice is weighed down by the heavy
dress, the "enormous" hat, and seems to need the support of the table to stand
still, to face her present and her future. Her life is described through objects,
her future unhappiness is reflected in a lifeless statue as if it were Alice's mir-
rored image. Signification is displaced in the narrative from language to objects: the pictures and the still life surrounding Alice's portrait. She is the
embodiment of the epitome of female silence since the reader can barely
guess about her hidden gift of creativity. For Elsa, instead, there is a short
interlude with art that allows her to travel in Italy accompanied by Alba. In
a photo of the time "they both look into space with wide open eyes that, one
could even say, were full of fear" (68). Cialente interprets their expression as
an indication of the girls' awareness of their precious independence and fear
for the risks they will face. The narrator is searching for a signified, for the
voice of maternal creativity that is suffocated by what Cialente calls a "banal"
matrimony. In the picture, the mother's creativity has not been silenced yet,
and Fausta and Alice can be read as pioneers of women's future freedom:
"They generously want to show people of their era that they are initiating a
new one—and they are its shy but courageous models" (68).[15]

Indifference and acceptance belong both to Elsa and her sister Alice. The author describes the effects of marriage on the young Elsa: "The suddenly decided engagement and wedding seem instead to have succeeded in erasing from her and her family's memory the events and hopes of those few years dedicated to studies and a career. Events and hopes that soon, incredibly soon, drown and disappear in the mysterious fog of a strange indifference— and acceptance" (63).[16] Their married lives are filled with humiliation and betrayal: Alice's husband can afford to pay for a mistress; Elsa's husband chooses from among the servants who wash themselves, at least. For years the two sisters remain passive and silent. By their silence, they, in turn, educate their daughters to silence: "They are two prudent bourgeois ladies who accept the status quo and the limitations of their class and, in spite of their unhappy experiences, they are preparing themselves to educate their children— mainly the little girls—to self-denial and sacrifice" (73).[17] At this point the author states the purpose of the autobiographical act: to construct a female subject, herself, as daughter and narrator of this autobiography and to separate her identity from that of her silenced mother(s). The constant intervention of the narrator in the text reminds the reader of the narrating subject's presence, of a woman who describes her maternal origins as the beginning of a female *Bildungsroman* that incorporates Elsa's and later Fausta's experience. Memory and imagination are one in this semifictional representation of the mother. Imagination plays an important role in writing another's autobiography; Elsa is a somebody recognized as same because she is "mother," and a somebody recognized as other. Reading the mother as a text in order to write the text of the daughter's life creates a distance between the maternal character and the protagonist of the autobiography. The task of the narrator, who is fulfilling the dual role of writer and reader, is to incorporate the idea of mother as an open text from which to separate herself and to become "different." The search for that "difference" is carried out by Fausta, the daughter, in the public sphere where she actively participates and finds a "public" role distancing herself from the closed private sphere of the mother.

In the description of her life, Fausta, as protagonist of the autobiography, is very distant from the passive woman her mother had been. Fausta, in fact, acquires the ability both to be part of, and to act forcefully in order to modify, the patriarchal discourse in which she once felt trapped. She acquires power, as it is defined according to Carolyn Heilbrun: "Power is the ability to take one's place in whatever discourse is essential to action and the right to have one's part matter."[18] The newly constructed concept of a female identity is initiated by looking at the mother as same and different in order to create a third term, the adult Fausta, who becomes the desired representative of an independent female subjectivity within the narrative. Luce Irigaray states: "As *two* women, defining each other as both like and unlike, thanks to a third 'body' that both by common consent wish to be female."[19] This new "female body" is represented not only by the woman Fausta becomes but also by the resulting triangular structure in which mother, daughter, and the construction of a new female identity can be found. The concept created by the dialectical relationship between mother and daughter not only constructs the future adult character of Fausta; it also modifies the rigid structures of the past and totally changes the mother's traditional acquiescence to her husband's will. In fact, later in life Elsa leaves her husband, who cannot understand why "his wife would not stop playing a part in this comedy of separation" (227).

The first part of Cialente's autobiography reconstructs Elsa's memory and brings to light the potential of women's creativity. Together creativity and memory acquire a special meaning since it is within the literary creation of the daughter that the mother's memory is shaped. The daughter's creativity is therefore already the elusive center of the first section of Cialente's autobiography; the mother's biography is a pre-text for the daughter's autobiographical project. The imaginary world of someone else's biography, as created by the narrator, brings to surface the tension between "historical truthfulness and aesthetic design in autobiography";[20] it is not a historically precise genealogy intended in the traditional sense. The need for a wider definition of memory is the core of Cialente's construction of gynealogy. The familial maternal story is a fictional search for the roots of the "self" that is gradually constructed in the second part of Cialente's autobiographical act.

The first of the two parts into which I have divided Le Quattro Ragazze Wieselberger reveals the four sisters' inability to become subjects of their own lives. Only Alba can be said to rebel, but her rebellion is mute; she refuses marriage but remains trapped within the familial boundaries and spends her life caring for her aging father. She then becomes a "strange" spinster, defeated in her struggle against the brothers-in-law whom she publicly accuses of infidelity and neglect. Cialente remarks: "None of the sisters have learned how to float more freely, not even Alba, and that would have been logical and possible even at that time if they had been born in a different sort of family. The four Weiselberger girls, therefore, still and always appear to be four, despite the fact that one of them is gone" (22).[21] The metaphors of drowning, of the girls' inability to float, of their loss of self, and of the mysterious fog are repeatedly presented in the description of the sisters' lives. They remain girls, unable to construct an identity as women; they are unable to detach themselves from a fictitious peaceful "golden age" in which they lived; they are unable to float since they are weighted down by the idea of motherhood, wifehood, and femininity as constructed by patriarchy. The end of *Le Quattro Ragazze Wieselberger* is instead dominated by the surfacing of a female identity partly inherited from the mother and passed onto the daughter and the daughter's daughters. This newly created chain is visually represented as walking along the shore: they move in an orderly line, from Fausta to the grandchildren. They walk along the beach where water and earth come together; it is a no-man's-land appropriated by woman in order to construct her identity in time and space. In this new narrative context, women's "life/lines" cannot be "washed out" any more by a patriarchal telos that drowned Fausta's female ancestors into nothingness.[22] The sisters' private tragedy is reflected by their mother's death. Her awkward big and heavy body, her straight hair, her resigned expression "seem to reveal that she has given up on everything" (66). It is this picture the three daughters keep to remember their mother, as if their lives were doomed to become like hers and, as Cialente says, they thus forget even that their mother had once been as young as they. The picture of the old mother on her deathbed is discarded by the grandchildren, who choose to remember her as she looked in an older photograph, in which she appears younger and less defeated. A different female story is ready to be told; it is a narration in which the representation of women is signified neither by passivity and silence, nor by disappearance.

The second part of the autobiographical text, the author's memories of childhood, begins with an image of winter: "It was winter most of the time," says the narrator (79). She remembers the feeling of being a stranger in different places where the family had no roots. Fausta Cialente writes: "only the names of those towns, their cold weather, and their blizzards are left in my memory as if they never had milder seasons" (79).[23] She portrays herself as a "stranger" to these unfriendly lands. This description of an initial feeling of unhappiness is complementary to a long passage from Scipio Slataper's *Il mio Carso* (My Carso), quoted at the beginning of Fausta Cialente's new chapter. In Slataper's book another stranger is portrayed: it is the "S'ciavo" ("slave"/ Slovenian) who, in this context, is allowed to acquire the dignity denied him by the racism of the Triestini (78). The beginning of Cialente's autobiography, therefore, reintroduces the problematic definition of otherness that was a thematic core in the narrative of her mother's life. The narrator is thus searching for a definition of self that adopts the "other" as its point of departure; in Fausta's childhood, the other is the mother from whom she has already inherited the gift of "silence." The author comments: "But who dared to say anything? Both Renato and I have already learned to keep silent, we are a nice pair of hypocrites" (80).[24]

The first person plural, in which the memories of infancy are narrated, describes Fausta's and her brother Renato's common experiences. Within gynealogy the silent other is also related by both the male and the female children. Fausta and Renato share a common plot, reflected also in their feelings toward the mother and the father. Renato is just a few years older than his sister and they have in common fantasies and experiences: "despite the fact the we insulted and hit each other like all brothers and sisters in the world have always done, we were above all accomplices, probably without even realizing it" (95).[25] Marianne Hirsch in her book *The Mother/Daughter Plot* introduces the idea of the representation of the brother as a maternal substitute.[26] She uses the term "fraternal plot" to refer to a fictional dimension in which the brother becomes "the man who would understand" (79). Fraternal traces are scattered in Cialente's construction of the past and they form a plot that begins with the silence of both siblings and ends with the public recognition of their creativity. The narrative contains the story of the discovery of a tongue and the development of creative expression. Hirsch describes the "brother's tongue" as "a tender form of discourse which revises both the coldness of paternal authority and the rage or anxiety underlying maternal silence" (80). Thanks to the brother's tongue, Fausta can enter and mimic the language of patriarchy and acquire the power to develop her own creativity. Fausta and Renato are often temporary guests in their grandfather's house where they feel uncomfortable as they do not share the language and the political ideas of the Weiselbergers. Their reaction to the foreign atmosphere is similar to their mother's: their "feminine" silence brings them together and isolates them from Gustavo Weiselberger's patriarchal realm:

> I believe that Renato was less troubled than I was and he urged me not to worry [*bazilar*], a term that we used after adapting it to the first conjugation, "io bazilo," "tu bazili." The fear that talking to the cousins we would say something we were not supposed to, would sometime isolate us, and what happened was that we would end up playing together as if we were in Italy and not guests at the villa in "Via dell'Istria." (108)[27]

When together, Fausta and Renato can move from silence into linguistic experimentation that develops into what they call "the game of words" (108).

For their game they choose a forbidden location: a pond nearby, considered a dangerous place for children. They disobey orders and sit near the water allowing themselves to transgress the limitations of their everyday language. The game starts with one of the children saying "mangeresti" (would you eat . . .); anything disgusting could be the answer to such an introduction. The narrator admits:

> I was faster in creating combinations and Renato used to look at me a little suspiciously, seeming to believe that I had begun the game after having practiced, and that probably was not true. Once, when I succeeded in putting together something in which I had also included crushed cockroaches and legs of centipede, Renato was overwhelmed by disgust but nevertheless, expressing something between surprise and envy, exclaimed: "well, today, you win!" (109)[28]

The brother's tongue is, in this context, a language that can be defeated by the sister's ability at "the game of words." Fausta's consciousness of her creative ability is born, and accepted by her brother. Both children are, however, expelled from the place of discovery that has allowed them to create a common linguistic plot. The momentary sanctuary near the pond has permitted them to step aside from silencing rules. This symbolic place, once abandoned, becomes an untouchable locus of creativity that will develop in different ways for Fausta, the future writer, and Renato, the famous actor.

Silence is, nevertheless, Fausta's and Renato's answer to the father for whom Fausta feels an "unconfessed terror" that is accompanied by an "unconfessed pity for the mother" (95). The acute sense of separation from both parental figures slowly changes as in the narrative of her childhood Fausta gradually discovers the overdetermined concept "femininity" and attempts to develop a new relationship with the women of the family. The regular visits to the child's house made by other officers' wives (Fausta's father is an officer in the Italian army) bring the child in touch with the overcodified concept of femininity that is so important in the "casta" (the caste) to which she belongs (87). The wives are divided according to degree of respectability. Among them, there is a group of women Fausta has to ignore, as if they did not exist; they are of course the ones the child prefers to all others. Fausta investigates the inherited ideas about femininity and strives to revise them as a result of her curious exploration of real and imaginary territories that are officially forbidden to her. The initial transgressive sympathy for the "fallen wives" of the officers is the prelude to an episode that constitutes a rite of passage for the young girl: the discovery of prostitution. The exploration of a faraway area of the city is initiated by Renato, who leads her to an unknown neighborhood. Renato's behavior and statements determine the hidden sig-nificance of this place where women publicly sit on doorsteps or are seen through windows. As he tells her who they are, his voice is soft and low, he holds his sister's arm "as if he wanted to run away from that place and those women" and he says: "Can you see them! They are the whores" (126). By transgressing the father's law, Fausta learns of a hidden world of otherness, considered as a signifier to which Fausta supplies, later in her life, a new signi-fied that connects all the oppressed—the "sciavi," the Wieselberger girls, the "fallen" wives and the prostitutes.

The narrator's search for the meaning of otherness is carried out by stress-ing the discrepancies in the "golden cage" of the grandfather's bourgeois life. It is an alternative paternal literary voice that appears in Fausta Cialente's text to comment upon and contrast Gustavo Weiselberger's racist ideology. The narrator quotes from Scipio Slataper's words: "*S'ciavo* (slave/Slovenian) do you want to come with me? I will make you the master of the large fields by the sea. . . . You have come from lands where nobody wanted to live, and you cultivated them. . . . For many years they have slapped you in the face with your slavery, but now your time has come. It is time for you to become a master" (77).[29] The Slovenians, seen by the *irredentisti* as the unwelcome barbarians on Italian soil, can acquire in this fictional context a new meaning as suggested by Scipio Slataper's words. To speak of "otherness" in this con-text means to reflect on the voices that are able to rewrite both a public history and a private story. Breaking the silence and disturbing the dominant historical discourse is expressed on various levels in the narrative. The con-cepts of "slave" and "slavery," which could be interpreted either as the op-pressive enclosure of women within the private sphere or as the open racism against the "s'ciavi," is also personified in a third element, the character Alì (42–43). The Weiselberger girls refer to a turning point around which many of their memories are constructed. It is the time when Alì was the young, black servant in the neighbors' house. A rebellious boy brought back from a trip to Africa, he could only communicate in "triestino" and was thus com-pelled to speak a language that was not his own. Alba attempted to teach him Italian with little success. Soon Alì disappeared and a stray dog was adopted in the house and named after the black boy. The silenced Alì, whose name is a floating signifier which, within the language of patriarchy, can sig-nify a human being or a dog, brings to the surface the role of language as a means to negate and to oppress. Alba felt that it was her duty to "teach" him the language of white patriarchy without recognizing the role of Alì as mirror of her own oppression. She is, along with her sisters, silenced by the same patriarchal rules that she cannot defeat by disappearing, like Alì, into a different "original" land. It is only Fausta who finds a new locus of creativity in her voluntary exile.

Fausta's search for the hidden meaning of otherness in the private sphere is echoed by the silence of the mother. This silence is broken infrequently by moments when Elsa becomes again the artist she was, and successfully sings for a few friends: "Strangely, the applause would make her grow pale rather than make her blush and we could feel that she was upset as if singing did not give her any pleasure. Her song was sometimes joyful and illuminated by a mysterious happiness that used to make me feel weightless in a world framed by light and happiness. Maybe the world that she had given up in order to choose the marriage that had given us birth" (90).[30] The sudden glimpse of her mother's creativity and the hidden message acts a prelude to the different woman Elsa will become when, years later, she removes the yoke of her marriage and shows the family her strength by rescuing her husband from bankruptcy. Once her family's finances are saved by her creativity, Elsa returns to her music and becomes, as a music teacher, the family's main support. The short moment of closeness and understanding Fausta feels for her mother's hidden richness is destroyed by the implacable laws of gender dictated by patriarchy: as women, everything must be abandoned in order to become wives and mothers. The pity she felt previously for Elsa is too simple a feeling to express the new relationship that slowly develops between mother and daughter. Elsa's singing hides a maternal message that is interrupted by the father, but that will slowly surface throughout Cialente's autobiography. It reaches its climax in the final chapter where the construction of matrilinearism becomes the only possible way of creating a woman's future and reconstructing the past.

Fausta's time in Trieste provides the precious occasion to investigate the world her mother left behind. The young girl is intrigued by the bizarre character of the grandmother who used to refuse to eat chickens that she had "looked in the eyes" when they were still alive. It was, writes the narrator, "an adorable sensitivity that I felt I could totally approve of made her, in my eyes, pleasant and nice, and to talk about her seemed to be the best way to celebrate her memory" (115).[31] The curiosity about the mother is followed by a keen interest in all the Weiselberger girls. In this context, Cialente reveals her interest in the chronology of her retrospective narrative, which she calls the "prima" and "dopo" in her memory (116). It is in the "prima-dopo" sequence, in the "story," that Fausta acquires a voice and discovers the hidden message in the silence of her mother(s). The construction of memory fulfills the role of rescuing the dead from disappearance by turning them into the components of the text of Fausta's life, "So everything that was left was entrusted to my memory alone . . . nothing could change or destroy it" (243).[32] The autobiography, thanks to its fragmented structure, becomes the safe womb for memories.

Even the relationship between Fausta and her father is subject to profound change. The terror she feels for him is accompanied by the never-voiced awareness that her humble mother is culturally superior to the father. The child feels a weak link to her father's family and their past and is instead attracted to the Trieste family. The language of the father, Italian, is, however, the only means Fausta has to communicate with the branch of the family she prefers. She can understand the dialect, but it is a language she cannot speak; speaking a different language signifies the objective separation between her maternal ancestors and the young girl. Triestino comes to be associated with *irredentismo*; it becomes the symbol of the patriarchal structure in which the Weiselberger girls are "linguistically" trapped. In Cialente's literary production the solution to the problem of acquiring a linguistic and political identity is the choice of a physical and metaphorical exile. The narrator displaces language from its patriarchal cradle into a new social and narrative context. She writes in Italian from Egypt and uses her literary and oratorical skills against the fascist motherland. The image of fascist Italy as motherland accurately describes once more the destruction of both the rigid dichotomy between male and female characteristics, and the representation of the father as Father, as the embodiment of patriarchy. It is the mother who profoundly sympathizes with the regime and is, once again, trapped within a patriarchal structure that she blindly accepts. The paternal heritage slowly surfaces in Fausta Cialente's autobiography. As an adult, Fausta's *Weltanschauung* is constructed on her father's political ideas, on a complete refusal of her mother's *irredentismo* and, later, of her blind faith in Mussolini:

> We had always heard our father talking with contempt (he was a peculiar officer, being angrily antimonarchical); whenever he mentioned the king he would call him "that evil and deformed little man" (but only when the relatives from Trieste were not present; our mother had begged him not to do that) . . . and as far as the queen went he was happy to exclaim ironically: sure, the one who breastfeeds all her children, the glory of the nation! (105)[33]

Her father's demystifying approach to reality puts Fausta in touch with a pragmatic antimilitarism and anti-*irredentismo* that exposes the ideological fanaticism of Fausta's favorite members of the family.

The father she has previously rejected now becomes an important component in her construction of a discourse on women's subjectivities. In fact, the
father character is fragmented so that his pacifism and his ideals are absorbed
and transformed by the female protagonist in the autobiographical act. The
core of the problematic construction of womanhood practices in *Le Quattro
Ragazze Wieselberger* lies in its attempt to create a nonmythical woman who
can be the daughter of both the father and the mother. Absorbing the paternal positions and point of view within the public sphere, from which the
mother is excluded, allows Fausta to acquire a privileged position within the
text as "reader of the father." This also helps the protagonist to leap intellectually beyond the father and understand the limitations of his ideological
discourse. The narrator comments: "The anger and indignation that I always
saw within him originated from his contempt toward the rulers and the career
that he had never got used to and that had made him suffer. But as far as I
realized, his rebellion and his criticism were not linked to the reality of social
turmoil that was foreign to him and whose best sides he never understood"
(181).[34] The pity for the mother, which has been such a consistent part of
Fausta's approach to the parental figures, is displaced and shifts from the
mother to the father, who becomes pathetic in his personal unhappiness, his
anti-Semitism, and his only partially enlightened political ideas. This new
text that the author constructs is a new personal history in which "traces of
the father" are important.

It is finally the father who, as an ex-officer, begins "intendere i problemi
sociali" (to understand social problems) and becomes, through his antimilitarism and republican ideals, a fictional "feminine father." The paternal image
is in fact understood by Cialente as the same but, at the same time, different
from the patriarchal construction of the paterfamilias. It is by privileging that
difference that the narrator can construct the fictional father who is acceptable in her creation of a personal memory. If the father is seen as transgressing
the rules established by patriarchy, then the paternal character acquires characteristics of "otherness" that create a link between the daughter, the mothers, and the father. Cialente constructs the fictional father by fragmenting his
life and privileging his antimilitarism and antifascism, which he proclaims
even when still an officer in the Italian army. Through the filter of memory
and the autobiographical fiction the father is seen as an intermediate figure
between female "otherness" and marginalization and the patriarchal estab-

lishment. This newly created "feminine father" is a hybrid character, an image of transition between two binary oppositions.[35] He becomes a social and ideological *métis*. He retires into a private life of failures as he is not successful in his attempt to create a career after leaving the army, and his loneliness and marginalization are stressed by the narrator. He is also abandoned by his wife, is unable to take care of himself, and needs a companion as a nurturing substitute for his wife. When he is no more identified by his uniform, his ideological transgression is neutralized by his isolation. Trapped within a domestic sphere, the father as an "old man" becomes an approachable identity that can be manipulated within the fictional structure of an autobiographical act. The genealogical analysis of Fausta's past is therefore structured within a form of textual *métissage* in which maternal and paternal images are closely interwoven to create the braided genealogy of the protagonist.[36] The fragmentation of the father's ideological inheritance is reflected in Cialente's active role in the public sphere, which follows the death of the father within the narrative time frame. Fausta puts into practice the heritage from the father and, at the same time, comes closer to the mother through her own motherhood. The matrilinear chain slowly builds within the text while male characters disappear from the narrative. "Since my mother's death," writes Fausta Cialente, "I had only had one wish: to find myself again with my daughter" (250). What remains is the new woman whose memories are reflections of a double influence.

The point of contact between the mother's private sphere and the paternal public sphere is found in Fausta's writing, in her creativity. Creativity is, in *Le Quattro Ragazze Wieselberger*, always linked to some kind of public performance. The mother proves to be an artist in front of large audiences before her marriage. Later, it is a smaller public of friends that applauds her domestic performances after her marriage. For Fausta's brother, creativity is reflected in his theater performances through which he acquires national notoriety. While the mother fails to succeed because other priorities are imposed on her life—marriage and maternity—Renato's short but brilliant career as an actor is not impeded by the rules of society. While still proclaiming the importance of her role as mother in the private sphere, Cialente succeeds in portraying the domestic realm as a fictionally "plastic" space. Her aim is to destroy and then reconstruct the boundaries that limit the traditionally female sphere that had frustrated Elsa's creativity. As a child Fausta had, in fact, witnessed her mother's efforts to arrive at a "compromise" between creativity and her destiny as wife and mother. Only in the daughter's life can such a "compromise" be found. Without sacrificing the importance of motherhood the narrator stresses her role as writer, journalist, and antifascist, thus achieving that mobility between spheres that the mother had sought.

The mother's life as a pre-text to the daughter's life appears to be a correct reading of Fausta Cialente's construction of a double autobiographical act that contains the "biographical autobiography" of the mother/daughter and the construction of a self. It is only the mother's marriage that is described in *Le Quattro Ragazze Wieselberger,* as if to prove the repetitiveness of women's negative experiences in marriage. The mother's unhappiness in marriage functions as a mirror for the other female characters, including Fausta, the daughter. The narrator talks about her marriage as "una fuga" (an escape) a way to flee from the patriarchal Italian society and to begin a "new" life in Alexandria where her marriage soon fails (216). Yet, the man she marries barely appears as a character in the narrative. He is relegated to the background and Fausta's marriage is covered by a silence that is broken in a different context, in an interview in which she talks about her husband: "He was a person who allowed me to gain access to the world of modern music, which fascinated me right from the beginning. However, he was my teacher in many other fields: in culture and in politics, for instance. The final judgement on my married life is positive, even if, at one point, I decided to leave both Egypt and my husband."[37] The point of contact between Fausta and her husband lies in creativity and in their political involvement in the public sphere. Their relationship within the familial sphere is revealed as secondary within the narrative. The disturbing note in Fausta Cialente's positive portrayal of the man she "had" to leave is the husband's role as "teacher in many things" who is appreciated because he supplies the means to enter the public realm, but must be abandoned once the woman acquires the power to rewrite the silenced images from her maternal past. The separation is thus described: "It became necessary after the tragic death of my brother, the actor Renato Cialente; my mother was left alone, I had to devote myself to her."[38] The story of the husband is suffocated by the private story of discovery in which living with the mother and preserving the brother's memory become priorities. The husband is initially silenced as he becomes one with the character of the grandfather; they both love music and give Fausta a musical education. Their creativity is "taught" but not shared. However, the husband acquires a "different" voice because he is inscribed in the plot of the "exile," an imaginary place where woman can gain power and enter the public sphere represented by the world of creativity and politics. The husband's political voice is heard several times in the narrative and it is in contrast to the racist ideals of his bourgeois family. In his transgression, the husband can become an ally to the

woman's antifascist battle and share a common context of difference, of "otherness."

In the new social context, Egypt, Fausta is faced with a new kind of "otherness." Egypt is again a land of the father(s). The original "patriarchal land"
is reflected in the new country where the separation between the dominators
and the dominated is again clearly cut. Cialente writes: "I had grown fond of
the country and the people, a new experience for me . . . my affection or
sympathy originated, at least in part, from my reaction against the barely hidden racism that the Europeans and the Levantines, including the Jewish family, showed toward the natives" (220).[39] Her description again is of victims
and victors and we only have a glimpse of the private sphere where the blind
racism of the husband's family is portrayed. "Otherness," the natives, becomes
the subject of Cialente's creativity in novels like *Cortile a Cleopatra* (Court-
yard in Cleopatra) (1936), *Ballata Levantina* (The Levantines) (1961), *Il
Vento sulla Sabbia* (Wind on the sand) (1972), and many short stories; her
writing is however interrupted by the war and her active participation in
antifascist propaganda. She works to broadcast antifascist programs from a
radio station in Cairo. At her father's death Fausta feels "una grave, definitiva
lacerazione" (a severe, definitive laceration) that helps the process of separation between Fausta and her father's land (288). The narrator confesses that:
"the habits of Italians are such that I almost always feel the desire to leave
the country" (246).[40] In a recent interview, Fausta Cialente added: "I have
never felt Italian, anyway, partly because of my origins and partly because of
the kind of life that I have led."[41] The language inherited from the father is
separated from the fatherland, so even while writing in Italian Fausta Cialente remains in voluntary exile from Italy.

In her introduction to the book *Women's Writing in Exile*, Angela Ingram
writes:

> Voluntary exile, something of a luxury when we consider it closely,
> constitutes for a number of writers an escape from the entrapping do-
> main of the silenced mother-under-patriarchy, the manifestation of
> women's internalized exile/estrangement: a "matricidal" intent is writ
> large through some of the text of exile. Such an escape into the world
> of the apparently liberating word, the world of culture, of adulthood,
> though often means entry into the confines of patriarchal languages
> and heterosexual and heterosexist imperatives. Enabled, on one hand,
> to write, to create new worlds and to create what should have been
> home, many writers find the other hand shackled by the expectations

and rules of the world of words they have chosen to inhabit. For some, however, the ambiguities and paradoxes inherent in finding a place to write are at least partly resolved by finding a "home" in writing itself.[42]

Fausta's voluntary exile is her solution to the "matricidal" tension in the narrative. It is her reaction to the mother's double exile from Trieste, which she leaves to follow her husband into the Italian kingdom, and from creativity. In the privileged condition of émigrée and in the context of gynealogy, the narrator creates a context in which the silenced mothers can find their voice. Cialente's choice of voluntary exile becomes a protracted choice of marginality, because a new land to inhabit permanently is never found. Home then becomes the fictional context of "literature," and above all, it is the locus of the construction of a gynealogical past. It is, however, a realm not recognized by the fatherland of patriarchal language. In the context of Italian literature, Cialente has been marginalized and labelled as a minor female author of the twentieth century. To "inhabit the words" becomes the only way to construct the marginalized, but disturbing, voice that aims to destroy the rigid oppositions within patriarchy by creating an intermediate, hybrid place in which to dwell. It is her voluntary exile, as portrayed in the autobiographical act, that is not a completely controllable locus in either the public or the private spheres.

Creativity for Fausta Cialente partakes of both private and public spheres. Her public involvement in propaganda, her political role during the Second World War and fiction writing are presented as an important part of her life. In the final chapter of *Le Quattro Ragazze Wieselberger*, Fausta Cialente returns to the private sphere of family life where the creation of a different self is successfully carried out. Surrounded by her daughter and granddaughters Fausta encloses herself in a familial atmosphere and leaves the public struggle behind. She steps out of the political diatribe in the postwar world where the oppressed sometimes prove that they have learned to imitate and become the oppressors. "I saw the miserable camps for Palestinian refugees," admits Cialente "for the refugees from the first war with Israel. I reacted with indignation and that probably surprised my travel companions" (250).[43] The concern, voiced by Fausta's anti-Zionist husband, about the new Jewish state is welcomed with sympathy, but detachment, by the narrator:

> Create another nationalism? Are not there enough of them? Have not they brought enough bad luck? If only they at least founded a state that was really democratic and modern, I mean tolerant! But

> with the money from the rich American Jews, the epitome of conser-
> vatism (they would never even consider moving to Israel) they will
> do the opposite, do you want to bet on it? (251)[44]

"I myself would not have been able to bet on anything," answers Fausta, in her mind, to her husband's rhetorical question while she is already flying to join her daughter. Public thoughts and private choices become intertwined in the text. The attraction of a public involvement is surpassed by the desire for a private life with her daughter. However, after a private parenthesis Fausta Cialente succeeds in constructing a fictional intermediate sphere that unifies the opposites. While choosing a life with the daughter and rejecting a political, public role, she returns to writing in order to participate publicly in the cultural life of a country she can accept only from her voluntary exile. This semipublic, semiprivate realm allows Fausta Cialente to construct a "floating self" that can be, within the narrative, the daughter of both a public and, simultaneously, a private sphere. She becomes the element of rupture within a rigid oppositional structure.

The final chapter of Fausta Cialente's autobiography contains the cathartic moment of closure in the construction of female subjectivities. Fausta joins her daughter in Kuwait. It is after the end of the war and she feels "tired" and "exhausted"; she wants only to rest and live with her daughter and the grandchildren (255). The new temporary home in Kuwait becomes a female Garden of Eden from which woman cannot be expelled. The land described does not belong to any historical-geographical place, it is an atemporal and mythical location. In the primordial landscape of a deserted beach the protagonist feels that she is breaking all limitations; she has the feeling of "taking the first steps in the limitless solitude of a new world, recently surfaced from the ocean" (260).[45] Her footprints on the sand create a new path in the discourse on matrilinearism as a hybrid and fragmented entity. The reconstruction of the past and the construction of an identity within Fausta Cialente's autobiographical text are only starting points in the construction of a female future: "These dear figures, who walk ahead of me, are really mine, I thought looking at them with tenderness; They were doubles of myself. . . . The fact that they represented for me the continuity of life could only make for a severe re-awakening to reality" (262).[46] By representing the daughter and the grandchildren simultaneously as same and other, the narrator expresses the possibility of creating a never-ending discourse on female identities who cannot be enclosed within the text of her autobiography.

In this temporal line that tends toward things to come, the past can find its true place. Fausta interrupts her walk on the beach and, turning, she sees and hears her dead mother: "I still love you, but leave me alone, now, and try to live making the fewest possible mistakes. We made so many of them" (263).[47] Her mother's message, delivered against this mythical landscape, between the amniotic fluidity of the ocean and the desolate land, creates the concrete reality of matrilinearity in which the death of the mother can be accepted, because it is not final and is not signified by silence and disappearance. The mother's words, delivered in the plural, include a multiplicity, a collective past of which she only represents the symbolic unity translated in the text—thanks to a *métissage* of traces. Fausta's walk continues into creativity toward "the open page of this sea and this sky, behind my three distant little figures" and into her text, her autobiography, her newly constructed gynealogy and braided genealogy (263).[48]

# Notes

I would like to thank Fausta Cialente's daughter, Lionella Muir Terni, for reading this essay and for her suggestions. This chapter was completed in the fall of 1991.

1. See Françoise Lionnet, "*Métissage*, Emancipation and Female Textuality in Two Francophone Writers," in *Life/Lines: Theorizing Women's Autobiography*, ed. Bella Brodzki and Celeste Schenck (Ithaca: Cornell University Press, 1988), 260–81; and Françoise Lionnet, *Autobiographical Voices* (Ithaca: Cornell University Press, 1988). My construction of gynealogy is also based on the representation of male and female traces in Sidonie Smith's *A Poetic of Women's Autobiography* (Bloomington: Indiana University Press, 1987) in which the author attempts to "elaborate . . . a theoretical framework through which to understand women's self writing" (19). In the introductory chapter of her book, Smith supplies her definition of a woman's past as a polyvalent metaphor constructed thanks to an interweaving of traces:

> the woman who chooses to write her life story must negotiate the figures of "man" and the figures of "woman" promoted by the cultural discourses that surround her. . . . This framework posits certain dynamics that structure women's life writing, including [the] way in which the autobiographer who is a woman must suspend herself between paternal and maternal narratives, those fictions of male and female selfhood that permeate her historical moment. (19)

2. I am using the term *life/lines* as Germaine Bree defines it in the foreword to *Life/Lines: Theorizing Women's Autobiography*, ed. Brodzki and Schenck:

> Life/lines: the metaphor is ambiguous and invites us to ponder its relation to the subtitle. Lifelines, ropes thrown to ships or persons floundering in deep waters nearby; lifelines, ropes that link the deep-sea diver to the mother-ship; lifelines, more metaphorically, essential routes of communication between mutually dependent communities; but again, and differently, lifelines, those lines in the palm of the hand that in palmistry, dictionaries tell us, supposedly reveal facts about a person's life to the person who can decode the meaning. (ix)

The multifaceted metaphor of life/lines allows a wide range of interpretations and use in the discussion on women's autobiographies. Bree calls it "more than a metaphor; it defines a critical space or scene and suggests a purpose" (ix). It is a loose metaphor that encompasses the various techniques and strategies adopted by women to translate their lives into the fictional world of autobiographical writings. It is a "polyvalent metaphor" (ix) that describes the translation and transformation of life roles into "invented" lines, newly created roles and female identities in autobiographical spaces. Life/lines supplies the "metaphorical" context in which "gynealogy" can be created. Constructing a "gynealogy" involves a redefinition of a woman's past that is reflected into the narrative of her present life and is translated into a new metaphor of a female future.

3. The narration of the mother's life is not only a biography in Cialente's autobiography; it is also the daughter's indirect autobiography. Elsa, Fausta's mother, is described by the narrator as trapped in a marriage portrayed as an institutionalized prison where woman's creativity is silenced. When talking about her own marriage, Fausta takes refuge in silence. She creates a narrative void. The mother's life can fill such void if we consider her experience as complementary to the daughter's failed marriage. Elsa leaves her husband late in life and Fausta's marriage soon fails. She, however, does not write about her marriage as if her "self" is already hiding in the character of her mother. What is created is Elsa's "autobiographical biography," which plays an important role in the construction of matrilinearism within Cialente's autobiography. To create another's woman's biography, transforming it into an "indirect autobiography," is a technique used by several writers. The most famous is Gertrude Stein's *The Autobiography of Alice B. Toklas* (New York: Harcourt and Brace, 1933). See also Kim Chernin *In My Mother's House* (New York: Tickor and Fields, 1983). Rosellen Brown's *The Autobiography of My Mother* (New York: Doubleday, 1976) can be considered a parallel text to Fausta Cialente's autobiography. The mother, described as same and at the same time other, becomes the character through which a daughter can construct her self. The mother's life becomes the starting point in the construction of an independent feminine self in an autobiographical act.

4. See Stephanie A. Demetrakipoulos, "The Metaphysics of Matrilinearism in Women's Autobiography: Studies of Mead's *Blackberry Winter;* Hellman's *Pentimento;* Angelou's *I Know Why the Caged Bird Sings;* and Kingston's *The Woman Warrior,*" in *Women's Autobiography,* ed. Estelle C. Jelinek (Bloomington: Indiana University Press, 1980), 180–202.

5. Fausta Cialente, *Le Quattro Ragazze Weiselberger* (Milan: Mondadori, 1976), 19. All future references to this text will be indicated by the page number following the quotation in the text. All the translations are mine.

6. *Babe* is a word in the Triestino dialect. It is a derogatory term as it transforms women into worthless female identities. In this context naming women as "babe" has the power of depriving them of individual identities and of never allowing them to become "women."

7. "Le sere in cui l'orchestra veniva a suonare in casa la famiglia doveva cenare assai più presto del solito perchè la signora e le ragazze . . . avessero tempo sufficiente per sbarazzare la tavola della sala da pranzo . . . , la grande porta a vetri che le separava dall'entrata dovendo rimanere aperta. Bisognava tenere ben chiusi, invece, tutti gli usci verso la cucina e i 'servizi' giacchè il padre non voleva sentire durante l'esecuzione gli strepiti delle rigovernature e le chiacchiere, le *ciacole,* delle serve."

8. "Di lei sono rimaste sbiadite fotografie in abito da ballo in cui veramente sembra una fata, ma dove ha pure nella bocca amaramente piegata in giù una strana sembianza dolorosa, come se già sapesse che deve morire sui ventisette anni d'un male a quei tempi misterioso."

9. In Triestino dialect "s'ciavi" means Slovenians, but also "slaves." The Weiselberger "girls" have "the despicable habit of calling them in dialect *s'ciavi* or better these damn *s'ciavi*" (48).

10. The "girls" witness the hard life of the women working at the market who, after hours in the cold, can only face more hours in such weather after drinking the local alcoholic beverages. Like well-instructed schoolgirls they superciliously disapprove: "Those drunkards—the sisters used to say with contempt" (21).

11. "e già s'impinguava una borghesia rapace e reazionaria ch'egli, ingenuo musicista, non era in grado di giudicare e ancor meno di condannare, tanto più che da quei ranghi eterogenei uscivano le caste che riempivano i teatri, le sale dei concerti e l'amatissima Filarmonica."

12. "ed era con una sprezzante invidia che gli irredentisti giungevano fino ad esclamare: questi cafoni! che diventano avvocati, dottori e dirigenti! —quasi fosse inammissibile il loro diritto a studiare per progredire e senza rendersi conto di quanto razzista fosse invece il loro disprezzo."

13. "la guerra alla quale assistevo mi aveva non solamente stomacata, ma suscitava in me un odio che sentivo inguaribile: l'odio contro qualsiasi forma di nazionalismo o razzismo (" 'sti maledeti s'ciavi, 'sti maledeti austriacanti, 'sti maledeti ebrei"), contro ogni sopraffazione, quindi; in più avevo già imparato che i primi a pagare e ad essere travolti sono sempre i poveri, le guerre sembrano inventate per loro, giacchè è la miseria che meglio insegna a resistere e a durare."

14. "[Alice] è una signora imponente; . . . in un'istantanea, certamente presa in casa, indossa un tetro abito scuro, ha un cappello enorme e minaccioso posato in cima alla bionda testa e s'appoggia a un tavolinetto a tre piedi su cui è in mostra una statuetta confusamente inquietante, che sembra predire qualcosa di molto funesto alla dama immobile, altera e triste: il suo stesso destino, forse."

15. "Vogliono generosamente mostrare al prossimo della loro epoca che ne stanno principiando un'altra—della quale sono il timido ma coraggioso esemplare."

16. "Il fidanzamento e un matrimonio, repentinamente decisi e conclusi, sembrano invece aver cancellato dalla sua memoria e da quella dei familiari gli avvenimenti e le speranze di quei pochi anni di studio e di carriera, che presto, incredibilmente presto annegano e scompaiono nella misteriosa nebbia d'una strana indifferenza—e accettazione."

17. "Sono due prudenti signore borghesi che accettano l'ordine e i limiti della loro classe e nonostante le tristi esperienze si preparano a educare i figli—le femminucce soprattutto—alle rinunce e ai sacrifici."

18. Carolyn Heilbrun, *Writing a Woman's Life* (New York: Norton, 1988), 18.

19. Luce Irigaray, *Speculum of the Other Woman* (Ithaca: Cornell University Press, 1985), 35.

20. James E. Breslin, "Gertrude Stein and the Problems of Autobiography," in *Women's Autobiography*, 162.

21. "Nessuna delle sorelle ha preso a galleggiare più liberamente, nemmeno Alba, e ciò sarebbe stato logico e possibile anche a quell'epoca, se fossero uscite da un ceppo diverso. Le quattro ragazze Wieselberger sembrano quindi essere ancora e sempre quattro, nonostante una d'esse sia sparita."

22. I am here referring to Carolyn Heilbrun's statement: "But, at least insofar as women's lives are concerned, it is wrong. Lines can be cancelled and washed out" (*Writing a Woman's Life,* 19).

23. "di quei paesi m'è rimasto solo il nome, il freddo, le bufere come se non avessero mai altre stagioni più clementi."

24. "Ma chi osava dire niente? Abbiamo già imparato a tacere Renato ed io, siamo un bel paio di ipocriti."

25. "nonostante c'insultassimo e ci picchiassimo come tutti i fratelli di questo mondo e di ogni tempo, eravamo sopra tutto complici, probabilmente senza rendercene conto."

26. Marianne Hirsch, *The Mother/Daughter Plot: Narrative, Psychoanalysis, Feminism* (Bloomington: Indiana University Press, 1989), 73.

27. "Credo che Renato fosse meno turbato di me e m'invitasse a non 'bazilare,' termine che adoperavamo adattandolo all prima coniugazione, 'io bazilo, tu bazili,' e il timore che parlando con i cugini ci sfuggisse qualcosa che invece non dovevamo dire a volte c'isolava, e accadeva che finivamo per giocare insieme come se fossimo in Italia e non ospiti della villa in via dell'Istria."

28. "Io ero più svelta nelle combinazioni e Renato mi guardava con un po' di sospetto avendo l'aria di credere che cominciavo il gioco essendomi già preparata, il che probabilmente

non era vero; e una volta ch'ero riuscita a metter insieme qualcosa in cui avevo introdotto anche polpa di scrafaggi e zampe di millepiedi, stravolto dal disgusto e mostrando nondimeno non so se stupore o invidia, Renato esclamò: 'bè, per oggi hai vinto!'"

29. "S'ciavo vuoi venire con me? Io ti faccio padrone delle grandi campagne sul mare. . . . Sei venuto nelle terre che nessuno poteva abitare, e le hai coltivate. . . . Per lunghi anni ti sputarono in viso la tua schiavitù, ma la tua ora è venuta. E'tempo che tu sia padrone."

30. "Stranamente quegli applausi la facevano impallidire piuttosto che arrossire e la sentivamo allora turbata come se non le recasse nessun piacere un canto che a volte era gioioso e in cui mi pareva balenasse una felicità misteriosa che mi faceva sentir leggera leggera in un mondo tutto orlato di luce e di gioia, quello, forse, al quale lei aveva rinunciato per un matrimonio che ci aveva fatti nascere."

31. "una tenerezza amabile che sentivo d'approvare completamente me la rendeva cordiale e simpatica, e il parlarne mi sembrava il miglior modo di celebrare la sua memoria."

32. "Così, quel che mi rimaneva era affidato soltanto alla memoria, nulla poteva più alterarlo e distruggerlo."

33. "Avevamo sempre udito nostro padre parlare con sommo dispregio (strano ufficiale, egli era, rabbiosamente antimonarchico); se nominava il re lo chiamava 'quel maligno stortignaccolo' (non in presenza dei parenti triestini, nostra madre l'aveva scongiurato di non farlo!) . . . e per la regina si accontentava di esclamare ironicamente: ma sí, quella che allatta tutti i suoi figli, la gloria della nazione!"

34. "La collera e lo sdegno che gli conoscevo da sempre gli venivano dal suo disprezzo per i regnanti e per la carriera alla quale non s'era mai adattato e l'aveva indubbiamente fatto soffrire; ma la sua ribellione, le sue critiche non si legavano—come dovetti giudicare più tardi—alla realtà d'un fermento sociale che gli era invece estraneo e del quale non riusciva a cogliere i bagliori."

35. I do not intend to create an easy equation that equals femininity to failure and patriarchy to fascism. I am naming the newly created paternal figure a "feminine father" because he comes to inhabit a space "in-between" in order to leave behind his role as paterfamilias and acquire a more "tender form of discourse" (Hirsch, 80) that becomes part of the daughter's text of her life.

36. See Françoise Lionnet, "*Métissage*, Emancipation and Female Textuality," 260–81, *Autobiographical Voices*.

37. Sandra Petrignani, *Le Signore della Scrittura* (Milan: La Tartaruga, 1984), 87. "E'stato lui a farmi entrare nel mondo della musica moderna, dalla quale fui subito fortemente affascinata. Ma è stato maestro anche in molte altre cose: nella cultura e nella politica, per esempio. Il bilancio della mia vita coniugale è positivo, anche se a un certo punto decisi di lasciare l'Egitto e mio marito."

38. Petrignani, 87: "si rese necessario per la tragica morte di mio fratello, l'attore Renato Cialente; mia madre era rimasta sola, dovetti dedicarmi a lei."

39. "M'ero affezionata al paese e alla sua gente, cosa nuova per me . . . l'affetto o la simpatia venivano, almeno in parte, dalla mia reazione contro il mal celato razzismo che europei e levantini, la famiglia ebrea compresa, manifestavano agl'indigeni."

40. "il costume deg'Italiani è quasi sempre tale che ho quasi sempre voglia di andarmene."

41. Petrignani, 85: "Non ho mai sentito, del resto, di essere italiana, un po' per le mie origini, un po' per la vita che ho fatto."

42. Angela Ingram, introduction to *Women's Writing in Exile*, ed. Mary Lynn Broe and Angela Ingram (Chapel Hill: University of North Carolina Press, 1989), 5.

43. "Vidi i miserabili accampamenti dei rifugiati dalla Palestina, quelli della prima guerra con Israele, ebbi un moto d'indignazione che forse meravigliò i miei compagni di viaggio."

44. "Creare un altro nazionalismo? Non ce ne sono già abbastanza? Non ci hanno portato sufficentemente scalogna? Se almeno fondassero uno stato davvero democratico e moderno, cioè tollerante! Ma con i quattrini dei ricchi ebrei statunitensi, il fior della reazione, che si

guarderebbero bene, loro dal venir a vivere in Israele, faranno esattamente il contrario, vuoi scommetterlo?"

45. "muovere i passi nella solitudine sconfinata d'un mondo nuovo, appena sorto dall'oceano."

46. "Queste care figure che camminano davanti sono proprio mie, pensavo guardandole con tenerezza; erano un me stessa sdoppiato. . . . Ch'esse rappresentassero per me la continuità della vita poteva essere solo un severo richiamo alla realtà."

47. "vi voglio ancora bene, ma lasciatemi in pace, adesso, e pensate a vivere sbagliando il meno possibile. Noi abbiamo tanto sbagliato."

48. "la pagina aperta che sono questo mare e questo cielo, dietro le mie tre lontane figurine."

# Works Cited

Bree, Germaine. Foreword. *Life/Lines: Theorizing Women's Autobiography*. Edited by Bella Brodzki and Celeste Schenck, i–xii. Ithaca: Cornell University Press, 1988.

Breslin, James E. "Gertrude Stein and the Problems of Autobiography." In *Women's Autobiography*, edited by Estelle C. Jelinek, 158–79. Bloomington: Indiana University Press, 1980.

Cialente, Fausta. *Ballata Levantina*. Milan: Feltrinelli, 1961.

———. *Cortile a Cleopatra*. Milan: Feltrinelli, 1962.

———. *The Levantines*. Translated by Isabelle Quigly. London: Faber and Faber, 1962.

———. *Le Quattro Ragazze Wieselberger*. Milan: Mondadori, 1976.

———. *Il Vento sulla Sabbia*. Milan: Mondadori, 1973.

Demetrakipoulos, Stephanie A. "The Metaphysics of Matrilinearism in Women's Autobiography: Studies of Mead's *Blackberry Winter*, Hellman's *Pentimento*, Angelou's *I Know Why the Caged Bird Sings*, and Kingston's *The Woman Warrior*." In *Women's Autobiography*, edited by Estelle C. Jelinek, 180–202. Bloomington: Indiana University Press, 1980.

Heilbrun, Carolyn G. "Non-Autobiographies of 'Privileged' Women: England and America." in *Life/Lines: Theorizing Women's Autobiography*, ed. Bree, 62–76.

———. *Writing a Woman's Life*. New York: Norton, 1988.

Hirsch, Marianne. *The Mother/Daughter Plot: Narrative, Psychoanalysis, Feminism*. Bloomington: Indiana University Press, 1989.

Ingram, Angela. Introduction. *Women's Writing in Exile*. Edited by Mary Lynn Broe and Angela Ingram, 1–16. Chapel Hill: University of North Carolina Press, 1989.

Irigaray, Luce. *The Speculum of the Other Woman*. Ithaca: Cornell University Press, 1985.

Lionnet, Françoise. *Autobiographical Voices*. Ithaca: Cornell University Press, 1989.

———. "Metissage, Emancipation and Female Textuality in Two Francophone Writers." In *Life/Lines: Theorizing Women's Autobiography*, ed. Bree, 260–81.

Petrignani, Sandra. *Le Signore della Scrittura*. Milan: La Tartaruga, 1984.

Smith, Sidonie. *A Poetics of Women's Autobiography*. Bloomington: Indiana University Press, 1987.

# 11

## Ethnic Matriarchy: Fabrizia Ramondino's Neapolitan World

*Maria Ornella Marotti*

"Damned be Neapolitan mothers who bring us up to keep us children; they would sleep with us, if they could and they do it when they can, in the same bed, until their own and our extreme old age," complains the protagonist and narrative voice of Fabrizia Ramondino's short story, "La Bassura." He continues:

> I have seen some who seem to enjoy the fact of having disabled children because in this way they can push them around in a carriage even when they are adults; they feed us with spaghetti to make us soft like bread dough and take away our virility and vigor, like eunuchs. Whether they be fat or bony, or whether their children be fat or bony, the result is the same; their souls and ours are malleable like bread and pizza dough, and similarly amorphous. They are so jealous of our virility that they intimately gloat when they see us become effeminate. Love, for them, is the carnal vicinity to their big body and to the family clan.... And sex is for them, therefore, the means by which they reproduce eternally this situation. And damned be Nea-

politan fathers, and their husbands! Their virility and their airs of command are only a show.[1]

The nameless narrator of "La Bassura," while venting his anger at Neapolitan mothers, gives voice to a recurrent theme in Fabrizia Ramondino's work: the peculiar position of women inside the Neapolitan family within which they enjoy an ambiguous power. Even though they perpetuate patriarchal dominance in their homes, Neapolitan mothers are powerful matriarchs who rule over their children. Rather than subverting male dominance, they indirectly undermine it through their own power in the family.

Ramondino's treatment of the Neapolitan matriarchal system is consistent with some anthropological studies of matriarchy. In studying societies in which matriarchy developed, both Ida Magli and Ginevra Conti Odorisio notice that matriarchy never means absolute power to women, but rather only power in certain well-delimited spheres of action. Even in societies ruled by matrilinearism, that is where the law of heredity is linked to the mother rather than the father, women never gain access to the symbolic order.

However, in her argument against matriarchy Ramondino differs from some recent trends in Italian feminist thought that, while placing a special value on the maternal, tend to reevaluate some aspects of women's domestic governance. Although she acknowledges women's power, in her Neapolitan stories Ramondino describes both the immobile nature of the system and the perpetuation by the matriarch of the symbolic order of the father, rather than the symbolic order of the mother, as Luisa Muraro would have it.[2]

Few writers have been more interested in depicting the crossing of ethnicity and gender than Fabrizia Ramondino has in most of her works: a collection of short stories, *Storie di patio* (1983); a fictional autobiography, *Althenopis* (1981); and a recent collection of autobiographical essays, *Star di casa* (1991). In writing about Naples and its culture she joins a rich literary tradition that includes Salvatore Di Giacomo, Matilde Serao, Eduardo De Filippo, Giuseppe Marotta, Domenico Rea, Raffaele La Capria, Giuseppe Patroni Griffi, and Luciano De Crescenzo. Ramondino holds a special position among this group. None among those who have dealt with ethnicity in the Neapolitan area have placed themselves in the position of partial outsiders to the culture and the language as she consistently does throughout her works; she plays the role of observer more than participant. From the vantage point of the outsider, the one who is not completely Neapolitan, she observes the mores of the middle and upper bourgeoisie, with the class consciousness of a materialist. She describes these social classes, their homes, and social mannerisms with a love for detail that reminds one of Balzac's realistic decors in "La Comédie Humaine."[3] From the masters of great realistic fiction, Ramondino also learns detachment, the impassible mode of her narration. Such mode of detachment also signals her ethnicity from the most canonical forms of the Neapolitan literary tradition.

Ramondino approaches the Neapolitan language with the same outsider's attitude; she uses it neither in her prose, nor as the language of her characters. Only occasionally she inserts words of Neapolitan origin: for example, "guantiera" instead of "vassoio" (tray), "forestiero" instead of "staniero" (foreigner). In *Althenopis*, she even uses footnotes to explain the meaning and origin of Neapolitan words, as one would in a philological essay rather than in a fictional autobiography. In contrast, several stories in the collection, *Storie di patio*, are interspersed with dialogues and quotations in Catalan, the language that she claims as her true origin. The daughter of Neapolitan parents, Ramondino spent the first years of her life in an island off the coast of Spain. The rest of her childhood was spent in a small town on the Neapolitan coast, in Naples and in France. However, if the Neapolitan dialect is not her true language and Naples is not her origin, the city becomes for her the place of inevitable return, more a state of mind and a dimension of the human spirit than a geographical location. In *Star di casa*, she writes:

> And fleeing Naples, to pursue a mythic North, which almost never extended itself beyond Rome, [young Neapolitan intellectuals] were in turn followed by Naples, as if from a secret obsession. Because, Naples is used to follow its citizens everywhere, like a shadow, if they move elsewhere. . . . Thus Naples, where it is so difficult to live and which entices one so much to leave, which is so difficult to abandon and which compels one to always come back, becomes, more than other places, the emblematic place of a general human condition in our time: to find oneself on an inhabitable planet and yet to know that this is the only one that for the time being we can call home.[4]

While, like other Neapolitan writers, Ramondino stresses Naples's hold on its citizens, her approach to Neapolitan life differs from theirs in another way: instead of emphasizing the feeling of communality in the city and Neapolitans' flexibility and capacity to survive under impossible circumstances, Ramondino focuses on the inherent despair of life in Naples, a despair that is, however, the essential human condition—life on an "inhabitable planet" which is our only home. In *Star di Casa* she refers to the 1980 earthquake as the turning point in the city's decline. The earthquake itself becomes a metaphor for the instability of Neapolitan life, a condition that has always been latent due to the vicinity of the volcano Vesuvius, and the seismic activity of its underground. Ramondino views Neapolitans as caught between magic enchantment at the natural beauties of the bay and the warm and sunny climate, and a feeling of suspension over an abyss. The result is a metaphysical approach to life. The other side of the coin is what Ramondino calls "accidia": a combination of passivity, laziness, and incapacity to act that she sees as predominant in Neapolitan upper classes.

Naples permeates personal lives with the complexity of its social signs, the rituals, the food and the many layers of civilizations and historical eras, thus creating an inescapable web. Ramondino entitles her own fictionalized autobiography, *Althenopis* (old woman's eye), the Greek name by which the invading German soldiers called the city—as if her personal life could only be told in relation to the surrounding environment. She herself, like her characters, springs out of it. Even the places from which and to which she moves—Spain and France—are linguistically and historically related to Naples. And so are the other civilizations that are objects of her intellectual speculations: the Greek, the Roman, and the Arab.

However, despite Ramondino's connections to and deep understanding of the various historical layers of the city, throughout her work, she expresses also her repugnance toward women's retrograde condition in Campania. She personally rebels against it and escapes it. She describes it in *Althenopis* and alludes to it in *Star di casa* and again in several stories of *Storie di patio*. She goes one step further. Unlike other Neapolitan writers, Ramondino deconstructs the myth of Neapolitan matriarchy by showing the feeling of enclosure that such a social structure generates for both females and males. Among her characters, the innocent narrator, Perfetta D'Ayala, in "Perfetta's Day" ("Una giornata della bambina Perfetta D'Ayala") is the one that more effectively captures the contradictions inherent to family matriarchy.

The use of a child narrator is widespread in world literature. The innocent voice tells with absolute frankness what is usually unspoken of. Narrating children's perception of situations is defamiliarized by their ignorance of a general context. This defamiliarization makes their observations more poignant and candid. Perfetta's perspective functions in the narrative as both a mirror and a lamp that throws a new light on reality.[5] From her position, sitting on the floor, often forgotten by the adults, she observes the human comedy that unfolds around her. She is a rather precocious preschooler whose poignant observations and explanations provide us with a new interpretive key to Neapolitan matriarchy.

The title itself alludes to her position in the space that surrounds her. "Una giornata . . . ," in the original Italian title, alludes to the better known Solzhenitsyn novel *A Day in the Life of Ivan Denisovich*. Like Ivan, Perfetta is a prisoner, except that her captivity can only be recognized as such through her narrative. Her "gulag" is a Neapolitan apartment inhabited by fourteen people: eight adults and six children. As the daughter of a single working mother, Perfetta is left during the day in the care of her eighty-five-year-old great-grandmother, the matriarch of the family. Considerations of space and time are indeed important when reading the story. The narrative unfolds over two time levels: Perfetta narrates a day before the old woman's death; she then resumes and concludes the narration a short time after the death. Perfetta's day thus stretches over a second day that proves to be a repetition with few variations of the first one. We are thus allowed to see the inescapable repetition that governs her life.

Perfetta, the youngest female member of a group of nuclear related families living in the same apartment, spends her days sitting on the floor of the dining room together with her great-grandmother. The highest and the lowest— the old woman, sitting on a chair from which she cannot move, and the child, on the floor, illustrate the paradoxical structure of the system that incarcerates them both. The great-grandmother controls Perfetta's every move. She exhorts the child: "Eat! Eat!" or she asks: "What are you doing? Why aren't you playing?" (155). Perfetta can only temporarily escape such incessant control by pretending to abide by the rules of matriarchy, that is, by pretending to play a maternal role with her doll. From her comments we learn, however, that she has already decided to break the matriarchal chain: she does not want to have children; she does not want to perpetuate matriarchy, and therefore has ceased to play seriously with her doll.

Despite her absolute power in the household, the great-grandmother is also a prisoner. Perfetta, who observes her during her last living week, and has a premonition of her impending death, points out: "Nonna will never go to heaven. Even if she dies, she won't be able to leave this room, this house, and this world" (155). The old woman's physical size—so enormous that she cannot lift herself from the chair without help—epitomizes her inability to leave in several senses: physical, emotional, and spiritual. We are reminded again of the narrator of "La Bassura" who calls Neapolitan mothers: "true antagonists of God" ("veri antagonisti di Dio") because of their hold on the physical world. The great-grandmother reveals prophetically to Perfetta that even after her death she will not leave her house because her role will be continued without interruptions by her own daughter. Her personal identity, indeed her survival beyond death, are inextricably connected to the role she plays.

Perfetta, on the other hand, argues that her great-grandmother already inhabits the entire world, while being paradoxically unable to leave even her chair. Her power (rather, her omnipotence) is expressed through her total control of vocabulary and grammar. One of the activities in which she engages herself is to test her grandchildren's knowledge of verbs and idiom. The old woman attaches enormous importance to grammatical structures: "It seems that if there weren't any verbs, the entire castle of words would crumble," observes Perfetta (158). Because of the linguistic assumptions on which it rests and the tools that it employs, the vocabulary game that the great-grandmother plays with the child reveals the implicit significance of the upbringing that the old woman imparts. Indeed, the dictionary that she uses is the most traditional and antiquated one that one could possibly use and her linguistic assumptions, reinforced by the solemn tone of her voice when dealing with verbs, show that what she is trying to pass on is the law of the father, the cornerstone of patriarchy. Even though she expresses skepticism toward men, the old woman does not challenge the ideological basis of patriarchy.

Perfetta, however, enjoys the vocabulary game because the words give her a glimpse of the world outside, a world that she cannot see any more from inside her apartment: ever since the curtains were broken by one of her cousins, the great-grandmother has had the blinds lowered in order to protect the family's privacy. In her position of captive, Perfetta has the illusion of gaining, through the acquisition of language, temporary access to the symbolic order of the father, from which she is actually excluded because of her gender. Quite poignantly, Adriana Cavarero observes that "Women have no language of their own, but instead use the language of the other" (52).

The enclosed world of the large decaying apartment—yet another emblem of the deterioration of Neapolitan life—is a self-contained signifying system. From her vantage point of observation on the ground, Perfetta notices similarities: the legs of the almost unbreakable and ancient dining table resemble those of the grandmother; they bulge in the upper parts and are frail in the lower ones. The imprisoned huge dog who is kept in the small closet-room also resembles the old woman, both in his physical size and in his double position of captive and jailer. On one occasion the dog is able to escape his cell and he keeps the great-grandmother paralyzed with fear for a few hours. That is, however, the only time when Perfetta enjoys, at least potentially, a total freedom of movement. Yet her own inner compulsion to observe, brings her back to the room where she contemplates the sight of her great-grandmother together with her own double.

Like all doubles, and like all the somewhat anomalous beings that preceded him in the closet-room, the dog, Moby-Dick, is also the repressed element that needs to be kept under control for the system to work. His presence functions in the microstructure of the matriarchal family in the same way as matriarchy itself functions in the macrostructure of patriarchy. The power of the female, just like that of the dog, is repressed through domestication and captivity.

Matriarchy only works inside patriarchy through an unspoken agreement with the male-dominated system. Inside this system, women carve for themselves a sphere of influence. Through their representative, the matriarch, they control family life and succeed in feminizing the males. To this purpose, the narrator of "La Bassura" observes:

> Just in the opposite way of the Elizabethan theater, where males played female roles and where males, disguised as females, acted on occasion the role of females disguised as males, we, Neapolitan males, real females in our souls, play male roles; this is why in our city there are so many transvestites; [they are] females in their souls, with male appearance, [who are] disguised as females.[6]

Through the feminization of males, matriarchy acts upon Neapolitan society in an indirect way that is perceived by the narrator of "La Bassura" as a form of sabotage of male identity compelling males to waver between genders. However, because the characteristics socially connected with the feminine have been devalued in the eyes of the society, the male narrator expresses his concern about the emergence of the feminine in himself and other Neapolitan males.

Despite its indirect power over males, matriarchy perpetuates women's subjection and the status quo. Indeed, the private sphere (woman's sphere) is ultimately controlled by the public sphere, as the Diotima feminist philosophers observe (Fischer et al., 31). Matriarchy does not increase, therefore, women's power in the society at large; it does not even foster solidarity among women. In *Althenopis*, Ramondino recalls that in her own matriarchal family, the few women who had distinguished themselves for their high level of education were looked at with suspicion and even spite by other women. This attitude is evinced also by the great-grandmother who explains to Perfetta that while men can easily be divided into two categories, the boring ones and

the irresponsible ones, women are almost always boring: "Almost all of them
are tedious, many are mental. But the tediousness of women is different from
that of men, I think. It's much larger and deeper, it's ancient, ancient like
that which comes to me from the crust of the earth. Luckily every so often
they go mad" (171). In her condescending remarks about women, the great-
grandmother also alludes to the unchangeable quality of the matriarchal system (the boredom of repeated actions) and its ancient origin (the crust of
the earth).

The only deviant to the enclosed system of matriarchy is Giulia, the servant to the family for more than forty years. She is the only one who sees
herself as a separate individual, the only one that "didn't come from Nonna,"
as Perfetta puts it. However, she speculates: "maybe she came from Nonna's
shadow" (156), thus evoking the Jungian image of a dark aspect of the psyche, the old woman's unacknowledged side. Giulia complains about overpo-
pulation both in the apartment, which is becoming every day dirtier and dirtier, and in the outside world, every day more and more densely populated.
She observes: "if you didn't know that people always come out from the same
place, you'd ask where do they all come from? . . . I stayed just the way
Mamma made me. One I was and one I've stayed" (157). Giulia has no pa-
tience with children and does not allow them in her private territory, the
kitchen. Whenever Perfetta tries to invade her sphere, Giulia complains
loudly and monotonously with her mistress: "You know our pact. And you
also know why I insisted on it. I raised four of my mother's kids and when the
fifth was born, I had had it. I said, 'Mamma, I am going out to work as a maid
and I'll give you my whole salary, but I'm done with raising children'" (168).
As unattractive, and somewhat grotesque, Giulia might appear, Perfetta fa-
vors her model ("One I was and one I stayed") over the matriarchal one.
Using words that echo Giulia's, she states: "I don't want to become anything
more than what I am" (159).

After the great-grandmother's death Perfetta observes the fulfillment of the
old woman's prophecy: her place is immediately taken over by her grandmother. The child notices a sudden and complete change in her grandmother: in assuming her mother's role, she accepts both her own aging and
her domestication. She retires from her job to devote herself completely to
the administration of the family; she does not color her hair any more, nor
does she use makeup. She wears black. Perfetta is determined to avoid such a
repetitive model and, linking matriarchy to ethnicity, she decides: "When
Zia-Nonna dies, my mother will have to sit at the table. Then, according to

the rule, it would be my turn. But I'm going to leave this house and Naples, too" (175).

Yet, as we learn from other works by Ramondino, Naples is hard to leave because its memory follows its citizens everywhere. Even harder is for a female to leave behind her own femaleness, when this is so inextricably connected with the structure of matriarchy. Perfetta observes poignantly: "My only fear is that Nonna may have occupied the whole world. Even the face of the moon, if you see it close up, resembles Nonna" (175). Her words reveal that she has already internalized what she would like to evade; it has become her own femaleness (the face of the moon) and her entire perception of reality (the whole world). Just like Naples is inescapable for Neapolitans because it epitomizes the human condition, matriarchy is unavoidable for those who have experienced it in their family.

The nameless male narrator of "La Bassura" and Perfetta both link matriarchy to a feeling of deprivation of personal identity: the merging of individuals into the great maternal body of the matriarch, or the clan that she dominates. While the male narrator perceives that, through a process of feminization, his virility has been diminished, the young female narrator experiences oppression deriving from the linking of personal identity to the matriarchal role. Both recognize a close connection between the family structure and Naples. Matriarchy is the cornerstone of the Neapolitan family and the hidden source upon which the city's mores rest. Because of its fixity it acts indeed as a corrective to the physical and social instability of Neapolitan lives.

One may ask at this point: How does Ramondino differ on this topic from the Neapolitan literary tradition? Strong female images emerge throughout Neapolitan literary and cinematic texts. Yet, if Ramondino's descriptions of the situations of women inside the family may not differ substantially from those of other writers from the region, the point of view that she allows her characters to express deviates from that of more canonical authors. The difference appears clear when one compares her works with other texts. As an example I have chosen to look at Eduardo De Filippo's drama, *Filumena Marturano* (1946), his best-known work and one in which his views about the maternal emerge most unequivocally. In De Filippo's drama, after having shared her life for twenty-five years with philandering Domenico Soriano, former prostitute Filumena Marturano tricks him into marriage by pretending to be on her deathbed. She has a plan: she wants Soriano to adopt her three children. Once he discovers that he has been cheated into wedlock, Soriano decides to have the marriage annulled. Yet Filumena's revelation that one of her children is his son touches him deeply. Even though, to the very end, she refuses to tell him which one of her three children is his, he decides to marry her again and adopt all of her children.

Throughout the drama, and even in the author's foreword, Filumena appears powerful, dignified, responsible, and intensely tragic. Domenico, by contrast, appears powerless, superficial, self-indulgent, ultimately vulnerable, and comic. She is and always has been the efficient administrator of both his household and his business. He has spent all his life betting on horses and chasing women. Now that he has started to age, the only thing left to him is to reminisce on his past glories with his submissive and foolish servant. She is surrounded by other women who recognize her authority and deep warm humanity. Filumena is a matriarch who lives inside patriarchy and ultimately succeeds in molding the male subject; she transforms him by initiating him into the values of the maternal, into the symbolic order of the mother. Indeed, Filumena's main claim to the status of admirable character, in the eyes of the other characters and supposedly of the audience, is her heroic motherhood; that is, her choice to have, and then support her own children against all odds. The line: "e figlie so' ffiglie" (children are children) is repeated more than once in the drama and it becomes the sign of Domenico's change of heart when he himself repeats it at the end of the drama: "Children are children. . . . And they are all equal. . . . You're right, Filumena, you're right!"[7] In adopting all of Filumena's children, Domenico transcends the biological link of fatherhood and accepts the implicit equality of all human beings. He gains access to a higher moral level that is epitomized by Filumena's maternal role.

Similarly to De Filippo's Filumena, the great-grandmother is a provider and administrator for her family. Although, unlike Filumena, she never had to face predicaments created by extreme poverty, she too is a survivor. Yet Ramondino's approach to the maternal and its symbolic order greatly differs from that of De Filippo. Instead of looking at matriarchy from the perspective of the mother, Ramondino through her narrators and characters, adopts the point of view of the children. Although her descriptions of the warm, assertive, and imperious ways of the matriarch may not greatly differ from those inscribed in Neapolitan tradition, her analysis and the conclusions she allows her characters to draw mark a major deviation. Eduardo De Filippo leaves the matriarchal role unchallenged. He recognizes and appreciates women's inherent power; he ascribes such a power solely to women's maternal role. In her deconstruction of gender roles in Campania, Ramondino observes, instead, the debilitating effect that the familial power of women causes in an overall patriarchal society. The feminization of the males does not break down gender polarization, even though it deprives males of their traditional social prerogatives; the sabotage of the symbolic order of the father does not result in a liberating androgynous acceptance for males of femaleness as a valuable component of one's own humanity. Feminized males take on the powerlessness that, in patriarchy, is connected to femaleness. On the other hand, females create inside the household an authoritarian order that is not meant to subvert patriarchy but instead to perpetuate it. Inside the family, they take on responsibilities that the disempowered males have abdicated, and therefore create for themselves an oppressive system. For Ramondino's characters, only such extreme solutions as renunciation of the maternal role or exile seem to provide alternatives to the structure.

In her autobiographical pieces, Ramondino distinguishes between the matriarchal structure and the maternal chain existing between mothers and daughters and, for that matter, between all younger and older female members of the family. In *Althenopis* such a link is solidly based in the female body where the connection between sexuality and death is unequivocal. In the final episode of the book, the narrator's dying mother's last, although unaware, message to her daughter is a gesture—touching her vagina:

> That gesture, which for so many years had remained buried, alighted in her lap, to reclaim her rights and assert them, to peel away from the old dying body and enter the soul of her who grasped it, to lift the ban and make her fertile, that others born of woman might see the light. (261)

Although in her autobiography Ramondino illustrates the powerful link uniting females and its inextricable connection to women's sexuality, she also creates characters who refuse to play the maternal role—exemplified by Perfetta's refusal to play with her doll—as a form of rebellion against an imprisoning system that uses maternity to compel women to renounce personal identity and perpetuate patriarchy. In her analysis she evinces a skepticism that contrasts with Muraro's celebration of the symbolic order of the mother, by showing that, at the social level, such an order has been infiltrated and contaminated by patriarchy. In questioning the basis of her own society, and in challenging those views concerning the maternal that are inscribed in the Neapolitan literary tradition, Ramondino pushes toward a revision of that tradition.

# Notes

1. Fabrizia Ramondino, "La Bassura," *Storie di patio* (Turin: Einaudi, 1983), 206. Translations from "La Bassura" are mine. The original version reads as follows: "Maledette . . . le madri napoletane che ci allevano per conservarci bambini; dormirebbero con noi, se lo potessero, e lo fanno quando possono, nello stesso letto, fino alla loro, e alla nostra, estrema vecchiaia; ne ho viste alcune che sembrano godere di avere figli paralitici perchè così possono spingerli anche da adulti in carrozzina; ci nutrono di spaghetti per renderci morbidi come la pasta del pane e toglierci ogni virilità e vigore, come eunuchi. Siano esse grasse ossute, o lo siano i loro figli, il risultato è lo stesso; le loro anime e le nostre sono malleabili come la pasta della pizza e del pane, e nello stesso modo amorfe. Sono così gelose della nostra virilità che nel loro intimo godono quando ci vedono diventare effeminati. L'amore, per loro, è la vicinanza carnale al loro grande corpo e al clan familiare. . . . E il sesso è quindi, per loro, il mezzo per riprodurre in eterno questa situazione. . . . E maledetti i padri napoletani, e loro mariti! La loro virilità e le loro arie di comando sono solo teatro."

2. In another essay, "Filial Discourses; Feminism and Femininity in Italian Women's Autobiography" in *Feminine Feminists: Cultural Practices in Italy,* ed. Giovanna Miceli Jeffries (Minneapolis: University of Minnesota Press), I argue that Ramondino values the link between generations of women and bases that link in the female body. Her position is not far from Luisa Muraro's in *L'ordine simbolico della madre* (Rome: Editori Riuniti, 1991). However, when dealing with the social and ethnic aspects of women's domestic governance, her position is more skeptical than that of Muraro and other Italian feminists, as for example, Alessandra Bocchetti.

3. Erich Auerbach's observations in *Mimesis* concerning Balzac's characters and their metonymic relation to the environment from which they spring could almost be applied to Ramondino's handling of characters and environments. Erich Auerbach, *Mimesis: The Representation of Reality in Western Literature*, trans. Willard Trask (New York: Doubleday, 1957), 413–25.

4. Fabrizia Ramondino, *Star di casa* (Milan: Garzanti, 1991), 59–60. Translations are mine. "E fuggendo Napoli, per inseguire un Nord mitico, che quasi sempre non oltrepassava Roma, [i giovani intellettuali napoletani] venivano a loro volta inseguiti da Napoli, come da una segreta ossessione. Ché Napoli usa seguire i suoi concittadini dovunque, come un'ombra, se si trasferiscono altrove. . . . Così Napoli, dove è così difficile vivere e che invoglia tanto a partire, che è così difficile abbandonare e che costringe sempre a tornare, diventa, più di molti altri, il luogo emblematico di una generale condizione umana nel nostro tempo: trovarsi su un inabitabile pianeta, ma sapere che è l'unico dove per ora possiamo star di casa."

5. In an analysis of Mark Twain's and Henry James's children narrators, Tony Tanner argues that children's outlook can function in narrative either as a mirror that reflects objects accurately and without mediations or a lamp that throws a new light on reality; "The Literary Children of James and Clemens," *Nineteenth-Century Fiction* 16 (December 1961): 205–18.

6. Fabrizia Ramondino, "La Bassura" in *Storie di patio* (208). The translation is mine. The original Italian reads as follows: "Proprio all'inverso del teatro elisabettiano, dove i maschi impersonavano ruoli femminili e dove maschi, travestiti da femmine, impersonavano quindi all'occorrenza il ruolo di femmine travestite da maschi, noi maschi napoletani, femmine in realtà nell'animo, impersoniamo ruoli maschili; perciò nella nostra città ci sono tanti travestiti; femmine nell'animo, con sembianze di maschio, travestite da femmine."

7. The translation is mine. The original reads as follows: "E figlie so' ffiglie. . . . E so' tutte equale. . . . Hai ragione, Filume', hai ragione tu! . . ." (92).

# Works Cited

Auerbach, Erich. *Mimesis: The Representation of Reality in Western Literature*. Translated by Willard Trask. New York: Doubleday, 1957.

Cavarero, Adriana. "Per una teoria della differenza sessuale." *Diotima: Il Pensiero della differenza sessuale*. Milan: La Tartaruga, 1987.

De Filippo, Eduardo. *Filumena Marturano*. Turin: Giulio Einaudi, 1964. Reprinted Milan: Arnoldo Mondadori, 1966.

Fischer, Cristiana, Elvia Franco, Giannina Longobardi, Veronica Mariaux, Luisa Muraro, Anita Sanvitto, Betty Zamarchi, Chiara Zamboni, Gloria Zanardo. "La differenza sessuale: da scoprire e da produrre." In *Diotima: Il Pensiero della differenza sessuale*. Milan: La Tartaruga, 1987.

Magli, Ida, ed. *Matriarcato e potere delle donne*. Milan: Feltrinelli, 1978.

Marotti, Maria O. "Filial Discourses: Feminism and Femininity in Italian Women's Autobiography." In *Feminine Feminists: Cultural Practices in Italy*, edited by Giovanne Miceli Jeffries. University of Minnesota Press, 1994.

Muraro, Luisa. *L'Ordine simbolico della madre*. Rome: Editori Riuniti, 1991.

Raimondino, Fabrizia. *Althenopis*. Translated by Michael Sullivan. Manchester: Carcanet Press, 1988. (Original published 1981)

———. "La Bassura." In *Storie di patio*. Turin: Einaudi, 1983.

———. "Perfetta's Day." In *New Italian Women*, translated by Barbara Dow Nucci, edited by Martha King. New York: Italica Press, 1989. (Original published 1983)

———. *Star di casa*. Milan: Garzanti, 1991.

Tanner, Tony. "The Literary Children of James and Clemens." *Nineteenth-Century Fiction* 16 (December 1961): 205–18.

# 12

# Mythic Revisionism: Women Poets and Philosophers in Italy Today

*Lucia Re*

Does it make sense to talk about "women poets" rather than "poets" tout court? There are strong disagreements on this issue and women poets are often the first ones to tell you that true poetry is gender-blind. I outline briefly here the current debate on the notion of sexual difference in order to reconsider "écriture féminine" in terms neither reductive nor metaphysical. Two Italian philosophers whose work I find challenging and useful have influenced my thinking on this subject:: Aldo Gargani and Adriana Cavarero. In particular, a 1984 text by Gargani entitled "La voce femminile" (The Feminine voice) and a recent book by Cavarero entitled *Nonostante Platone* (Despite Plato), will be focal points. In outlining a possible strategy for reading contemporary Italian women poets, I examine "mythic revisionism" as a practice of poetic writing that many—though certainly not all—women poets share; a practice that may amount to a specifically, though not exclusively, feminine aesthetic pursuit.

My strategy of reading women poets in terms of "mythic revisionism" has a threefold goal: (1) to contribute to the present inquiry among feminist critics into the specificity of women's writing; (2) to call attention to the complex relationship between Italian women poets and the (mostly) male canon in both stylistic and thematic terms; and (3) to see how through its probing of some of the fundamental mythologies of Western patriarchal culture, the work of women poets acquires a philosophical depth and symbolic import that make it one of the fundamental discourses through which humanity (not just women) is rethinking itself at the end of a millennium dominated by patriarchy and its symbolic order.

I refer mainly to the work of the contemporary Italian women poets Rossana Ombres, Maria Luisa Spaziani, Rosita Copioli, and Amelia Rosselli, as well as to the philosophical work of Cavarero and Luisa Muraro. In my readings of their texts I demonstrate what are the stakes involved, for Italian women poets and for the canon of modern Italian poetry, as well as for certain mythologies of Western patriarchal thought, in the critical-creative practice of mythical revisionism. Why mix a discussion of philosophical texts with the analysis of poetic texts? I believe that the tasks of poetry and philosophy are never separated, but proceed hand in hand as elaborations of and responses to the logic of the symbolic order. As Cavarero's and others' critiques of Plato show, both discourses help to shape and perpetuate certain mythic constructions of gender and sexual difference entrenched in the practices of and reflections on human existence throughout history. They shape our intelligence, our sensibility, and our lives.[1]

First, then, does it make sense to speak of "women poets"? The Italian language itself, like French and English, seems to reject this concept. The word *poeta* is used for both women and men. There is, as Xavière Gauthier has pointed out in a famous piece, in all three languages the word "poetess," but it is a "ridiculous word . . . synonymous with foolish innocence . . . or old-lady respectability There are, however, women who write. Is their writing different from men's? In what ways does their writing call attention to the fact that they are women?" (160). The answer for many Italian women writers is: in no way. Giulia Niccolai, for example, gives an implicitly negative answer to the question when she says, provocatively: "I propose to use some texts as guinea pigs: texts by men and texts by women mixed up without the audience knowing which is which; and the audience will have to guess which ones are by men and which ones by women, independently of the subject matter."[2] Maria Luisa Spaziani—an altogether different poet—is also unwilling to accept the label "woman poet." Answering the same question, she asserts that "the individual voice of a woman poet was and is valuable in and of itself, for its emotional and moral uniqueness, the same singularity that differentiates important books written by men."[3]

Why should Italian women poets be so reluctant to accept this label, or to formulate a link between writing and gender? One answer lies in the way the word "feminine" has traditionally been used, with a host of connotations that women poets would understandably like to do without. Maria Luisa Spaziani is a case in point. Her voice has been called "feminine" because it is "lyrical," "singing," "graceful," and "melodious," and because her poetry reappropriates the dimension of the private and the experiential with a renewed ability to communicate them through language.[4] The stereotype of women's poetry as effusive, sentimental, and autobiographical is implicit here, a stereotype that has an uncanny ability to creep into the discourse of even well-meaning critics when they discuss poetry by women.[5] Another facet of this stereotype is the attribution to women's poetry of certain supposedly feminine qualities such as intuition and sensitivity. We need to free the word "feminine" from these stereotypical associations and explore its possible meanings in relation to poetry written by both men and women. What we need is, in effect, a new way of thinking about sexual difference and its impact on writing.

In her response to the same question, Amelia Rosselli gives a more thoughtful, if tentative, view of the question of writing and gender difference. She says that although in her work she has never felt compelled to specify or refer to her feminine identity as an author, there is a strong and voluntary link between her writing and her femininity, particularly visible in her early long poem, "La libellula," where she refers to the arduous psychosocial condition of women by picking up a theme first found in Rimbaud. But besides thematic concerns, is there a specifically linguistic difference in women's writing? Rosselli argues that this may not be so far-fetched as it appears: "That there exists a feminine linguistic differentiation is a strong possibility, in my view, whether it be a 'fourth world' kind of phenomenon or even of biological origin. It is obvious that in their writing women imitate men, and women's finding of artistic forms which are more genuinely, or even chemically, their own remains an open problem. But if a woman is conscious of this problem of course her writing becomes much more laborious!"[6] Femininity in writing by women, then, is not something that can be assumed, a biological or biographical given. It is rather a possibility, something to be uncovered or unveiled or, conversely, pursued and constructed.

Let's assume then, for the sake of discussion (although I realize my contention is far from proven) that it is legitimate to speak of "women poets" not because there are poets who incidentally happen to be women, but because something specific in their writing makes it different from men's. How does this difference become visible or readable?[7] It is only because women writers subscribe for the most part to a "masculine" system of signification—as Gauthier argues—that "men and women seem to speak approximately the same language; in other words women find their 'place' within the linear, grammatical, linguistic system that orders the symbolic, the superego, the law. It is a system based entirely upon one fundamental signifier: the phallus" (162). The destabilization of this system of signification then, may itself be seen as a mark of the feminine in writing. It has been argued that a woman author like Marguerite Duras, who writes of a restless, shifting and mysterious interiority, is an example of "feminine writing" in that she refuses to translate this interiority into a "masculine," clarifying, authoritative—and authoritarian— psychology (Di Battista, 288). Yet writing itself for Duras means to take on a masculine posture. "The woman who writes," she says in Les Parleuses, "disguises herself as a man." As writers, Duras feels, women are always clandestine: they exist, but almost in secret, as saboteurs and underground agents. Theirs is a kind of self-conscious mimicry and parody, or transgression through mimicry, of the institution of "male" authorship. Feminine writing as a specific discourse of femininity does not yet have a form: rather, it manifests itself only as deformation; it becomes audible or visible in the "holes in discourse, in the un-said, or in the non-sense" (Gauthier, 163). It often appears as a kind of madness.

This way of describing feminine writing, interesting as it is, makes it look much like the poetic practice of experimentalism and the avant-garde, from futurism on. And since the exponents of the avant-garde have mostly been men, we come to the paradox that feminine writing may after all belong—at least thus far—more to men than to women. This argument is not new; it is Julia Kristeva's. She claims that the subject experiences sexual difference not as a fixed opposition—man/woman—but as a process of differentiation. Only very recently have a few women writers produced work where the dissection of language reaches levels comparable to those of the real subverters of phallic dominance in discourse, Mallarmé, Lautréamont, Joyce, and Artaud. Kristeva is not alone in this view of the relation between writing and gender difference. Even Hélène Cixous, in "The Laugh of the Medusa" (which is itself one of the first examples of self-conscious feminine writing and mythic revisionism), states that, with a few exceptions, there has not yet been any writing that inscribes femininity; that is, a writing that does not subscribe to a masculine economy. The few exceptions include Kleist and Genet, whom she places alongside Colette and Duras. For Cixous, feminine writing, then, is not necessarily the domain of women writers, though of course she wishes that it would increasingly become so. Instead, feminine writing is often the domain of poets, "rather than novelists, allies of representationalism. Because poetry involves gaining strength through the unconscious and because the unconscious . . . is the place where the repressed manages to survive: women, or as Hoffmann would say, fairies" (250).

To speak of women poets, therefore, does not necessarily mean to speak of feminine writing, and vice versa. There are some obvious problems with this position, first and foremost, political. If feminine writing can be attributed to male writers, especially poets, it is all the easier to continue to ignore women poets, to continue to exclude them from symposia, anthologies, the literary canon. Therefore, while I am skeptical of positions such as Irigaray's, who argues the irreducibility of anatomical and physiological difference as a basis for gender difference in writing, I prefer to opt strategically for a compromise that allows me to pursue the question of gender difference in relation to writing and to read Italian women poets at the same time. This is dictated not by any firm hermeneutical faith, but rather by the specific historical circumstances of feminist theory and criticism on the one hand, and the problem, on the other, of the conspicuous glossing-over of the presence, authority, and importance of women poets in modern Italian literary culture.

A second reason for such a move is the hypothesis that although there might not *appear* to be any fundamental differences between the destabilizing rhetorical and stylistic strategies of the historical avant-gardes and what has been called "écriture féminine," this lack of difference may be due to a lack of serious scrutiny of texts—especially avant-garde texts—by women.[8] While it may be (rather trivially) true, as Rita Felski remarks, that "linguistic playfulness and nonlinear syntax are in no sense unique or specific to women" (37), is it true that James Joyce's and Dorothy Richardson's experimentations with the novel form amount to the same thing, and that gender plays no role in the differences detectable between their styles? How can we even begin to address such a question when the study of Richardson—as of most experimental women writers (even Stein, not to mention Italian writers)—is still in its infancy? Felski contends, as do other critics, that "the gender-specific qualities [of écriture féminine] can only be sought in [its] particular *content*, in representations of the female body or recent explorations of mother-daughter relationships for example, rather than in any stylistic features which can be designated as uniquely feminine" (38). This statement ought to give us pause. For how can we really go back to such a distinction between form and content, especially when we discuss poetry? Thematics make it easier to distinguish a male-authored from a female-authored text, true, but thematics are always imbricated with rhetoric, style, language. And language itself, as Patrizia Violi has shown, is far from being gender-blind, but rather bears the semiotic traces of the sexed nature of the speaking subject (209–11).

I prefer therefore to side with the philosophers Aldo Gargani and Adriana Cavarero. From Gargani I borrow a provocative definition of "feminine voice" that I believe can contribute to discerning a common thread or ethical tendency in the work of some Italian women poets today. From Cavarero I borrow (or steal) the notion of a feminine symbolic order, which will help me define what I have called the practice of mythic revisionism. "The feminine voice (in either written or spoken language)," writes Gargani, "is characterized by a tone that is fundamentally that of interrogation. The language of women for the most part does not build systems, does not put forward theses, it does not even tend toward the possession of facts. It lets itself be defined, rather, by its difference from all those attitudes. The style of the feminine voice manifests itself more in the form of interrogation, of questioning, than in that of statement. . . . It does not yearn for and it does not accept the mastery of facts claimed by men (that mastery by which one always ends up being mastered), because it senses in such mastery the blockage of intention, of will, of sense. . . . It discovers—beyond the facts, the theses and the systems built by men—the space of contingency, of intention, of sense. . . . The ethical nature of the feminine voice shines forth in the call it puts out to reach for all the signs, traces, and voices which have been forgotten or ignored."[9] Gargani is one of the foremost Italian critics of Western paradigms of rationality and metaphysics, whose "crisis" has led in turn to radical responses such as those of Gianni Vattimo and so-called *pensiero debole*. Gargani's suggestion, therefore, that what he calls the "feminine voice" points in the direction of different modes of (nonpatriarchal) thought is intended as a positive assessment of the alternate means the feminine voice offers for thinking and living beyond the crisis of (patriarchal) reason. Gargani points in particular to the work of Virginia Woolf and Ingeborg Bachmann as examples of feminine writing. Given the apparent stylistic disparity between these two writers, what are the qualities they share, what makes their voices feminine? "What constitutes the specificity of the feminine voice which diverse women writers share," writes Gargani, "is the tendency towards a sense which, faced with the resistance of the contractual truth ordinarily underwritten by men, fatefully manifests itself as a call, as a cry, as grieving. In every case it manifests itself as a propensity to describe, to go from a condition of truth to a condition of the sense of that truth, rather than the paranoid, systematic argumentation that fulfills the need for affirmation and mastery which normally motivates men."[10] The otherness of the feminine voice for

Gargani resides in its ability to probe the past, to recall and scrutinize the obliterated and forgotten, and to perceive alternate senses behind and beyond the official history and truth by which patriarchy abides. I am interested in showing how this otherness (*alterità*) of the feminine voice as defined by Gargani finds expression in the interrogation, undoing, and tentative reshaping of certain key mythic moments or figures (especially but not exclusively feminine ones) that are particularly significant in the symbolic order of Western patriarchal culture.

Adriana Cavarero points to some of these moments and figures in her book *Nonostante Platone*, and to their successive reinterpretations: the Greek gods and myths, then Homer's Odysseus, the Oedipus of Greek tragedy, Faust, Don Juan; and then the metamorphoses of these figures: the Oedipus of Freud, the Ulysses of Dante and Adorno, the Don Juan of Kierkegaard. Although the symbolic order can and does find other forms of expression, such as the philosophical treatise or lawbook, the power of a symbolic figure is incomparable for its communicative and evocative force. These mythic fugures, argues Cavarero, have the power to concentrate within themselves, in a sort of paradigmatic incarnation, the symbolic order that informs them. Their metamorphoses, however, take place within the historical development of the same symbolic order, which from the beginning is under the sign of patriarchy.[11] In it, a masculine subject, claiming to be neutral and universal, speaks its own centrality and locates around itself a world configured in its own image. Feminine figures have their place within this system as well, but always in reference to the masculine subject. For Zeus there will therefore be Hera, for Don Juan, Zerlina, and many others.

What happens, asks Cavarero, if one begins to reject the claim that this symbolic patriarchal order configures and gives meaning to the experiences of humanity as a whole? Once we question the centrality of male subjectivity, the entire symbolic structure of Western culture with its male and especially female figures begins to fall apart. The need for symbolic and mythic figures, however, remains. Where should a feminine symbolic order find these figures? There are two possibilities, Cavarero suggests. One is to create them. The imagination of women poets is one of the places where this creation occurs. The other is to steal them. To steal them, that is, from their "original" contexts, and in so doing to transform them, to invest them with different functions and meanings; to invent different subtexts for them. This is indeed the prerogative of the feminine voice in Gargani's view. And this is exactly what Cavarero herself does, taking up a series of female figures who occupy a very minor place in Plato's texts: Penelope, Demeter, Diotima, a young Thracian servant girl. Cavarero's entire project, which includes the unraveling of some complicated philosophical questions, is under the sign of Penelope, of her work of weaving and unweaving, which comes to symbolize at the same time the undoing of Western patriarchal thought and the construction of a feminine symbolic order.[12] For in Cavarero's revisionist version of her story, Penelope works on two different looms. On the first one she weaves the figures of a feminine symbolic order, while on the second she undoes the worn-out tapestry of the fathers.

I argue that there is a common project among several otherwise extremely different contemporary Italian women poets. This project I call mythic revisionism, whereby these poets "steal" old stories and change them utterly, so that they can no longer stand as foundations of collective male fantasy,[13] and become, rather, part of a feminine symbolic order. My first example is the myth of Orpheus and Eurydice. Orpheus is, from Ovid to Rilke and beyond, the quintessential figure of the male poet and his privileged object of desire and representation: woman. Why this myth should be particularly disturbing to women poets is made clear by an American poet, Alta. Of the passive Eurydice who exists only as the tragic object of Orpheus's love, she says:

> All the male poets write of orpheus
> as if they look back & expect
> to find me walking patiently
> behind them. they claim i fell into hell.
> damn them, i say.
> i stand in my own pain
> & sing my own song.[14]

Rossana Ombres's 1975 "Orfeo che amò Orfeo" (Orpheus, lover of Orpheus), a long poem that includes sections in both prose and verse, is an irreverent parody of both the classic myth of Orpheus and some stylistic features of canonical male poetry and poetic prose of the twenties and thirties. In Italian literary culture these two key decades of the seizure of power and the consolidation of the fascist regime coincided with the era of *ermetismo*, a poetic tendency coupling rarefied, evocative, but often impenetrable lyrical diction with an elegiac tone, and celebrating the "secrets" of self-made, small-scale, and unassuming personal mythologies. Although politically and ideologically ambiguous, such mythologies (Montale's "Occasioni," although not strictly a work of the hermeticist "school," would be the primary example) were interpreted retrospectively as poetic strategies of indirect "resistance" against the loud and violent mythologies of the regime, with its emphasis on the collective, the heroic, and the grandiloquent. Orpheus's journey into the underworld, his attempt—through poetry—to rescue the dead Eurydice and bring her back into the light became an allegory of *ermetismo*'s *mise en crypte* of poetic discourse and its retrospective salvific claims vis-à-vis Italian literary culture in a season of obscurity and political oppression.[15] A poem entitled "Dialogo" (Dialogue) by Salvatore Quasimodo, published in the 1949 volume *La vita non è sogno* (Life is not a dream), gives a clear sense of the persistence of the myth of Orpheus and Eurydice in this salvific key and its political significance in the years immediately following the fall of the fascist regime. The poem's speaker is a soldier coming home from the war, but he is also Orpheus mourning his Eurydice. Quasimodo skilfully superimposes the image of the loss of the lover on that of the loss and devastation brought by the war and the parallel loss of the Orphic poetic power to reclaim the dead. But this situation of loss is reversed by the end of the poem, when through the revivifying contact with the places of his youth and the recovery of his poetic voice, the poet envisions himself as capable of bringing Eurydice back to life and regaining his role as redeemer:

> Euridice è viva . . .
> E tu sporco ancora di guerra, Orfeo,
> come il tuo cavallo, senza la sferza,
> alza il capo, non trema più la terra:
> urla d'amore, vinci, se vuoi, il mondo.

> (Eurydice is alive . . .
> And you, still soiled from the war, Orpheus,
> like your horse, without a whip,
> raise your head, the earth is no longer shaking:
> scream with love, win, if you want, the world.)

The symbolic function of the mythic material of Orpheus and Eurydice is not limited to the hermeticist "period," however. Dino Campana's *Canti Orfici* (1914) constitutes one of the most powerful and idiosyncratic occurrences of the myth in Italian twentieth-century poetry. The entire text is written in a visionary mode inspired by a Nietzschean version of orphism, and tells of the poet's journey of initiation and purification from earthly passions. While the repertory of female characters runs the gamut of misogynist turn-of-the-century stereotypes, the virulence of some of Campana's sadistic fantasies about women's bodies points in the direction of futurist and fascist misogynist violence: "E allora figurazioni di un'antichissima vita libera, di enormi miti solari, di stragi di orge si crearono avanti al mio spirito. Rividi un'antica immagine, una forma scheletrica vivente per la forza misteriosa di un mito barbaro, gli occhi gorghi cangianti vividi di linfe oscure, nella tortura del sogno scoprire il corpo vulcanizzato, due chiazze due fori di palle di moschetto sulle sue mammelle estinte" (15). ("Then figurations of an ancient free life, of enormous solar myths, of slaughters of orgies were gathered in front of my spirit. I saw once again an ancient image, a skeletal form living through the secret strength of a barbaric myth, the eyes iridescent whirlpools shining with dark lymphs, in the torture of a dream to discover the vulcanized body, two stains two musket-ball holes in the extinguished breasts.") In the 1960s, Campana was celebrated by the new (male) poetic avant-garde (especially Sanguineti) as its only authentic predecessor and a true innovator. The persistence of the myth of Orpheus in the Italian poetic tradition reveals an ideological continuity in the articulation of the male poet's (Orpheus) relation to his ambiguous female object of love, loss, and representation (Eurydice), which transcends otherwise profound stylistic, thematic, and political differences.[16]

In explicit opposition to hermeticist pretenses of timelessness, Ombres sets her poem in a contemporary, historically marked present: the era of the triumph of consumer capitalism and selfish self-interest after the loss of postwar illusions. In so doing, however, Ombres does not set narrow limits to her poem's critique. She roots her Orpheus in the present in order to reach all the more effectively into the past and question the presuppositions of the myth as well as its significance and uses within the patriarchal symbolic order. In Ombres's irreverent version, Orpheus is a narcissist in love only with the image of himself as a young man. Women are repugnant to him, and he looks at Eurydice in disgust: "La verità è che Orfeo aveva sempre pensato che le donne fossero insolenti, buie e miserabili." ("The truth is that Orpheus had always thought that women were insolent, dark and wretched.") This fall of Orpheus from his exalted rank to a narcissist and misogynist is not just a sign of the times for Ombres. Rather, this latter-day Orpheus finally unmasks a syndrome that was always deeply embedded in patriarchy throughout the myth's metamorphoses from Ovid to Cocteau and after.

According to Cavarero the homosexual self-love advocated in Plato's *Symposium* reflects a fear of death and an obsession with the immortality of the soul whose corollary is a pervasive contempt for women as life-givers through the body, for bodies are destined to die. This contempt is coupled with a form of womb-envy (evident in the language of midwifery used by Plato's Socrates and echoed by poets from Dante to D'Annunzio), whereby the ability of women to give life is both an object of jealousy and of scorn because material rather than spiritual. The life-giving power of Orpheus in the classical myth, and especially his ability to give back to a woman, Eurydice, through poetry, is on the one hand a symbolic usurpation of the life-giving role of women, and on the other hand a stigmatization of it as worthless because—unlike poetry—it is material rather than spiritual. Orpheus's ultimate loss of Eurydice is a punishment for his inability to transcend completely (the desire for) the material, for the body and its life. In Ombres's poem Orpheus refuses to take Eurydice back out of Hades because he finds her pregnancy revolting and threatening. She is, he feels (and actually imagines that he can see), about to give birth to a monster: "Il feto che porta nella pancia la traspare. . . . La terra non deve avere più mostri!" (345). ("The fetus that she carries in her belly is clearly visible. . . . Earth must no longer have monsters!")

In Ombres's poem there is no attempt to glorify Eurydice, however. Ombres's Eurydice—a fashion model who loved money and fast cars (she died in an automobile accident) and earned a living posing for ads for "Jesus" shorts—is a grotesque example of feminine alienation, of the debasement of woman when she becomes nothing but the prostituted embodiment of male desire. The loss of Orpheus's mythic identity in Ombres's poem and his dismemberment by the frenzied Maenads (a motley group of Roman whores from the "Raccordo anulare" taking their revenge because he does not want to have sex with them) corresponds to a loss of voice: "la sua voce chissà dov'è, forse è, già sulla terra, finita nella gola di un uccello o, per estrema punizione, squittisce in un topo di chiavica." ("Who knows where his voice is, perhaps on earth, ended up in the throat of a bird or, as extreme punishment, in the squeaking of a sewer rat.") The voice of the poet here is not Orpheus's: rather it belongs to her, Rossana, who puts herself on stage with a flourish in signing her text:

> Orfeo amò Orfeo
> e la morte col suo infuriato esercito
> offensiva e ributtante
> abolì un amore così perfetto.
> Con l'anima tutta rattristata
> Rossana poetessa questa storia ha scritto.


> (Orpheus loved Orpheus
> and death with its furious army
> offensive and disgusting

abolished such a perfect love.
With a saddened soul
the poetess Rossana wrote this poem.)

Ombres's poem is shocking for at least two reasons. One is its grotesque debasement of a classical myth that concerns the very origins of poetry. The second is its low diction and obscene tone: both are as removed as possible from the kind of lyrical sensitivity associated with women poets. Indeed, the very writing of a long poem runs counter to the common expectations about women poets. Implicit in Ombres's revisionist retelling of the myth of Orpheus is a sweeping indictment of a kind of male-authored poetry that in twentieth-century Italy is associated particularly (but not exclusively) with the tradition of *ermetismo* and its aftermath. Implicit here is the notion that such poetry and much of the lyric belonging to the Western patriarchal tradition is but a cover-up for self-indulgent narcissism and misogyny.

Ombres's critique extends to the language in which these contents are embedded, taking issue with its ambiguity as a cover-up for the violence of representation:

> Solo il vento ha la spavalderia
> di dire Orfeo nei suoi ululati
> ma così criptico è il suo linguaggio
> una carezza può essere una feroce percossa.
>
> (353)

> (Only the wind has the boldness
> to say Orpheus in its howlings
> but so cryptic is its language
> that a caress could be a ferocious beating.)

Her own language has none of the ambiguity she chastises. Its violence is not the hidden violence of symbolic representation but the direct, explicit sarcasm of a latter-day Juvenal or Parini. Along with the mythology of Orpheus the male poet, Ombres rejects both the rarefied, cryptic diction of the hermeticist mode and the play with the polysemic potentials of language of *neoavanguardia* poets such as Sanguineti. This is in no way a "beautiful" poem; in many ways it is a very "ugly" poem, with a strong scatological undercurrent and an uncomfortable tendency to dwell on the most grotesque aspects of the body and its potential disfigurements, with none of Bosch's visionary appeal.

But then, the kind of aesthetic prejudice that makes me say this is precisely what Ombres's poem sets out to subvert. In all fairness to Ombres it must be said that I have chosen to focus on this poem[17] because it is one of the clearest examples I know of a sharply *critical* mythic revisionism.

Ombres's version of mythic revisionism in "Orfeo amò Orfeo" is satiric and savagely critical but, for all its demystification of the myth and the language in which it is embedded, it does not provide either a countermyth or a counterlanguage capable of articulating a feminine symbolic order other than in negative, "destructive" terms. As in Montale's famous lines, what this poem tells us is only "ciò che non siamo, ciò che non vogliamo" ("That which we are not, that which we do not want"). There are, however, at least two other strategies of mythic revisionism in Italian poetry by twentieth-century women. One—which we might call the "constructive" approach (as opposed to the "destructive" one taken by Ombres)—subverts a powerful patriarchal myth by replacing it with a myth that "founds" (or restores) a feminine symbolic order. The poets who pursue this second strategy, while at odds with the dominant male tradition of poetic language, do not reject it completely. Rather, they take from it what they need to forge their own language and symbolic framework. The third strategy, which we might call "deconstructive," pursues the same kind of radical, demystifying critique as the first, but it neither believes that a radical break with the dominant male tradition and language is possible nor does it trust its own capacity for (re)creating alternative mythologies, even though it relentlessly pursues this possibility. Its language does not seek to expose or explode hermeticism and ambiguity, nor does it attempt to restore a fullness of signification capable of giving myth a firm grounding in truth or belief. Rather, it engages in strenuous, painful play with the resources of language and the poetic tradition to eviscerate them from within, to lay bare their ideological stratifications as well as their potential for difference. None of these strategies is necessarily superior to the others in my view, and while the third, typified by the work of Amelia Rosselli, holds the fascination of being the most complex and arduous, the second—for which I have chosen as paradigmatic examples the work of Maria Luisa Spaziani and Rosita Copioli—has the appeal of clarity, rhetorical efficacy, and a sharp political edge.

A short poem by Spaziani entitled "Mitologia" (Mythology) from the 1966 collection *Utilità della memoria* (Usefulness of memory), may serve as an introduction to the second, "constructive" strategy of mythic revisionism. Spaziani takes mythic female figures associating woman with death (the Parcae or fates), destruction (Penelope unweaving at night what she wove during the day), and emasculation (the Danaids who killed their husbands with daggers and were punished by having forever to carry water in leaking jars), and turns these figures upside down. In her version, the Parcae's work of death turns out to be that of life itself. Unlike the thread-cutting Parcae, women, Spaziani claims, are rather thread-weavers, like Penelope. At night Penelope does not in fact unweave but rather reweaves the threads that a "beloved hand" (presumably that of her husband, the warring Odysseus) has torn and cut during the day. And the Danaid's restless work, in another inversion, turns out to be not a futile act but one essential to life—the life that male violence constantly threatens. Spaziani rewrites these female figures not as destroyers but as saviors and life-givers. They are saviors, in particular, of other women, and of themselves. And it is male violence—sometimes the violence of the men closest to them—that has necessitated their taking on these roles. The truth, then, is the opposite of the "official" version. Spaziani's unassuming way of conveying her message (tentative at first but then, in stanzas 2 and 3, unambiguously affirmative) is particularly effective:

> Basta soltanto essere in vita, a volte:
> e simili alle Parche
> tagliamo i fili della vita altrui,
> avveleniamo il sangue di chi amiamo.
> Ma più sovente, forse, capovolte
> Penelopi tra gli ospiti nemici,
> ritessiamo di notte it cento fili
> che va strappando la diletta mano;
> come Danaidi senza mai riposo
> ricolmiamo le vasche del respiro
> che ci succhia (più stretto si fa il giro)
> l'uomo lupo agli uomini.

> (It is enough to be alive, sometimes:
> and like the Parcae
> we cut the threads of others' lives,
> poison the blood of those we love.
> But more often, perhaps, upended
> Penelopes among the enemy guests,
> we reweave at night the hundreds of threads
> that a beloved hand keeps tearing;
> Like Danaids without ever any rest
> we fill the basins of breathing

that (as the circle tightens)
is sucked from us by
man, wolf to other men.)

Spaziani's language, here and elsewhere, has the virtue of clarity and conci-
sion. Even in such a short poem the classical elegance of her style is evident.
"La diletta mano" (The Beloved hand) is a phrase that echoes Leopardi and
Carducci. Montale, Pascoli, and the *crepuscolari* are other important influ-
ences in her work, as she charges autobiographical detail and confessional
material with mythic resonance.[18] Contrary to her male predecessors,[19] however, Spaziani's central semantic axis—the mythic framework that persists
throughout her poetry—opposes an economy of life and affirmation to one
of death and negativity.

Spaziani's particular approach to re-vision consists of appropriating not
only traditional mythic figures of the patriarchal tradition, but also the language of her male predecessors, while reversing their message. This is visible
in another poem from *Utilità della memoria* entitled "L'antica pazienza," dedicated to the author's mother:

L'allegria rialza la sua cresta
di galletto sui borghi desolati,
come il lillà che ti cresce alle spalle
passo a passo, baluardo sul massacro.
Raccogli ancora e sempre il pigolante
nido abbattuto dal vento di marzo
e ripara le falle della chiglia.
Nessuno è senza casa se l'attende
a sera la tua voce di conchiglia.

(Joy raises once again its cockerel
crest over the desolate villages,
like the lilies growing behind your shoulders
step by step, bulwark against the massacre.
Pick up once again and forever the chirping
nest thrown down by the march wind,
and fix the leaks in the keel.
No one whom your seashell voice
awaits in the evening
is without a home.)

These lines (the last nine of the poem) interweave allusions to Pascoli ("il pigolante nido") and Leopardi ("galletto," "borghi desolati") and their respective semantic universes with, in the final five lines, an imperative and a closing *sententia* that are almost transparently molded from Montale, except that they carry a message of hope and being-at-home-in-the-world whose strength is alien to all three male poets. Although the centrality of maternal or life-giving figures in Spaziani's poems is hardly peculiar to women poets, male poets tend to celebrate maternal figures from the point of view of death rather than life.[20]

Whether the concern with death and negativity may be extended beyond Spaziani's three male predecessors to the entire corpus of Western poetry written by men is a question whose implications are beyond my scope here, but I shall nevertheless pursue it briefly in light of my discussion of mythic revisionism. In his poetically and philosophically charged essay "Il remo di Ulisse" (The Oar of Odysseus), the contemporary poet and critic Luigi Ballerini concludes his reading of Odysseus's second journey by stating that "La poesia si costituisce come esercizio di fronte alla morte" (138). ("Poetry is constituted as an exercise in the face of death.") For Ballerini, all of Odysseus's skill and resourcefulness never represent an epistemic breakthrough for him. His coming home is merely a *restoration* to his wife and land, the stuff of which *narrative* prose, not poetry, is made. He will be restored, that is, to a world of (implicitly inauthentic) *limits* and institutional meanings and feelings. Only with his second voyage, where, according to Ballerini, Homer intimates he will encounter death, will he also acquire a different form of cognition, coinciding with poetry: "Homer gives no more details about this second journey . . . but they are enough to suggest beyond the narrative ceremony—which, as we have seen, constitutes the 'matter,' the 'prose' of the first return—the 'necessary rituality,' the 'poetry' of the second, an activity whose meaning gravitates around, draws life from, a type of *cognition* that is separate from *recognition* and oftentimes antithetical to it."[21]

In *Nonostante Platone*, Adriana Cavarero expresses a similar view of the meaning of Odysseus's last journey as centering on the experience of the limit and of death, but she opposes to this an antithetical reading of Penelope and the symbolic significance of *her* experience after Odysseus's last departure. Her reading is based on an interpretation of the crucial image of the sea as *il limite*, which forms the core of a poem about Penelope by Bianca Tarozzi:

> Ora discesa
> sulla riva, dal mare risuonante
> sente voci lontane, antichi naufraghi,

fantasmi che la vogliono afferrare:
tutte le guerre che non ha perduto
nè vinto,
tutti gli amori che non ha vissuto
il dolore e il furore degli eroi,
che non le spetta:
scempio,
dolce urlare del vento
dentro l'anima.
Ritorna sui suoi passi.
L'esperienza
del limite per lei
è l'acqua incollerita della riva—
per Ulisse lo schianto
e la fine tremenda
contro gli scogli, verso la leggenda.[22]

(Now descended
on the shore, from the resounding sea
she hears far-away voices, ancient shipwrecks,
ghosts that want to grab her:
all the wars she has neither lost
nor won,
all the loves she has not lived
the sorrow and wrath of the heroes,
which does not belong to her:
devastation,
sweet screaming of the wind
inside the soul.
She retraces her steps.
The experience
of the limit for her
is the raging water against the shore—
for Ulysses the crash
and the awful end
against the rocks, toward legend.)

While the sea grants to Odysseus an ending adequate to the meaning of his existence (he cannot die at home, because he is, Cavarero says, the "else-where of eventful action"), for Penelope the seashore marks the experience of the limit. Penelope's and Odysseus's experiences of the limit are conceptually "asymmetrical," argues Cavarero. For Odysseus it is death that measures the limit. The sea is the place of that limit because the threat of death is always present in it, not only because the sea is dangerous but because it leads to occasions for death: Polyphemus, Circe, the Mermaids. Shipwrecks, transits, and arrivals turn, every time, into another potential death. Odysseus experiences the limit almost as the goal of his wanderings, before yielding to it once and for all. Each of his adventures is but one trial in a series that leads to the definitive one. Death constitutes the border, the limit of *his* realm. Yet death is also always present because it is always challenged, and is the measure of the challenger's strength. Indeed, Cavarero concludes, in Homer's world of "i mortali," only legend defeats the limit and gives eternal life, and only the human challenge to the limit can become legend.

For Penelope the sea represents the limit in an altogether different way. The realm of death borders on her house—her island—but only as a foreign region of "wars that she has neither won nor lost," events that do not concern her and that she does not know. For her, the place of the experience of the limit is not the whole sea, with its irresistible ambush of death, but only the circumscribed shore. Although this limit may be seen as a confinement imposed by the patriarchal order, this is so only if we adopt that order's critical perspective, Cavarero claims. If we look at it with Penelope's eyes instead, we see the shore not as a prison, but as that which excludes, holds at a distance, an alien world inhabited by men. Penelope knows that the sea is Odysseus's, and lets him go and stake the meaning of his being on his confrontation with death. She, for her part, does not resign herself to the confined role Odysseus has imposed on her. Penelope turns her room into her own legend: "La vedo ridere con le ancelle mentre insieme tessono vesti ad esse confacenti, narrando di come tennero in scacco i Proci insieme scoprendo la letizia di quello stare fra di loro lavorando e pensando. La vedo, le vedo, in quell'isola, che ora straordinariamente separa con mitica chiarezza due mondi estranei, parlare di nascita e di radicamento piuttosto che di morte e di avventura, guardando dalle finestre quel limite di acqua incollerita che le separa dalle gesta degli eroi e consente loro di stare su una terra ben ferma dove il gesto tesse un primo luogo non più minacciato di libertà femminile. Un primo orizzonte di appartenenza il quale lascia altrove il maschile affaccendarsi in quel regno della morte che esso ha scelto a sua misura e a limite estremo dei suoi sanguinosi orizzonti" (23). ("I see her laugh with her maidens while together they weave garments that suit them, telling of how they kept the suitors at bay and discovering the joy of their being together, working and thinking. I see her, I see them, on that island that now extraordinarily separates with mythic clarity two worlds foreign to each other, speak of birth and of rootedness rather than of adventure and death, looking through the windows at that limit of raging waters that separates them from the deeds of heroes and allows them to stay on dry land where a gesture weaves a first, no longer threatened, place of feminine freedom. A first horizon of belonging that leaves elsewhere man's bustling with death, which he has chosen as his measure and the extreme limit of his bloody horizons.") Cavarero's text on Penelope is indeed, as is apparent from this passage, a prose poem, and as such it intends to mark a different way of "thinking," of doing philosophy, outside or on the margins of the patriarchal tradition. The image of Penelope with her maidens in the house, laughing and thinking ("laughing" as a form of demystification of the "foundational lie" of Western philosophy forms the subject of the second chapter of Cavarero's book), may be read as an allusion to the Diotima group (or rather, as they call themselves, "philosophical community") of women philosophers, which includes Cavarero and Luisa Muraro. Cavarero's and Muraro's philosophical works are attempts to delineate that "other" mode of thinking and that "first horizon of belonging" that Cavarero attributes symbolically to Penelope and her women.

Central to such a new mode of thinking is Hannah Arendt's notion that throughout the history of Western philosophy we find the persistent, singular idea of an affinity between philosophy and death (to which Arendt wishes to oppose a form of thought rooted in the life-giving). The first philosopher to express such an idea is Plato in the *Phaedo*, when he says that the philosopher appears to those who do not do philosophy as someone pursuing death. Although orphism is the direct predecessor of the Platonic theory of "living for death," it is Plato's thought that comes to have a determining influence on the entire course of Western philosophy, argues Cavarero. And it is to the *Phaedo* that Cavarero turns to show that death is as central to the project of Western metaphysics as it is to the wanderings of Odysseus. The (male) poet (Ballerini's Odysseus, but also the poet as Orpheus of the hermeticist tradition) and the (male) philosopher yearn for a form of cognition only death can yield.[23]

Plato argues that philosophy, by taking thought toward the eternal objects (ideas) suitable to it, *unbinds* the soul from the mortal body. Those who lament death (Socrates' death is imminent) are bad philosophers, because death is but the definitive unbinding of soul from body. Plato compares these bad philosophers to Penelope, because they want to bind again that which they have unbound with philosophy, in an endless work that renders vain

what has been achieved. Cavarero notes that the metaphor is strange, because it uses an inversion: the absurd act for the philosophers is to reweave
what they have undone, while for Penelope it is absurd to unweave that
which she has already woven. But Plato's strange or inverted use of the metaphor allows Cavarero to make Penelope the symbolic figure of a philosophical
mode antithetical to Plato's. Plato's metaphoric play allows us to see Penelope's weaving as a reuniting of the soul with the body. As with Penelope and
her women, there is in Plato a notion of dwelling or home, but it is not, like
the weaving room at Ithaca, on this earth; it is not a being-at-home-in-the-
world. On the contrary, for Plato this world and the life to which one is born
represent a form of estrangement. Birth itself is seen as negative, the *fall* of
the soul into the body, matter, passions, desire. For the soul this sojourn in
the body represents an imprisonment from which the exercise of philosophy
can begin to free it in expectation of that definitive liberation that death will
bring by lifting up the soul once again to the realm of ideas.

Plato's philosophy, Cavarero points out, is based on a semantic estrangement separating the concept of life from those of birth and death, although
the latter belong to every living being's experience of life. It is the life of
the soul, an eternal life without birth or change or death, that becomes the
paradigm, so that life loses its connotations of birth and death, leaving these
to the body, which is correspondingly devalued. This complex operation of
semantic estrangement and devaluing of the body marks the crucial beginning of a process of "de-signification of the necessarily corporeal dimension
of living, which in turn inhibits the symbolic translation of sexual difference"
(27). "In other terms," she continues, "a corporeality that is separated and
de-realized lends itself more easily to not being seen in its sexual connotation,
always marked by difference, so that the male sex can more easily pretend its
neutrality and universality." The work of Cavarero and the other women of
the Diotima group seeks to restore to thought a series of dimensions (first and
foremost that of sexual difference) which the "foundational lie" of Western
metaphysics has systematically excluded since Plato. Opposing the devaluing
of the real and of material experience inherent in Platonic thought, Cavarero
and the Diotima group seek to elaborate a form of thought in which the fundamental categories are, along with sexual difference, the experiences of
birth, receiving and giving life, the link with the mother, the body, and the
notions of dwelling, at-homeness and rootedness. Penelope the weaver, after
Odysseus's last departure, becomes the symbolic figure for such thought:
"Penelope is in effect a weaver, and now perhaps, thanks to Plato, we know
what she kept on weaving, with her handmaidens, when the last event was

consummated at sea leaving her quietly with the experience of the limit which marked her horizon of belonging. She kept weaving that singular wholeness of body and thought that was already manifest in her *métis*, that reality where to live is above all to be born and then, only at the end, also to die. Hers is that interweaving of intelligence and sensibility where every living human being—not eternal soul fallen into a body, of any kind or sex— exists in his or her kind and gender: she, like the handmaidens, a woman keeping woven together their thoughts and their bodies in a home of their own that leaves elsewhere the male gymnasium of death."[24]

In Cavarero's outline of a feminist mode of philosophical thought, the categories of birth—being born, and giving birth—and the figure of the mother are paramount. Cavarero proposes a new reading of the myth of Demeter. The myth tells that when Demeter's only daughter, Persephone, is taken away from her to marry Hades and live in the underworld, Demeter withholds her gifts from the earth, which becomes sterile. The threat of sterility and death convinces Hades to send Persephone back to her mother for a brief period each year, in the spring when fecundity returns to the earth. The central theme of the myth, according to Cavarero, is maternal power, inscribed in the whole of nature; the power, that is, not only to generate, but *not* to generate, to give and to withhold life. The devastation and silence Demeter's grief brings to the earth, are to be read as figures of a traumatic response to the violation of an original maternal order. Hades, with the complicity of other male divinities, raped Persephone and deported her to the kingdom of death. The symbology could not be clearer: to the feminine order of birth and life- giving is opposed a masculine order of death. Toward the end of her book, Cavarero cites *The Passion According to G. H.*, a work of poetic prose by the experimental Brazilian woman writer Clarice Lispector. Cavarero takes Lispector's itinerary of self-discovery as an emblem of a philosophical itinerary radically different from that of patriarchal thought. Taking the form of a daughter's address to her mother, Lispector's reflection on life and death succeeds in "destructuring the centrality of the omnipotent and bodiless self which had grown up feeding on the metaphysics of nothingness. Lispector does descend into the neutrality of impersonal life, but not in order to find simply the annihilation of the self there. On the contrary, she finds once again that maternal and sexed root that binds itself to impersonal life itself, and every living being to its beginning" (117). The fundamental coordinates for retracing a feminine symbolic order, Cavarero concludes, consist in taking the here and now of the living singular human being and looking backward, to the past: "towards a rootedness that preserves the meaning of origin, rather than forward, foreseeing and pro-jecting limits and obsessive ways of de-feating individual mortality" (119). The backwards glance of the singular human being encounters first of all the figure of a mother who has given birth to him or her. And the mother, Cavarero says, paraphrasing Lispector, is in many ways the *threshold* "between the irreducible and full given of each singular living individual and the world from which this singularity comes and against which it takes relief: a world that already is, that exists before (and also without) this singularity" (120).

With its rejection of Cartesian skepticism as well as of Platonic Idealism, and its richly suggestive notions of the need to look back to an origin, of the mother as threshold, and of a feminine economy of gazes that alone can mediate the recovery of a feminine symbolic order, Cavarero's text lays the foundations for a feminine/feminist metaphysics. For indeed, despite its emphasis on the body, experience, and the incontrovertible reality of sexual difference, hers is not a traditionally secular and materialist mode of thinking. Although Marx, Gramsci, Freud, and Nietzsche have all visibly influenced her thought, the crucial step of positing sexual difference as a fundamental category of thought is not the only discriminant between her way of thinking and theirs. Unlike them, she is essentially not so much a secular thinker as a "religious" thinker. I do not mean that she posits the existence of a God or that she falls into any recognizable theological "school." Yet it is from Irigaray's work that Cavarero, and other women philosophers of the Diotima group develop a sense that feminist thought needs to believe in belief, and particularly in the belief in an origin—hidden and sacrificed—from which alone the meaning of a (repressed, displaced) feminine symbolic order can issue. In Cavarero's reading of the myth of Demeter, for example, the possibility of a feminine economy of gazes and a mother-daughter bond is predicated on that bond having been there originally, and on its having been hidden and sacrificed by patriarchal violence. This is precisely Irigaray's version of the "myth of origins." The hidden act of violence that stains (and founds) Western civilization is not—as Freud thought—a patricide, but rather (as Euripedes suggests in the *Oresteia*) a matricide. Reinterpreting Heidegger's diagnosis of the destiny of Western metaphysics and its fulfillment in a modern world plagued by the triumph of technology, Irigaray points to the sacrifice of the mother and the rejection of living nature as the beginning of that collective forgetting of being which has led the world to its self-destruction, because it has forgotten its vital origin. The sense of this vital origin can be recuperated only through the restoration of a female genealogy, that mother-daughter bond for which—to Irigaray as well as Cavarero—the myth of Demeter and Perse-phone is the most pertinent figure.[25]

While Cavarero maintains a degree of reticence vis-à-vis the restoration of a metaphysical dimension to philosophical thought, and the need for a grasp of the "sacred," and prefers elegant literary allusiveness to direct state-ment, Luisa Muraro is an unabashed advocate of metaphysics, and openly discusses mysticism in her short book, *L'ordine simbolico della madre* (The Sym-bolic order of the mother). This strange, partly autobiographical book is writ-ten in a straightforward, colloquial, and at times almost pedestrian style that intentionally breaks with the traditional difficulty of philosophical jargon. The book includes its own commentary and self-critique, in the form of end-notes, and thus rejects the traditional format of the finalized, polished philo-sophical tract, taking on an appearance that, following Bakhtin, we might call "dialogical" in that it is constantly open to (self-)questioning and seeks to incorporate the perspectives of other women. "The unruly appearance of my writing," Muraro explains, "is due to the fact that my writing obeys rules that are still little known or not yet established" (64). The language Muraro seeks to adopt evolves in part from the author's experience of dialogues with other women and the so-called *pratica dell'autocoscienza* of the Italian feminist movement: "The practice of consciousness raising [*presa di coscienza*] leads one to discover that the real world is that which is given in our experience through the word and in the word through experience. This discovery is equivalent, in my view, to the rediscovery of the point of view of the origin, when the world was born along with us and our learning how to speak" (80). Muraro's book is based on a basic, fundamental "intuition" (as she calls it), that represents a turning point in her thinking and writing. For Muraro the entire history of Western philosophy is the story of the alteration and there-fore the *oblivion* of the meaning of being initially glanced at in the Greeks' most ancient thought (Parmenides' fragments in particular). This oblivion, Muraro claims, is due to one cause: the cultural repression (*rimozione*) of our relationship with the mother, by which she means literally the woman who gave us birth as well as, symbolically, the matrix of life itself.

The loss of the mother and the loss of the truth of being are one and the same for Muraro. Hers is an unabashedly metaphysical statement, and she acknowledges metaphysics as the proper sphere and tradition from which her discourse stems: "Metaphysics is where truth rules as the meaning of being" (25). Muraro defines being for metaphysics as "the energy capable of driving back [*respingere*] nothingness [*il nulla*] away from itself" (26). "I accept metaphysics," Muraro states at one point, "but I reject that which in metaphysics tends to render superfluous the work of the mother and to invalidate its authority" (73). Muraro rejects, that is, all forms of nihilism, which she perceives to be the tragic consequence of the repression and loss of the mother.

Nihilism takes three major forms, in Muraro's view. One conceives of being as originally limited by nothingness and destined to end in nothingness—a being that is absurdly indifferent to being or not being. The second form separates being from thinking and conceives of them as mutually independent. Finally, the third conceives of being as indifferently true or false. It is a nihilism of being as fiction, of being as simulacrum, whose principal resource is that of being *believed* to be true (29).[26] The authentic sense of being must be rescued from these three forms of nihilism. Muraro, like Cavarero, cites *The Passion According to G. H.* as a crucial feminist text. For Muraro, it is an example of a mystical-poetic discourse that succeeds in recovering the pure presence of being (the unsayable) through an experience of the failure of language. Mysticism, Muraro asserts, is a "shortcut" to the recovery of being to which women often resort (she points out that the mystical tradition is mostly a women's tradition).

Muraro is careful to distinguish between her notion of "the mother" and her symbolic authority and a theological notion of God: "The maternal greatness of which I speak is of a symbolic, not of an ontological order. . . . I do not see greatness in the fact of putting children into the world. . . . The woman who has put me into the world is great because of her precedence, for her being upstream of every one of my choices and my greatness, which gives her a unique and unmatchable greatness, not substantial in itself but for the position she definitively occupies" (129). Muraro's is a metaphysics of the origin, fully inscribed within the tradition that poststructuralist philosophers such as Derrida and Vattimo have sought to deconstruct or "weaken." Paradoxically, metaphysics, which has come to be viewed in the postmodern era as fundamentally mystifying and oppressive, acquires, from the point of view of Muraro's feminism, an unexpectedly radical and liberatory potential for women.

What leads women mystics, asks Muraro, to skip altogether the "step of beginning to tell the truth, and to aim instead directly at the unsayable in order to leave fiction [the fiction of nihilism] behind?" (33). And, she asks, "what leads those who do instead commit themselves to the regime of mediation [language], much too often, to failure?" One answer is the inadequacy of patriarchal language to serve as a tool for women's self-signification. But the inadequacy of language as mediation is due first and foremost to a lack of an authentic symbolic authority for women, the authority to affirm "what is"— which language does possess and which we acquire when we learn how to speak. While it is true that language, as a social product, reproduces the historical condition of the female subject in the system of social relations, "language is not reducible to a product, being in turn a producer of the social, and this from the time of the exchange of life and the word with the mother. As such, it is capable of assisting effectively women's coming to consciousness [presa di coscienza] and to the word" (130). The apparent inadequacy of language, Muraro affirms, thus arriving at the core of her theory, can be overcome only by recovering in our adult lives the original relation with the mother and adopting it as a principle of symbolic authority. It is the original relation with the mother that "gives us a lasting and true point of view on the real . . . , true in accordance with the metaphysical truth that does not separate being from thought and nourishes itself with the reciprocal interest of being and language" (46).

One of the fundamental myths of patriarchal culture (a kind of original "theft of language") is, according to Muraro, the notion that "as culture separates itself and us from nature, so it is necessary that we separate ourselves from our mother and turn our back on the experience of our relation with her, in order to enter the social and symbolic order, the principal agent of this separation being the father" (42).[27] On this myth is predicated the notion that "it is a structural characteristic of the symbolic order that our experience of our relation with the matrix of life cannot be expressed and does not therefore constitute a point of view. This perspective—the cornerstone of the Lacanian concept of language and the symbolic order—is in Muraro's view false, because "we learn to speak from our mother or someone who functions as mother . . . and we learn to speak as part of our vital relationship with her" (42). Contrary to Julia Kristeva, who in Revolution in Poetic Language posits the loss of the original relationship with the mother and the separation from her (the "thetic cut" or "break") as necessary for the child's entry into the symbolic, Muraro argues that the symbolic order necessarily begins to establish itself in the relationship with the mother, and that the "break" which separates us from her is not an inherent structural necessity of the symbolic. Rather, the "thetic break" describes a historically determined, contingent symbolic order, the symbolic order of patriarchy where, as stated by Luce Irigaray, men have usurped the power of the mother, destroyed her genealogy, and inserted women, one by one, into male genealogies instead.[28]

Can the symbolic order be changed, asks Muraro? Yes: a change can occur in the symbolic through the practice of *autocoscienza*, which amounts to a revolution:

> In order to understand what this revolution is, we need to reconsider the symbolic order by not limiting it to reconstructible codes (such as the economic system and the political one, the law, etc.) . . . We need to reconsider it in terms of its actuality, as a system of mediations on which I depend in order to say what I am saying and what I am unable to say and in general all that is sayable and desirable for me, etc. It is at this level of mediation . . . that the symbolic order reproduces itself and can be changed. . . . But can we *plan* to change the symbolic order? That it can change is shown by history. But does it make sense to conceive of a politics for its modification, as I suggest on the basis of the women's political movement? I think yes. The symbolic order belongs, without doubt, to the deep structure of human reality, which makes us be this way or that way unbeknownst to us. This, however, does not exclude, I believe, the possibility that it can become the object of a modifying intention. (93–94)

As Muraro acknowledges, her idea of an *accordo* among being, the real, and language—mediated by the mother—echoes the notion of an original concord between subject and world formulated by the German philosopher of language von Humboldt. Paul de Man identified the symbol-allegory dichotomy in preromantic and romantic literature as the difference between, on the one hand, a world—the world of the symbol—in which it would be possible for language and image to coincide with being, and for the self to identify with the world (or nonself) from which it springs; and, on the other hand, the world of allegory, where no such identification is possible—allegory "designates primarily a distance in relation to its own origin, and, renouncing the nostalgia and the desire to coincide, it establishes its language in the void of this temporal difference" (207). Unlike Muraro, whose entire project is precisely under the aegis of the symbol, de Man himself denounces the symbol as a mystification and attributes to allegory authenticity and truth: "[Allegory] prevents the self from an illusory identification with the non-self, which is now fully, though painfully, recognized as non-self. It is this painful knowledge that we perceive at the moments when early romantic literature finds its true voice" (207). Muraro's perspective—which would inscribe de Man's stand within the forms of nihilism she denounces—allows us to rethink the ideological (patriarchal) bias of de Man's preference for allegory as a rhetorical strategy. Allegory is the dominant figure of the historical avant-gardes first, and of modernism and the postmodern.[29] But allegory is also, in Benjamin's influential definition, the figure of death and mourning, which seeks to destroy all "illusion" of organicity and totality of being. In this light, the apparently retrograde return to the symbol as a rhetorical strategy, and the antimodernist, anti-avant-garde stand of a poet like Rosita Copioli, assume a particular interest, especially since she seems to have taken Muraro's impassioned philosophical manifesto to heart, and to have placed her entire poetic endeavor under the sign of the mother.

"My youth having been afflicted by the avant-gardes of the 1960s," writes Rosita Copioli in a recent autobiographical statement, "I remained faithful to myself with my work on myth, nature, and the imagination" ("Per l'anniversario," 100). Copioli's second volume of poetry, *Furore delle rose* ("Wrath of the roses," an expression, Copioli explains, that gardeners use in some areas of the Emilia-Romagna region of Italy to refer to the peak of roses' blooming season in May), starts with a section (significantly entitled "Origini") that in turn begins with a long poem devoted to a mythic mother, "Mater Matuta." Impressive for its formal elegance, elevated style and diction, and complex rhetorical figurations, this poem takes the form of an address and prayer to the mother comparable in intensity and sustained breadth of vision to the highest compositions of two of Copioli's male predecessors: D'Annunzio and W. B. Yeats.

Copioli's admiration for Yeats is documented by her excellent critical work on him.[30] The strength of D'Annunzio's influence is less obvious, due in part to D'Annunzio's peculiar history of reception in modern Italian literary culture, where, for reasons that have little to do with the intrinsic value of his texts, he became associated with "decadent" fin-de-siècle excess and shallow formal versatility on the one hand, and with reactionary politics on the other. No Italian poet as a consequence openly admits D'Annunzio's influence, although no one writing poetry in Italy in this century is unmarked by his poetic presence. It is curious that Copioli should find in D'Annunzio and Yeats—whose exploitation of a repertoire of degrading images of women is well known—a source of inspiration. I do not mean that Copioli is in any way a "D'Annunzian" poet. What she does take from D'Annunzio (I am thinking of the epic D'Annunzio of *Maia* and the "Laus Vitae"), and, to a lesser extent, from Yeats, is a propensity to speak poetically in an elevated, visionary style, of matters pertaining to the sacred, the origin, and myth, and at the same time of the lyrical self.

Copioli avoids the fragmentation and syncopation of neo-avant-garde poets such as Sanguineti, opting rather for a full syntax, distended rhythms, and a sumptuous imagery. Like D'Annunzio, Copioli makes abundant use of complex figures such as paronomasia, oxymora, and chiasmus, in ways that are creative (in the sense that these figures help to generate new, surprising consonances of meaning) rather than simply decorative. She also avoids the rhetoric of the unpoetic that marks many exponents of the neo-avant-garde. Unlike Giulia Niccolai, for example, she avoids the postmodern tic of shunning traditional poetic diction and imagery by resorting to the visual impact of advertising and the mass media, or alienation devices such as multilingual diction and extreme forms of colloquialism.[31] Like D'Annunzio, Copioli fuses personal mythology with universal cosmology, and her work is studded (again like D'Annunzio's) with allusions and references to classical literary texts, myths, and narratives. Hers is not just a commentary *on* myth, but an attempt to *create* myth. In "Mater Matuta" in particular, a threshold poem to the book, Copioli seeks to create the myth of an empowering female figure—a mother and muse—who will give her the strength to speak and to be at one with being and the world.

While this is a common enough move in romantic and late romantic poetry by male authors (D'Annunzio inserts his own "Inno alla madre immortale" [Hymn to the Immortal Mother] in the *Laus Vitae*), it is uncommon among women poets. There is something perhaps uncanny (in that it might disclose the return of the repressed) in a woman poet addressing a woman mother-muse. This is indeed one occasion when the gender of the poet and of the subject of enunciation (in Benveniste's terms: the one who says "I"), does make a glaring difference. For the apparition of this mother-muse in a poem by a woman dispels the patriarchal myth that all women are destined to inscribe themselves in an Electra-like scenario. Copioli, instead, envisions a scenario in which the very origin of poetic language, the ability to speak poetically, is predicated upon restoring the lost link with the mother that patriarchy has repressed. (It is due to the difficulty of restoring such a link for women that Kristeva has stressed what she supposes to be their inability to tap the resources of the imaginary [the "semiotic" in her terms] and to produce writing comparable to that of such male avant-garde authors as Joyce and Mallarmé.)

The Mater Matuta is the Greek goddess of the dawn, and Copioli's poem is about the dawn in more ways than one. The occasion, the epiphany or "intermittance du coeur," which coincides with the fictional moment of enunciation is in fact the moment immediately before dawn during a journey by train along the seashore somewhere in Southern Italy, when the eyes of

the poet are struck by the first presages of sunlight on the water. She remembers a similar moment when, as a child, she used to see a glimmer of light
reflected in the bedroom mirror from the barely open door and feel the gaze
of her mother coming in to watch over her sleep. The traditional, but here
creatively reinterpreted, paronomasia—"madre-mare"—plays an important
role in the poem and may be said to be the implicit subtext of the epiphany
that triggers the enunciation:

> Madre mattutina, dalle porte
> dei tamerici, nata dal tessuto
> della pietra serena,
> madre antica, ora remota, che mi appari
> dalla finestra d'alba d'un treno
> precoce
> che corre sul mare, prima del risveglio
> del sole, si alza appena il primo
> taglio grigio dell'acqua, e non è ancora
> luce, e come allora, ricordo,
> mi custodivi il sonno, entravi
> a guardarmi, sentivo dallo specchio
> una luce, avevi dita di mandorle
> e carminio, e ora, nel buio più alto
> in cui sei, forse dischiudi altre porte,
> sei custode di porti, mutata d'egida
> come la vedetta prima, con gli occhi
> di rapace; i piedi ti fremono
> sul mare stellato.
> Madre mattutina, da queste pozze
> algide che fuggono, dove la terra
> perduta pare donarci le stelle,
> ricordi, sussurri ancora:
> "inizia",
> e mi prendi sul fianco,
> e spingi il mio piede:
> "va?"

(7)

(Morning mother, from the doors
of the tamarisks, born from the tissue

of stone,
ancient mother, now remote, you who appear to me
from the dawn window of an early train
running by the seashore, before the awakening
of the sun, the first grey edge of the water
is just rising, and it is not
light yet, and like then, I remember,
you watched over my sleep, you came in
to look at me, I felt from the mirror
a light, you had almond and crimson fingers,
and now, in the highest darkness
where you are, perhaps you open other doors,
you are guardian of harbors, having changed your aegis
like the first lookout, with the predatory
eyes; your feet tremble
on the starry sky.
Morning mother, from these algid
pools that fly past, where the earth,
lost, seems to give us the stars,
remember, you still whisper:
"begin,"
and you take me by your side,
and you push my foot:
"go?")


The theme of the mother's gaze—as in Cavarero's notion of a feminine economy of gazes—coupled with the image of the mirror where mother and daughter recognize each other, recurs throughout the poem and becomes the symbol of the empowering poetic identity which the mother alone can confer on the daughter, and vice versa: "Madre mattutina," the poem concludes in a final imploration to her for poetic power,

> madre della polvere
> del latte e dell'argento,
> che fai nascere il sole dal cavo
> della notte delle onde
> infinita,
> guardami, con te sulle sponde

di questo vetro
dove seguo un nastro di luce,
luce,
ti inseguo.

(Morning mother, mother of dust
of milk and silver,
you who make the sun come to life in the depth
of the night of the waves
infinite,
look at me, with you on the edge
of this glass
where I trace a ribbon of light,
light,
I am pursuing you.)

The vision of the cosmic body of the mother culminates in the spectacle of the universe encircled by "un ovario immenso" (12) ("an immense ovary").

In explicit and polemical opposition to the Lacanian theory of the mirror phase, according to which the formation of the subject (and its gaining access to language) is a process of estrangement from the (m)other, Copioli sets up an alternative identity, one that binds once again the daughter not only to the mother but also, through her, to the entire universe, altogether undoing the Lacanian paradigm. Through a complex process that Gayatri Spivak has called "rememoration," the symbolic reworking of the meaning of one's being a daughter or son (195), Copioli projects the possibility that her mother is a link between her and the great body of Indo-European myth. "Madre Matuta," Copioli tells us in a note explaining the poem's more arcane allusions, is a conflation of a complex genealogy of feminine figures and goddesses, including Carna, the Roman goddess of food (but also of entrails and the most "secret" parts of the human body); Tacita, the goddess of silence; the Egyptian goddess Thueris, giver of milk; Nemesis, who, raped by Zeus, generates Helen in vengeance; Helen herself, "torch of tragic beauty"; Minerva-Athena, the goddess of wisdom, war, and all the liberal arts; the Mediterranean Maya, originally an androgynous Libyan goddess of the sea and the source of all creative impulses in nature; and finally Aphrodite-Venus, her game of love and death understood not only in the terms of Lucretius and Homer, but of the Upanishads, in which the universe is born from death and hunger.

This intricate network of mythic figures, while covering with a characteristically D'Annunzian sweep the entire structure of the human experience of nature and culture, the body, time, desire, and the mind, is also beautifully simple in leading everything back to a feminine and maternal principle. Copioli's metaphysics of the mother, however, is more subtle and less simplistic than Muraro's admittedly tentative statement about the need to return to the mother as a fundamental principle of being. Copioli, for one thing, although confident of the power of the symbol (and of a "maternal" language) to signify fully the presence of being, expresses some doubt in her poems about her ability to extricate herself from the realm of patriarchy. In effect, all the mythic feminine figures she refers to, while symbols of a maternal and feminine realm, are also known almost exclusively through their problematic representations in patriarchal culture, and are therefore essentially ambivalent.

None is more so than Nemesis, whose very name defines her in terms of mimetic revenge against the violence of patriarchy. Nemesis *is* that revenge and nothing else. Copioli feels that she herself is, at least in part, a daughter to Nemesis, that her bond with the mother does not exonerate her from the destructive compulsion of male-generated violence—which for a woman becomes, in the end, self-destruction:

> Anch'io nell'illusione del mondo,
> violenta, raddoppio le vendette
> contro di me . . . Nemesi,
> slitto dal litorale lastricato
> senza che l'alba fasci una speranza
> (11)

> (I too, in the illusion of the world,
> violent,
> redouble the acts of vengeance
> against me . . . Nemesis,
> I slide down from the paved littoral
> without the dawn wrappings any hope)

Violence and death are important themes in Copioli's poetry, and the face of the mother is, like that of Janus (the other presiding deity of *Furore delle rose*), always double, doubly posed to look toward life on one side, and death on the other. Yet life and life-giving remain—as in Spaziani, Cavarero, and Muraro—dominant principles in Copioli, and death enters into it not as the most authentic moment, from the anticipation of which all thinking and poetry springs but, on the contrary, only a *part*, a natural part, of life. The overall sense of this visionary poem is of an extraordinary *life* that emanates, through the poetic work of rememoration, from the word of the "madre-mare."

While Copioli shares with Spaziani and, in different ways, also with Cavarero and Muraro, the notion that a feminine symbolic order can be constructed or restored through the appropriation and alteration of existing mythologies or the creation of alternative ones, Amelia Rosselli takes a more skeptical, disenchanted approach to the question of mythic revisionism. Her approach may be called "deconstructionist" in that while it works to dismantle the assumptions of patriarchal discourse on women, it does not share the metaphysical beliefs of the Diotima philosophic community and of poets such as Spaziani and Copioli, although it gestures toward the possibility of a different language that might not be entrapped in the logic of the patriarchal symbolic.

At least three poems in Rosselli's work deal explicitly with mythic feminine figures: "Perchè il cielo divinasse la tua ansia di morire," "Nel letargo che seguiva l'ingranaggio dei," and "Mare del bisogno, Cassandra." All three poems are from *Variazioni Belliche*, and involve three mythic Greek heroines: Electra, Antigone, and Cassandra. I shall focus my analysis on the Antigone poem, because it is there that the philosophical and political implications of Rosselli's approach appear most clearly. Since the poem is short, I will cite it in its entirety:

Nel letargo che seguiva l'ingranaggio dei
pochi, io giacevo, felice e disonorata, disordinata
all'estremo; e le lingue del serpi s'avventavano
come fuoco vicino al capezzale. Vicino al capezzale
moriva un drago, salumiere con i suoi salumi, le
sue code che pendevano molto puzzolenti, ma delicate
nel loro odorare insieme.

E se l'antigone che vegliava silenziosa, molto silenziosa
ai miei poderi i miei prodotti disordinati, disadorni
di gloria, se essa fosse venuta col suo gradito grido
d'allarme, io morivo, molto silenzioso allarme.

(88)

(In the lethargy that followed the engaging gears of
the few, I lay, happy and dishonored, disordered

to the extreme; and the tongues of snakes hurled
    themselves
like fire near the deathbed. Near the deathbed
a dragon was dying, delicatessan seller with his cold cuts,
his tails hanging and stinking, but delicate
in their smelling together

And if the antigone that silently kept watch, very silent
over my farm and my disordered products, unadorned
with glory, if she had come with her welcome cry
of alarm, I was dying, very silent alarm.)

As usual with Rosselli's poems, a first reading is rather forbidding, and the text presents an opaque, almost impenetrable surface until we perceive the "formal messages" that sound patterns and other repetitions and correspondences generate at the level of the signifier. The key organizing principle of the text appears indeed to be phonetic, a kind of "grid" centered on the repetition of a hard *g* sound: "Letargo," "seguiva," "l'ingranaggio," "drago," "gloria," "gradito," "grido." This is, however, also the central sound of the word "antigone," which begins the second stanza after the central caesura of the poem, so that the poem's phonetic rotation around this sound implies its being centered semantically on the figure of Antigone and what the poet sees as central and essential to this figure. The other dominant pattern at the level of the signifier is an emphasis on the privative prefix *dis-* which occurs four times: "*dis*onorata," "*dis*ordinata," "*dis*ordinati," "*dis*adorni." The repetition of this prefix, with its negative force, suggests that the theme of being dispossessed is also crucial.

Unlike Copioli's text, where the integrating, organic symbol is the dominant rhetorical figure, Rosselli's poem is essentially allegorical in the fragmented, montagelike and nonorganic manner characteristic of the avantgardist work of art.[32] Death and mourning—elements inherent in the allegorical by definition, according to Walter Benjamin—are the key concerns of this poem's revision of the Antigone story. The one who says "I," whom I will call, in light of her reference to her poetic work later in this highly self-reflexive text, "the poet," describes her state as one of "letargo": a condition of unconsciousness or semiconsciousness, like sleep, and like, or even near, death. The poem that follows in the collection (which, as throughout *Variazioni belliche*, is linked to the preceding poem thematically and phonetically), opens with the line, "Se dalle tue lunghe agonie e dai miei brevi respiri," where the word "agonie" not only echoes "antigone," but also spells out the theme of agony that in the previous poem is only alluded to. The second half of the long opening sentence, "e le lingue dei serpi s'avventavano come fuoco vicino al capezzale," reinforces the sense of lying near death while it evokes an odd scene of martyrdom seemingly taken from early Christian iconography. This would explain to some extent the series of seemingly contradictory adjectives: "felice e disonorata, disordinata / all'estremo." The "extreme" dis-order and dis-honor of the martyr's tortured, scattered body in this moment of agony ("all'estremo" both qualifies the adjectives that precede it and also means "at the end, near death") produces a sort of ecstasy, a happy abandon.

Although it is risky to try to track down referential or autobiographical allusions in Rosselli's poetry, one cannot help thinking about the effect of electroshock administered in a modern hospital as the equivalent of the ancient martyrdom evoked here. "L'ingranaggio dei / pochi," this mysterious thing that is the cause of dis-order and dis-honor, but also of happiness and sleep, may then refer to the machine used to administer electroshock—electroshock being a privilege granted only to few. But the poem, like a perverse image-producing machine, at this point shifts gears and confronts us with *another* agony. (Doubling in an estranging form is a key device in Rosselli.) As in a postmodern pastiche, the body of a dying dragon is juxtaposed metonymically to the martyred body on its deathbed: "Vicino al capezzale moriva un drago." The dragon in its agony projects us into the realm of fairy tales or, keeping to the code of Christian iconography, evokes Saint George slaying the dragon, as in Carpaccio's famous painting at the Scuola di San Giorgio. The lower left foreground of that painting is taken up by the disturbing sight of the scattered limbs of a young woman the dragon has torn to pieces, miraculously leaving intact, however, her beautiful head and torso. As in the first two lines of Rosselli's poem, here too there is a striking contrast between the dis-order and the dis-honor of this violated feminine figure, torn apart and dismembered, and the peaceful tranquility of her closed eyes and delicate feminine breasts, as if she, too, were happily sleeping in her agony. But the rest of the line immediately dispels the somewhat perverse beauty evoked by this bit of necrophiliac voyeurism by plunging us, again with a sudden shift of gears and a swift change of register, into the prosaic: "Moriva un drago, salumiere con i suoi salumi, le / sue code che pendevano molto puzzolenti." The phallic tension of the dragon (which Carpaccio emphasizes in his depiction of the monster's duel with Saint George and his spear, two phallic powers confronting one another) is comically deflated. Not only is the heroic struggle reduced to the vulgar buying and selling of meat but—were there any room for equivocation—the poem tells us exactly how rotten this activity is, how much it *stinks*. What is bought and sold in the symbolic economy of patriarchy is always and still the body of women. As soon as it is defeated, however, deprived of its phallic tension, "deflated," the body of the dying dragon becomes *feminized*, one and the same with the scattered limbs of the victims. Carpaccio's other painting, "San Giorgio vittorioso sul drago," depicts the dragon thus reduced, lying harmless on the ground with his neck in a leash in the saint's left hand, while the right hand, holding a sword, is about to decapitate (i.e., castrate) him, and thus (according to the patriarchal logic by which the female is only a castrated male) "feminize" him. The dragon becomes feminized as one of those "monsters," like the Sphinx or Medusa, who are only obstacles on the male hero's path to manhood.[33] This feminization in death redeems the dragon in the logic of the poem: "puzzolenti ma delicate nel loro odorare insieme." The second corpse in the lower foreground of Carpaccio's painting—that of a young man, also dismembered and strangely peaceful—is also delicate and effeminate: a double of the young girl, as if in death femininity prevailed over masculinity, or as if there were something connatural between femininity and death—a myth the Antigone story in many ways seems to confirm.

The "delicate" smell of rotting flesh, the feminine agony, martyrdom, dishonor and dis-order of the opening lines are all geared toward the evocation of Antigone. Agony-Antigone: the assonance is all the more powerful in English. Even the duel alluded to through the image of the dragon points to Antigone. It is the duel between Polyneices and Eteocles, and their reciprocal killing, that leads Sophocles' Antigone to her own confrontation with Creon. Like the duel of Saint George and the dragon, Antigone's duel with Creon takes place amidst the smell of rotting flesh; Antigone refuses to leave Polyneices's body unburied. In Rosselli's poem, whose body is Antigone called to bury?

As Rossana Rossanda has pointed out, of the many interpretations of the Antigone story (those of Hegel, Kierkegaard, Hölderlin, and Brecht are among the best known), none highlights or problematizes the fact that Antigone is a woman.[34] All see in the story a paradigm of conflict in which the feminine plays only a subsidiary role. Or, when femaleness is highlighted (as with Hegel), it is in terms of the most traditional patriarchal vision of "women's roles." In Hegel's *Phenomenology of Mind*, the conflict between Antigone and Creon is one between the knowledge of oneself acquired within and through the family, and the superior, broader knowledge acquired as part of the multirelational system of the state: as a woman Antigone "stands for" the

family and the home.[35] For Kierkegaard, Antigone's femaleness corresponds
to another gender stereotype: she is the figure of a dangerous seduction by the
deepest and most ambiguous secret hidden in her being (her knowledge
of Oedipus's true predicament). Lacan, influenced by both Hegel and Kierkegaard, subordinates Antigone's femaleness entirely to the male plot of psychoanalysis; she is the incarnation of desire in its "pure" state (that is, in
essence, *male* desire), the desire for the other as desire of the forbidden, the
(m)other. Thus there is no real difference between Antigone and Hamlet.
Sophocles's tragedy, Lacan argues, "presents man [sic] to us and interrogates
him on the path of solitude."[36]

Because her revision of the Antigone story is by a woman poet speaking
in the first person, Rosselli's is neither so phallocentric as those of her male
predecessors, nor so ready to gloss over Antigone's status as a woman. The
first stanza frames the apparition of Antigone by evoking the martyrdom and
agony of an unambiguously female-gendered speaking subject. The poem,
while not espousing a male-centered system of signification, does not try to
do away with it either. Rather, it mimics and parodies it by alluding to the
death of the dragon and its stinking tails (and tales, for it is in these tales—
such as the Carpaccio cycle of Saint George and the Dragon—that the commerce, death, and dismemberment of women's bodies is represented again
and again).

I said that Antigone "appears" in Rosselli's poem, but this is not altogether
correct. Rather, she is evoked, or *invoked*: "se essa fosse venuta col suo gradito
grido/d'allarme." "If only she had come." Antigone is elsewhere, not here.
Unlike her male predecessors, who thought they could *represent* Antigone,
speak for her, make her reappear on the stage of their texts in her truer being,
Rosselli makes no such claims. She even deprives the name of the capital
"A," the first letter that marks the proper name. "E se l'antigone che vegliava
silenziosa . . ." Why this diminution to the lower case? The "real" Antigone
(if this term may be adopted for a literary character) belongs, for one, in
Sophocles's text, nor can it be re-presented except as a pale simulacrum or
as another (in which case the proper name is a misappropriation). Rosselli's
Antigone, then, is but one of many sumulacra of the original; she is only an
"antigone," as if the name had to be changed into a common noun. Indeed,
nothing is proper to Antigone. She has through the ages been expropriated
of everything, she has become common property, used differently—albeit always within the same masculine economy—with each successive rewriting.
The conversion of the name to the lower case denounces—even as it un-
avoidably partakes in it—the violence of writing against woman, the turning

of woman into an object of representational exchange within the patriarchal symbolic.

While not implying that hers is the true Antigone, Rosselli does assign to Antigone a place, a position: "E se l'antigone che vegliava silenziosa, molto silenziosa / ai miei poderi i miei prodotti disordinati, disadorni / di gloria, se essa fosse venuta col suo gradito grido / d'allarme, io morivo, molto silenziosa allarme." Antigone is elsewhere, in a place other than the scene of the poet's agony, keeping watch over something that belongs to the poet, the products of her labor ("i miei prodotti"). A number of connotations interweave here by virtue of the vocabulary and the associations that Antigone's figure calls to mind. First, the poet's "products" cannot but be her texts. Antigone, then, is keeping watch over the agonizing poet's poems. These are associated with the earth, and with the products of the earth, through the use of the word "poderi" (which also, antithetically, evokes "poteri," the power of writing). This association of poems with the earth reminds us that Antigone's rite of burial is indeed, as Hegel remarked, a literal reenclosure of her brother in the womb of the feminine earth, and echoes Cavarero's reading of the story of Demeter and Persephone, in which the feminine earth withholds her products (buried within her body) in protest against the masculine violation of her daughter's body. Because Antigone watches over them, these poem-products are implicitly linked to human remains, the remains of her brother Polyneices, which are also "disordinati, disadorni / di gloria," for they lack the glory and dignity of a proper burial, and are exposed to vultures and dogs. (Sophocles's Antigone, in her mercy, has covered them with a thin veil of dust in defiance of Creon's orders.) The dyad "disordinati, disadorni di gloria" also echoes the paired "Disonorata, disordinata" from the second line of the poem, linking the poem-products of the second stanza to the agonizing feminine body of the incipit. Body and texts are conterminous. Both are dis-ordered, and dis-honored; both share the stigma of the prefix "dis-," its expressing privation, dispersion, and separation. But the texts differ from the body in having the privilege of Antigone's silent watch. They are dead and (almost) buried, mercifully covered with a thin veil of dust—and rendered invisible. It is precisely that privilege, the honor of being—like her poems—mourned by Antigone, that the poet invokes: "se essa fosse venuta col suo gradito grido / d'allarme, io morivo, molto silenziosa allarme." In Sophocles's text, Antigone sends out her cry of alarm when, on returning to her brother's burial site, she finds that he has been left unburied. Were Antigone's cry to be heard again it would mean that the poet, like her poems, would be free to die (to fulfill the bliss promised by her "happy" agony) with the knowledge that her body would be buried with the poems, and return to be one with them.

What is the meaning of this wish-for-a-burial, and in what sense are the poems already buried? Is it simply a death wish, a "feminine" self-erasure in the face of patriarchal violence evoked in the first stanza? Antigone's centrality as the rebellious heroine who defies the laws of the city and of patriarchy seems to argue against this, although her predicament remains highly ambiguous in Sophocles's play: she kills herself by hanging (like her mother Jocasta) in the cave-tomb where Creon has ordered that she be buried alive, and in dying she calls into question all she has done. To answer these questions we must look at another reading of the Antigone myth.

Although deeply influenced by both Hegel and Lacan—hers is indeed a *gloss* of Hegel's interpretation of the myth, and it pursues the Lacanian question of desire, although in the direction of an exploration of *female* desire—Luce Irigaray's reading of Antigone in *Speculum: De l'autre femme*, centers on the question of Antigone's femininity and its ambiguous status in Sophocles's play. While the "pure" relationship between brother and sister is idealized by Hegel as a relationship of sameness of blood without desire and therefore without violence, "this moment is mythical, of course, and the Hegelian dream . . . is already the effect of a dialectic produced by the discourse of patriarchy. It is a consoling fancy, a truce in the struggle between uneven foes, a denial of the guilt already weighing heavily upon the development of the subject; it is the delusion of a *bisexuality* assured for each in the connection and passage, one into the other, of each sex" (217). In Sophocles, however, "things are not yet that clear," for his work "marks the historical bridge between matriarchy and patriarchy [and] no decision has yet been made about what has more value" (217). Antigone's defiance of Creon is a rejection of the roles that patriarchy, at that particular stage of development in Greek civilization, imposes on woman. Refusing to be wife or mother, Antigone chooses to die a virgin. For Irigaray, the allegiance Antigone pledges to "another" law, the *unwritten* law (as opposed to the written ones of the city of men) of the "gods below," who uphold the sacredness of blood ties, is a form of transgressive desire: "Better to die than to refuse service to the divine law and to the attraction she feels for the gods below. There her jouissance finds easier recognition, no doubt, since her allegiance to them frees her from the inventions of men. She defies them all by/in her relationship to Hades. In her nocturnal passion she acts with a perversity which has nothing in common with the wretched crimes that men stoop to in their love for money" (218).

Antigone's nocturnal passion, argues Irigaray, isolates her, makes her an outcast, places her outside of patriarchy and condemns her to annihilation: "Without friends, without husband, without tears, she is led along that *forgotten path* and there is *walled up* alive in *a hole* in the rock, shut off forever from the light of the sun. Alone in her crypt, her cave, her den, her womb, she is given just enough food by those who hold power to ensure that the city is not soiled and shamed by her decay" (218). But this path to self-destruction is also, ambiguously, a path back to the mother, and to all that patriarchy has tried to suppress: "By killing herself [does Antigone] anticipate the decree of death formulated by those in power? Does she duplicate it? Has she given in? Or is she still in revolt? She repeats, in any case, upon herself the murderous, but not bloody, deed of her mother. Whatever her current arguments with the laws of the city may have been, another law is still drawing her along her path: identification with her mother" (219). This path back to the mother marks the deadly uncertainty of a woman who, although rejecting the laws of patriarchy, cannot find a role or place for herself outside its violent economy. For what the mother is can no longer be grasped outside of the patriarchal order, even though for Sophocles this order is far from being fully in place, nor is it unambiguously positive (as it is for Hegel). For Irigaray, the fact that both Antigone and Polyneices have "doubles" in the play indicates that "this is still a transition in which the extremes—which will later be defined as being more masculine or more feminine: i.e. Eteocles and Ismene—seem almost like caricatures" (217). Unlike her tearful and submissive sister Ismene, Antigone never "becomes a woman" by the logic of Creon's patriarchy (indeed, he fears that she might usurp his manhood), but "she is not as masculine as she might seem if seen from an exclusively phallic viewpoint—for it is tenderness and pity that have motivated her" (219). For Irigaray it is clear that Antigone "is a captive of a desire whose path has reached a dead end, has never been blazed" (219).[37]

A thorough unpacking of the allegorical logic of Rosselli's poem leads to a similarly oxymoronic reading. As in Irigaray, the question of the relationship between patriarchal violence and feminine desire or jouissance is central. The woman poet in agony who faces her own extinction with a sense of jouissance is, like Irigaray's Antigone, rejecting the violent logic of patriarchy. With their extravagant, obscure imagery and semantic opaqueness, Rosselli's poems place themselves on the margins of the symbolic and of "communication." They are, like Antigone herself, en-crypted, buried in the underground of writing. Although inscribed in an economy of writing that inevitably belongs to the patriarchal culture of mid-twentieth-century society, Rosselli's poems denounce this economy of writing as a betrayal. Her poems are, like the remains of Antigone's brother Polyneices, "disadorni di gloria," because they shy away from the monumentality of more ambitious poetic endeavours. They run counter to the tradition of the text as *testament* and *monument*. Rosselli's Antigone poem may be seen as a response to Foscolo's "I sepolcri," the greatest poem in the Italian tradition where the notions of literary testament and funerary monument are explicitly linked to the author's desire to find glory and eternal life through his writing. By placing Antigone in the role of silent guardian to her poems, Rosselli implicitly wishes that they might be un-written, be allowed, like Polyneices's remains, to decay and disintegrate without being *seen* and preyed upon.

This is, of course, impossible. Although (like her) Rosselli's poems denounce the violence of the Law and of the symbolic, and although (like Antigone) they pursue a *different* path (dictated by unwritten laws, which do not participate in the violent economy of patriarchal writing), there is no writing—except in madness—outside the symbolic, and writing exposes the text to the violence of interpretation. The desire that speaks in the poem, therefore, a desire that body and text be coterminous, and that both be mercifully buried by Antigone, remains "a desire whose path has reached a dead end, has never been ablaze." There is no indication, contrary to Irigaray's reading of Antigone's desire, and to Muraro's and Copioli's metaphysical impulse, that a return to the mother as origin and authentic locus of being might provide the symbolic framework for a new feminist politics. Ultimately what the poem expresses, through the oxymoron of the "silent alarm" (*silenziosa allarme*) is the contradictory wish both to be dead and silent, like Antigone, and to retain, like *Antigone*, the disruptive power of a cry of denunciation and rebellion against the violence of patriarchy.

The oxymoronic logic of Rosselli's deconstruction of the Antigone myth holds little promise of a radical change in the structures of the symbolic and of patriarchy. Like Antigone herself, Rosselli increasingly refuses any compromise with politics, or with writing itself. Silence surrounds her verses, and constantly threatens to obliterate them. Her approach, therefore, differs substantially from the more positive logic of the poets and thinkers associated with the Diotima group. While Rosselli's dark vision has the appeal of an uncompromising formal and epistemic rigor, and her highly "writerly" texts generate their own, difficult aesthetic pleasure, its political impact is bound to be extremely circumscribed. It is, to use Adorno's phrase, the impact of a "negative dialectics." The aesthetic rigor and strange beauty of her poetry are a critique of the intolerability of the real, and a metaphor of how things should be otherwise. But for all its denunciation of the violence of writing, this poetry does not attempt to imagine a way of mediating between writing and other spheres of experience. It remains *in* writing, and in a way this is the principal reason for its deconstructionist rigor and beauty. Such rigor and beauty are—like the admirable stubborness of Antigone—politically suspect to other women. Irigaray herself, in her 1984 *Ethique de la différence sexuelle*, states the need to go beyond Antigone (and the deconstructionist version of her parable she had given in *Speculum*) to embrace the project of a new feminine subjectivity and ethics. In her commentary on this further revision of the Antigone story, Gloria Zanardo—a member of the Italian feminist group "Il filo di Arianna," which is closely associated with the Diotima group—concludes on a note indicating how these women see the entire project of mythic revisionism from a philosophical and political perspective: "Lo sforzo di Antigone risulta inutile e destinato al fallimento, come ha fallito Antigone stessa, se le donne non contrappongono alla legge della città una loro legge. . . . Il mondo comune delle donne articola una struttura etica affinché le donne si riapproprino della vita e dell'energia che a loro appartiene, piuttosto che spenderla per dare vita a un morto" (90–91). ("Antigone's effort turns out to be useless and destined to failure, just as Antigone failed, if women do not oppose to the law of the city a law of their own. . . . The shared world of women must articulate an ethical structure in order that women may regain the life and energy that belongs to them, rather than wasting it on restoring life to the dead.")[38]

Whatever one thinks of the advantages and disadvantages of the various strategies of mythic revisionism I have discussed, as a whole (and despite their different formal, epistemic, and political approaches), they represent one of the most compelling ways through which Italian women writers—poets, philosophers, critics—are calling into question the ideological underpinnings of a male-centered tradition while at the same time opening up a space for a feminine symbolic, a symbolic where the feminine is no longer always subordinate, secondary, or negative, but takes on legitimacy and significance in its own right.

# Notes

1. Some of the most convincing discussions of this subject are de Lauretis's "The Technology of Gender," and Judith Butler's *Gender Trouble*.

2. The Italian original reads as follows: "Propongo di usare dei testi come cavia: testi maschili e testi femminili mescolati all'insaputa del pubblico. Il quale dovrà indovinare quali sono gli

scritti di origine maschile e quali sono gli scritti di origine femminile, indipendentemente dall'argomento" (Frabotta (161). All translations from the Italian in the text are mine, unless otherwise noted.

3. The Italian original reads as follows: "La singola voce di un poeta donna valeva e vale di per sè, per una sua unicità sensibile e morale, la stessa che differenzia i libri importanti scritti da uomini" (143).

4. Luigi Baldacci, introduction to Spaziani, *Poesie*, 9 and passim.

5. See for example Antonio Porta's review of Patrizia Valduga's *Medicamenta*, 86.

6. The Italian original reads as follows: "Che esista una differenziazione linguistica femminile è da sospettarsi, sia essa da quarto mondo o biologica, addirittura in origine, anche se rimane da studiare in campo sperimentale, secondo me. Che la donna imiti l'uomo nello scrivere è ovvio, e forse un suo rintracciare forme artistiche sue originarie o perfino chimicamente più sue, resta problema aperto. Ma se la donna ne è conscia, il suo scrivere si fa davvero più laborioso!" (159–60).

7. Luce Irigaray and Hélène Cixous are traditionally associated with the notion of "écriture féminine." Irigaray is actually suspicious of the notion of writing and prefers to speak of a "parler femme," a writing that has the fluidity and (in)formality of speech; see especially her "Quand nos lèvres se parlent," in *Speculum de l'autre femme*. She emphasizes the need for women authors' self-representation of their own sexed body and subjectivity, or what she calls "a morphologic appropriated from the body." The classic text by Cixous on feminine writing is "Le Rire de la Meduse." See also Conley, Shiach, and Jones. For critiques, see Jacobus and Felski. For a broader, rigorous, and fascinating study on language and sexual difference using a sociolinguistic and semiological approach, see Violi.

8. This lack of being remedied slowly by studies such as Cixous's on Clarice Lispector; see, for example, "*Coming to Writing,*" and *Breaking the Sequence,* ed. Friedman and Fuchs. Suleiman's *Subversive Intent* is also a pioneering work in the study of women and the avant-garde.

9. The Italian original reads as follows: "La voce femminile (della lingua femminile scritta o parlata) si caratterizza per un tono che è fondamentalmente quello dell'interrogazione. La lingua delle donne in linea di massima non costruisce sistemi, non avanza tesi, non tende nemmeno al possesso dei fatti; si lascia piuttosto definire mediante la differenza rispetto a tutti quegli atteggiamenti. Lo stile della voce femminile si estrinseca più nella forma della interrogazione, della domanda, che non in quello dell'affermazione. . . . Non brama e non accetta il possesso che sui fatti rivendicano gli uomini, quel possesso dal quale si finisce per essere posseduti, perchè avverte nel possesso lo sbarramento dell'intenzione, della volontà, del significato. . . . Essa scopre al di là dei fatti, delle tesi e dei sistemi eretti dagli uomini lo spazio della contingenza, dell'intenzione, del senso [. . . e] un arbitrio originario. [. . .] L'eticità della voce femminile risplende nella chiamata che essa rappresenta nei confronti di tutti i segni, tracce, voci, che sono state dimenticate e disattese" (16).

10. The Italian original reads as follows: "Ciò che costituisce la specificità della voce femminile tra scrittrici fra loro diverse è la tensione verso un senso che, di fronte alla resistenza eretta dalla verità notarile sottoscritta dagli uomini ordinariamente, fatalmente si estrinseca come richiamo, come strazio, come grido. In ogni caso si estrinseca come propensione alla descrizione, al passaggio da una condizione di verità alla condizione del senso di quella verità, anzichè, all'argomentazione sistematica paranoide che assolve al bisogno di affermazione e di possesso che spinge normalmente gli uomini" (16).

11. Cavarero's notion of the symbolic order is loosely based on the Lacanian notion of the Symbolic, via the mediation of Irigaray. See also Muraro, 111.

12. A founding member, along with Muraro, of the Italian feminist group of philosophers called "Diotima," Cavarero partakes of the specifically Italian tendency—within feminism—to attribute to sexual difference a fundamental role that many Anglo-American critics have called "essentialist." On the virtues and vices of essentialism, see de Lauretis, "Essence."

13. See Alicia Ostriker, "The Thieves of Language." This essay, in many ways a pioneering

work in feminist criticism, inspired many of my own thoughts. I owe an earlier debt to Harold Bloom on revisionism in poetry. "A poem is not writing, but *rewriting*," Bloom says (3). The notion of writing (and reading) by women as "revision" originates with Adrienne Rich's "When We Dead Awaken." On the revision of classical myths by modern American women poets, see Du Plessis, 105–41.

14. Alta, "euridice," quoted in Ostriker, 318.

15. See for example Sergio Solmi's claims, cited in Petronio, 896–97.

16. Evidence of this continuity may be found in the "Congedo" to Luigi Ballerini's recent *Che figurato muore*: the loss of Eurydice becomes an allegory of the desirable, even necessary, loss of literal referentiality in poetic discourses; in other words, the beloved has to be dead for the poetry to be good.

17. For two different revisionist rewritings of the myth that attribute to Eurydice an empowered role, see Copioli, "Euridice," in *Furore*, 23, and Splendore, "Orfeo e Euridice" in *Elena*, 41–43.

18. For an overview of Spaziani's work, see West.

19. Montale is of course rather a contemporary of Spaziani than a predecessor *strictu sensu*. Spaziani also happened to be, for a time, Montale's lover and the poetic beloved, under the name of "Volpe" of a number of Montale's poems.

20. Pascoli's poems "Il morticino," "L'agonia di una madre," "Colloquio" (all from *Myricae*) and "Mia Madre" (from *Canti di Castelvecchio*), are cases in point.

21. The original Italian reads as follows: "Di questo secondo viaggio Omero non dà che gli accenni menzionati. . . . Essi sono tuttavia sufficienti a suscitare (al di là della cerimonia narrativa, che, come si è detto, costituisce la materia, la prosa, del primo ritorno), la ritualità necessaria, la poesia del secondo, intesa, quest'ultima, come attività il cui senso gravita intorno a, e trae vita da un *conoscere* distinto dal *riconoscere* con cui è, anzi, in antitesi" (136).

22. "Variazioni sul tema di Penelope," cited in Cavarero, 21.

23. Hannah Arendt points out in *The Life of the Mind* that "even the younger Heidegger of *Sein und Zeit* still treated the anticipation of death as the decisive experience through which man can attain an authentic self and be liberated from the inauthenticity of the They" (80–81). See also Blanchot.

24. The original Italian reads as follows: "Penelope è appunto tessitrice, e ora forse, per merito di Platone, sappiamo cosa continuò a tessere, con le ancelle quando l'evento ultimo si compì per mare lasciandola quieta nell'esperienza del limite che tracciava la sua appartenenza. Continuò a tessere quell'interezza singolare di corpo e pensiero che già nella sua *métis* si era manifestata, quella realtà dove vivere è soprattutto nascere e poi, solo alla fine, anche morire. Quell'intreccio di intelligenza e sensibilità dove ogni umano vivente—non anima eterna caduta in un corpo qualsiasi, di qualsivoglia specie o sesso—esiste nella sua specie e nel suo genere; lei, come le ancelle, donna, a tenere insieme intessuti i pensieri e i corpi loro in una propria casa che lascia altrove la palestra maschile della morte" (31).

25. One of the more dubious though appealing implications of Irigaray's theory is that women are somehow outside the rule of technology and its nihilistic results, and that women therefore constitute a reservoir of hope for the world's salvation.

26. Muraro is critical of poststructuralist modes of the thought, and especially critical of feminist thinkers such as Joan Scott who think that poststructuralist theory can fulfill the needs of feminist theory. Muraro also finds most modern critiques of metaphysics (she cites Derrida, Foucault, and Vattimo) ineffectual.

27. Muraro specifies, citing Adrienne Rich, that when she refers to "the father" as the third member of the Oedipal triangle she is not talking about the actual father, nor about the father in a purely symbolic sense, but about the patriarchal power (45).

28. Muraro cites Irigaray's *Sexes et parente*.

29. See Burger, esp. 68–82, and see Luperini.

30. See Copioli's volume of essays *Anima Mundi*.

31. By Niccolai, see "Harry's Bar Ballad" (1977) in *Harry's Bar e altre poesie*, 137–38.

32. See Burger, 68–82.

33. See de Lauretis, *Desire in Narrative*, 116–21.

34. See Rossanda, 14. For a comprehensive account of the metamorphoses of Antigone, see Steiner. A few women have written about Antigone: George Eliot, Virginia Woolf, Margaret Drabble; see Joseph. The most notable Italian revision of the Antigone story by a woman is Liliana Cavani's 1970 film, *I cannibali* where, however, Antigone's female identity is secondary to her role of political opposition.

35. See Rossanda, 26, and Steiner, 28–42. See also Derrida's critical gloss in *Glas*, 108–14, which highlights the gender polarization in Hegel's interpretation.

36. *Le Seminaire: L'ethique de la psychanalyse*, 7:328–29 and 331.

37. For a less nuanced feminist interpretation of the Antigone story, partly based on a reading of Irigaray, see Feral, 2. For a critique, see Du Bois.

38. See also the section entitled "Antigone la custode del corpo" in Izzo.

# Works Cited

Arendt, Hannah. *The Life of the Mind: Thinking*. New York: Harcourt Brace Jovanovich, 1971.

Ballerini, Luigi. *Che figurato muore*. Milan: All'insegna del pesce d'oro, 1988.

Benjamin, Walter. *The Origin of German Tragic Drama*. London: NLB, 1977.

Bimbi, Franca, Laura Grasso, and Marina Zancan, Gruppo di filosofia femminile "Diotima." *Il filo di Arianna: Letture sulla differenza sessuale*. Rome: Utopia, 1987.

Blanchot, Maurice. *The Gaze of Orpheus and Other Essays*.

Bloom, Harold. *Poetry and Repression: Revisionism from Blake to Stevens*. New Haven: Yale University Press, 1976.

Burger, Peter. *Theory of the Avant-Garde*. Translated by Michael Shaw. Minneapolis: University of Minnesota Press, 1984.

Butler, Judith. *Gender Trouble: Feminism and the Subversion of Identity*. New York: Routledge, 1990.

Campana, Dino. *Canti Orfici e altre poesie*. Milan: Garzanti, 1989.

Cavarero, Adriana. *Nonostante Platone: Figure femminili nella filosofia antica*. Rome: Editori Riuniti, 1991.

Cixous, Hélène. *"Coming to Writing" and Other Essays*. Edited by Deborah Jenson. Cambridge: Harvard University Press, 1991.

———. "Le Rire de la Meduse" (originally published in *L'Arc* [1975]: 39–54). Revised version in Marks and De Courtivron, 245–64.

Conley, Verena Andermatt. "An Exchange with Hélène Cixous." In her *Hélène Cixous: Writing the Feminine*, pp. 129–61. Lincoln: University of Nebraska Press, 1984.

Copioli, Rosita. *Anima Mundi*. Parma: Guanda, 1988.

———. *Furore delle rose*. Parma: Guanda, 1989.

———. "Per l'anniversario di Colombo, in Giamaica." *Tuttestorie: Racconti Letture Trame di Donne* 3–4 (November 1991): 100.

de Lauretis, Teresa. *Alice Doesn't: Feminism, Semiotics, Cinema*. Bloomington: Indiana University Press, 1984.

———. "The Essence of the Triangle or, Taking Essentialism Seriously: Feminist Theory in Italy, the U.S., and Britain." *Differences* 1, no. 2 (1990): 3–37.

———. "The Technology of Gender." In her *Technologies of Gender*, 1–30.

de Man, Paul. "The Rhetoric of Temporality." In *Blindness and Insight: Essays in the Rhetoric of Contemporary Criticism*, 187–228. 2d ed., revised. Minneapolis: University of Minnesota Press, 1971, 1983.

Derrida, Jacques. *Glas*. Lincoln: University of Nebraska Press, 1986.

Di Battista, Maria. "The Clandestine Fictions of Marguerite Duras." In Friedman and Fuchs, 284–97.

Du Bois, Page. "Antigone and the Feminist Critic." *Genre* 19, no. 4 (1986): 371–82.

Du Plessis, Rachel Blau. *Writing Beyond the Ending: Narrative Strategies of Twentieth-Century Women Writers*. Bloomington: Indiana University Press, 1985.

Felski, Rita. *Beyond Feminist Esthetics: Feminist Literature and Social Change*. Cambridge: Harvard University Press, 1989.

Feral, Josette. "Antigone or The Irony of the Tribe." *Diacritics* 8, no. 3 (1978): 2–13.

Frabotta, Biancamaria, ed. *Donne in poesia: Antologia della poesia femminile in Italia dal dopoguerra a oggi*. Rome: Savelli, 1977.

Friedman, Ellen G., and Miriam Fuchs, eds. *Breaking the Sequence: Women's Experimental Fiction*. Princeton: Princeton University Press, 1989.

Gargani, Aldo. "La voce femminile." *Alfabeta* 64 (September 1984): 16.

Gauthier, Xavière. "Existe-t-il une écriture féminine?" (1974). Translated as "Is There Such a Thing as Women's Writing?" by Marilyn A. August, in Marks and de Courtivron, 161–64.

Hegel, Georg Wilhelm Friedrich. *The Phenomenology of Mind*. Translated by J. B. Baille. New York: Harper Torchbooks, 1967.

Irigaray, Luce. "Quand nos lèvres se parlent" ("When Our Lips Speak Together"). *Signs* 6, no. 1 (1980): 69–79.

———. *Speculum of the Other Woman*. Translated by Gillian C. Gill. Ithaca: Cornell University Press, 1985.

Izzo, Francesco. "Immagini del soggetto moderno: Etica e soggettivita." in *Reti*, nos. 3–4 (1989): 304–6.

———. "Il materno tra origine e storia" (Review of Luce Irigaray's *Sexes et parente*), in *Reti*, no. 2 (1989): 23–26.

Jacobus, Mary. "The Question of Language: Men of Maxims in *The Mill on the Floss*." In *Writing and Sexual Difference*, edited by Elizabeth Abel, 37–52. Brighton: Harvester, 1982.

Jones, Ann Rosalind. "Inscribing Femininity: French Theories of the Feminine." In *Making a Difference: Feminist Literary Criticism*, ed. Gayle Greene and Coppelia Kahn, 80–112. London: Methuen, 1985.

———. "Writing the Body: Toward an Understanding of *l'écriture féminine*." *Feminist Studies* 7, no. 2 (1981): 247–63.

Joseph, Gerhard. "The *Antigone* as a Cultural Touchstone: Matthew Arnold, Hegel, George Eliot, Virginia Woolf, and Margaret Drabble." *PMLA* 96 (1981): 22–35.

Kristeva, Julia. *Revolution in Poetic Language*. New York: Columbia University Press, 1984.

Lacan, Jacques. "The Mirror-phase as Formative of the Function of the I." *New Left Review* 2, no. 51 (1968): 71–77.

———. *Le Seminaire*. Vol. 7, *L'Ethique de la psychanalyse*. Paris: Seuil, 1986.

Luperini, Romano. *L'Allegoria del moderno*. Rome: Editori Riuniti, 1990.

Marks, Elaine, and Isabelle de Courtivron, eds. *New French Feminisms: An Anthology*. New York: Schocken Books, 1981.

The Milan Women's Bookstore Collective (Libreria delle donne di Milano). *Sexual Difference: A Theory of Social Symbolic Practice*. Bloomington: Indiana University Press, 1990.

Muraro, Luisa. *L'Ordine simbolico della madre*. Rome: Editori Riuniti, 1991.

Niccolai, Giulia. *Harry's Bar e altre poesie, 1969–1980*. Milan: Feltrinelli, 1981.

Ostriker, Alicia. "The Thieves of Language: Women Poets and Revisionist Mythmaking." In *The New Feminist Criticism*, edited by Elaine Showalter, 314–88. New York: Pantheon Books, 1985. (Originally published in *Signs* 8 [1981])

Petronio, Giuseppe. *L'Attivita letteraria in Italia*. Florence: Palumbo, 1980.

Porta, Antonio. Review of Patrizia Valduga's *Medicamenta*, published in *Il corrietre della sera* (26 September 1982). Reprinted in *Il progetto infinito*, 85–86. Rome: Edizioni Fondo Pier Paolo Pasolini, 1991.

Quasimodo, Salvatore. *La vita non è un sogno*. Milan: Mondadori, 1966. (Originally published 1949)

Rich, Adrienne. "When We Dead Awaken: Writing as Re-Vision" (1971). In *On Lies, Secrets, and Silence: Selected Prose, 1966–1978*, 33–49. New York: Norton, 1979.

Rose, Jaqueline. Introduction to *Feminine Sexuality: Jacques Lacan and the Ecole Freudienne*, 27–58. New York: Norton, 1982.

Rossanda, Rossana. Introduction to *Antigone*, by Sophocles, 7–58. Translated into Italian by Luisa Biondetti. Milan: Feltrinelli, 1987.

Rosselli, Amelia. *Variazioni belliche*. Milan: Garzanti, 1964.

Shiach, Morag. "Their 'Symbolic' Exists, It Holds Power—We, the Sowers of Disorder, Know It Only Too Well." In *Between Feminism and Psychoanalysis*, edited by Teresa Brennan, 153–67. London: Routledge, 1989.

Spaziani, Maria Luisa. *Poesie*. Introduction by Luigi Baldacci. Milan: Mondadori, 1979.

Spivak, Gayatri. "Sex and History in The Prelude (1805): Books IX to XIII." In *Post-Structuralist Readings of English Poetry*, edited by Richard Machin and Christopher Norris, 193–226. Cambridge: Cambridge University Press, 1987.

Splendore, Carmen. *Elena Ippolita e le altre*. Palermo: Dharba, 1992.

Steiner, George. *Antigones: How the Antigone Legend Has Endured in Western Literature, Art, and Thought*. Oxford: Clarendon Press, 1986.

Suleiman, Susan. *Subversive Intent: Gender Politics and the Avant-Garde*. Cambridge: Harvard University Press, 1990.

Ungaretti, Giuseppe. *Vita d'un uomo: Tutte le poesie*. Milan: Mondadori, 1992.

Violi, Patrizia. *L'Infinito singolare: Considerazioni sulla differenza sessuale nel linguaggio*. Milan: Essedue Edizioni, 1987.

West, Rebecca. "Maria Luisa Spaziani." Forthcoming in *Dictionary of Literary Biography*, edited by G. De Stasio.

Zanardo, Gloria. "Lettura dell'Antigone di Sofocle in *Etica della differenza sessuale*." In Bimbi et al., *Il Filo oli Arianna: Letture della differenza sessuale*, 82–92. Rome: Utopia, 1987.

# Part V

## Women as Filmmakers

Images of Women

Images by Women

Images for Women

# 13

## Monica Vitti: The Image and the Word

*Marga Cottino-Jones*

According to Lucy Fisher in "The Lives of Performers: The Actress as Signifier," the role as an actress is a very significant one for women who, "cast as
the *Other* to the male norm . . . have been urged to embody a wide range of
dramatis personae; from earth mother to temptress, from madonna to
whore."[1] As Luce Irigaray maintains, the role of "mimicry [is] historically assigned to the feminine";[2] hence the importance given to the acting profession
among women's activities. Actresses, therefore, are perfectly legitimate topics
of scholarly investigation within the field of women studies and the subfield
of women in cinema.

Within the area of women in Italian cinema, there is no doubt that Monica Vitti holds a remarkable position. She is in fact recognized as one of the
most talented and accomplished actresses in Italy today, for both stage and
screen, with a powerful mastery of both dramatic and comic performing skills.
In addition, in the past few years Vitti has added a new dimension to her
acting by writing the script for each of her three latest films: *Flirt* (1983),
*Francesca è mia* (1986), and *Scandalo segreto* (1989);[3] this last one she also
directed. And yet, notwithstanding her accomplishments and the popularity

she enjoys not only in Italy, but all over Europe, there has been little critical assessment of her.[4]

In this essay, I shall briefly analyze Vitti as an actress, particularly in Antonioni's films, and then concentrate on her work as a scriptwriter and a director. I intend to show her development from a female character constructed by the camera look of male directors (as the object of the male characters' and the male spectators' gaze and desire), to more ambiguous and complex female roles, reflecting the point of view and the look of a woman writer and director. In this analysis, I am basing my critical discourse on the latest critical theories about women in cinema that I have found useful for this study,[5] without losing sight of the specific historical context in which Vitti has worked and refined her performing skills and her feminine sensibility; that is, the Italian contemporary film industry and the social and cultural codes that control Italian cinema and culture.[6] Because of the heavy pressure of its patriarchal structure, feminism in Italy, as Laura Mulvey has correctly stated in her introduction to the essays in *Off Screen*, has "evolved alongside a close attention to practice and a highly politicized, militant culture." At the same time, it has also shown a particular concern with a theme that Mulvey calls "woman's relationship to love, or rather to the *sogno d'amore* or dream of love," which "offers a starting point for understanding woman's complicity with her oppression . . . and acts as a resistance to the negativity inherent in woman's binary position" (*Off Screen*, xii). This theme is a constant in Vitti's films and its function in the film narratives is essential in inscribing her, her roles, and her filmic discourse in the stream of contemporary Italian feminism. A special 1972 issue of *Bianco e Nero* dedicated to interviewing women in cinema, including actresses, scriptwriters, costume designers, director assistants, etc., regarding their experiences in the cinema world, throws some light on this particular matter. Vitti, one of the women interviewed, shows, already at that time, a keen awareness of women's repression and conditioning within the context of patriarchy both in their private lives and at work. In answer to the question Do you think that it may be possible for an actress to accept the roles that are imposed on her and then undermine them from within? Vitti replies:

> It is incredible how very few Italian directors and scriptwriters are seriously interested in what a woman thinks or by what a woman is moved. . . . In cinema, when they write a script, nobody writes for women characters. How many times a scriptwriter has told me: "But, my dear Monica, how can I write stories for you? You are a woman

and what does a woman do? She does not go to war, she has no profession . . . see how few professions? What can I have you do? Only a
love story can I make you do; that you have children, suffer, he leaves
you, you are desperate . . ." You see, this is the only function they give
me. I have tried many times to say: "But why don't you turn inside
out this character and you'll have a woman!" "Ah, no! That's impossible!" That was the answer! If you could see the enormous difficulties
that I have to face in trying to make a film that deals with a woman![7]

That was in 1972. Only in 1989, Vitti will eventually be able to make such
a film.

As a graduate of the Accademia d'Arte Drammatica of Rome, Vitti started
her career as stage actress, combining already at that time her dramatic skills
in classical roles from the Greek theater and Shakespeare, with her comic
brillanti ones in Molière, Brecht, contemporary pieces, and even the music
hall. Monica held a steady job as a professional at dubbing, an activity in
great demand in the Italian film industry. She had great success in dubbing
because of her, as she puts it, "strange voice," suitable especially for popular
characters, such as "prostitutes, color women, drunkards, etc." (Colli, 22).

The great step into the world of cinema was taken with Michelangelo Antonioni, even if she had already tried out her comic talent earlier in films
with well-known actors and actresses, such as Aldo Fabrizi, Paolo Stoppa,
Giovanna Ralli, Sandra Mondaini, etc. The first film with Antonioni, and
the one that catapulted both of them to international fame, was L'Avventura
(1960). After that followed La Notte (1961), L'Eclissi (1962), and, a few years
later, Deserto rosso (1964). The last film she did with Antonioni was Il Mistero
di Oberwald (1980), a very powerful drama of love, political intrigue, and
death, where she plays the key female role. Throughout the period between
1965 and the early '80s, she is nearly exclusively involved in roles within the
genre of the commedia all'italiana,[8] playing mostly the female counterpart to
the male comic stars of our cinema, such as Alberto Sordi, Ugo Tognazzi,
Nino Manfredi, etc.[9] Probably her best-known roles were Assunta Patanè, as
the sedotta e abbandonata in La Ragazza con la pistola by Mario Monicelli
(1968); Adelaide Caprocchi, the beautiful girl at the center of the love triangle in Dramma della gelosia: Tutti i particolari in cronaca, by Ettore Scola (1970);
and the multiple roles, including the romantic girl, the mother, the slave for
love, the war correspondent, the nun, etc., in Noi donne siamo fatte così, by
Dino Risi (1971).

Before concentrating on her last three films (the first two directed by Ro-

berto Russo) let us investigate how Monica was cast as an actress by one of
the masters of Italian film, Michelangelo Antonioni, in two of his earliest
films, and by far the most important, L'Avventura and Eclisse. Even if Antonioni's films have always been regarded as much more sensitive to women's
issues than those of other equally talented Italian film directors, such as Vis-
conti or Fellini, a close re-reading of his framing of women characters may
reveal an equally male-dominated handling of the female image. The success
of L'Avventura was not so "absolute and unquestionable as will be for Blow-
up."[10] The film was in fact censored in several countries and its projection
suspended for six months in Milan for oltraggio al pudore because of the several
scenes showing women, and particularly Monica, undressing in front of the
camera. These reactions to the film encoded a patriarchal sanction against
the uncovering of the female body, viewed as a transgression to the social and
moral system controlling women's activities in Italian society. At the same
time, the severity of these reactions revealed the deep patriarchal fear of the
visual impact that scenes presenting the uncovering of the female body could
have on the film's viewers, thus confirming the need for sanctions aimed at
diffusing the disturbing sexual power that woman may have on a male audience.[11] It is quite clear, therefore, that the censoring operation activated
against the film has established "the ideal spectator (of the film) as male and
the typical object of spectacle as female."[12]

Cinematically, the image of woman undressing reveals the male's gaze,
framing woman in a static image, as the object of that look and, through her
desirability, also as the object of his desire. The "unmasking" of this image,
then, uncovers the underlying presence of the main activator of all action in
the film; that is, male desire, working through the look of the camera. In
L'Avventura, this look reveals the gaze of the main male character, Sandro,
while directing also the look of the male spectators from outside the film.
Thus, in de Lauretis's words, "the look of the camera, the look of the spectator
and the look of each character within the film intersect in a complex system
which structures vision and meaning," and in so doing "governs its representation of woman" (Alice Doesn't, 138). That woman in L'Avventura is reduced
exclusively to the object of the male's desire is implied in the event that acti-
vates the diegesis of the film narrative: Anna's disappearance. The only thing
the spectators know about Anna, prior to her disappearance, is that she is
involved romantically with Sandro, and hers is the first female body that we
see undressing on the screen, prior to making love to him. This scene frames
her as the object of both Sandro's look and desire. Shortly after, there is another undressing scene on the yacht, before Anna's disappearance, involving

both Anna and Claudia (played by Monica Vitti), where the camera's look together with the spectators' concentrate also on Claudia, as if to suggest that the next time an object of desire attracts the male character's look, it will be Claudia. And, indeed, shortly after that scene, Anna disappears and, nearly instantly Sandro transfers on Claudia both his look and his desire. Several scenes of undressing and lovemaking follow, through which Claudia is framed as the locus of the male's gaze, until, close to the end of the film, she is left alone in her room, while Sandro becomes the activator of an intersection of different looks, both female and male, that prepare for the transference of his desire onto another object, the *ragazza squillo* that he had previously met in Palermo. At the end of the film, Claudia is framed again by the look of the camera, in the image of a woman standing behind and touching delicately with her hand the head of a man sitting with his back turned to her and crying. The story closes then on an image of woman that is different from the one that has been projected throughout the whole film. Instead of framing her as the object of man's desire, here the screen reveals woman as a maternal image of compassion and understanding, encoded, also in this case, within the male's needs.[13] Both images of woman, as object of desire and as mother, are equally static and representative of the patriarchal codes of values that underlie the meaning of the film, so that, as in the classic Hollywood films, the female position "produced as the end result of narrativization is the figure of narrative closure, the narrative image in which the film . . . comes together" (*Alice Doesn't*, 140). With this closing maternal image of Claudia, superimposed on her previous one as object of Sandro's desire, *L'Avventura* hardly leaves woman any other space but those constructed for her within the patriarchal system in order to fulfill the male's needs.

The *Eclisse* presents a less conventional narrativization, even if the social and existential message conveyed by the environment and by the several characters therein playing is very similar to that of *L'Avventura*. Both films deal with unusual love relationships. But, instead of a male character being involved with two women, the *Eclisse* tells the story of one woman involved with two men. Vittoria (played by Monica Vitti) has two lovers; first Riccardo, whose love she cannot reciprocate, and then Piero for whose look and desire she becomes framed as a static image throughout most of the film. The end, however, is more contradictory and ambiguous than in *L'Avventura*. In a way *Eclisse* seems to end on the event that opens *L'Avventura*: the disappearance of the woman. Anna disappears from Sandro's and her friends' sight and throughout the whole film she is signified through absence. Vittoria has been present on the screen throughout the whole film, but at the end of the film, when she is supposed to meet Piero at the usual place and at the usual time, she is not to be seen anywhere in the sequence of scenes that stage their expected rendezvous. Thus here too the woman is absent. At the same time, also Piero, her lover, who was supposed to be there too, is absent. Consequently, the film's "narrative closure," rather than signified by the image of the woman framed in a traditional position, is evidenced throughout the absence of both the male character's look and of the object of his look. What is then the meaning of absence as "the end result of narrativization?" Is Vittoria's absence a consequence of her search for female subjectivity, and, therefore an assertion of her individuality and a refusal of her position as object of the male's desire? The narrative progression of the film and Vittoria's character focalization[14] hardly validate such a reading of the cinematic text of the *Eclisse*. Given the pattern of static image-framing in which woman is encoded in the film always as object of the male's desire and look, created by his narcissistic projection of desire, shouldn't absence be the only possible space in which to frame woman when the male's look is absent as well? Since here Piero and his look are *not* there, Vittoria, the woman-object of the male's look, cannot be but absent.

In Antonioni's films, then, Monica Vitti, even if playing the role of the female protagonist, was constantly constructed as the object of the male's look and desire, as "woman . . . inside the rectangle." Things did not change too much in the following years, as Monica Vitti became the heroine of *commedia all'italiana* plots that frame woman even more "as narrative image, object, and ground of cinematic representation" (de Lauretis, *Technologies*, 114). Only in the 1980s has her collaboration with Roberto Russo given her the opportunity to make three films about women as she sees them, women who, although caught in conflicts still controlled by desire and domination, "tell stories resisting the drift of narrativization (the operation of narrative closure)" and show "the practice of self-consciousness, that particular kind of ideological analysis which begins from and always refers back to the experience of gender and its construction of subjectivity" (de Lauretis, *Technologies*, 114, 121). All three films for which she wrote the script with Russo, *Flirt*, *Francesca è mia*, and *Scandalo segreto*, still adopt the conventional strategies of narrative that address the relationship between the text and the spectator on the level of "visual pleasure." In all these films, the narrative plot is centered on the classical situation of *commedia all'italiana* films; that is, on marriage, where Monica plays the traditional wife still in love with her husband, even when she has to deal with his infidelity with a usually powerful rival. Typical triangle situations develop also in these cases, where the male's desire is the activator of the films' action, even if the women's desire, differently in each of the three films, interferes with it, producing less conventional alternatives for the outcome of the narrative process. On the whole, these three films convey a new concern with "address (whom the film addresses, to whom it speaks, what and for whom it seeks to represent, whom it represents)" that "translates into a conscious effort to address the spectator as female, regardless of the gender of the viewers"; this is what de Lauretis calls "feminist cinema" (*Technologies*, 119).

Flirt, a film that, as Monica herself says, "Roberto and I have written, rewritten, thrown out, started again, corrected, changed idea about for several years,"[15] was produced in 1983 in collaboration with RAI, the state-run television network. The narrative here works on a level of comic irony though the traditional triangle situation activated by the husband's desire, which is here pushed to the boundaries of the absurd by positioning his new object of desire, his beloved Veronica, in the realm of the hallucinatory, and as such invisible to anyone but him, and yet no less real to him than if visible. At this level of meaning, the film, through the invisibility of the object of Giovanni's desire, works out an amusing satire of man's narcissistic drives and of male analysts' inability to recognize them. And yet, there is another level of meaning in the film, that works out through the character of Laura, the wife (played by Monica Vitti), and the conflict that emerges from her maintaining the focus of her desire on the very visible character of Giovanni, even when his desire has shifted to the invisible Veronica. Through the strategies that Laura uses in order to impose her own desire and interfere with Giovanni's, so as to reshift his look and desire back on to herself, the narrative creates a discrepancy between the traditional framing of woman as image and the self-consciousness displayed by Laura in framing herself as the object of Giovanni's look while being the subject of the action that controls that look. In this conscious manipulation of desire, the text *addresses* its spectators in a contradictory way: it does not "repel [the] woman's gaze . . . or [the] feminist understanding of the female subject's history, of a-womanness, contradiction, and self-subverting coherence" (de Lauretis, *Technologies*, 124). The film closes on the image of the fulfillment of mutual desire with Laura and Giovanni making love with equal intensity and passion: "They hug and kiss with a frightful violence as if they had waited years for this moment."[16] Female desire and pleasure are therefore recognized as important elements in *Flirt*, capable not only of what Mulvey calls "subverting the dominant male-constructed discourse and gaze" (*Off Screen*, 13) but also of constructing, as de Lauretis would say, "the terms of reference of another measure of desire and the conditions of visibility for a different social subject" (de Lauretis, *Alice Doesn't*, 155).

More complex is the narrativization of the plot in *Francesca è mia*, where it is the triangle situation that is pushed to the boundaries of the absurd. Although her husband lives with his lover (who is also her best friend), Francesca, the wife (played by Monica Vitti), accepts without any contention, that he still is the controlling force in her life. In this context, it is the husband who stands at the center of the triangle situation as the manipulator of wife and lover, the two objects of his desire. Francesca is, therefore, represented as subjected to the dominant male-discourse controlling the marriage binary structure of female oppression and male dominance, even if her marriage is far from representing a normal situation. At this point, the film diegesis opens this closed structure and disrupts it. A fourth character, Stefano, is inserted in Francesca's life. After he has been seriously injured in a hit-and-run car accident, Francesca takes him to the emergency ward and watches over after his operation. With the insertion of Stefano, a second triangle situation is created, this time with Francesca at the center as object of desire. While the first triangle situation inscribes both women, and particularly the wife, within the typical representation of the passive woman totally subjected to the male's desire and dominance, the introduction of Stefano disrupts such representation by constructing a different frame for Francesca around the obviously Oedipal conflict between two men, one young and the other much older, over her.

The relationship between Francesca and Stefano starts on an equivocal level when Francesca is thrown into a maternal role toward the young man immediately following his accident. She is asked by the hospital staff to stay with him all night immediately after his operation, to watch over him as, his name being unknown, none of this relatives or friends can be notified. When she comes back the next day to see how he is progressing, she finds herself in the middle of another emergency situation since his condition has worsened and he is placed in intensive care. She is thus thrown again into the role of caretaker and, more specifically in this case, of life-keeper. Indeed she is entrusted by the nurse with the task of keeping the young man alive by constantly talking to him from late afternoon all through the night until early morning. At dawn, as if in response to Francesca's incessant flow of words, describing spaces she has seen and liked, events of her life she has particularly cherished, or telling stories about people she knows or about imaginary events, or encouraging him to hold on to life and to look to the future with optimism and joy, Stefano regains consciousness and utters the words she had asked him to tell her: "Mi chiamo Stefano." Francesca, therefore, has become the voice that brings Stefano back to life, thus fulfilling the maternal role of life-giver, ambiguously experienced by the young man in an obviously Oedipal transference. According to Kaja Silverman, it is the mother's voice that is identified by the child long before he or she can see her face or body, and it is her voice "that first charts space, delimits objects, explains and defines the external world" for the infant (76). The mother assumes therefore the role of "commentator . . . and . . . narrator" for the child, the same role Francesca plays for Stefano all through that long night when he hovers between life and death.

The "fantasy of the maternal voice," as Silverman calls it, gives rise, however, to contradictory interpretations and "takes on a different meaning, depending upon the psychic 'lookout point'; viewed from the site of the unconscious, the image of the infant held within the environment or sphere of the mother's voice is an emblem of infantile plenitude and bliss. Viewed from the site of the preconscious-conscious system, it is an emblem of impotence and entrapment" (73).[17] Stefano's fascination for Francesca displays the aspiration for total unity with her that the "unconscious . . . lookout point" may project; a unity, full of "plenitude and bliss," probably experienced by him earlier in his infancy, solicited now by Francesca's voice and, it is hoped, to be achieved by Stefano even without speaking and through visual contact. Indeed at first, Stefano constantly follows Francesca, carefully avoiding speaking to her. Thus also for Stefano, as Silverman has warned us, listening to Francesca's voice has not only been his connection with life for a whole night, but it has also provided him with the first stimulation for achieving that state of "plenitude and bliss" that he needs. After listening to her voice, then, his main motivation will be to look at her face and body in order to achieve and maintain the imaginary unity with her that he yearns for. And this is actually what Stefano will try to do as soon as he leaves the hospital.

There are three key scenes in the film—the mirror scene in the bar, the encounter with the older rival, and the dialogue with Francesca—that mark the development of Stefano's ambiguous relationship with Francesca, from the early imaginary phase, through the following symbolic or Oedipal stage, down to a post-Oedipal one. The first phase (which corresponds to the imaginary one and consists of purely visual contacts, when Stefano follows Francesca from far away without ever attempting to talk to her) is abruptly interrupted by the bar scene (the first of the key scenes), all projected through a large mirror that is in front of Francesca while she is sipping a cup of coffee. The eye of the camera is positioned behind her; consequently, the spectators watch Francesca through the mirror. Suddenly Stefano enters the bar and comes to stand next to Francesca, so that the mirror now reflects both of them together, looking at their image in the mirror. When Francesca takes her gaze away from the mirror and turns to Stefano to talk to him, Stefano turns away and walks out of the bar, this time with the camera—and the spectators—taking the position of Francesca's look; that is, still from behind her, but no longer in front of the mirror. This scene brings to mind the Lacanian mirror phase, when the child, faced for the first time with the complete image of himself and the mother through a mirror, projects his own identity on that image, while at the same time experiencing a sense of differentiation and loss.[18] In internalizing such an image, the child overcomes the sense of loss and narcissistically invests the whole image of himself and the "other" with his own identity. In applying this stage to Stefano, his encounter with the mirror image of himself and Francesca helps him in overcoming his fear of losing her by strengthening his sense of identification of her with himself, thus heightening his potential for a narcissistic misrecognition of the imagined unity with her.

The acquisition of language is also another way of overcoming the sense of loss or absence of the mother, while at the same time it moves the child into the symbolic stage, where the figure and the word of the father predominate. We have a second important scene in the film where this stage is reenacted in the encounter between Stefano and Andrea, Francesca's husband, at the door of her apartment, in a series of shot/reverse shots that heighten the conflict. When Stefano rings the bell, Andrea opens the door and, before calling Francesca, asks the younger man for his name twice: Stefano replies both times, but, when eventually Francesca comes to the door, he has disappeared. The filming of this scene on the liminal space of the entrance door to Francesca's apartment—Andrea is in the inside, while Stefano is kept outside—stresses the position of superiority that the older man holds over the younger, conferring on him the aura of the superior father figure (which later on will be reversed through a depiction of his weaknesses and impotence). It is at this particular point that the Oedipal triangle surfaces, when Stefano becomes aware of a rival in his desired unity with Francesca. It is after this encounter that Stefano speaks for the first time to Francesca, in the scene between the two that immediately follows, outside of her apartment building, in the rain. In this scene, he acknowledges the change in his own view of their relationship that has just taken place: "Indeed, at the beginning, I wanted to tell you 'Thank you' and I looked for you for that reason. Then, I changed my mind . . . and I felt the desire to look at you. And it was never enough. I had also thought that I would have never talked to you . . . maybe if you had not come down here, now, I would have never talked to you . . . but . . . I would have kept on looking at you . . . not following you . . . but looking at you. I have also tried to do other things. . . . Last Thursday, you must have noticed it . . . you didn't see me all day. But then I couldn't make it. On Friday morning, I was already sick, my stomach was hurting . . . I am here because otherwise my stomach hurts."[19] In the Oedipal phase, after a strong recognition of rivalry with the father, perceiving the threat of punishment coming from him, the boy child gives up his incestuous desire for the mother; he then identifies with the father and repudiates the mother's body and voice, accepting the voice and law of the father. However, in Stefano's case, his narcissistic misrecognition of his unity with Francesca displaces the normal Oedipal development. This condition pushes for a subversive solution by which he puts himself directly in the absent father's place, taking up his role and exercising his power over Francesca: "Come away with me" he commands her, "do not go back there. . . . Come with me . . . now and for ever."[20] Other scenes stress this subversive Oedipal trend, particularly the sequence of scenes inside Francesca's apartment where Stefano has entered unnoticed and where, unseen, he watches Francesca, alone at first, and then with Andrea who has unexpectedly come back to her in the middle of the night. In these scenes, the complexity of the narrative situation is indicated by the play of the different looks that work on- and offscreen: while, on-screen, Francesca looks at television, Stefano looks at her from behind a door, while the camera and the spectators watch both of them, from offscreen, through pans and zoom-ins and -outs. When Andrea joins Francesca, we have a series of shot/reverse shots between the two, with Stefano looking at both of them from different hiding spots in the apartment, while the camera and spectators look at all three of them at different length and distance. Eventually, with Stefano's drastic decision to prevent Francesca from leaving, by physically dragging her away from the train, the narcissistic structure that has been building up around his image of plenitude with her, closes upon his total misrecognition of the "other" as self. As a narcissistic subject, Stefano sees Francesca as part of himself and he wants her there in his totally isolated house, with him, for ever: "Now you stay here and I want you to stay here. . . . Throw away everything . . . your house, your mother, your brothers . . . your stupid fears . . . forget everything, pretend to have been born this morning . . . now!"[21] This narcissistic misrecognition of Francesca as his own, rather than as a being with her own needs and desires, reveals Stefano's fears of his inability to play out the role of the overpowering father; to this purpose, the absence, in his last speech just quoted, of any mention of her husband, is very revealing. This intensity of desire that the young man projects on Francesca and his uncontrollable need to reduce her to a mere object of his will and desire, seem indeed to disclose that feeling of "impotence and entrapment" that Silverman saw in "the fantasy of the maternal voice."

Francesca, on her part, while accepting to be framed for one night within Stefano's possessive desire, eventually distances herself from his enclosing narcissistic grip, establishing her own self also in matter of desire. The woman is therefore positioned in a contradictory interplay of signification: at the level of the male character's desire, she is constructed first as the confirming, narcissistic reflection of his ego identity and later on as a threat to it; at the level of the female character, then, she projects herself ambivalently both as the fixed image of woman subjected to male dominance as the object of his desire and violence (tied up to a chair and subjected to his physical abuse), and, at the same time, as an individual in need to establish herself as a separate subject. In her final conflict with Stefano, Francesca inserts herself into a contradictory discourse about female desire: "Now it is not like this morning . . . now you have made me understand . . . how squalid it was between Andrea and myself . . . at home. . . . It wasn't like that before, you know . . . but then, little by little . . . it is part of life. All the mistakes, the things to be forgiven . . . also for me. Maybe I do not have any clear reason to go back there, he is perfectly all right, even without me; but I know that I will go back, I realize it now. I am just like you . . . I cannot stand seeing him walking out of the door . . . when he leaves me, I too would want to tie him down . . . I love him."[22] Through this discourse, Francesca projects her desire over the image of the woman oppressed and subjected to male dominance; and thus she denies such an image through her openly voiced claim to desire, although her controversial achievement on the level of discourse provokes a tragic conflict on the level of the action. In fact, when left alone by Stefano, she does leave him and runs to the station to get a train back to Rome and to the one she loves. When Stefano finds her on the train and commands her to go with him, threatening her with his gun, Francesca, for the first time in her life, finds the strength to say no to a male's request. The conflict between the female voice, that finds the courage to stand by her decision and her desire, and the male's antagonistic action aimed at imposing his own narcissistic control on her, results in Francesca's death. Stefano never overcomes his narcissistic misrecognition of Francesca as his own "self." Spurred by his Opedipal fear to violate the law of the father requiring from him the elimination of the mother figure, he prefers to destroy her rather than admit to his own narcissistic deviation. His weapon is a gun, the phallic symbol of his male ego—and clearly a symbol cherished by him in his career as a trap-shooter champion. The final conflict between male and female is solved thus through the traditional supremacy of the male, who, although unable to control his own self, has power—signified here by the gun—over the female, who is devoid both of power and of defense against power, even if she is capable of acknowledging her own desire and identity. The film closes on a long shot of Stefano in the empty station, with his hands in his pockets, his eyes downcast, oblivious of the world outside, obviously projecting the image of himself as the ideal ego of the Imaginary realm "an ideal of narcissistic omnipotence constructed on the model of infantile narcissism (or investment of energy in the self) . . . in which images of "otherness" are transformed into reflections of the self."[23] This indifference to "otherness" and to the outside world, inscribed in his body posture and look, signifies Stefano's utter solitude and introversion, bringing the film to a narrative closure where gender conflicts remain unsolved and woman is the victim of male's narcissistic self-projection, even when she has finally established her own identity and found the courage to voice her own true desire.

With *Scandalo segreto*[24] (1989), Monica Vitti becomes a director and the film is a brilliant example of Italian feminist cinema in terms of both Italian feminism (and particularly of its concern with the "relations of power and domination in social and political structures, starting from the family . . . in order to reach definition of female identity, subjectivity, and pleasure" (*Off Screen*, 10), as well as in terms of women's cinema and contemporary theories of feminism. I have in mind particularly what de Lauretis calls "the contradiction constitutive of the female subject of feminism," deriving from the fact that "the female subject . . . is at once inside and outside the ideology of gender, or . . . is at once *woman* and *women*. In other words, *woman* is inside the triangle, *women* are outside; the female subject is in both places at once. *That* is the contradiction" (de Lauretis, *Technologies*, 114). Monica Vitti seems particularly aware of this contradiction in this film, when she positions herself both *in front of* the camera—as Margherita, the character of the wife, whose husband, Paolo, is a famous painter of *eyes*, involved in a love affair with her best friend Laura—and *behind it*, as Monica, the director. In this way, she is at the same time both *woman*, *inside*, framed by the gaze of the camera in a rectangular screen, and the historical woman who is telling the woman's story, *outside*. At the same time, Monica, the female director, with her long experience as an actress, unwillingly obliged by male directors to impersonate the traditional image of woman, seems to be well aware also of the contradiction that is constitutive of female characters. Thus she has Margherita, the character who is controlling the video camera, visually displaying such contradiction.

On her birthday, Margherita receives a video camera as a present from her friend Tony. From that point on, up to, but not including, the last scenes of the film, the narrative unfolds exclusively through the eye of this video camera, of which Margherita appears to be, most of the time, the controlling eye. Indeed, when the video camera is turned off, the screen goes blank. Margherita, then, as the main character of the film, positions herself, like the director Monica Vitti, both behind and in front of the camera, playing different roles according to her positioning in the narrative. When she is in front of the camera, she plays Margherita, the wife, with Paolo; Margherita, the mother, with her son—exclusively on the phone—and Margherita, the friend, with Tony; and, by herself, in the several scenes where alone, mostly inside her own home, she verbalizes her thoughts directly into the camera, playing a woman in search of her identity. When she is behind the camera, instead, she uses it as a regular filmmaker, often inserting an ironic dimension in her directing, as when she frames the male characters of Tony and Paolo in close-ups or full shots, commenting on their physical attractiveness; or when, in preparing the set for her encounter with Laura, she insists on camouflaging the camera in order to hide it from her friend, thus commenting on the problematics of cinema versus reality. In this double presence, both in front of and behind the video camera, Margherita the character—or Monica the actress—becomes inscribed in the contradictions of the female subject, positioned in this case in the specific social environment of the family and in the private space of her home; an environment and a space both particularly meaningful for Italian female spectators. The film shows indeed a conscious effort to address the spectator as female, building accordingly narrative patterns of woman representation easily recognizable to both male and female spectatorship. At the same time, the narrative subtly interweaves a more hidden network of meaning involving Margherita and the contradiction of the female subject inscribed in her character, employing strategies intended at disrupting traditional narrative.[25]

One of these strategies is certainly the complexity of the cinematic look and particularly the double positioning of the main character in relation to the camera eye. With this positioning, the typical plot involving a marriage situation is disrupted since the wife in this case is not always the object of the frame, but becomes often the eye through which other objects are framed. So, while with his paintings, Paolo, her husband, creates pictures that are images of the eye, Margherita becomes herself the eye of the image-creating camera. Furthermore, just as she cannot stand his painted eyes hovering over her, he cannot stand her camera eye focused upon him. If the male's look has always been the framing eye of the traditional film narrative, in this film, it is the female's look that is now the framing eye at the surface level of the narrative.

Sometimes, however, the eye of the video camera introduces a dimension of unpredictability in the narrative that contributes to its disruption, while undermining the main character's controlling influence. Another important device working disruptively within the narrative, is provided by the rough quality of visual presentation conveyed through Margherita's inexperienced use of the video camera, limited mostly to close-ups or full-length representation of people or short pans of interiors and exteriors, and subjected to the constant interruptions imposed by the personal whims of the would-be director or by decisions external to the diegesis of the story. This type of disruption, not uncommon in feminist films, besides increasing the effect of "decentering . . . the masculinity" from within the narrative, also invests with a stronger impact the film strategies of addressing the spectator as female; it undercuts the importance of cinematic smoothness and regularity to the advantage of a more feminine, emotional, and instinctive form of representation.

Through this subtle network of strategies, disruptive of both the narrative and the main character, the self-consciousness training process that Margherita undergoes acquires a stronger appeal for the spectator. The first stage of such a process is provided by the sequence of scenes where Margherita and Laura are facing each other as rivals. This encounter is impulsively arranged by Margherita, as soon as she becomes aware of Paolo's relation with Laura. The two women are framed in a series of shot/reverse shots, as two different sides of femininity; on one side, Margherita seems to stand for the typical image of femininity inscribed in the patriarchal code: frail, emotional, insecure, unprofessional, ideally content in the limited but comforting enclosure of her marriage situation and comfortable home. Laura, instead, is positioned as another side of femininity, in opposition to her: strong, independent, cold, secure of herself and her charm, self-centered and uncompromising. While Margherita's *sogno d'amore* is to be loved and needed by Paolo ("tell me," she asks him, "how long could you stay away from me? . . . Please, tell me you love me . . . louder, please"), Laura's relation with Paolo is purely physical, "without the shadow of a feeling."[26] Margherita, as expected, as soon as she confronts Laura, is unable to stand up to her; in her insecurity, she even believes she wants to become like her: "Teach me how to become like you," she asks her rival. "I want to be able to go out when I feel like, to go and enjoy a landscape on my own. To go to the seaside, to go where I want. And not share everything always with him!"[27] And yet, by the end of this encounter with Laura, she begins to realize that she is different and that her needs are different, thus catching a first glimpse of her own identity: "But what does it mean not to need anyone? How can I do without people, and mostly without him? I need everyone, even you."[28] From this first realization of her own difference, she goes through a process of alternative states, sometimes blaming herself for his unfaithfulness: "I had to love him better! Instead . . . all that talk about love me more, loving me better. You don't love me enough . . . I love you more . . . keep on bargaining about love as if we were at the market!"[29] sometimes openly admitting that, although still loving him, she cannot continue to live with him: "I know that I will not be able to live without you, but I leave you all the same."[30] And she does leave him, without giving him any explanation that might hint at her knowing of his affair with Laura or at the anguish that it has caused her. With this last statement, Margherita's self-realization has come full circle, from passivity to anger, to doubts, and eventually to a dignified, self-respecting acceptance of herself and her limitations, still in the context of that *sogno d'amore* that dominates her whole life. As long as that dream had been real for her, she had accepted the safe image of the good wife in which Paolo and all her friends had framed her for their own needs—especially Paolo for maintaining the right atmosphere for his *eye* paintings and the cozy family environment where to eat well and relax. But, as soon as her dream has been destroyed and she has realized the hypocrisy of the situation and the selfishness of his intentions, she does not accept that image any longer, even if it still greatly suits her own needs and she positions herself in front of him in a new image of independence and self-assertion.

The contradiction, however, inscribed in her character, between woman as object, in front of the camera eye, and as subject, behind the camera, is played out dramatically in the narrative toward the end of the film, when, standing in front of the video camera, Margherita accuses the camera of having been the cause of her fall from blissful ignorance to painful realization: "It's all your fault! There you stand with that black eye that stares . . . and criticizes . . . and provokes, but if you had not been there, always looking and criticizing, maybe I would not have known . . . and, even if I had known . . . and you had not been there, maybe, I would have accepted or forgotten."[31] This conflict that emerges here between the character in front of the camera and the camera eye that used to be identifiable with the eye of the character, dramatizes further the process of self-consciousness that Margherita has undergone because of her position behind the camera.

The most disruptive strategy in the narrative is climactically revealed at the end of the film, when the video camera ignores Margherita's attempt at turning it off, thus uncovering the complexity of the gaze apparatus of the film. It is at this point, that we, the spectators, find out for the first time that there is another look behind Margherita's, on the other side of the video camera; another ever-present look that has been controlling the camera and most of Margherita's operations as well, all throughout the film. It was the male look of Tony, determined to use Margherita and her life as the narrative text for his own film. Margherita becomes aware of this, even later than we spectators, when she is practically on the point of death, after having ingested several sleeping pills. This last disruptive strategy of the film disturbingly questions the independence of the female look, while addressing with a vengeance the problem of male domination with such a vibrant example of man's blatantly insensitive interference with a woman's life. In the last scene of the film, the second one framed exclusively by the woman director's look,[32] Margherita herself throws the video camera out of the balcony.

We may now be asking ourselves, What is the meaning of this text? What is our female director telling us with this narrative envisioned and projected by the superimposition of a male character's look over a female's and eventually of the all-encompassing female director's look on both of them? Is Vitti, the director, confirming our suspicions that the ambiguity of the woman's story here unfolded is inscribed into the codes that have controlled woman's life for centuries and that the gift of the mechanical eye of the video camera from man to woman is another way to make us, women, tell our story just as they, men, want us to do? If this is the message, certainly the only image woman is to be positioned in by the woman director, as the closing image of her film, is in her act of throwing away the male's present. And yet, we cannot forget that the male character's look was kept all the time under the supervision of the female director who controlled the accuracy of the representation, while obviously sharing in the contradictory positioning of the female character and in the concern for whom the film addresses. Could we then imply that for the female director the long tribulations Margherita had to endure were actually necessary for her self-consciousness to rise and fulfill its promises so as to inscribe her within the contradictory process that helped her become a female subject? And even if Tony's male look was there, seemingly to control Margherita's look and life, it actually worked as a catalyst to Margherita's self-realization, rather than as a hindrance to it, and it was always kept safely under control through the attentive surveillance of the female director's eye. Accordingly, Margherita's last enraged action of throwing the camera off the balcony, is her final act of self-accomplishment (also essential to her, because it physically helps her to keep active while waiting for the ambulance to come and ensure her survival!). With that action, indeed, the film closes on a very dynamic image of cathartic liberation from the control of the male's eye, thus establishing the woman's refusal to be the object of that eye; through that conscious refusal, she asserts her own identity and subjectivity.

We can then close our reading, by agreeing that Scandalo segreto's visual representation conveys what de Lauretis calls "the contradiction constitutive of the female subject of feminism . . . the female subject (that) is in both places (inside . . . and . . . outside the rectangle) at once." Monica Vitti has therefore come a long way from her beginning as a very talented actress, constantly framed by all male directors exclusively as a sexual object of the male's eye and desire. In her last three films, especially in Scandalo segreto, she has succeeded, as an actress, as well as a scriptwriter and director, to create female characters who, even if constantly inscribed in the contradictions of an Italian social environment, arrive, through painful awareness of their weaknesses and limitations, to assert their difference and self-identity.

## Notes

1. Lucy Fisher, "The Lives of Performers: The Actress as Signifier," in *Shot/Countershot: Film Tradition and Women's Cinema* (Princeton: Princeton University Press, 1989), 63–88, 64.

2. Luce Irigaray, *This Sex Which Is Not One*, trans. Catherine Porter (Ithaca: Cornell University Press, 1985), 76–77.

3. I want to take this opportunity to thank Monica Vitti for having provided me personally with the scripts of these three films and a videocopy of *Scandalo segreto* and for her cordial encouragement of my scholarly undertaking.

4. The only book combining a careful discussion of her career and a good bio- and film bibliography is Laura Delli Colli, *Monica Vitti* (Rome: Gremese Editore, 1987).

5. The most useful studies have been: Jessica Benjamin, "A Desire of One's Own: Psychoanalytic Feminism and Intersubjective Space," in *Feminist Studies/Critical Studies*, ed. Teresa de Lauretis (Bloomington: Indiana University Press, 1986), 78–101; Teresa de Lauretis, *Alice Doesn't: Feminism, Semiotics, Cinema* (Bloomington: Indiana University Press, 1984) and *Technologies of Gender: Essays on Theory, Film, and Fiction* (Bloomington: Indiana University Press, 1987; from now on de Lauretis's works will be quoted directly in the text); Lucy Fisher, *Shot/Countershot*; Mary Ann Doane, *The Desire to Desire* (Bloomington: Indiana University Press, 1987); Luce Irigaray, "The Gesture in Psychoanalysis," in *Between Feminism and Psychoanalysis*, ed. T. Brennan (London: Routledge, 1989), 127–38; E. Ann Kaplan, *Women and Cinema: Both*

*Sides of the Camera* (New York: Methuen, 1983); Annette Kuhn, "Textual Politics," in *Issues in Feminist Film Criticism*, ed. P. Erens (Bloomington: Indiana University Press, 1990), 250–67; Jurij Lotman, *Semiotics of Cinema* (Ann Arbor: University of Michigan Press, 1976); Marsha McCreadie, *Women on Film: The Critical Eye* (New York: Praeger, 1983); Judith Mayne, *The Woman at the Keyhole: Feminism and Women's Cinema* (Bloomington: Indiana University Press, 1990); Christian Metz, *Psychoanalysis and Cinema: The Imaginary Signifier* (London: MacMillan, 1982); Tania Modleski, "Time and Desire in the Woman's Film," in *Film Theory and Criticism: Introductory Readings*, ed. G. Mast, M. Cohen, L. Braudy, 4th ed. (New York: Oxford University Press, 1992), 536–48; Laura Mulvey, "Visual Pleasure and Narrative Cinema," *Screen* 16 (1975): 6–18 and her "Afterthoughts on 'Visual Pleasure and Narrative Cinema,' Inspired by *Duel in the Sun*," in *Psychoanalysis and Cinema*, ed. E. Ann Kaplan (London: Routledge, 1990), 24–35; B. Ruby Rich, "In the Name of Feminist Film Criticism," in *Issues in Feminist Film Criticism*, ed. Erens, 268–87; Peter Wollen, *Signs and Meaning in the Cinema*, 3d ed. (Bloomington: Indiana University Press, 1972).

6. A very useful study in this area is *Off Screen: Women and Film in Italy*, ed. Giuliana Bruno and Maria Nadotti (London: Routledge, 1988; from now on directly quoted in the text). For a diversified, but thorough historical view of the conditions of women in Italy, see the catalogue of the show, *Esistere come donna*, organized by the city of Milan in 1983 (Milan: G. Mazzotta, 1983).

7. *Bianco e Nero* 33, nos. 1–2 (January-February 1972): 1–112, 105. The translation is mine.

8. The best works I have found on this topic are Masolino D'Amico, *La Commedia all'italiana: Il cinema comico in Italia dal 1945 al 1975* (Milan: Mondadori, 1985); C. Salizzato and V. Zagarrio, eds., *Effetto Commedia: Teoria, generi, paesaggi della commedia cinematografica* (Rome: Di Giacomo Editore, 1985); and Mario Monicelli, *L'Arte della commedia* (Bari: Dedalo, 1986).

9. See Filmography at the end of this essay.

10. C. Biarese and A. Tassone, *I film di Michelangelo Antonioni* (Rome: Gremese, 1985), 45.

11. For a relevant discussion of the relationship between the female body and representation, see Mary Ann Doane, *Femmes Fatales: Feminism, Film Theory, Psychoanalysis* (London: Routledge, 1991, esp. the chapters "Woman Stake: Filming the Female Body," 165–77, and "When the Direction of the Force Acting on the Body is Changed: The Moving Image," 188–206).

12. Mayne, *The Woman at the Keyhole*, 17. For further arguments about the concept of the gaze, see Joan Copject, "The Delirium of Clinical Perfection," *Oxford Literary Review* 8 (1986): 57–65, and esp. "The Orthopsychic Subject: Film Theory and the Reception of Lacan," *October* 49 (summer 1989): 53–71; Christian Metz's "The Imaginary Signifier," in his *The Imaginary Signifier: Psychoanalysis and the Cinema* (Bloomington: Indiana University Press, 1982), 1–87; Constance Penley, "The Avant-Garde and Its Imaginary," *Camera Obscura* 2 (fall 1977): 2–33, and "Feminism, Film Theory, and the Bachelor Machine," in *m/f* 10 (1985): 39–59; Jacqueline Rose, *Sexuality in the Field of Vision* (London: Verso, 1986).

13. For the "maternal" in narrative and film, see especially Mary Ann Doane's "The Moving Image: Pathos and the Maternal," in her *The Desire to Desire*, 70–95; E. Ann Kaplan, *Motherhood and Representation: The Mother in Popular Culture and Melodrama* (London: Routledge, 1992); and Kaja Silverman's two chapters "The Fantasy of the Maternal Voice: Paranoia and Compensation," and "The Fantasy of the Maternal Voice: Female Subjectivity and the Negative Oedipus Complex," in her *The Acoustic Mirror: The Female Voice in Psychoanalysis and Cinema* (Bloomington: Indiana University Press, 1988), 72–140.

14. For the use of this term, see Gerard Genette's *Figure III*, trans. as *Narrative Discourse: An Essay in Method* (Ithaca: Cornell University Press, 1980).

15. Delli Colli, *Monica Vitti*, 41 ("con Roberto abbiamo scritto, riscritto, buttato, ricominciato, corretto, cambiato idea per anni"; my translation).

16. *Quando suona Veronica (Felici come pazzi!) Flirt*, script by Monica Vitti and Roberto Russo, 225. ("Si abbracciano e si baciano con una violenza da far paura come se avesse aspettato anni quel momento"; my translation).

17. Other critics discussing this particular association of the maternal voice either with "plenitude and bliss" or with "impotence and entrapment" are: Didier Anzieu, "L'enveloppe sonore du soi," *Nouvelle Revue de Psychanalyse* 13 (1976): 161–79; Michel Chion, *La Voix au Cinéma* (Paris: Editions de l'Etoile, 1982); Mary Ann Doane, "The Voice in the Cinema: The Articulation of Body and Space," *Yale French Studies* 60 (1980): 33–50; Jacques Hassoun, *Fragments de langue maternelle: Esquisse d'un lieu* (Paris: Payot, 1979); Julia Kristeva, *Desire in Language: A Semiotic Approach to Literature and Art* (New York: Columbia University Press, 1980, esp. chap. 10, "Place Names," 271–94); Guy Rosolato, "La Voix: Entre corps et langage," *Revue Française de Psychanalyse* 38 (1974): 75–94. A very interesting study on motherhood is E. Ann Kaplan's *Motherhood and Representation: The Mother in Popular Culture and Melodrama* (London: Routledge, 1992).

18. See Jacques Lacan, *Ecrits: A Selection* (New York: Norton, 1977), 1–7.

19. *Francesca è mia*, script by Monica Vitti and Roberto Russo, 87–88: "Infatti prima volevo dirti grazie . . . e ti ho cercata per questo. Poi però mi è passata la voglia di dirtelo . . . e . . . mi è venuta la voglia di guardarti. E non mi bastava mai. Avevo anche pensato che non ti avrei mai parlato . . . forse se tu non fossi scesa adesso, non ti avrei mai parlato . . . ma . . . ma avrei continuato a guardarti. Non a seguirti . . . a guardarti. Ho provato anche a fare altre cose. . . . Giovedì, te ne sarai accorta . . . non mi hai visto tutto il giorno. Ma poi non ce l'ho fatta. Venerdì mattina già mi sentivo male, mi faceva male lo stomaco . . . sono qui perchè se no mi fa male lo stomaco."

20. *Francesca è mia*, 88: "Vieni via con me . . . non salire su. . . . Vieni con me . . . subito e per sempre."

21. *Francesca è mia*, 137: "Adesso tu stai qui e voglio che resti qui. . . . Butta via tutto . . . la casa, tua madre, i tuoi fratelli . . . le paure cretine . . . dimentica ogni cosa, fai finta di essere nata appena stamattina . . . adesso."

22. *Francesca è mia*, 150–51: "Ora non è più come stamattina . . . ora m'hai fatto capire . . . quella cosa squallida che tu hai visto, io e Andrea . . . a casa . . . non era così, sai? Ma poi, piano, piano . . . fa parte della vita. Tutti gli errori, le cose da perdonare . . . anche per me. Forse io non ho nessun motivo chiaro per tornare là, tanto lui sta benissimo anche senza di me, ma so che lo farò, me ne rendo conto ora. . . . Anch'io, sai . . . non posso vederlo uscire dalla porta quando mi lascia . . . anch'io lo legherei . . . lo amo" (my translation).

23. For a very clear discussion on the Lacanian theory of the imaginary as applicable to film criticism, see R. Stam, R. Burgoyne, and S. Flitterman-Lewis, *New Vocabularies in Film Semiotics: Structuralism, Post-Structuralism, and Beyond* (London: Routledge, 1992).

24. Also for this film, Monica is responsible, together with Roberto Russo, for the subject and the script, while all dialogue was rewritten by her in conformity with the film direction, thus introducing several important changes and elisions in the script. One of the most important is the elimination of the romantic ending, which involved Margherita and her friend Tony.

25. Yvonne Rainer speaks of narrative strategies to be consciously deployed by feminist films in order to disrupt cinematic narrative, and suggests specifically to change the "glossy surface and homogeneous look of 'professional cinematography by means of optically degenerated shots,' refilming, blown-up 8 and video transfers." Yvonne Rainer, "Some Ruminations around Cinematic Antidotes to the Oedipal; Net(les) while Playing with DeLauraedipus Mulvey, or He May Be Off Screen, but . . . ," *Independent* (April 1986): 22, quoted in de Lauretis, *Technologies*, 122.

26. *Scandalo segreto*, dialogues by Monica Vitti, 53: "Dimmi, quanto tempo potresti stare lontano da me? . . . Dimmi che mi ami . . . più forte, per favore" (my translation).

27. Ibid. "Insegnami a essere indipendente," she asks her rival Laura. "Voglio poter uscire quando mi pare, andare a veder un paesaggio da sola. Andare al mare, andare dove voglio. Non dividere sempre tutto con lui!" (my translation).

28. Ibid. "Ma che cosa vuol dire non avere bisogno di nessuno? Come posso stare senza gente intorno a me, e sopratutto senza di lui? Io ho bisogno di tutti, anche di te" (my translation).

29. *Scandalo segreto*, 62: "Bastava che io lo amassi meglio. No! Tutto questo amami di più, amami meglio. Tu mi ami poco e io ti amo di più, stare lì a tirare con i sentimenti come al mercato!" (my translation).

30. *Scandalo segreto*, 71: "Lo so che non potrò vivere senza di te, ma ti lascio lo stesso" (my translation).

31. *Scandalo segreto*, 86: "E' colpa tua. Stai lì con quell'occhio nero fisso a . . . criticare, a provocare, ma se tu non fossi stata . . . sempre lì a guardare, a criticare, io forse non avrei mai saputo niente, lo sai? e, anche se l'avessi saputo . . . e tu non c'eri, io forse, lo avrei accettato o dimenticato" (my translation).

32. The other scene is the one when Tony and his assistants are framed in their trailer while filming Margherita's last attempt to turn off the video camera that they control. This is the scene that reveals to the spectators for the first time who is actually in control of Margherita's video camera.

# Filmography

*Ridere, ridere, ridere!* by Edoardo Anton (1955)
*Una Pelliccia di visone* by Glauco Pellegrini (1956)
*Le Dritte* by Mario Amendola (1958)
*L'Avventura* by Michelangelo Antonioni (1960)
*La Notte* by Michelangelo Antonioni (1961)
*L'Eclisse* by Michelangelo Antonioni (1962)
*Le Quattro Verità* by Alessandro Blasetti (1963)
*Chateau en Suède* by Roger Vadim (1963)
*Dragées au poivre* by Jacques Baratier (1963)
*Alta infedeltà* by Luciano Salce (1964)
*Deserto rosso* by Michelangelo Antonioni (1964)
*Il Disco volante* by Tinto Brass (1964)
*Le Bambole* by Franco Rossi (1964)
*Modesty Blaise* by Joseph Losey (1966)
*Le Fate* by Luciano Salce (1966)
*Fai in fretta ad uccidermi . . . Ho freddo!* by Francesco Maselli (1967)
*La Cintura di castità* by Pasquale Festa Campanile (1967)
*Ti ho sposato per allegria* by Luciano Salce (1967)
*La Ragazza con la pistola* by Mario Monicelli (1968)
*La Femme écarlate* by Jean Valère (1968)
*Amore mio aiutami!* by Alberto Sordi (1969)
*Dramma della gelosia. Tutti i particolari in cronaca* by Ettore Scola (1970)
*Ninì Tirabusciò, la donna che inventò la mossa* by Marcello Fondato (1970)
*Le Coppie* by Mario Monicelli (1970)
*La Supertestimone* by Franco Giraldi (1971)
*La Pacifista* by Miklos Jancsò (1971)
*Gli ordini sono ordini* by Franco Giraldo (1971)
*Noi donne siamo fatte così* by Dino Risi (1971)
*La Tosca* by Luigi Magni (1973)

*Teresa la ladra* by Carlo di Palma (1973)
*Polvere di stelle* by Alberto Sordi (1973)
*Le Fantome de la liberté* by Luis Bunuel (1974)
*A mezzanotte va la ronda del piacere* by Marcello Fondato (1975)
*Qui comincia l'avventura* by Carlo di Palma (1975)
*L'Anatra all'arancia* by Luciano Salce (1975)
*Mimì Bluette, fiore del mio giardino* by Carlo di Palma (1976)
*Basta che non si sappia in giro* by Nanni Loy (1976)
*L'altra metà del cielo* by Franco Rossi (1977)
*La Raison d'Etat* by André Cayatte (1978)
*Per vivere meglio divertitevi con noi* by Flavio Mogherini (1978)
*An Almost Perfect Affair* by Michael Ritchie (1979)
*Letti selvaggi* by Luigi Zampa (1979)
*Non ti conosco più amore* by Sergio Corbucci (1980)
*Il Mistero di Oberwald* by Michelangelo Antonioni (1980)
*Camera d'albergo* by Mario Monicelli (1980)
*Tango della gelosia* by Steno (1981)
*Io so che tu sai che lo so* by Alberto Sordi (1982)
*Scusa se è poco* by Marco Vicario (1982)
*Flirt* by Robert Russo (1983)
*Francesca è mia* by Roberto Russo (1986)
*Scandalo segreto* by Monica Vitti (1989)

# 14

# Signifying the Holocaust: Liliana Cavani's *Portiere di Notte*

*Marguerite Waller*

There are many subtexts to this paper, some of which I am probably not even aware of. One I am aware of is an ongoing project of analysis and art-making by a women's art-making collective to which I belong. We call ourselves Las Comadres (the Godmothers), and we work in the San Diego/Tijuana border region. In the fall of 1990, we created an installation called "La Vecindad/ The Neighborhood," in which we begin the task of unpacking the particular form of racism that seems to power the debates over the immigration of un-documented workers into Southern California. Here are a few sentences from a piece of hate mail sent to Roberto Martínez, an undocumented workers' advocate, by "The Holy Church of the White Fighting Machine of the Cross":

> The cops are going to start shooting you Mexicans wholesale soon, and there will be nothing you can do about it. Go back to T. J. (Tijuana) and watch the mule fuck the whore that will be better for you. . . . Stop criticizing the border patrol and the whites who are try-

ing to save our white country from the Jews and the Goy stooges in
the government who will not act in behalf of the white Aryan race.

(In our installation, we stenciled a blow-up of the text on a 10' by 6' piece
of fabric, which we used as a rug that museumgoers had to walk on or consciously avoid to get from one part of the installation to another.) What interests me here is the conflation of Mexican agricultural workers with Jews,
and the introduction into the equation of sexuality, fantasized as somehow
miscegenating, sterile, bestial, heterosexual, and misogynistic all at the
same time.


## The Holocaust as a Feminist Issue

In the first volume of his book *Male Fantasies*, Klaus Theweleit observes, "The
argument that a social democrat is not a communist, a communist not an
anarchist, and that none of these categories has anything to do with Jews,
has never had much effect. The fascist unconscious perceives an essential
sameness in all of the categories (and in the many others that made the spectrum of concentration-camp prisoners so diverse . . .)" (383–84). Topping the
list of threatening not-quite-others is woman, according to Theweleit's
provocative study of the diaries, poems, and novels of proto-Nazi German
Freikorps men. A sexual woman is a whore is a proletarian is a communist is
a Jew—or vice versa—regardless of the gender of the person in question
(383). In fifteenth-century Ferrara, archival and secondary sources suggest,
female prostitutes and male Jews had to contend together in a seminude foot-
race in the ruling family's annual *palio* (Shemek, 5, 10, 24). Red-light districts
and Jewish ghettos seem to have come into existence at about the same time
in several Italian cities, and Jews and prostitutes were legally required to con-
form to similar dress codes (Shemek, 24).[1] In Hungary, newly liberated from
Soviet and domestic Communist domination, the foreign minister, a member
of the ruling nationalistic Democratic Forum party, declared in public, in
September 1990, that the Hungarian Jews (who make up some of the membership of the more liberal Free Democratic party) are not authentically Hungarian and should not be taken to represent the interests of real Hungarians.
Is it coincidental that another of Democratic Forum's initiatives is the illegal-
ization of abortion, a transparently misogynistic approach, it seems to some,
to the problem of Hungary's declining population, which seems pretty obvi-

ously keyed, not to the dangers of female autonomy, but to the lack of available housing?

Except for Theweilet, and a handful of American feminists—including
Susan Griffin in *Pornography and Silence* (168–201) and Elly Bulkin, Minnie
Bruce Pratt, and Barbara Smith, whose book *Yours in Struggle: Three Feminist
Perspectives on Anti-Semitism and Racism* also makes the connection—commentators have not generally approached anti-Semitism as a feminist issue;
nor, conversely, have misogyny and male dominance been a central concern,
as far as I know, of historians and analysts of European anti-Semitism. In fact,
both Liliana Cavani's *The Night Porter* and Lina Wertmuller's *Seven Beauties*,
have been vehemently criticized by eminent male Holocaust survivors for
muddying our understanding of the "truth" with their sexual allegories of
concentration-camp power relations. In *The Drowned and the Saved*, Primo
Levi criticizes Cavani's film for confusing murderers and victims, beclouding
"our need for justice" (49). In his long *New Yorker* essay, "Surviving," published in 1976, Bruno Bettelheim objected to, among other things, the comedy of *Seven Beauties*, which, he complained, "neutralizes the horror" (31).
Both men, though, themselves deploy sexual imagery to elaborate their
points. Characterizing Cavani's film as "beautiful and false," an exemplifica-
tion of a "moral disease," Levi speaks of the terrain it explores—what he
calls the "gray zone . . . of prisoners who in some measure, perhaps with good
intentions, collaborated with authority" (20)—as not "virgin." "On the contrary it is a badly plowed field, trampled and torn up" (48). Bettelheim, too,
is concerned with keeping the horror pure, and the moral issues clear, while,
like Levi, he construes the woman filmmaker's intervention in the field as
allied with prostitution or pornography: "I must express my disgust that the
abomination of genocide and the tortures and degradations of the concentration camp are used as a special, uniquely macabre titillation to enhance its
(the film's) effectiveness. . . . [T]his depiction of the survivor . . . robs survi-
vorship of all meaning. It makes seeing the film an experience that degrades"
(31, 34)

Let me hasten to say that I in no way wish to discredit the historical and
emotional accuracy of these witnesses. On the contrary, the metaphorical
structures of their own arguments have heightened my curiosity about the
relevance of a feminist or gender-centered approach to the Holocaust and to
the questions of national and individual identity with which anti-Semitism
seems historically and conceptually linked. As fascist emotions are fanned by
recession in North America and, in Central and Eastern Europe, by the formerly Communist bloc's efforts to resurrect and reclaim pre–World War II

national and ethnic identities, films like *The Night Porter* and *Seven Beauties*, seem particularly prescient. Not attempting the kind of mimetic or documentary representation of what happened favored by Levi, Bettelheim, or Claude Lanzmann (director of *Shoah*), these films pointedly approach the questions of what happened, how it happened, why it happened, and what changes need to occur in order for it not to happen again through *non-Jewish* principal characters, unrealistic mise-en-scène and plotting, and, not coincidentally, exhaustive explorations of what might seem the peripheral issue of the constructedness of genders and sexualities. They both begin, that is, from the assumption that fascism cannot be subverted from within the moral and ethnic categories through which the world has come to know it historically. Whether one agrees or not with the analysis that each film, in its own way, performs—and, as I shall argue elsewhere, I think Wertmuller's film already takes issue with and revises certain aspects of Cavani's—I would urge that together they constitute a richly suggestive feminist revision of this chapter in modern European history. Here I shall comment on Cavani's film, in a reading that as feminist film theory has already so effectively taught us to do, will take into account not only what is shown, but how it is shown; not only the relations enacted between characters onscreen, but also the relations played out between the screen and the audience. I will return, then, to Levi and Bettelheim, to see whether, re-read through the lens provided by Cavani, the terms of their criticism begin to make a different kind of sense.

## Constructing a Subject

The spectator's relation to Cavani's Max, the impeccable, ex-Nazi night porter, played by Dirk Bogarde, is as problematic visually as it is morally; or rather, a major reason for our uneasy relationship with Max is the unstable relation between what the camera seems to be showing us and what we learn from the film's action and dialogue. It would be relatively comfortable were we first seduced by Max, then gradually or shockingly, disabused of our sympathy, as happens, for instance, in Costa-Gavras's more recent film, *The Music Box*. There the retired American factory worker and devoted family man turns out *really* to be a sadistic rapist/murderer, a member of the infamous Hungarian Arrow Cross. The Costa-Gavras film refuses, in other words, to entertain the problematics of subjectivity, to question the ontology (including the continuity and stability) of identity, in spite of the obviousness with which such material invites investigation. Throughout *The Night Porter*, on the other hand, the camera insists that we continually be re-seduced by Max. Lingering shots of his soulful brown eyes, his exquisite gestures while pouring tea, his vulnerability in the presence of his wartime cronies—of a complex range of mannerisms and expressions imperfectly masked by his nearly identical SS and night porter's uniforms—magnetically draw attention to Max as a sensuous, emotionally responsive figure whose next move is as unpredictable as it is eagerly anticipated. We are drawn to him, that is, *at the same time* that his career as a sadistic, murderous, phony camp doctor (only one of whose patients, Lucia, has survived) is also being unfolded.

As I have just intimated, though, Max's attraction differs from that of the stereotypical Hollywood male, who, as film theorists Laura Mulvey and Mary Ann Doane have persuasively argued, is visually portrayed as a kind of ego ideal. Visually Max is as often as not "feminized." (My reasons for putting the word in quotation marks will become apparent momentarily.) Like the classic Mulvey and Doane woman, he is shot in close-up, often centered on the screen, isolated from his context, and delivered up for voyeuristic scrutiny, even in sequences and individual shots where he is simultaneously portrayed, like the classic Mulvey and Doane man, as the origin and owner of the gaze (Mulvey, 19–20; Doane, 28–31). For example, when we see Max with a movie camera aggressively filming Lucia's thin, naked body amidst a crowd of other naked, newly-arrived camp prisoners, or, elsewhere, Max training a spotlight on Bert, the virtuosic, homosexual ballet dancer, it is also the image and performance of Max, onscreen almost as long as the images and performances his gaze frames, with which the film fascinates us.[2] Lucia, especially in the latter part of the film, is, in these terms, often "masculinized." Though observed by Max, she is shown framed in profile, placed at the edge of the frame, her face partly shadowed, signifying, relative to the "feminine" position described in feminist film theory, that she is also an agent: not only seen but seeing, not only acted upon but initiating and guiding the action (Mulvey, 22–23; Doane, 28).[3] As if to underscore this strategy, Cavani shows her smoking a pipe in one sequence in which Max, framed in the center of the screen, unpacks groceries and tells her he has quit his job. But, the film's mixing of conventions also implies, these categories of "masculine" and "feminine" do not inhere in the people they describe. The bodies and faces of both figures become the site of a dissonant and denaturalized visual language that, across the disturbing story of their past and present relationship, denaturalizes the legibility of sex and gender.[4]

There is good reason for anyone interested in "truth," clearly and morally represented, to be troubled by this twofold instability and multiplicity of Max's and Lucia's subject positions. Gender theorist Judith Butler suggestively describes the kind of signifying practice through which a substantive, knowing "I" (which is to say a subject situated in opposition to a knowable and recoverable Other) can appear; her terms seem equally useful for describing the subversion of such an "I" enacted by *The Night Porter*'s signifying practices. "Such appearances," like all subject positions in Butler's argument, "are rule generated identities, ones which rely on the consistent and repeated invocation of rules that condition and restrict culturally . . . intelligible practices of identity" (145). In ways that can and have been described both historically and philosophically, sex and gender have been among the most thoroughly naturalized, taken for granted, of the intelligible identity practices—practices that stabilize no less than they are stabilized by, the position or practice of the knowing "I." By proliferating sex and gender configurations on screen, Cavani's film, then, strikes at the heart of the rules that allow mutually constitutive identity *practices* to appear as, what Butler scornfully terms, "inert substantives" to a global subject (144). As we struggle to organize the slippery images on screen, we are prevented from mistaking ourselves for such a global subject, whose imperializing point of view and substantializing effects are, by contrast, vigorously maintained by Hollywood's consistent and unambiguous language of male and female, weak and strong, good guys and villains.[5] Instead, insistently ambiguous and open, the film offers too many possible readings of figures, actions, images, and sequences. The film as Other is not knowable and recoverable, and the more we try to dig into a position of voyeuristic domination, the less comfortable, intellectually and morally, this position becomes. As many feminist viewers have commented, a lot of this film is "hard to watch" (Stone, 41). My point is that this may have as much to do with the way we are watching it as with what is onscreen. To give one example, if we assume that everything is as it seems when we see a close-up of Lucia, with her hands chained above and behind her head, approached by Max, who grasps her torso, we may (many viewers do) find the images unbearable (Stone, 42, 44). Especially if her enigmatic passivity is read as acceptance or even pleasure, then viewers may find themselves wishing they were not watching, wishing the filmmaker were not showing us this, wishing Lucia would let us off the hook by appearing to suffer more.[6] Why should the film work this way? What do the political stakes of the subject matter—the Holocaust and its aftermath—have to do with how we conceptualize and experience identity? Or, to turn the question around, what cognitive, political, and psychological ends are served when we insist that identities be grounded in bodies and that those identities and bodies be understood as ontological essences? What *new* political possibilities emerge when we experience sexual, ethnic, and national identities—ours included—not as the ground, but rather as an effect, of the signifying situations through which they are articulated?

Let me interject here a corollary whose implications will be important for the rest of my argument. This global subject position, as I think Mulvey's work with Hollywood film codes aptly illustrates, is gendered male, whoever happens to occupy it. Truth, knowledge, and thus the very notion of identity are constituted *and* threatened by falsehood, ignorance, and impurity, which are consistently gendered female. To make a long story short, the subject whom Cavani's film will not let us be is implicitly misogynistic. It is also potentially anti-Semitic and racist, since it must see as wrong (to guarantee truth) anything it sees as different. Misogyny and anti-Semitism are, if you will, different vectors of the same kind of identity formation. But what other kind of subject is there?

To begin with, there is Max. Max, who is said to have "imagination," does not want to *be* anybody, but is drawn instead to playing roles and wearing costumes. We see him as a "documentary" filmmaker, an image that quickly becomes itself polyvalent. The images Max has made with his cameras are never presented as ideologically neutral, but the potential arguments embedded in them also change radically with the circumstances and the viewer. His nude photographs of Lucia, for example, can, and at first do, signify Max's power over her, but, later, in the hands of the ex-Nazis, the same photographs come to signify Lucia's power to expose Max. Max's images, then, might caution us against ontologizing Cavani's images as well.[7]

Max is also said to have had fun playing doctor during the war, and before that to have served in the entourage of a count. He accomodates both Burt (the insomniac ex-Nazi and closet homosexual) and Erika (the appetitive countess) in their elaborate psychosexual rituals. But most of all he revels in a relationship with one of his victims in whom he creates or discovers another avid role-player. It is interesting to speculate on how or why Lucia responds to Max, though I would interject the caveat that, with both Max and Lucia, I am indulging in a kind of explanation that the film itself problematizes as it reconfigures the notion of identity that produces the appearance of individual histories and psychologies. For this viewer, at least, the film does *not* offer "realistic" portrayals of character, and I see it full of traps and obstructions that discourage the impulse to translate the interaction between Max and Lucia into individual, psychological terms. I propose merely heuristically, then—the better to see where it takes us and what problems it presents us with—the following scenario: As mad Max's "little girl," Lucia, referred to and treated by everyone else as either "the daughter of the socialist" or "the wife of the American conductor," is not locked into the usual heterosexual conventions, the male-centered sociosexual identities, reserved for her in prewar Vienna or postwar North America. Ironically, it is from the hypermasculinist Nazi power structure that Max derives the power over Lucia that evokes and/or provokes—"legitimates" and/or enforces—her polymorphous, indeterminately active and passive, "male" and "female," masochistic and sadistic sexuality. Already, you will note, my narrative is in trouble. There is no appropriate verb to describe this interaction, since the way one would characterize it depends upon the relative positions of two subjects whose bond has to do very largely with the thrill they experience in constantly renegotiating their subject positions. And I say "ironic" of Max's point of departure because these renegotiations between Max and Lucia subvert the sexual and gender identity principles that are among the most basic of the rigid binaries, taken for absolutes, upon which Nazi (and other fascist) organizations of power and knowledge are founded.[8] Lucia's particular mode of collaboration, one might say, allows Max a respite from, and ultimately a way out of, the untenable role of absolute masculine authority—a role that cannot be a role if it is absolute and cannot be absolute if it is a role, and that is, paradoxically, a kind of passivity, culturally speaking. (This is a way out, it is intriguing to note, not available to poor Burt, the gay Nazi, who is trapped in the closet, as well as in the past, by his own fascist homophobia. In an instance of Cavani's little-noted, deadpan playfulness, Burt is costumed and made-up to resemble a movie vampire, one of the living dead. He comes brilliantly alive when he dances, I presume, because it is there that he *can* role-play. As a dancer he can "move" in several senses of the word.) The denaturalization of Max's position, then, allows Lucia a respite from and a way out of the subordinate and objectified position in which her role as prisoner—and perhaps as woman—places her. (Does her self-absorbed orchestra-conductor husband, a kind of authoritarian by profession, lock her into her perfect performance as bourgeois wife by his "unimaginative" performance as husband?)

I am not saying, nor do I think the film suggests, that Nazis and survivors are therefore, the same. Indeed, in this film not all *Nazis* are the same, nor, for that matter, are characters themselves self-identical. It is precisely the point that they occupy different positions simultaneously, as well as over time, in relation to different people, and even in relation to the same person, and that these positions are all contingent, frequently self-contradictory, and always in the process of being renegotiated. I am suggesting, on the contrary, that to distinguish ontologically between "guiltless victims" and "murderers," to try to cement the moral purity of these categories, is itself to deny difference in a way that, paradoxically, undermines the moral (and, I would argue, political) position of the "victim." As feminist theorists have discovered in their attempts to extend visibility and legitimacy to women, treating a term like "women" as a stable category, presumes and fixes the unfavorable status of the very "subjects" that they hope to represent and support. The legitimation of such "subjects," within a system that defines them as inferior and "other" then involves them in more of the same oppositional logic that produced them. Recall that the two male survivors, Levi and Bettelheim, unselfconsciously express their acceptance of the basic dichotomy they have been victimized by in misogynist terms. Like Theweleit's fascist unconscious, their discourse represents diverse categories of difference as essentially the same, as sexual, impure, and disorderly. If binary logic itself and the subjects it produces, remain in place, then "Jews" as well as "Nazis," women as well as men, remain burdened with the task of having to represent their positions as stable, coherent, and correct, a task that cannot but involve them in further representations of difference as opposition and threat.

## Signifying the Holocaust

How does Cavani signify the Holocaust, then, if not through binary logic? In the limited space of this essay, I can only begin to address that question. As an example, I shall conclude by "reading" part of the remarkable sequence, fairly near the film's beginning, that interweaves the reestablishment of Lucia's and Max's relationship in the present, flashbacks to their past in the camp, and a passage from Mozart's opera, *The Magic Flute*. As this sequence opens Max takes his seat several rows behind Lucia in the Viennese opera house as Pamina and Papageno on stage sing their duet about the joys of married life and Lucia's husband conducts the orchestra. Max and Lucia make eye contact, and Lucia has a flashback to her experience in the concentration camp where Max was the "doctor" and her lover.[9]

In the first fourteen shots of the sequence virtually every image is destabilized rather than stabilized, by its relation to the others. This is accomplished, in part, by the triple focus itself. Mozart's problematic opera, about a woman, Pamina, who first seems to be imprisoned and later "saved" within a rigidly hierarchical masculinist regime, becomes associated, through the complex intercutting of sound and image, with *both* Lucia's relationships—with her past *and* her present. These three-way associations undo the binary interpretation that, at this point in the film, we are strongly tempted to make. Surely a clean-cut American conductor is good, an uptight ex-Nazi sadist, torturer night porter is bad. But Papageno and Pamina sing the praises of heterosexual, companionate marriage right through the scene of what I take to be a male prisoner being raped by a male guard on the bed next to Lucia's in the concentration-camp barracks. A spectral group of prisoners helplessly watching is set up visually, by the rhyming of camera movements and framings, as the reverse shot of the Viennese audience watching the Mozart performance. The gorgeously sung phrases "Nothing is nobler than to be man and wife. Man and wife together attain godliness," are "married," as a sound mixer would say, with the rhythmic humping of the barely visible prisoner by the beefy guard. It may also be relevant that Papageno and Pamina sing their duet in praise of marriage just after the attempted rape of Pamina by a "Black Moor." The race of this character will eventually serve to distinguish the Moor's attempted rape from the right of the white male power structure, personified by the sorceror Zarastro, to use Pamina's sexuality for its own ends. Having abducted her from her mother, Zarastro will offer her, as a reward, to the hero Tamino, once both Tamino and Pamina have successfully weathered a rigorous, not to say sadomasochistic set of initiation rituals, designed to indoctrinate them thoroughly in the ideology of male-dominant heterosexuality. Along the way Pamina's mother and the Moor are thoroughly discredited as disorderly and untrustworthy, and women in particular are blamed for abusing "true" language by their useless but seductive chattering. Though the opera's representation of marriage could be read as a contrast to the rape enacted on screen, then, I think the film also suggests a certain congruence between the abuse we see and the familiar heterosexuality being celebrated (or exposed) in the opera—a heterosexuality whose misogynist and racist foundations are at least made more obvious by the comparison.[10] If the Viennese opera house and the concentration camp are seen as reverse images of each other, then it becomes more difficult simply to oppose Lucia's husband to Max. Lucia's husband is, in his own way, reproducing and naturalizing the white or Aryan male subject position that Nazism, the epitome of the patriarchal repression of women and "non-Aryans," tried to solidify to an absurd extent. The sexuality and the organization of power that we see in the camp are, in a fundamental sense, continuous with what we see in the eighteenth-century opera, as well as in the postwar culture for whom the opera remains a significant ruling-class ritual.[11]

The introduction of the third historical moment, the late eighteenth century when *The Magic Flute* was written, makes it equally difficult to indulge in binary historiography, to condemn a "bad" past from the perspective of a "good" present, or vice versa, as Klaus and the other ex-Nazis want to do. As cinema can so powerfully suggest, and does here with its constant reframings of characters, actions, and contexts, what we think we see, with its consequences for who and where we think we are, is an effect of a complex web of relationships with no particular point of origin and no necessary endpoint. The extent to which our readings of even these few images can proliferate over the course of a few moments offers some idea of how much the linear understanding of time produced by binary thinking limits historical understanding, concealing possibilities that could otherwise become visible and expressible.

One final observation: The continual reframings of characters—Max with others in the audience, Lucia with others in the audience and behind the conductor's hands, the audience with the figures on stage, Max the only one in focus, Lucia the only one in focus—are performed by a camera that does not purport to be objective. It pans and tracks, zooms, pulls focus: a conspicuous, haunting figure in its own right, which seems to want us never to mistake for mimetic representations its "signifying" plays on the images it gives us. Representations, in the sense that one position or effect can stand for another (whereby for example, Lucia could stand for women, who could stand for victims, who could stand for Jews) would require the inert, monocular vision enforced by binary logic that produces a kind of "truth" in which people and events appear to stay put.[12] (Another of Cavani's visual jokes or puns, like Burt's resemblance to Dracula, is Klaus's monocle, visually literalizing the one-point perspective of fascist logic.) In Cavani's film, positionality is relative and cannot be fixed or "clarified." The camera's restless comparison of every position with every other is among the film's most powerful and most disturbing strategies. These comparisons, I stress, do *not* serve to minimize the horrors of the Holocaust; on the contrary, they keep them relevant. They signify the Holocaust, not as the unthinkable Other, but as one distinctly possible effect of the misogynistic signifying situations through which we, who share this history and culture, are ourselves articulated.

# Notes

1. The superimposition of Jewish ghettos and red-light districts in Italian cities was described to me by Deanna Shemek in a conversation about her unpublished article "Circular

Definitions: Disciplining Gender in Italian Renaissance Festival," which describes the stigmatization of "both Jews and prostitutes in Ferrara and other cities by laws forbidding them to touch foodstuffs in public markets and requiring them to wear distinguishing signs on their clothing" (24).

2. The actual screen time given to Max is certainly longer (and differently framed) than that of a typical reaction shot. But since the shots of him with the camera or the spotlight are relatively "simple" with regard to the time it takes to "read" them, they do not have to be literally as long as, say a shot of Burt dancing, in order to carry the same affective weight. A long-shot customarily takes longer to read than a close-up and is therefore left onscreen longer in "real time" if a sense of equivalence in the "film time" is desired.

3. Cavani's "feminization" and "masculinization" of Max and Lucia differ from the gendering that occurs in the Hollywood film language analyzed by Mulvey and Doane, though, in not conflating the camera's gaze with the gaze of either character. The audience is not, in other words, rhetorically induced to identify with either character, with the result that the gendering of the characters on screen is that much more denaturalized.

4. My argument about sexuality and gender in The Night Porter thus differs in one crucial respect from that of Kaja Silverman in her book The Acoustic Mirror. She would read Max as a psychological character, a mimetic subject, who can then be said to take or not take actions, and whose "male" subjectivity she sees as "impaired" rather than as fluid, unstable, and performative from the start. She also discusses Max in isolation from Lucia, as if his behavior were autonomous and rooted in a single psyche. By characterizing Max as an individual Freudian subject, I would argue, this reading does too little with the film's destabilization of the categories of gender and sexuality that produce the appearance of phallic or nonphallic males. In other words, it essentializes, in a subtle way, the sexuality of the characters (or rather that of Max), while I would emphasize its status as relational and performative. Whichever position one takes as a spectator, I would call attention to the enormous difference that position makes to one's reading of the film and to one's relationship to the two figures. There are virtually two different stories here, and a completely different relationship to the cinematic image, depending upon where one finds oneself.

In an earlier discussion of the film in her article, "Masochism and Subjectivity," Silverman presents a compelling argument about the gap between "the fiction of the active male subject" and male identification with "negation, passivity, and loss" (8). Here she does take into consideration the interaction between Max and Lucia. Although she structures her case around the categories "male" and "female," much of what she says hints at the possibility of their nonessential ontological status (6).

5. An interesting variation on Hollywood's struggle to eliminate ambiguity and conceptual movement from its constructions of subjects is described by Amelia Jones in her fine article on Presumed Innocent, "'She Was Bad News': Male Paranoia and the Contemporary New Woman," in which she argues that several recent Hollywood films interestingly fail to contain a "phallic uncertainty," which they blame on the "new" career woman's expansion of "feminine identity" across traditional gender lines. Jones sees the failure of such films to contain the "new woman" as a moderately positive sign culturally. One could also draw more negative conclusions from this (lucrative) scapegoating of career women for the fundamental instability of the phallic male subject.

6. Mirto Golo Stone cites herself and Teresa de Lauretis, among others, as spectators who find the film unbearable. Both commentators construe Lucia as a conventional, psychological subject, similarly to the way Silverman construes Max. De Lauretis in 1976 wrote of the presentation of Lucia, "It is a harsh, unadorned, cruel view of the depth of one's self" (38). My point is that the film destabilizes the position of the spectator in ways that make such certainty about what one is seeing impossible.

7. For her eye-opening discussion of the power relations involved in the reading as well as the making of photographic images, I am indebted here to Martha Rosler's essay "In, Around,

and Afterthoughts (On Documentary Photography)" in Richard Bolton's edited volume *The Context of Meaning: Critical Histories of Photography*.

8. For a brilliant, multifaceted discussion of the collusion between the binary thinking of gender and sexuality and "knowledge" as it has been constructed and construed in the West, see Eve Sedgwick's *The Epistemology of the Closet*, where she touches on the relation between fascism and the assumption of historically stable, internally coherent sexual identities (154–55).

9. Laura Pietropaolo gives an excellent verbal transcription of this sequence in her article "Sexuality as Exorcism in Liliana Cavani's *Night Porter*" in the context of her persuasive argument for the importance of seeing the flashback, the opera, and the film itself as versions of ritual, which she defines as "a formalized re-enactment with a cathartic purpose" (75–76). Her sense of ritual and my sense of performance are, I think, closely related. She describes the scene as follows:

> As the text of the duet is tenderly expressing that "the gentle love of man and woman shows that humans are a race apart" (Schikaneder 82) and the melody fills the theatre ever more rapturously, the camera moves back to the audience to close upon Lucia's profile. She turns full face feeling that someone is watching her. Next, for several seconds we focus on the magnetic stare on Max's face, then again on Lucia's tense profile. At this moment we have a flashback to the lager. As the duet spills into a cold, dingy dormitory, the camera again pans slowly, this time not over the composed, attentive members of Viennese society sitting in the theatre hall, but over a group of prisoners all sitting huddled together on rows of metal beds, all staring out with empty eyes. Then the camera lingers for several long seconds on one of the dormitory beds where an SS officer is sodomizing a male prisoner while in the background Papageno and Pamina are joyfully reiterating: "While love is ours, we'll freely give. . . . It's love that sweetens every sorrow. . . . With love we need not fear tomorrow, we feel its universal power" (Schikaneder 82). The camera then closes up on Lucia resting on a mattress. Max comes in and drags her away (74).

10. For a provocative, polemical feminist reading of the opera from which I have borrowed here, see Cathérine Clément's rueful commentary on it in *Opera; or, the Undoing of Women* (70–77).

11. Teresa de Lauretis particularly emphasizes this aspect of the film in her important 1976 *Film Quarterly* review: "Cavani's love story is not only the story of the relation between two individuals, but of the world around them, of the culture and history in which they exist, of the values, conflicts, and inner contradictions of a society which is, whether we want to see it or not, our own" (36).

12. Here Cavani's film seems to anticipate Craig Owen's excellent discussion of the "crossing of the feminist critique of patriarchy and the postmodernist critique of representation" in his well-known "The Discourse of Others: Feminists and Postmodernism" (59).

# Works Cited

Bettelheim, Bruno. "Reflections: Surviving." *New Yorker* (2 August 1976): 31–52.

Bulkin, Elly, Minnie Bruce Pratt, and Barbara Smith. *Yours in Struggle: Three Feminist Perspectives on Anti-Semitism and Racism*. Brooklyn, N.Y.: Long Haul Press, 1984.

Butler, Judith. *Gender Trouble: Feminism and the Subversion of Identity*. New York: Routledge, 1990.

Clément, Cathérine. *Opera; or, The Undoing of Women*. Foreword by Susan McClary. Translated by Betsy Wing. Minneapolis: University of Minnesota Press, 1988.

de Lauretis, Teresa. "Cavani's *Night Porter*: A Woman's Film?" *Film Quarterly* 30 (1976–77): 35–38.

Doane, Mary Ann. "Film and the Masquerade: Theorizing the Female Spectator." In *Femmes Fatales: Feminism, Film Theory, Psychoanalysis*, 17–32. New York: Routledge, 1991.

Griffin, Susan. *Pornography and Silence: Culture's Revenge Against Nature*. New York: Harper and Row, 1981.

Jones, Amelia. "'She Was Bad News': Male Paranoia and the Contemporary New Woman." *Camera Obscura: A Journal of Feminism and Film Theory* 25/26 (1991): 297–320.

Levi, Primo. *The Drowned and the Saved*. Translated by Raymond Rosenthal. New York: Summit Books, 1988.

Mulvey, Laura. "Visual Pleasure and Narrative Cinema." In *Visual and Other Pleasures*, 14–26. Bloomington: Indiana University Press, 1989.

Owens, Craig. "The Discourse of Others: Feminists and Postmodernism." In *The Anti-Aesthetic: Essays on Postmodern Culture*, ed. Hal Foster, 57–82. Seattle: Bay Press, 1983.

Pietropaolo, Laura. "Sexuality as Exorcism in Liliana Cavani's *Night Porter*." In *Donna: Women in Italian Culture*, ed. Ada Testaferri, 71–79. University of Toronto Italian Studies 7. Ottawa, Canada: Dovehouse Editions, 1989.

Rosler, Martha. "In, Around, and Afterthoughts (On Documentary Photography)." In *The Context of Meaning: Critical Histories of Photography*, ed. Richard Bolton, 303–40. Cambridge: MIT Press, 1989.

Sedgwick, Eve Kosofsky. *The Epistemology of the Closet*. Berkeley and Los Angeles: University of California Press, 1990.

Shemek, Deanna. "Circular Definitions: Disciplining Gender in Italian Renaissance Festival." Unpublished essay.

Silverman, Kaja. *The Acoustic Mirror: The Female Voice in Psychoanalysis and Cinema*. Bloomington: Indiana University Press, 1988.

———. "Masochism and Subjectivity." *Framework* 12 (1980): 2–9.

Stone, Mirto Golo. "The Feminist Critic and Salome: On Cavani's *The Night Porter*." *Romance Languages Annual 1989* (1990): 41–44.

Theweleit, Klaus. *Male Fantasies*. Vol. 1, *Women, Floods, Bodies, History*. Foreword by Barbara Ehrenreich. Translated by Stephen Conway et al. Minneapolis: University of Minnesota Press, 1987.

# Notes on Contributors

BEVERLY ALLEN is associate professor of Italian and comparative literature at Syracuse University. She is the author of *Andrea Zanzotto: The Language of Beauty's Apprentice* (Berkeley and Los Angeles: University of California Press, 1988), which has also been translated into Italian, and editor of *Pier Paolo Pasolini: The Poetics of Heresy*. In her numerous articles and lectures, she has dealt with contemporary Italian poetry, film, and Italian women's studies.

FIORA A. BASSANESE is professor and chair of the Italian Department at the University of Massachusetts at Boston. She is the author of *Gaspara Stampa* (Boston: G. K. Hall/Twayne, 1982) and *Marginal Women: Letters of Renaissance Courtesans* (New York: State University of New York Press, 1992).

MAURIZIA BOSCAGLI is assistant professor of English at the University of California, Santa Barbara. She is a specialist in literary theory and has written articles and lectures on Italian feminism and other theoretical issues. She is the author of a book on the modernist period.

JOANN CANNON is associate professor of Italian at the University of California, Davis. She is the author of *Postmodern Italian Fiction: The Crisis of Reason in Calvino, Eco, Sciascia, Malerba* (Rutherford, N.J.: Fairleigh Dickinson University Press, 1989) and *Italo Calvino: Writer and Critic* (Ravenna: Longo Editore, 1981).

MARGA COTTINO-JONES is professor of Italian at the University of California, Los Angeles. She is the author of seven books and fifty articles, among them: *Order from Chaos: Social and Aesthetic Harmonies in Boccaccio's Decameron* (Washington, D.C.: University Press of America, 1982) and *A Student's*

*Guide to Italian Film* (Dubuque: Kendall/Hunt, 1983). She specializes in medieval and Renaissance poetry and narrative, theater, film, and women's literature.

NANCY HARROWITZ is assistant professor of Italian at Boston University. She has written numerous articles on Italian Jewish writers, popular literature in Italy, and the detective novel. She is the editor of two collections and author of a book on Mathilde Serao.

RENATE HOLUB is associate director of the Center for German and European Studies at the University of California at Berkeley. She is the author of *Antonio Gramschi, Postmodernism, and Feminism* (New York: Routledge, 1992) and of numerous articles on Italian feminist theory.

CONSTANCE JORDAN is associate professor of English at Claremont Graduate School. She is the author of *Renaissance Feminism: Literary Texts and Political Models* (Ithaca: Cornell University Press, 1990) and of numerous articles on the Renaissance.

BERNADETTE LUCIANO is assistant professor of Italian at the University of Auckland, New Zealand. She has written articles on Carlo Porta and resistance novels.

ELISE MAGISTRO is a lecturer at Scripps College. She is a specialist on Italian regional writers, in particular Grazia Deledda and Maria Messina.

MARIA O. MAROTTI is a lecturer in Italian at the University of California, Santa Barbara. She is the author of *The Duplicating Imagination: Twain and the Twain Papers* and editor of *Identità e Scrittura* and of articles on Italian women writers.

GRAZIELLA PARATI is assistant professor of Italian at Dartmouth College. She has written articles on Italian women autobiographers and a book on female genealogies in Italian literature (Minneapolis: University of Minnesota University Press, forthcoming).

LUCIA RE is associate professor of Italian at the University of California, Los Angeles. She is the author of *Calvino and the Age of Neorealism: Fables of Estrangement* (Stanford: Stanford University Press, 1990) and of numerous articles on modernist and contemporary Italian literature.

MARGUERITE WALLER is associate professor of English at the University of California, Riverside. She is the author of *Petrarch's Poetics and Literary History* (Amherst: University of Massachusetts Press, 1980) and of numerous articles on theoretical issues, film criticism, and feminism.

# Index